P9-DTG-987

HOTEL
PLANNING
AND DESIGN

OVERLEAF

Nova-Park Élysées, Paris. *This handsome Second Empire facade, which once fronted the* Paris-Match *magazine's office building, now houses a luxurious 73-suite hotel.* *(See the section on adaptive reuse in Chapter 10 and page 124 for more on this hotel.)*

ABOVE

Nova-Park Élysées, Paris. *The fanciful decor in the hotel's Jardins des Muses restaurant sets the stage for its unique luxury image. This tiered and sculptured inner court is also the scene of classical music concerts on summer evenings.*

RIGHT

Hotel Inter-Continental, Paris. *The frescoed ceilings of the Napoleon Ballroom in this hotel, which was restored in 1968, are designated as a national landmark. This room has been the scene of such historic occasions as Victor Hugo's 80th birthday celebration in 1883.* *(See the section on restoration in Chapter 10 and page 120 for more on this hotel.)*

ABOVE

The Royal Hawaiian, Honolulu, Hawaii. *A symbol of grace among its modern highrise neighbors, the Royal Hawaiian continues to accommodate guests in a grand manner, today as part of Sheraton's Waikiki complex. (See the section on the beach resort in Chapter 4.)*

RIGHT

The Petra Forum Hotel, Wadi Mousa, Jordan. *Built from the local sandstone to serve visitors to the ancient walled city, the 80-room hotel and visitor's center blends discretely into the landscape nearby the 300-foot high (92-meter) carved red-rock tourist site. (See the section on the sight-seeing resort in Chapter 4 and page 82 for more on this hotel.)*

OPPOSITE PAGE ABOVE

Boca Beach Club Hotel and Cabanas, Boca Raton, Florida. *Complementing Addison Mizner's historic hotel across the bay with all the charm and grace of today's idiom, this extensively landscaped contemporary resort overlooks the ocean, intercoastal waterway, and surrounding recreation amenities. (See the section on the beach, golf, and tennis resort in Chapter 4 and page 67 for more on this hotel.)*

OPPOSITE PAGE BELOW

Mauna Lani Bay Hotel, Big Island, Hawaii. *Designed to maximize views of the unusual lava-formed coast, most of the resort's land has been preserved as open space to protect its indigenous beauty. (See the section on the beach, golf, and tennis resort in Chapter 4 and page 63 for more on this hotel.)*

ABOVE

The Mayfair Regent, New York. *Located on residential upper Park Avenue, many of the hotel's rooms and suites are permanently rented. This residential atmosphere is reflected in the intimate lobby with its elegant lounge, recalling the grand drawing rooms of European hotels. The hotel also includes Le Cirque, one of the world's finest restaurants. (See the section on renovation in Chapter 10 and page 107 for more on this hotel.)*

RIGHT

The Mayfair Regent, Chicago. *The hotel's residential character is emphasized by such attention to interior detailing as the Louis XVI desks in the lobby, the hand-painted Chinese murals in the lobby lounge, and the extraordinary simplicity of the rooftop Ciel Bleu restaurant. (See the sections on renovation and restoration in Chapter 10 and page 117 for more on this hotel.)*

ABOVE AND LEFT

Golden Nugget Boardwalk, Atlantic City, New Jersey. *Offering opulent decor in its gaming rooms (left) and lavish suites (above), the Golden Nugget attracts the more affluent gaming public, often luring its high-roller guests with complimentary hotel suites. (See Chapter 13, The Casino Hotel, and pages 144–145 for more on this hotel.)*

OPPOSITE PAGE

Harrah's at Trump Plaza, Atlantic City, New Jersey. *On a central Boardwalk site adjacent to its convention center, the $250 million, 614-room complex became the tenth and largest casino hotel in the community's rebirth as a gaming and entertainment center. (See Chapter 13, The Casino Hotel, and page 146 for more on this hotel.)*

ABOVE AND OPPOSITE PAGE

Campton Place, San Francisco. *This residentially scaled lobby with its French period furniture sets the tone of understated elegance and establishes a counterpoint to its contemporary atrium shown on the right. The impressive merging and restoration of two older downtown structures was paradoxically responsible for creating this strikingly contemporary atrium court. (See Chapter 9, The Super-Luxury Hotel, and pages 108–109 for more on this hotel.)*

RIGHT

Helmsley Palace, New York. *The Villard Houses, famous for their superb contribution to New York's architectural heritage, were rescued through a dramatic transformation to become the entrance motif of the multistory Helmsley Palace hotel. The Madison Room confers old-world graciousness on the hotel by its restoration.(See the section on adaptive reuse in Chapter 10.)*

LEFT

Las Salinas Sheraton Hotel, Lanzarote, Canary Islands. *The lush terrace planting on its stepped facade blends this hotel well with its natural environment. (See the section on the beach resort in Chapter 4 and page 68 for more on this hotel.)*

ABOVE

Ramada Renaissance Hotel, Atlanta Airport, Georgia. *The dramatic glass-roofed lobby with its garden setting provides an oasis of tranquility in the 10-story, 505-room hotel, relieving the stress of air travel in the midst of one of the world's busiest airport. A string quartet gives concerts in the hotel's atrium. (See the section on the airport hotel in Chapter 3 and page 58 for more on this hotel.)*

ABOVE

United Nations Plaza Hotel and Tower, New York. *Combining an international agency office building with a 290-room hotel built in 1976 and a 115-apartment tower completed in 1984, this mixed-use complex was master-planned to offer all the amenities of a well-appointed hotel to visitors and diplomats wishing easy access to the United Nations across the street. (See Chapter 7, Residential/Condominium, and pages 98–99 for more on this hotel.)*

RIGHT

Four Seasons Hotel, Philadelphia, Pennsylvania. *The hotel and adjoining office building encircle a well-scaled courtyard and overlook Logan Square, the site of several major museums and other public buildings. The colored granite facade complements these, while the hotel interiors recall Philadelphia's Federal-period history. (See the section on the downtown hotel in Chapter 2 and page 41 for more on this hotel.)*

OVERLEAF

Credit Lyonnais Tower, Lyons, France. *The turretlike motif of this cylindrical Francotel hotel, which sits atop an office building, merges it sensitively into Lyons' medieval skyline. (See the section on mixed-use in Chapter 12 and page 134 for more on this hotel.)*

COLOR PORTFOLIO

HOTEL PLANNING AND DESIGN

BY WALTER A. RUTES, FAIA, AND RICHARD H. PENNER

WHITNEY LIBRARY OF DESIGN
an imprint of Watson-Guptill Publications/New York

For our wives
Helene Rutes and Cathy Penner

and our children
Daniel Rutes, Linda Kastner, Robert Kastner,
and Anne Penner

First published 1985 in New York by Watson-Guptill Publications,
a division of Billboard Publications, Inc.,
1515 Broadway, New York, N.Y. 10036

Library of Congress Cataloging in Publication Data
Rutes, Walter A.
Hotel planning and design.
Bibliography: p.
Includes index.
1. Hotels, taverns, etc.—Planning.
I. Penner, Richard H. II. Title.
NA7800.R87 1985 728′.5 84-21906
ISBN 0-8230-7274-6

Published in Great Britain by The Architectural
Press Ltd, 9 Queen Anne's Gate, London SW1H 9BY

ISBN 0 85139 857 X

Manufactured in U.S.A.

1 2 3 4 5 6 7 8 9/89 88 87 86 85

DISCLAIMER

The information and statements herein are believed to be reliable, but are not to be construed as a warranty or representation for which the author or publishers assume legal responsibility. Users should undertake sufficient verification and testing to determine the suitability for their own particular purpose of any information or products referred to herein. *No warranty of fitness for a particular purpose is made.*

For other information on interactive computerized facilities and area programming (SHAPEE), please contact the authors in care of Richard Penner, School of Hotel Administration, Statler Hall, Cornell University, Ithaca, N.Y. 14853.

Acknowledgments

This book is the result of many years of experience in the specialized field of hotel architecture and interior design—the experience of scores of people who generously provided us with their insights about design and with examples of their work. We credit the architects, designers, photographers, and others who encouraged us and provided us with material about their projects in the List of Hotels and Credits because there are more than we can suitably acknowledge here.

Although we both were trained in architecture at Cornell University, our careers took divergent paths. Wally Rutes moved directly into architectural practice, where among his many colleagues and associates none has been more influential than the late Richard E. Smith, a pioneer of modern hotel architecture. Dick Penner has taught hotel design at the School of Hotel Administration. Both careers have offered us the opportunity to work with and learn from the *real authors of this volume*, the architects, designers, and specialists whose work we illustrate.

We owe a special debt to two giants in the industry, William B. Tabler and Joseph Baum, who agreed to introduce the book with personal observations about their distinguished careers and with projections about the future of hotel design and management.

We can't offer enough thanks for the patience and enormous good judgment of the editors at the Whitney Library of Design: Stephen Kliment for first helping us organize the project, Susan Davis for painstakingly reviewing the manuscript and shepherding it through the publishing process, and Damien Alexander for laying-out and designing the book.

Our own associates provided helpful comments throughout the writing of the book. Thanks go especially to Michael Loughran, David Oswald, David Cutliff, John Brannon, Zohair Neemuchwalla, Nadine Papon, Rick Bishop, Alec Oumov, Arthur Nave, Jim Powell, Henrik Bull, George Rockrise, Peter Chermayeff, Mort Bernstein, Joseph Fuller, Terry Holt, Emmett Gossen, Robert Bitner, Alan Lapidus, Richard Kramer, Frank Solano, Trisha Wilson, Jeff Howard, Hubert Wilke, and Rich Warnick for sharing ideas and experience.

Over the past decade and more, many students at Cornell took on individual research projects or assisted with the many drawings that illustrate the book. These include David Black, Henrietta Cheng, David Colle, Dana Dishel, Ruth Drab, Rob Glazier, Katy Heath, Carol Ann Holland, Armand Iaia, Lee Kanter, Beverly Kay, Maria Mak, Michael Merriman, John Nicolls, Susan Sheldon, Dan Stewart, Rob Stiles, Bill Tom, Vic Vesnaver, and David Wheeler. Their interest and enthusiasm for the details of hotel planning issues are infectious. Also, we recognize with sincere thanks the contributions of Dan Rutes, Bob Kastner, and Linda Kastner to the diagrams and space allocation programs included in the text and of Cathy Schlosberg for her tireless dedication to assembling the credits and appendices and for research into hotel operations.

There are too many individual contributors to acknowledge each. We want to thank, however, the many hotel executives who identified their company's most exciting new properties, the representatives of the scores of architectural and interior design firms who provided material, the photographers who culled their very best shots, all of whom willingly met our endless requests for additional information.

Others have helped by making time available to us to complete this book: Deans Robert Beck and Jack Clark of the Hotel School and those at Sheraton and Ramada who offered encouragement from the outset. Howard Hirsch and Michael Bedner provided Dick Penner the rewarding experience of a sabbatical working with their expert staff. And our families have provided the support and good cheer to enable us to spend the hours necessary to complete the manuscript.

We are also indebted to everyone at Trufont Typographers who worked above and beyond to turn a very complex manuscript into this handsome book.

CONTENTS

FOREWORD

by Joseph Baum, creator of many of the world's leading restaurants

While lodging and dining are the literal expressions of our medium, we in the hospitality industry know that our real product—the measure of our success—is pleasure. We're in the pleasure business. We're organized, equipped, and staffed to sell pleasure at a profit. Certainly we analyze markets, we conduct feasibility studies, we plan, build and operate beautiful facilities. Yet as we try (and God knows we try) to improve our industry, the ephemeral but absolute phenomenon called "pleasure" is too often not built into our equations. We may have become more efficient than ever before, but never before have we been able to sell efficiency—and we can't today either.

Refueling, sure. Shelter, of course. But whether it's a grand hotel, country inn, ski lodge, mega-resort, conference center, or caravansary, when all is done, what our guests remember is pleasure, whether they came for business, relaxation, or a little of both. Grand and glorious pleasure, that's what brings them back. Because what our public wants is that special pleasure that hotels alone have provided ever since the world began—that special controlled experience that gives each guest the sense of being pampered with a professional skill that is humanly concerned, which is exactly right for the occasion, which meets the needs and expectations of the moment. That experience can't be achieved only with bits and pieces, but must have harmonious character that *expresses the personal statement of intelligent, interested professionals.*

The customers we now seek are not the customers of the 1950s, grateful for simply being able to dine out once in a while, nor from the 60s when better and better hotels and restaurants sprang up and they were dazzled by them. The customers we're after are the sophisticated, more sensuous product of the 70s and the 80s. They've learned (because we taught them) how a good restaurant or hotel elevates a human need to a subtle and sophisticated pleasure.

They now set the pace and rhythm and are the true target of all major marketing campaigns. Why? Because they've traveled—slept and eaten—around the world in 80 ways. Because they respond to the media: the publications they now read devote limitless space to food and personal pleasures. Because they are forced by their normal style of life to eat out and to travel well at some company's expense. Because pleasure, once purely personal, is now being peddled as a commodity by critics, columnists, advertising, even inflight magazines and hotel entertainment guides.

As a result of all these and other factors, today's customers—at every level—are not only the most knowledgeable in our history, they are also the first market generation to be *consumed with the consumption of pleasure.* In the headlong rush to meet their demands and their awesome appetite for hotel services, it was inevitable that much of our industry initially responded by trying to mass-produce and prepackage pleasures. The results were often faddish and, like all fads, were quickly exhausted.

Confronted by its largest accumulation of affluent customers, our industry's response too often jeopardized many of the real pleasures that our hotels must provide. The customer wanted distinction, yet the operator tried to avoid risk while still selling expectancy. Too often we got short-range design solutions and copycat "features" that were guaranteed to have limited life-cycles due to overuse. It was far too easy to get lost in *sameness,* not just accidentally, but through unthinking or uncaring. Too often machine thinking replaced brilliance and a sense of delight, dictating facile solutions only because they were expedient and had worked before, misreading the meaning of mass market, groping for solutions that limited choices by appealing to the common denominator—inoffensive to all, objectionable to none—applied everywhere, so you couldn't tell where you were half the time, the repetition causing hotels to become so generic that the value of the experience to our customers was in danger of becoming secondary to the convenience of location.

As a restaurateur, I can think that what's been true of hotel architecture has been equally true of hotel restaurants. Distinction in the mouth has been watered down terribly by the so-called specialty restaurant—offering a limited choice in a souped-up atmosphere—efficient in kitchen production perhaps, but lacking in character on the plate. You've heard it before, but let's say it again. Both in the design of hotels and the character of hotel dining, *it became a case of the bland leading the bland.*

Perhaps if this extraordinary book had been around earlier there would have been fewer such missteps. Its authors, Walter Rutes and Richard Penner, have long believed that mass market does not necessarily mean mass taste and they recognized the enormous new market of pleasure-seeking consumers that use hotels is, in fact, made up of many, large, different groups. They analyze the trend toward market segmentation in this exhaustively researched, painstakingly organized, and encyclopedic work, and they identify some 30 hotel types and distinct market segments. They then describe the hotel's facilities program for each of these segments in terms of individual desires. Putting the customer at the center of the planning process—which is one of the great strengths of this book—they provide the specific requirements in relation to the individual guest and between the different design elements. They illustrate exactly how designs can and must function as operational parts of each solution: Of great importance, for no matter the size of demand, it will be varied and highly competitive and the battle for market share decided increasingly by how accurately hotels identify their target segments and how imaginatively they provide for their needs.

The problem of the numbing bigness of our industry and of operating on a grand scale is well understood by the authors. They know that the diseconomies of size cannot be overcome by marketing strength alone. The challenge is to transfer the benefits of size into personal pleasure for the guest through sensitive planning, innovative design, and better service—combating inhuman bigness by manacling the monolith in the service of the customer.

Another threat to pleasure and therefore to success is addressed: the misuse of the marketing phrase "perception of value." Too many of our executives today seem to think it means: How much can we take away before the customer reacts? Or if we give a special hand soap and a different bath soap will the customer accept a higher room rate? I think we have confused being fancy with having style and false symbols of luxury with true pleasure. Having the maid make pretty origami sculpture with the toilet tissue *may* strike customers as a perception of luxury—maybe once, maybe even twice. But it's no substitute for the pleasure of a telephone next to your bed instead of across the room where some hotels now put them to save wear and tear on the mattress. The perception of value is not enough. Our public now demands evidence of skill and proof of value. We need to become more expressive in our products and services—less stereotyped. We must plan every opportunity to increase, not diminish, the chances for pleasurable human encounters and service.

But too often, while invoking efficiency, we have lost touch with this human principle. Too often our industry has said: "Keep employees away from customers as much as possible

Let machines automatically wake up the guests. We'll let them know we're human by sticking a piece of candy on the pillow." Frankly, I am tired of sliding into bed with a slippery slab of chocolate, and I'm not amused by saying "good morning" to a machine.

Now, efficiency is very nice. It saves money and helps satisfy customers. With today's high costs of construction, labor, and supplies, management systems and controls must be a keystone of our planning. But let's transfer the values of these efficiencies and savings into guest services. Let's not confuse efficiency with excellence, but use efficiency to create a higher level of excellence, giving the guest more service. This efficiency must work as a "silent technology" that operates so quietly that its presence is only evident by the obvious benefits it provides. It is from such planning that good hotel architecture and design evolves, ideally expressing the notion and life of the hotel so perfectly and with such clarity of intent that when completed it all appears to have been inevitable—that it could not have been done any other way.

Rutes and Penner in this book emphasize the marketing value of dramatic, "worth-a-special-trip" architecture and design. Certainly we all know by now that exciting hotel architecture sells rooms. Trend-setting hotel architects such as John Portman and Ricardo Legoretto, among a host of others, must surely be given credit for the new highs in occupancy rates of hotels all over the world. In this time of burgeoning hotel building, great talents such as these have worked their wondrous ways with space and rich materials, creating shining products of the imagination that rival the hotels of an earlier, grander age. The boom in high-syle luxury, all-suite, and resort hotels reflects the success in today's affluent economy of the happy combination of dramatic design, innovative facilities, and personal amenities. The right hotels at the right time.

With hotel marketing so focused on architecture and design, there is the usual pushing and straining for recognition and impact in the crowded marketplace. Here again, we must be wary of inappropriate design blockbusters and the "schlock value" of hotels furnished in "Cattle Baron Baroque" or incongruous "skyline Williamsburgs" designed as distracting theatrical stage sets. No. *Nothing exceeds like excess.*

Design as entertainment, by definition, is of transient character. The very literalness of shallow themes and merchandising artifices masquerading as style limits the imagination and leaves no elbow room for the mind as times passes and tastes change. If appropriate at all, it's just for the moment. We must beware of all this, for it comes perilously close to obliterating the recognizable, socially spirited hotel experience and risks the guest feeling confused, out of place, unsure of the hotel's intent and his or her own response. What we're getting at is that we're just as concerned with *how the hotel guest feels in specific situations*, as we are with what he or she looks at. What he *infers* from his surroundings is what is important.

We care that the environment is evocative; that it excites the senses and the mind, conjuring up memories and recalls, both spiritual and real, always encouraging the sharing of the experience. The atmosphere should clearly project the hotel's desire to please, expressing the sum of the guest's needs and illusions that are so absolutely right for these times that they flow naturally with the future. And we need success that lasts. Hotels must be born with enough "good bones" to have an enduring character, yet must be sufficiently flexible to stay alive with continual "reinnovation", always sprightly and fresh yet with the grace of tradition that comes with the years.

Obviously, no book alone can design such hotels for us. Nor should it try. Pat formulas would at best be merely generalizations and would quickly become clichés. No, we still need our creativity, insight, talent. But what this book does is *provoke creativity, awaken insight, liberate talent.*

Because its authors are always respectful of the large investment needed to create a successful hotel, they take pains to provide us, in remarkably accessible ways, the information and the insight to prevent costly mistakes. To borrow a word from the world of computers, this book—with its exceptionally clear organization and its pages and pages of discipline-reinforcing checklists, standards, and guides—is *user-friendly.* It gives us solid ground to stand on, so we can safely begin to apply our imagination. Moreover, because this book is also *guest-friendly*—consistently directing us to think of our market always in multiples of one—it encourages us to see our hotel as a guest would see it, hearing its hum through his ears, catching the way people move within it out of the corner of her eye. And if we have done this listening and watching, we will also share the delight of the guests' surprise at something never-before-encountered but immediately recognized. Something that makes us say, "Yes, this is the way it should be. Why didn't someone think of that before?"

Finally, when all that we've been imagining comes together in our hoped-for, harmonious whole, I think we will sense our guests right there in the midst of it all. "Yes, yes," we will feel with them, "This is the right place. *What a pleasure!*"

Prologue

by William B. Tabler, FAIA, designer of hundreds of hotels over the past 45 years—far more than any other architect

Walter A. Rutes and Richard H. Penner, both recognized authorities in their subject, are to be commended and congratulated for undertaking this book on hotel architecture and design. Writing it has been a far more difficult and demanding effort than anyone can appreciate who has not actually designed a hotel. I'm sure that the proven principles this book contains will become a valuable asset to the hotel industry, long plagued by the fact that too many hotels have been designed by otherwise competent architects who know too little about the intricacies of planning a hotel structure for efficient operation and profitability.

I know of no competent textbook on hotel design that has been published previous to this one. No book can answer all the problems in design arising from ever-changing public tastes, fluctuating economic conditions, and other variable factors. However, this one lays down the basic principles that are enduring and should provide the architect with valuable guidance that in the past he or she had to learn by painful experience.

Thus, in the future, this book should help eliminate designs that impede function, distress management, discourage patrons, and lead to financial debacles. An especially graphic example is a well-known hotel in a large Midwestern city, whose developers engaged a famous designer with no previous hotel experience to provide a "fresh viewpoint" and incorporate "new, different, and exciting ideas." The architectural firm may well have accomplished this, but the trouble was that their ideas were so unrealistic and impractical that the hotel suffered financial disaster, passing through half-a-dozen ownerships.

The authors of this book have identified some 30 hotel types popular with today's increasingly sophisticated public. Prior to this, designers may not have been aware of the wide variations between these categories and that, through an understanding of them, they could develop even more appealing models.

Perhaps the most basic difficulty for the neophyte hotel designer is learning that the hotel operation must earn a profit *out of its building.* Unlike the Lever House or the Seagram Building on New York's Park Avenue, hotels do not have profits from soap, whiskey, or other such products to support monuments. Also, it is infinitely more difficult to create a successful hotel than an office building or shopping center, where the owner gets profits from leasing large spaces on a long-term basis to other businesses. In a hotel you are both leasing to the public *every night* and catering to their *every need.* Therefore, rather than a monument or mere rental space, a hotel must provide a total living environment, with all the needed multicomplex functions and activities. The designer soon realizes that he or she has to, in effect, create the equivalent of a compact community. Years after I was born and raised in a little town in Illinois of some 2500 people, when our firm was designing the ballroom for the Pittsburgh Hilton, I suddenly realized that I could seat everybody from my hometown in that ballroom. In our design for the New York Hilton, every resident of my little town of Momence, Illinois, could have a private room, with food, drink, entertainment, clothing, recreation, medical attention, books and personal necessities, laundry, beauty shop, and a telephone system large enough for a city of 50,000 people.

Aside from its many complex functions, hotel planning must anticipate the public's changing tastes and shifting economic and social trends as well as incorporate enduring qualities for it to survive as a viable operation over the long term. In the Depression of the 30s, only one small 200-room hotel was built between the opening of the Waldorf-Astoria in New York in 1931 and the Washington Statler completed a dozen years later, while four-fifths of the nation's hotels went through the bankruptcy wringer, as did all major hotel operators, except the Statler Company, with its tight controls and emphasis on efficiency. Statler then resolved to make its first new hotel a model of efficiency. As *Hotel Monthly* predicted, it would have "a profound effect on the future of hotel construction." Featuring simple, contemporary lines and "studio rooms" with beds that turned into sofas during the day, the guestrooms became sitting rooms or working spaces lit by wide picture windows, the first in urban commercial hotels. While wide hallways and towering ceilings were eliminated, the hotel provided impressive dining and meeting areas and Washington's largest ballroom.

During the early years of its operation, the Washington Statler produced almost three times the profit of the Waldorf-Astoria in New York. As a result, most new commercial hotels for the next two decades followed the Statler's principles. Now called the Capital Hilton, the hotel is being remodeled to convert its 850 guestrooms into 500 larger ones since the public now demands such accommodations. But the reason this 41-year-old hotel can be recycled rather than replaced is that its enduring planning qualities and large public spaces continue to make it a formidable competitor, although the economic climate is far different from that in which the hotel was originally conceived.

Today's hotels are glamourized with towering atriums, glass-enclosed elevators, exotic areas for relaxation, and glittering meeting spaces. The room rate for one of the first of these spectacular hotels was originally projected at $20 a night. But by the time it opened in the early 60s, escalating construction costs had forced the average room rate up to $53 a night. Yet guests paid the inflated rates that would have been impossible to obtain in the 50s. Thus, inflation of the 60s made a profitable hotel out of one that during the 50s would have been a financial catastrophe.

While inflation has greatly helped the hotel industry up to now, the slowing down of inflation is likely to create serious financial problems in paying for and operating luxury hotels. One example is New York's Helmsley Palace Hotel, charging up to $2,500 a night for its more prestigious suites. But even such hotels cannot afford the high ceilings, ornate lobbies, and ballrooms of the 20s. Behind their impressive facades, efforts to increase efficiency continue. Without this, even the inflated rates could not keep them in business. It is therefore the task of the hotel architect to devise cost-saving innovations while still improving guest satisfaction.

For example, staff salaries have escalated even more than building costs. While hotel services of the past depended mainly on squadrons of subordinates, waiters, and uniformed minions, present-day hotels must maintain a higher level of service, with a steadily decreasing staff. Hotel planners therefore must offset these staff reductions with improved technology, often resisted by the hotel's management.

While some cost-saving experiments have turned out to be impractical, the well-conceived ones not only have reduced the number of employees, but have often resulted in improved service and better guest relations. Early examples adopted over the objections of some hotel managers were dial telephones and automatic elevators. Many luxury hotel managers believed their guests would strongly object to such "automated" services (which eliminated approximately 40 staff members in a large hotel)!

Several years ago, I was asked by the management of the fashionable Dorchester Hotel in London to survey its operations with the idea of reducing costs. I found that the Dorchester had about five employees for every guestroom, while we were designing hotels with from one-half to two employees per room at most. Our efforts were initially met with the expected outcries of dismay by the management. For instance, one group worked on each floor arranging bouquets of flowers for the guestrooms on that floor. When I pointed out that this could be done more economically and effectively by the banquet department, which arranged flower displays for the public rooms, all sorts of objections resulted. But we eventually reduced the staff by 30 in that one operation and were able to cut down the Dorchester's staff to two-and-a-half to three employees per room *with the guests receiving even better service.*

People appreciate personal attention and service, and hotels fill this need, becoming in effect "the common man's palace." The successful hotel must, therefore, retain this image while continuing to make a reasonable profit through ever-increasing efficiency. Designing hotel structures to answer these requirements, in the face of changing tastes and economic conditions, is today's challenge and *why* this book makes such an important contribution.

Another important factor that determines a hotel's success is achieving community support. The backing of the leading people in a city is almost as important to a hotel's fortunes as the approval rating of its patrons who temporarily reside there. The building must reflect the personality of the area of which it is a part, becoming a place to which civic and social organizations, as well as individuals, are psychologically drawn for meetings and entertaining. Such a hotel can inspire enthusiastic support by the community, infusing energy and excitement into the city, and becoming more of a public institution than even the City Hall or library. It is therefore up to the architect to develop that mystique enjoyed by the most successful hotels.

While building their first hotel, the head of a giant development corporation once told me: "Although we have built hundreds of commercial buildings, the public never heard of us until we did a hotel. Somehow, there *must* be a unique fascination about hotels."

PREFACE

In his Foreword, Joseph Baum highlights the *pleasures enriched by hotels* and William Tabler, in his Prologue, emphasizes the hotel's *technical efficiency.* Equally important is the *marketing* of hotels. As keenly concerned creators and decision-makers in the hotel planning and design field, we are well aware that *the guest* makes the ultimate decision when choosing a hotel. How well do we truly understand his or her needs and desires? By the time we think we do, customers have changed. Therefore, each time we plan and design, we must again ask, *"What would the customer really like in a hotel?"* The most up-to-date answers come from market research, tracking guest experience, and long-range forecasting of social and economic trends, combined with common sense, logic, and pure intuition. All these factors forge the most effective tools for advancing hotels that best anticipate guest needs through *creative design and marketing.*

In this process, nothing is more essential to formulating successful and appealing hotels than continuous, comprehensive consumer feedback; and to this end most major hotel companies increasingly employ market research, including scientific surveys and in-depth interviewing techniques to better identify and confirm actual guest preferences and trends. Such data are essential for sound hotel design as well as effective marketing aimed at the following triple goal: attracting more guests, new guests, and repeat guests, or, in business terms, increasing *market share*, developing *new markets*, and improving *guest satisfaction.*

Market share

The value of such research was clearly demonstrated by one major "trend-spotting coup" of the past decade. Surveys discovered that Holiday Inns' market had shifted dramatically from family to business travelers and, moreover, that emerging life-styles had significantly altered guest preferences since the 1950s, when the chain began its unparalleled growth. Responding to this new market environment, the company modified its basic plans to include more specialized facilities and upscale hotels in the 80s, plus an immediate multi-million-dollar renovation program to convert many of its standard formula double-double rooms to more luxuriously designed single-kings. Also, by retiring its famous flashing road sign the company signaled its changing image and new design strategy, aimed at reversing a declining market share. A combination of astute social and economic forecasting and opportunity also drew the chain into the growing casino hotel market (see Chapter 13, The Casino Hotel) through acquisition and expansion of Harrah's, which soon became its most successful division.

Other consumer trends include recreational sports centers, health spas, condominium hotels, timesharing resorts, vacation villages, restored country inns, suburban conference centers, video conferencing facilities, business service centers, office suites, increased in-room amenities (such as expanded audiovisual entertainment and educational programs, computers, exercise equipment, and even in-room casino gaming), multiresort communities, and mixed-use commercial centers integrated with hotels, all of which are discussed in Part 1.

But when all the research, financial feasibility studies, facilities programs, technical standards, and management systems are completed, it is the specific *design* that makes the big difference. Even Holiday Inns has begun featuring its upgraded architecture in its ads. It may have been said: "If the bed was hard and if the eggs were cold in the morning, how nice the building was makes very little difference." But since so many hotels now feature a high standard of service, cleanliness, fine cuisine, and varied amenities, it becomes the architecture and design that count today. True, a hard mattress may still lose more points for occupancy than a "hard-edged design," but modern technology has increasingly eliminated such possible pitfalls, bringing *design ambience* to the forefront of the competition for guest occupancy.

As Paul Goldberger, architectural critic for *The New York Times*, stated: "The ads for another new building proclaimed 'A Touch of Class,' and spoke of the building's four-story atrium. Architecture has become, in short, a marketing tool." For example, the Warwick Post Oak Hotel in Houston boasts that it was "Designed by I. M. Pei." Taking this premise as a challenge, this book offers the following vital data needed to design popular, viable hotels: (1) examples of successful prototypes and their standards, (2) a background of required technical information, and (3) data on guest desires reflected in market research and attitudes of experienced developers.

New markets

Hotel demand is driven by a variety of factors beside travel. For example, in Philadelphia in the late 70s, when that city's hotels were dismal and tired, visitors would do their business quickly and head home the same day. Given newer, well-designed hotels such as the Franklin Plaza and Four Seasons, people are now attracted to stay overnight. Like other consumer products, *better hotels can create new demand.*

From banking to airline services, businesses are becoming segmented in the biggest entrepreneurial wave since the 20s, when the mass market was first discovered. Better-educated, more sophisticated postwar baby-boomers are demanding ever-widening choices for their individual tastes and varying moods, such as shopping on Rodeo Drive one day and at discount warehouses another. Since the "typical" consumer is now virtually extinct—only 7 percent of today's population now falls into that traditional mold—more diverse services are offered to satisfy their demands and get their attention. Surveys of recent successful hotels as well as long-range forecasts clearly confirm an accelerated trend toward what's called "market segmentation"—that is, isolating a particular consumer need and creating a special facility to tap it—*through a new type of hotel or by improving on an existing concept.*

Beginning primarily in the past five years, specialized prototypes include the "suites-only" hotel (Chapter 8, The Suite Hotel), which has rapidly become popular. Note how media ads, based on market research, clearly reveal such trends: "You Don't Live in One Room at Home. Why Live in One Room away from Home?" notes Guest Quarters; and "Welcome to the Suite Life" invites Granada Royale. The discovery that two rooms can be offered for virtually the same price as one, through an all-suite hotel containing efficient, well-designed suite units, may be the most revolutionary design concept to emerge in the industry since Kemmons Wilson discovered the 12 × 18-foot (3.7 × 5.5-meter) standard double room for Holiday Inns in the early 50s. What customer will go back to a single room after trying a suite? Already, subsegments of the suite market are proliferating, illustrated by such rapidly growing chains as Guest Quarters, which focusses primarily on downtown areas, and Granada Royale, targeting the suburban market.

Towers or concierge floors, a form of "in-hotel segmentation" featuring so-called old-world luxury, spread from its original marketer, New York's Waldorf Towers, to Boston's Sheraton in the 60s to the "new-image" Crowne Plaza Holiday Inns of the 80s. "On top of our great Boston Hotel there's an intimate little hotel" informs Sheraton; and "Manhattan has a very private hotel within a hotel" advertises the Executive Tower of the New York Hilton. All contain private elevator service to special upper-floor registration desks and lounges as well as more luxurious decor and amenities on those floors. The popularity of the towers and the suite ideas also illustrates the "trickle-down" principle, where *luxury preferences enter the mass market over time.*

"On display in each hotel is an original masterpiece by a contemporary artist" boasts Holiday Inn Crowne Plaza. Previously, only super-luxury hotels offered such unique appointments. Which luxury element should next be adopted by a budget motel to improve its guest appeal?

As in other fields, where increasingly sophisticated consumers generally choose more customized products, guests often prefer specialized hotels that are better designed for their specific needs and tastes. *Segmentation offers the public a much wider variety of choice and clearer recognition of brand images.* To exploit this proven concept, major chains have established new subchains with more individual personalities such as Ramada Renaissance; Courtyard-by-Marriott; three new, different priced brands by Quality Inns; Howard Johnson's Plaza brand; Inter-Continental's Forum line; Trust House Forte's Travelodge subchain; Holiday Inn's Crowne Plaza, their all-suite subsidiary Embassy Suites, and their budget chain Hampton Inn; and Accor's four brands: Sofitel (deluxe), Novotel (midscale), Mercure (roadside), and Ibis (budget).

Among the totally new companies spawned by segmentation are La Quinta with a loyal following for its no-frills approach with a Mexican design flavor and its more sophisticated and upscale counterpart, La Mansion. Occupancies tend to be higher and more recession-proof for chains with clearly perceived images and a faithful clientele than those with broad, but lukewarm support. Habitat Inns and Brock Residence Inn feature residential townhouse atmospheres, while Charlie Clubs offers health spas and special health food menus. Their focus gives them an edge with different types of travelers or with the same travelers on different types of trips. The search for new market niches therefore continues as the industry's latest gold rush.

Guest satisfaction

Contrary to previous theory, the guestroom's overwhelming importance clearly rises above any other element in creating the hotel's bottom-line impression. Until this was proven by market surveys, many leading designers and their hotel clients had neglected the guestroom design, concentrating their efforts and budgets on the main public areas. But when the guest's true perception became known, based on in-depth interviews, design improvements followed quickly.

Other interviews revealed guests' deep concern over fire safety, hastening further improvements in fire protection systems beyond those merely required by codes (discussed in Chapter 21, Special Systems). Safety devices were visually emphasized rather than esthetically obscured because, contrary to many designers' prior belief, guests felt more comfortable psychologically with such equipment in plain view.

Survey methods have also been used to test specific features during the design phase, with the findings ultimately influencing the final plans. In one case, Holiday Inns prepared renderings, illustrating alternative lowrise and highrise designs, which were shown to guests so that their comments could help determine the final building configuration of a 300-unit Holiday Inn expansion in Orlando (they selected the lowrise model). In another example, an experimental restaurant was installed in the Marriott Burlington to test guests' reactions to a proposed self-service concept being considered for the company's new hotels.

Also useful in improving details, a questionnaire administered to Inter-Continental guests first established the standard that phones should have long cords so they could be moved to nightstands or desks. But guest preferences may not always be consistent with the industry's responsibilities. For example, in spite of guest polls favoring carpet in bathrooms, management still wisely continues to provide tile for hygienic protection. Often, such conceptual questions as new hotel prototypes require in-depth discussion with selected cross-sections of guests in order to probe their psychological reactions to the proposed new facilities illustrated by drawings and sketches. For example, such tests continue to confirm the overwhelming desire of consumers for a residential type of ambience and more intricate decor, in effect reinforcing the postmodern trend.

Some long-range economic forecasts have shown a possible flattening of overall demand and potential oversupply of rooms in the luxury market in the late 80s. This has caused several chains to reenter the budget motel field with a vigor reminiscent of that of the 50s. The resulting competition clearly helps serve a large public, neglected to date, by the lack of well-designed facilities with good price values in this market.

Greater focus is also being placed on what hotel design can do to better accommodate such expanding groups as women travelers and the elderly. For example, of the almost 20 percent of business travelers who are now women, a large percentage prefer room service rather than eating out, suggesting increased attention to the quality of this service and of price values in this area. Some women may prefer separate women's floors and also fold-up wall beds to avoid having the bed in view during business meetings.

Age demographics also need to be considered as closely in hotel planning as in other consumer fields. For example, since the 65-and-older group will increase almost 20 percent by the early 1990s and since they spend more time in their rooms, they clearly ought to be offered more space, possibly by folding wall beds, electrically operated for their convenience. With the 20- to 35-year-old group still increasing in number, expanded bar-lounge facilities can be expected in the 80s. Also, through nonsmokers floors, better exercise facilities, and more varied menus, today's increased health consciousness and other life-style changes, will be better satisfied.

Fortunately for the industry, its most frequent and highest spending customers—the 25- to 44-age group—will increase by over 20 percent through 1990. Coupled with a worldwide economic rebound, about 3 to 4 million new rooms as well as the complete remodeling of another 1.5 to 2 million existing rooms will be needed to meet demand through the end of the century. With this vast market ahead, uncovering guest preferences through research, no matter how costly, provides a potent tool for marketing and design; and such data ensure that valid consumer desires are not overlooked.

But only major chains can support even partial studies of the marketplace, with such data highly fragmented and confidential. Nevertheless, *all design professionals can keep abreast of the valid trends by reading between the lines, as it were, of some of the key media campaigns noted here, which are based on market research, and by maintaining an awareness of the latest and most successful designs and standards that are illustrated in this book.*

Part 1
HOTEL TYPES

While prior to World War II, downtown hotels and elegant resorts virtually monopolized the lodging industry, today's contemporary hotels are as rich in variety as they are in location, with new specialties being created almost daily. Part 1 reviews more than 30 types of hotels now thriving in today's increasingly differentiated market, with a chapter devoted to each of 12 major categories. For example, the suburban hotel includes several subdivisions as diverse as airport hotels are from country inns. Resorts also encompass a wide range of types as unique as the seaside marina is from the ski lodge. And the old downtown structure has made a comeback through innovative renovation, restoration, addition, and adaptive reuse.

Determining what makes the conference center different, for instance, from the convention hotel, resort, or mega-hotel is clearly addressed in terms of specific location, design options, and planning considerations, as well as social and cultural implications, while future trends are also outlined for each category. Targeting a particular market to fulfill the hotel's function is a continuing theme. For example, luxury resorts and super-luxury hotels absolutely must have superb restaurants to attract their more affluent clientele.

This part begins with an overview tracing the hotel's evolution and forecasting the industry's future development. This historical perspective, summarized in a chart on hotel milestones, becomes another theme threading through these chapters.

1

OVERVIEW

"Enjoy it for a day, a week, or a lifetime"

invites the Turnberry Isle Yacht and Country Club in Miami

Arriving in Isfahan centuries ago, you could stay outside the city gates at a roadside *caravansary* now called the Sha Abbas. Or desiring better service, you might continue to The Khan, an in-town hotel. As a "frequent traveler" journeying to Rome, you could stay at a downtown *mansione,* a boarding house on the Appian Way, or at a spa resort.

While the quality of hotels improved immeasurably over several centuries, the basic categories remained almost as simple and familiar as in ancient times. But in the last few decades the competition created by the continuing hotel boom has spawned a series of more diverse and complex hotel types responding to an ever-growing variety of carefully discerned guest preferences.

Among the thirty hotel types discussed in this part of the book, many have evolved only in the past decade. The more prominent forms expanding on the market today include suite hotels, condo hotels, hotel/office buildings, hotel/shopping malls, timesharing resorts, vacation villages, marina hotels, casino hotels, and health and sports resorts. At the same time, hotel restorations, country inns, and small downtown hotels have enjoyed renewed popularity. Other variations include airport/conference centers, casino/convention resorts, and one new breed with facilities so broad that it can only be described as a "mega-hotel." Like Henry Ford's Model-T, following years of sameness and complacency, hotels have sprouted new models designed to please almost every taste and pocketbook, as might be expected of an industry dedicated to guest satisfaction.

Driven by growing consumer sophistication and demand, intensive competition of various chains, and a better understanding of what the public wants, the hotel industry has committed itself to supplying an ever-widening spectrum of varied new product lines. This has been further stimulated by recognition of the increased marketing potential of hotels when imaginatively packaged and designed to create and satisfy a variety of needs.

VARIETIES

While it was once possible to divide hotels into a few major types—downtown, roadside, and resort—there are so many varieties today, each with its own standards and special features, that previous classifications are inadequate. Even professionals specializing in a few of these categories may be surprised by the number of different types proliferating on the market today and the wide variations in their facilities' programs. For example, less than a decade ago, suite hotels did not exist, while today there are several types. With changing economic conditions, the residential hotel has become the condo hotel, while new lifestyles have spawned the casual vacation village and the fitness spa. The casino hotel has continued to develop its own new form while the mega-hotel is just in its infancy. Convention hotels have grown dramatically to keep up with increasingly larger groups, while another new breed, the conference center, has responded to the changing needs of the business world. Mixed-use complexes have reshaped our communities, while planned community developments and multi-resort complexes have developed vast new territories from Hilton Head in South Carolina and Harbour Island in Tampa, Florida to Cancun, Mexico, and Kaanapali, Maui.

Part 2, Design Guide, provides information on how to program and develop the various types of hotels, while the latest examples of each category are illustrated and included in later chapters of this part. To be familiar with the different features of each type of hotel, visiting the hotels illustrated and discussed in this book is recommended. For representative examples of the various types, including architects and interior designers, see the list of hotels in the Appendix.

GENEALOGY

Visualize, in the shape of an evolutionary tree, the historical roots and branches of the various forms of hotels as they flower into the 21st century. For example, the modern motel is descended from the coach inn and posting station, which was in turn rooted in the monastic inn and *caravansary* during the Middle Ages and the *mansione* of ancient times—all catering to the travel modes of their eras. As more contemporary illustrations of this process, the new suite hotel was developed as a hybrid of the residential hotel and the condominium, while the timesharing resort combines the condo with the resort. For a historical review, see the table of hotel milestones and accompanying tree diagrams of hotel types.

An understanding of how these different forms of hotels evolved is essential for developing improved new hotel types and projecting future growth trends in the field. For example, in 1981, the People's Republic of China embarked on a long-overdue major expansion of downtown hotels and tourist facilities, providing the infrastructure needed to serve international business travelers as well as gain much-needed foreign exchange credits. The Chinese have benefited from worldwide experience in the design of their initial hotels catering to foreign travelers. As their economy develops, they will also be able to better plan for the many other types of hotels eventually needed by adapting today's innovative hotel typology to their own cultural standards.

In the industrialized nations, *familiarity with new types of hotels is essential to developers in planning overall expansion strategies and devising more imaginative prototypes to attract new groups to hotels.* Since some types are as different as a single family house is from a highrise apartment tower in the residential field, *it is essential for the designer to understand the variations in facilities, areas, and circulation patterns required for each new form of hotel.* Also, an overall familiarity with all types encourages the cross-fertilization of ideas (for example, introducing health clubs to fill relaxation needs at conference centers, adding meeting rooms to create mini-conference retreats out of country inns, or using elements of super-luxury hotels such as private registration desks and original artwork to upgrade other types of hotels).

New and better ideas for different kinds of hotels will continue to come from all members of the consulting team, ranging from market researchers to food and beverage experts and including a variety of disciplines from consumer polling to systems technology, as well as design professionals themselves. (The use of different consultants in these fields is discussed in Chapter 24, Professional Practice, in Part 3.)

CLASSIFICATIONS

Since hotels are generally classified by location, function, and other special characteristics, a given hotel may fall into more than one category—for example, the Nova Park Elysée in Paris is both a downtown hotel and an example of adaptive reuse. However, this overlap should not impair the usefulness of the classification system, which permits easy access to information by subject headings generally used in the hotel field and understood by the public.

While hotel classifications are necessary for purposes of organizing and referencing information, they are by no means perfect and no substitute for specific knowledge of the individual character and detailed ingredients of a hotel. As the *New Haven Register* of September 18, 1983, lamented: "Along with new hotel types and almost infinite combinations and varieties, it is increasingly difficult for guests to select a hotel when labels are inadequate or misleading. Downtown hotels have as many tennis courts, pools, and saunas as resorts. Resorts have as many convention or conference guests as downtown convention hotels or airport meeting centers. Motor inns are not necessarily superior to motels. And 'Inns' are not necessarily old. 'Lodge,' 'spa,' 'guest ranch' are also unclear labels. Price is no indicator—expensive hotels may have small rooms, while budget hotels have larger, better appointed rooms. Buying on the basis of ingredients looks like the new wave."

In other words, it's not so much what you call it, but what's in it that counts. In this book we deal *with what's in* different types of hotels as well as *what's "in" with* different types of hotels.

PLANNING AND DESIGN CONSIDERATIONS

Since each hotel type has a different goal as to the kinds of guests it seeks, its planning requirements will vary by the location selected, size, image, space standards, circulation, and other characteristics. For example, convention hotels and conference centers require closeness to airports, while vacation villages and ski lodges do not. Airport hotels and roadside motels need high visibility and signage, while conference centers, country inns, and vacation villages seek seclusion. And super-luxury hotels must be small to create an intimate atmosphere, while luxury hotels must be large enough to justify the large number of restaurants, lounges, and banquet rooms required by first-class or five-star international standards.

Design considerations also vary by type. For example, resorts require larger rooms, closets, and drawer space than downtown hotels due to the longer stays of their guests and higher numbers of occupants per room. Roadside motels may require larger restaurants than other hotels for peak periods such as breakfast, but no room service. Casino hotels require a glittering design, while conference center decor needs to be understated. Also, similar design concepts are *expressed* differently in each type of hotel. For example, the social pastime of people-watching in the downtown or suburban hotel is accommodated by its lobby or atrium space. In a resort, the same purpose is served by the pool deck, the sun deck at the ski lodge, the commons area at a conference center, the outdoor bar in the piazza of the vacation village, or the tea lounge of the super-luxury hotel.

While the specific facilities, area programs, and technical requirements are discussed in Part 2, Design Guide, and Part 3, Special Concerns, this part summarizes the main *variations and trends* in current planning and design for each distinct type of hotel.

Union Hotel, Saratoga Springs, New York. *Taken from "Frank Leslie's Illustrated Newspaper," July 25, 1868.*

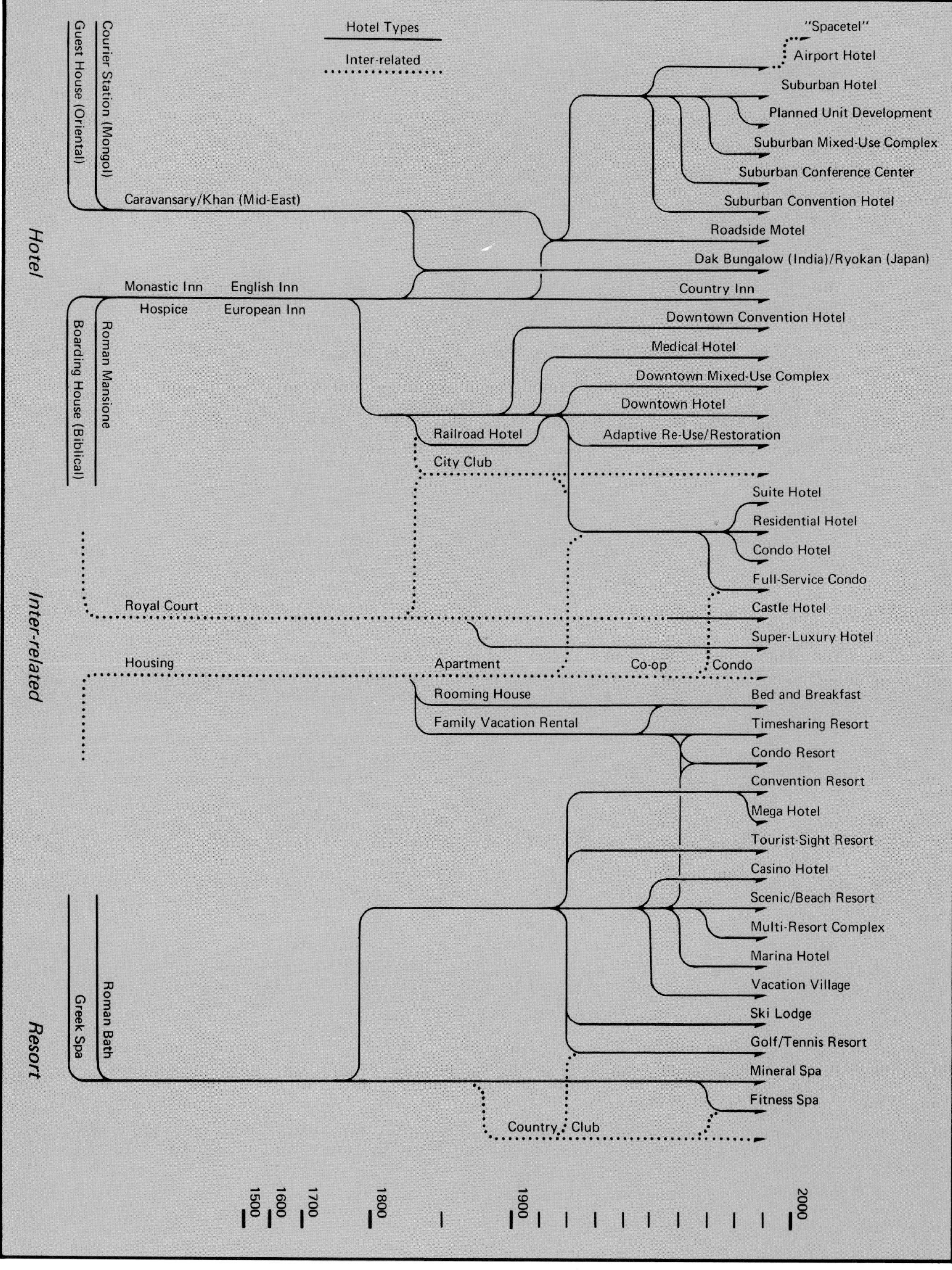

Hotel Types
Inter-related
Guest House (Oriental)
Courier Station (Mongol)
Caravansary/Khan (Mid-East)
Hotel
Monastic Inn
English Inn
Hospice
European Inn
Boarding House (Biblical)
Roman Mansione
"Spacetel"
Airport Hotel
Suburban Hotel
Planned Unit Development
Suburban Mixed-Use Complex
Suburban Conference Center
Suburban Convention Hotel
Roadside Motel
Dak Bungalow (India)/Ryokan (Japan)
Country Inn
Downtown Convention Hotel
Medical Hotel
Downtown Mixed-Use Complex
Downtown Hotel
Railroad Hotel
Adaptive Re-Use/Restoration
City Club
Suite Hotel
Residential Hotel
Condo Hotel
Full-Service Condo
Inter-related
Royal Court
Castle Hotel
Super-Luxury Hotel
Housing
Apartment
Co-op
Condo
Rooming House
Bed and Breakfast
Family Vacation Rental
Timesharing Resort
Condo Resort
Convention Resort
Mega Hotel
Tourist-Sight Resort
Casino Hotel
Scenic/Beach Resort
Multi-Resort Complex
Marina Hotel
Vacation Village
Ski Lodge
Golf/Tennis Resort
Resort
Greek Spa
Roman Bath
Mineral Spa
Fitness Spa
Country Club
1500
1600
1700
1800
1900
2000

Hotel Milestones

BIBLICAL
500 B.C. Boarding houses existed.
First resorts at mineral and hot springs in Greece.
Mansiones approved by government built along Roman roads to lodge government sanctioned travelers; some inns existed for others.
Romans spread spa resorts to England, Switzerland, Mideast; introduced *campona* (inns) in England. Riviera popular with Phoenician and Greek traders.
Caravansaries, cloistered courtyard caravan stops, provided by government along roads in Middle East.
Khans, small inns, established in Middle East towns.

MIDDLE AGES Manorial lords, abbeys, and monasteries sheltered some travelers.
Monastic inns run by religious orders. Hospices built as hospitals and shelters for travelers.
Some inns developed in larger towns (no meals).
Rooming houses used as relay stations for mail, government transport, rest stops, changing horses.
Hospitalers created shelters for Crusaders and pilgrims traveling to Holy Land.

1100s Travel became safe in Europe. Inns prospered with freedom and right to travel, declined in times of lawlessness.
The European inn gradually developed.
The Three Kings Inn in Basle, Switzerland, opened—earliest inn still operating.

1200s Guest houses, courier mail stations in China, Mongolia.
Rooming and relay stations for mail, government transportation, rest stops.
Cour St. Georges Inn opened in Ghent, Belgium.
Angel Inn opened in Granthan, Lincolnshire, England.

1300s The English country inn developed; some London inns.
Castle Inn founded in Taunton, Somerset, England.
French law required innkeepers to replace stolen property plus three times damages to victims.

1400s French law required hotel register.
English law established regulations for inns.
The Krone Inn in Solothrun, Switzerland, is earliest adaptive reuse—converted from residence.

1500s European spas revived in Carlsbad, Marienbad.
Stagecoaches developed, using Roman road system; teams changed, carriages checked, and travelers rested at posting houses.
English innkeeper set pattern for Europe and America to follow; 6000 inns in England.
Inn plan took form of enclosed cobble court with arched entrance, rooms along two sides, kitchen and public rooms at front side, stable and storage at rear.
First travelers' guide rating inns in France.

1600s Hotel industry developed in Europe with well-placed and reliable cuisine "at sign of insignia on a metal plaque, grating its rugged hinges in every wind."
Seaport inns developed in American cities, for example, The Blue Anchor in Philadelphia.
Village inns developed as required by Massachusetts law in all towns, for example, Old Yarmouth Inn in Yarmouthport.
First scheduled coach service established in England.

1700s Clubhouses similar to British clubs and Masonic lodges developed in America.
Spa resorts developed in Yellow Springs, Pennsylvania, and White Sulphur Springs, West Virginia.
Boodles and Coventry Clubhouses opened in London.
Market Square Taverne founded in Williamsburg, Virginia.
Place Vendome in Paris is first mixed-use complex.

OPPOSITE PAGE

Evolutionary Tree Diagram of Hotel Types *Charted here is the development of diverse hotel types, mostly emerging in the last few decades, as well as their relation to other building types.*

LEFT

Hotel Milestones. *Reflecting social change as well as new technology, this list traces the most significant events in the development of lodging, from Biblical times to today's worldwide advances.*

Hotel Milestones (continued)

1780s
Dessien's in Calais, France, is early large inn.
Covent Garden Inn in London is early large inn.

1790s
Industrial revolution stimulated hotels in England, Europe, and America; resorts developed.
Corre's Hotel and City Hotel in New York were first downtown hotels.
Hotel d'Angleterre opened in Copenhagen, Denmark, is earliest large adaptive reuse.
Saratoga Springs, New York, developed as spa resort.

1800s
White Hart Hotel opened in Salisbury, England.
Royal Hotel founded in Plymouth, England.
Luxury "swagger hotels" established in major cities.
Early resorts built along French and Italian Riviera.
Imposing clubhouses built.
Fulton's Cleremont steamship launched.
Exchange Coffee House in Boston is first atrium hotel.

1810s
Ryokan guest houses developed in Japan.
Dak bungalow, 24-hour guest stops, run by government in India.

1820s
Catskill Mountain House in New York State is early major resort.
City Hotel in Baltimore, Maryland, is first with partial gaslight.
B & O Railroad began passenger service.
Tremont House in Boston is first luxury downtown hotel with indoor toilets, door locks on rooms, and à la carte menu.

1830s
Saratoga Springs Hotel opened in New York State.
American Hotel in New York City is first with gaslight throughout.
Astor House opened in New York City.
St. Charles and St. Louis Hotels established in New Orleans, Louisiana.
Holt's Hotel opened in New York City is first with an elevator for baggage.
Reform Club in London had courtyard roofed in to become an early atrium.
Euston Station Hotel opened in London is early example of railroad hotel.

1840s
Railroads replace coaches; coach-route inns declined.
Shepheards Hotel opened in Cairo, is early major adaptive reuse.
Hotel des Trois Couronnes founded in Vevey, Switzerland.
Bar au Lac Hotel opened in Zurich, Switzerland.
New York Hotel in New York City is first with private baths.
Planters Hotel founded in St. Louis, Missouri.
The Homestead established in Hot Springs, Virginia.
Resorts developed in Coney Island, New York.

1850s
Spa resorts reached height of popularity.
Resorts developed at Niagara Falls, New York, and New Jersey shore.
Mills House opened in Charleston, South Carolina (rebuilt in 1970.)
Parker House established in Boston (rebuilt in 1927).
Fifth Avenue Hotel in New York City is first with passenger elevators.

1860s
Railroad terminal hotels such as Charing Cross in London were main type of hotels developed through 1920s.
Mohonk Mountain House established in the Catskills in New York State.
Central and Union Pacific Railroads were joined.

1870s
Palmer House opened in Chicago is largest of time and first built with a fireproof structure (rebuilt 1925).
Palace Hotel opened in San Francisco is earliest hotel with a large atrium.
Sherman House founded in Chicago.
Grand Hotel built in Point Clear, Alabama.
Continental opened in Paris (restored in 1970 by Inter-Continental).

1880s
Hotel Del Monte established in Monterey, California.
Hotel Everett in New York City is first with partial electric light.

Sagamore Hotel at Lake George in New York State is first with electricity in all rooms.
Chelsea Hotel in New York City is first large residential hotel.
Mountainview House established in Whitefield, New Hampshire.
Ponce De Leon Hotel in St. Augustine, Florida, is first built of concrete.
Grand Hotel in Mackinac Island, Michigan, has largest veranda.
Victoria Hotel in Kansas City, Missouri, is first with baths in all rooms.
Hotel Del Coronado opened in San Diego, California is largest resort of its time.
Whiteface Inn and Golf Club founded in Lake Placid, New York.
Savoy in London is first hotel with theater, chapel, print shop, laundry.

1890s The Broadmoor opened in Colorado Springs, Colorado.
Brown Palace in Denver, Colorado, has early atrium still operating.
Copley Square Hotel opened in Boston.
École Hoteliere in Lausanne, Switzerland, is first hotel school.
Hotel Netherland in New York City is first with phones in all rooms.
The Breakers opened in Palm Beach, Florida (rebuilt 1906, 1926).
Lake Placid Club established in Lake Placid, New York.
Original Waldorf-Astoria in New York City (on site of Empire State Building) was 17 stories—tallest of time.
Wentworth-by-the-Sea opened in New Castle, New Hampshire.
Claridges, Berkeley, Connaught all opened in London.

1900s The Ritz founded in London.
The Willard opened in Washington, D.C.
The Plaza built in New York City.
Taj Mahal Hotel opened in Bombay, (restored 1972 by Inter-Continental).
Statler in Buffalo, New York, set main principles of modern hotel circulation flow.
First cross-country U.S. auto trip.

1910s Grand Central Terminal in New York City is early mixed-use complex.
Boarding house resorts developed in Catskills in New York State.
Bellevue Stratford opened in Philadelphia.
Copley Plaza built in Boston.
Beverly Hills Hotel established in California.
The Greenbrier opened in White Sulphur Springs, West Virginia.
Asilomar near Carmel, California, is first nonprofit conference center.
Kahler Hotel in Rochester, Minnesota, is first medical hotel.
First trans-Atlantic flight and first scheduled airline.
Hotel Pennsylvania in New York City has 2200 rooms—largest of time.

1920s "*Hotel Boom #1*" generated by economic prosperity.
Grand Central in New York City is example of further developed hotel complex.
Miami Beach developed with Mediterranean-style architecture, for example, Flamingo, Pancoast, Roney Plaza hotels.
School of Hotel Administration established at Cornell University.
First nonstop cross-country plane flight.
Baker and Adolphus hotels opened in Dallas, Texas.
Royal Hawaiian established in Honolulu.
Prohibition caused decline of hotel/restaurant business.
The Ritz-Carlton opened on the Boston Public Gardens.
The Statler in Boston is first hotel/office building.
Ahwanee Hotel built in Yosemite National Park in California.
Biltmore founded in Santa Barbara, California.
Stevens Hotel in Chicago has 2700 rooms—largest of time.
The Cloister opened in Sea Island, Georgia.
Arizona Biltmore built in Phoenix.

1930s Depression forced most U.S. hotels into receivership.
The new Waldorf-Astoria in New York City, largest of its time, built during depression.

Hotel Milestones (continued)

1940s Statler in Washington, D.C., is one of few hotels built during World War II.
Flamingo in Las Vegas is a first casino hotel.
Statler Hotels in Los Angeles, Hartford, Connecticut, Dallas, Texas, first post-war hotels.
San Souci in Miami is first new post-war resort.

1950s "*Hotel Boom #2*" generated by mass travel.
Resorts developed in Caribbean.
Vacation village concept developed by Club Med.
Holiday Inn is first motel with large rooms.
Casino hotels developed in Las Vegas, Nevada.
Fountainbleau opened in Miami Beach.
First commercial trans-Atlantic jet service.
Airlines began developing hotels.

1960s 23,000 hotels, 40,000 motels, 170 chains operated in U.S.
Resorts developed in Spanish Mediterranean, Portugal, Balearic Islands, Scandinavia, Greece, Yugoslavia.
Hyatt Regency in Atlanta, Georgia, reintroduced atrium.
Arden House of Columbia University, Tarrytown House in Tarrytown, New York, and General Electric Co. in Crotonville, New York, are first conference centers used extensively by businesses.
Sheraton at Prudential Center in Boston is first major hotel/mixed-use complex.
Hilton Palacio del Rio Hotel in San Antonio, Texas, was first built with concrete prefabricated modules.

1970s Boeing 747 introduced; airlines became active in hotel development through subsidiary chains.
New hotel expansion took up slack caused by demoliton and conversions of hotels to apartments and office buildings.
Walt Disney World in Orlando, Florida, opens as first major hotel amusement destination center.
Extensive hotel development in Middle East generated by oil prosperity.
Luxury condominiums developed offering hotel services.
Hotel restorations extensively developed.
First suite hotels converted from condos.
Timesharing and condominium resorts developed.
Peachtree Plaza in Atlanta, Georgia, has 70 stories—tallest hotel.
Multiresort complexes developed in Maui, Hawaii, and Cancun, Mexico.
China opened to foreign tourists; international hotel experts invited to participate in development of facilities.

1980s "*Hotel Boom #3*" generated by innovative marketing and development of specialized types of hotels; many combined with large-scale complexes such as Copley Place and Lafayette Place in Boston.
Airport hotels, conference centers, suite hotels, vacation villages, health spas, marina hotels, ski lodges, timesharing and condo resorts expand rapidly.
Casino hotels developed in Atlantic City, New Jersey.
Condo hotels developed such as The Ritz-Carlton and Four Seasons in Boston and U.N. Plaza in N.Y.
Limited service budget motels continue rapid growth.
Popular revival of country inns.
Marriott Marquis in Atlanta is largest convention hotel.
Marriott Marquis in Times Square in New York City is highest cost hotel project.
Hyatt and Marriott open mega-hotels in Orlando, Florida.
Hotel Boom in China; 50 major hotels under construction or design including 2000-room Lidu in Peking; increase from 200,000 visitors at beginning of decade to 5,000,000 per year expected by end of century.
First comprehensive book on hotel planning published by Whitney Library of Design.

2 THE DOWNTOWN HOTEL

"In the Heart of it All"

lures The Bostonian

A product of the burgeoning American city, the earliest downtown hotels made their debut on Broadway in New York City in the early 1790s. The French word *hôtel,* meaning mansion, was adopted to distinguish their new form from the early European inns, American seaport inns, and New England village inns from which they were descended. The downtown hotel was much larger than any inn, had more comfortable rooms, served food as good as any restaurant, and provided a center for fashionable social and business occasions.

During the early 1800s, hotels of this type spread to the main U.S. cities including Boston, Philadelphia, and Baltimore, culminating in the most luxurious commercial structure of its time, the Tremont House in Boston. Containing 173 rooms, an impressive lobby, a restaurant with French menus, and space for meetings and gatherings, this elegant, advanced four-story granite structure located on a prominent downtown site gained worldwide attention and set the course of future hotel development. The Tremont established the precedent that hotels exemplify the best in design and take the lead in introducing the latest public conveniences and fashions, which, in 1829, included door locks and indoor bathrooms as well as French cuisine. In later years, this precedent continued, as guests would try their first electric lights, elevators, phones, color TV, and teleconferencing in hotels.

Within a few decades after the opening of the Tremont House, most major cities had at least one prestigious hotel. The Astor and Waldorf hotels were developed on New York's Fifth Avenue. The Palmer House and the Sherman House, the largest hotels of their time, became the pride of Chicago's State Street, while The Palace on San Francisco's Market Street and the Brown Palace in downtown Denver, Colorado, displayed their impressive atriums.

But with the advent of the railroad, most hotel development for the next half-century took place near terminals, with coach-route inns declining. London produced the Savoy, the first hotel with a theater, chapel, and laundry. Not to be outdone, America established the main principles of modern highrise hotels when the Buffalo Statler was built in 1908 in New York State, bringing the service departments up to the ground floor, surrounding them with restaurants, bars, and banquet facilities, and connecting them to the guestroom floors by means of service elevators.

Based on this new prototype hotels boomed in the wave of economic prosperity

THE BOSTONIAN
LOBBY LEVEL

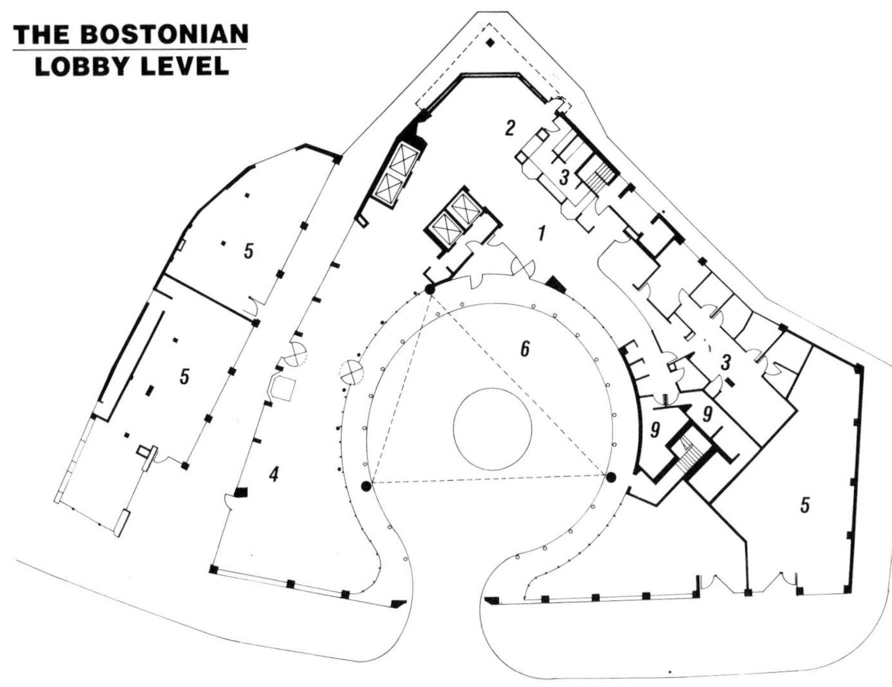

THE BOSTONIAN
3rd FLOOR

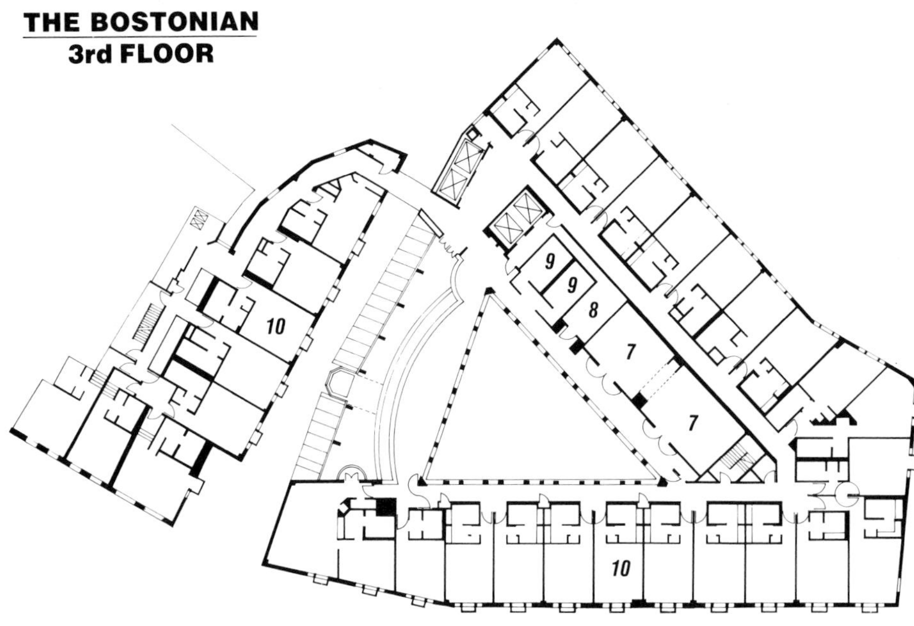

PRECEDING PAGE AND ABOVE

The Bostonian, Boston, Massachusetts. *The native brick and granite Bostonian provides a perfect companion to the adjacent Quincy Market entertainment area, one of the nation's foremost downtown restorations. Carved out of the odd-shaped block's center, a circular drive emphasizes the arrival experience, and its granite paving and sculptural fountain provide instant upscale ambience. Period pieces are integrated with stainless steel modernity; for instance, individual French Provincial registration desks are combined with a glittering glass elevator that rises to a 120-seat gourmet restaurant overlooking historic Faneuil Hall. Primarily serving business travelers and tourists, rather than groups, 100-seat meeting room is available.*

Wooden French windows open on small balconies with wrought-iron railings, and flower boxes blend the new wings with the adjacent restored facade dating back to the mid-1800s. The ground floor retail spaces and bar/lounge harmonize with the neighboring streetscape and its varied shopping and entertainment facilities.

Key: ***(1)*** *lobby,* ***(2)*** *registration,* ***(3)*** *administration,* ***(4)*** *lounge,* ***(5)*** *lease space,* ***(6)*** *porte cochere,* ***(7)*** *meeting rooms,* ***(8)*** *pantry,* ***(9)*** *toilets,* ***(10)*** *guestrooms.*

following World War I. The massive downtown construction of the 1920s produced such leading lights as New York's towering Waldorf-Astoria and Boston's Ritz. But following the economic collapse, the prolonged recession of the 30s and World War II caused a hiatus of almost two decades in hotel construction.

A second postwar boom was triggered by the increase in mass travel, with new, long-overdue hotel construction beginning first in the United States and spreading throughout the major cities of the world, finally reaching mainland China in the 80s. But the final two decades of the century are ushering in a third new boom, stimulated largely by creative marketing and development methods, which treat hotels as "destinations," featuring new, expanded types of facilities often combined with mixed-use complexes.

Social and Cultural Implications

People love to go to hotels, even more so than in earlier times when the Archbishop of Glasgow in the early 1600s recommended them as "the best places to die" and Samuel Johnson expressed his love for inns in the 1700s—"nothing else can produce such happiness." Similar strains have been heard from a former psychologist and hotelier, René Hatt, who defines today's downtown hotel as a "happy house." Since much happiness is found in bed, the hotel clearly has a head start. Also, due to a concentrated effort by the industry, hotel food has never reached a higher art form than in the past decade. Another desired criterion is happiness of mind and body. For this, more audiovisual entertainment and computerized self-improvement programs have been established, including a greater role in business education. Following these objectives, downtown hotels have increasingly provided conference center facilities, as well as office suites and audiovisual, secretarial, computer, and communications services, while fitness clubs have also become standard amenities.

Political and Economic Implications

From Atlanta to Zambia, hotels continue to play a pivotal part in the political life of nations and their cities. For example, during the height of international crises in such cities as Dacca, Pakistan, Kabul, Afghanistan, Managua, Nicaragua, and Teheran, Iran, Inter-Continental Hotels provided oases of relative calm and security where diplomats and press corps could continue to function and maintain communications with the outside world despite the surrounding chaos. In Managua, moreover, the hotel provided the meeting place for the peace negotiations that ended the civil war there in the 1970s.

In third world nations, hotels are frequently used for governmental meetings, diplomatic conferences, and state banquets. In capital cities such as Dar Al Salaam, Tanzania, Lusaka, Zambia, and Monrovia, Liberia, they form an essential part of the official infrastructure, hosting visiting heads of state as well as high-level negotiating bodies. For example, in Riyadh and Jeddah, Saudi Arabia, Inter-Continental manages downtown hotels as conference centers used by the government on a priority basis.

Developing nations also need hotels to house visiting business executives and technicians in the process of evaluating and inspecting potential investments. At the same time, the hotels themselves create substantial employment and exchange credits and stimulate future tourist growth.

American hotels have also been traditional political hubs—the scene of conventions, party meetings, and "power" lunches, with the original "smoke-filled room" most certainly in a downtown hotel. Each party machine had its headquarter's hotel during and between campaigns. The Muehlbach in Kansas City, Missouri, became synonymous with "Boss" Prendergast and President Harry Truman. Other traditional party strongholds included the Parker House near Boston's State House and the Palmer House in Chicago, named for the powerful politician who owned it. The Palace in San Francisco was owned by a U.S. senator, as was the first group of Florida hotels, while the Shoreham Hotel, built by a Vice-President, became Washington's center of political intrigue.

Boston provides a model of the benefits of interaction between a city and its hotels. From the first luxury hotel of the early 19th century to the latest in mixed-use complexes of the 80s, no city has contributed more to advanced hotel concepts nor gained more recognition for its fine hotels. In addition to the Tremont House, examples include the Statler (earliest hotel/office development), the Sheraton at Prudential Center (first major post-war mixed-use complex), the Meridien conversion of the Federal Reserve Bank (pioneering adaptive reuse), the Marriott Long Wharf and The Bostonian (trend-setting seaport revitalization), the Ritz-Carlton and the Four Seasons (pioneering condo-hotel designs), and Copley Place and Lafayette Place (latest in hotel/shopping malls and urban renewal). Confident in its hotel expertise, Boston has revitalized several downtown areas, stimulating its economy in the 80s by its encouragement of new hotel expansion.

As a business, political, and social center, "guestroom to the city," and international safehaven, oblivious of normal business hours or outside interferences, as well as shaper of neighborhoods and catalyst for multiuse development, the downtown hotel has continued to play increasingly vital roles in the city's life.

For new creative examples of downtown hotels see the list of hotels in the Appendix.

The Ramses Hilton, Cairo, Egypt. *The design of Cairo's Ramses Hilton, recalling Pharaonic design forms in the shape of its guestroom tower, produces an effective solution that blends a new highrise structure with its traditional architectural surroundings.*

PLANNING CONSIDERATIONS

Just as a city's prestige is symbolized by its skyline, bright lights, museums, or even superdome, its hotels provide a clear sign of its quality and character. Atlanta, Georgia's image soared after its first atrium hotel, the

Stanford Court Hotel, San Francisco, California. *The impressive stained-glass skylight, granite entrance drive, and traditional fountain, marking the arrival to the Stanford Court Hotel on San Francisco's Nob Hill, exemplify the effectiveness of spacious and attractive porte cocheres.*

Hyatt Regency Atlanta, triggered a wave of new development. Impressive new hotels have helped shape Houston's and Dallas's destinies in the 80s just as the Waldorf-Astoria and The Drake contributed to New York's and Chicago's glow in the 20s.

Through their designs, downtown hotels have interpreted their cities' dominant themes as in the ultra-modernity of Atlanta's Hyatt Regency and Westin Peachtree Plaza, the sophistication of San Francisco's Stanford Court and Compton Place, the massiveness of New York's Hilton and Marriott Marquis, and the traditional charm of Boston's Marriott Long Wharf and The Bostonian. Not only have restorations and new hotels sparked innercity revitalization as, for example, in Memphis, Tennessee's Peabody Hotel and Baltimore, Maryland's Hyatt Regency, but hotels have been used to reshape the character of entire neighborhoods, as, for example, New York's Marriott Marquis on Times Square.

Size

While the small hotel has long been treasured by a sophisticated minority, San Francisco, always a laboratory for advanced planning concepts, has in the mid-80s demonstrated a major reaction against bigness in downtown hotels. This trend also parallels the renewed popularity of other more personal types of hotels such as the country inn, the vacation village, and the conference retreat, all discussed in later chapters.

While America developed the large hotel in the mid-19th century, Europeans cherished their small hotels, resisting the construction of major hotels above 500 rooms until well into the 1960s. For example, even today most hotels in Paris, such as the Ritz, have fewer than 100 rooms. Ironically, as European chains have invaded the American market with big hotels such as the 35-story Meridien in San Francisco, Americans have developed small so-called European hotels in their wake, including several in San Francisco. (For example, the Hotel Bedford there advertises: "The small European-style hotel that only looks expensive.") Showing cultural maturity, both European and American societies have come full circle in their approaches to downtown hotels: Many Europeans now favor larger, less personal-type hotels, while a growing number of Americans prefer their hotels cozy and individualistic, proving, regardless of nationality, *chacun a son gout.* If this trend keeps up, as sophisticated Americans tell their agents to book them into European hotels abroad, foreign tourists may begin requesting American hotels here.

Average room rates in major U.S. cities have more than doubled between 1978 and 1984. But while Europe maintained its small downtown hotels as moderately priced choices, the main budget alternative in America was the roadside motel. For example, what Holiday Inns offered in their small suburban hotels of the 50s is provided by Days Inn in the 80s, while the former budget chain concentrates today on luxurious services in their larger downtown hotels, including special "concierge floors."

Nevertheless, small restored downtown hotels can afford to provide upscale service and personal attention while still maintaining reasonable rates. For example, in San Francisco, the Bedford and Vintage Court, both under 150 rooms, were purchased and renovated for half the cost per room of larger new hotels and charge half the rates of their bigtime neighbors. Although their ratio of employees to guests is much lower than that at a large hotel, "you get more of a smile, and the clerk at the front desk remembers your name," proving the effectiveness of smaller hotels.

The optimum-size hotel is often determined by "threshold" factors, or points beyond which:

1. An extra elevator or second bank of elevators must be added.
2. An additional restaurant is needed.
3. A computerized front desk system becomes mandatory.
4. The extra building height requires a more

sophisticated structural system.
5. The added loads dictate more complex foundations.
6. Another cooling tower, chiller, or boiler becomes necessary.
7. Structured parking is needed.

But while such elements influence optimum sizing within a range of 50 to 100 rooms, they are relatively minor factors when compared with the inherent *administrative efficiency* of small versus medium- or large-size hotels.

Two hundred rooms is a threshold beyond which management begins to shift from a direct "mom-and-pop"-style operation to a more intricate system of multidepartment heads and assistant managers. In the under-200-room hotel, the management style can be more personal, with fewer supervisors required, more productive and happier employees, better satisfied guests, and reduced operating expenses. Any economies of scale to offset this are not usually achieved until a size of 500 to 600 rooms is reached. In other words, labor productivity peaks at 200 rooms, declines, and is not overtaken by size economy until there are at least 500 rooms.

Note that among the vast range of independent nonchain hotels, most are under 200 rooms. This proves their size is basically efficient and profitable even without the marketing and reservation advantages of the large chains. Moreover, large hotel restaurants tend to be overstaffed and have oversized, overequipped kitchens, while small hotels often lease out their restaurants to more effective individual operators.

Although less efficient to manage, hotels in the 200-to-500 range are often more convenient to market and finance; for example, lending institutions often prefer to invest in two 500-room hotels in different cities than in one more efficient 1,000-room facility, no matter how great the market demand. But midsize hotels need to economize more on their capital costs to offset their lower efficiencies. Conversely, the more optimum-size hotels can translate their superior profitability into more attractive designs, such as atriums or more elegant decor.

Location

Hotels traditionally have been built in prestigious locations convenient to main business centers and fashionable shopping districts—New York's Grand Central area and Chicago's "Magnificent Mile"—or identified with major city plazas and parks—the Plaza Hotel on New York's Central Park, the Westin St. Francis on San Francisco's Union Square, and the Ritz-Carlton on Boston's Public Gardens.

Four Seasons Hotel, Philadelphia, Pennsylvania. *Through its lowrise profile and native masonry facade, the Four Seasons Hotel respects its historic setting by blending one of the city's largest commercial complexes into the cultural and architectural heritage of Logan Square. (See also page 15 in the Color Portfolio.)*

Railroad terminals were also the focus of hotels for over half a century through the late 20s, when New York's Waldorf-Astoria provided its own siding for its millionaire guests arriving by private railroad car. Fortunately for such hotels, many terminal locations remained prime sites even after the decline of the railroads. Grand Central's hotels, for example, became the center of the midtown business district, as Park Avenue residential areas gave way to office skyscrapers and the railroad terminal became their commuter station. Downtown hotel restaurants and lounges often cater largely to commuters, as exemplified by the Vista Hotel at New York's World Trade Center, serving traffic generated by the adjacent PATH trains to New Jersey. Located over a major terminal, the Menzies Hotel in Sydney, Australia, provides 20 different bars and restaurants catering mainly to commuters.

But with office developments outcompeting hotels for prime locations today, cities have provided the following forms of assistance to promote needed hotel development: (1) zoning bonuses and tax abatements to encourage developers to include hotels as part of their mixed-use office or retail projects; (2) city-provided hotel sites in new "seaport" developments (for example, as in Baltimore, Maryland, Halifax, Nova Scotia, Boston and San Francisco) to attract suburban visitors and tourists; (3) city-planning assistance in providing new hotel sites to upgrade "porno," or "combat" zones usually rejected by office expansion (for example, in New York's Times Square, Boston's Lafayette Place, and south of San Francisco's Union Square area); and (4) increased interest in secondary centers such as in New York City's lower Manhattan World Trade Center, Brooklyn's Academy of Music district, and Long Island City's expanding movie studio colony.

Recognizing the overall benefits that hotels return to their cities, hundreds of government grants and loans as well as revenue bonds and other incentives have continued to be extended to subsidize restorations and make valuable sites available to hotel development projects.

Entrance and service drives

While, due to the lack of adequate site areas, existing downtown hotels often forego off-street entrance courts, they are extremely desirable for receiving and welcoming guests. Stanford Court in San Francisco and The Bostonian have wisely provided spacious off-street entrance courts and porte cocheres to enhance the guest's arrival. Effective methods of incorporating entrance drives, even on tight urban sites, are also illustrated by the Crowne Plaza Holiday Inn in New Orleans and the Inter-Continental Cairo.

Enclosed off-street loading for at least three trucks is also essential. It must be visually well separated from the guest entrance and compactly planned without deducting too much from the hotel's public facilities.

Parking

With the exception of convention hotels, parking requirements for downtown hotels are lower than those for suburban and roadside hotels since downtown hotels are usually conveniently located within walking distance of major offices, stores, and tourist attractions, and guests would often rather not drive in congested downtown areas. Employees' parking requirements are also reduced by available rapid transit. Some luxury hotels, such as the 650-room Inter-Continental in New York, offer no on-site parking, since their guests primarily use taxis and limousines. But where possible, hotels should provide parking of at least 1 space per room.

While larger cities such as San Francisco and New York discourage parking garages in order to prevent further downtown congestion, smaller cities such as White Plains, New York, and Stamford, Connecticut, typically require parking spaces of 1.5 per room, since traffic congestion is less in smaller cities and guests rely more on cars. But due to high land values in large cities, the excessive cost of providing garages on downtown sites is often unsupportable, with leased off-site parking a more viable alternative. For example, the Crowne Plaza Holiday Inn in New Orleans has provided parking in a neighboring multistory garage. Parking requirements for downtown hotels are thoroughly detailed in Part 2, Design Guide.

Exterior signage

San Francisco is one of the rare major cities that has achieved the elegance made possible by eliminating rooftop signs. But in most cities, where signs on hotels and other commercial buildings are the rule, they must be planned to be compatible with the architecture, incorporating such easily recognizable hotel logos as monograms carefully placed within the architectural silhouette, rather than looking like hastily conceived signposts.

Limited in size and number by ordinances, signage locations must be surveyed for op-

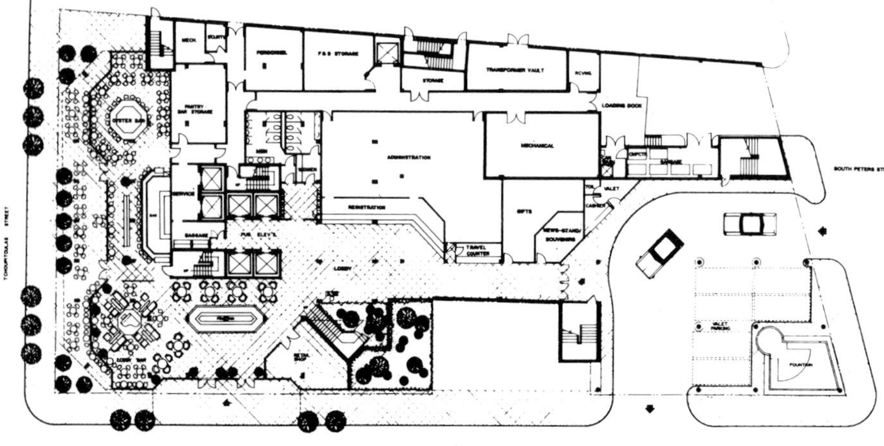

Holiday Inn Crowne Plaza, New Orleans, Louisiana. *Facing the Piazza d'Italia along New Orleans' growing corporate row, Poydras Street, the 21-story, 450-room Holiday Inn Crowne Plaza hotel provides the most efficient public layout and guest floor plan that could be adapted to a tight ⅔-acre plot. The octagonal plan includes 16 standard 12′ × 18′ (3.7 × 5.5 m) rooms plus eight special corner rooms on each guestroom level.*

ABOVE

Semiramis Inter-Continental Hotel, Cairo, Egypt. *The stepped-down tower of the Semiramis Inter-Continental Hotel blends with the surrounding cityscape and preserves the unobstructed views enjoyed by its famous neighbor, Shepherds Hotel, across the street. The terraces of the 32-story structure recall those of older buildings along the Nile and accentuate the magnificent views of the river. The 260,000 square feet (24,180 square meters) of public and service space include three restaurants, four bars, a casino, and a night club as well as a swimming pool and major health spa equipped for Egyptian loofah baths. The 1,700-seat main ballroom provides the special function area needed for traditional weddings and other local festivities. The Egyptian cafe at street level and outdoor rooftop nightclub recall the features of an older hotel that once occupied the site.*

RIGHT

Akasaka Prince Hotel, Tokyo, Japan. *The first major hotel by renowned master architect Kenzo Tange, the staggered V-shaped, 761-room, 40-story Akasaka Prince Hotel provides spectacular views of its historic surroundings, including the Imperial Palace, from the corner-angled windows of its upper guestroom floors. Twelve restaurants and lounges, each with a distinctive character, and 27,000 square feet (2500 square meters) of meeting and banquet space, including an executive conference room on each tower floor and a large business service center, cater to business travelers.*

timum visibility from main traffic approaches as well as for sightline interference from surrounding buildings. For visitors' and guests' convenience, signs are required at main entrances and separate restaurant and lounge entrances, in addition to the upper-level identification sign. Initiated by the architect, with assistance from appropriate graphic consultants, signage can be used to add liveliness and character to the overall design.

Design Considerations

In giving the downtown hotel its earliest and most influential form in the Tremont House and Astor Hotel, architect Isaiah Rogers combined rich and dignified materials on the exterior with exciting, grand spaces on the interior. Embellishing Rogers' concept, John Portman brought exterior light and view into the public spaces, as exemplified by the Atlanta Hyatt Regency and such earlier predecessors as The Palace in San Francisco and the Brown Palace in Denver, Colorado.

The work of Curtis and Davis revived historical context as a further environmental blender in such examples as Stanford Court in San Francisco, the Mills House in Charleston, South Carolina, and Royal Orleans in New Orleans, Louisiana.

It was a nonarchitect, E. M. Statler, who first gave the downtown hotel its efficiency in the operation and preparation space known as the hotel's "back-of-house" areas in the Buffalo Statler. But more than any other architect, William B. Tabler has advanced Statler's approach, improving on efficiency and economy in hundreds of hotels and widely influencing functional design over four decades.

The most recent mainspring of downtown hotel design has been the mixed-use complex. Through such large-scale developments, the influences of leading architect/planners including I. M. Pei, Romaldo Giurgola, Araldo Cossutta, TAC (The Architects Collaborative), John Portman, Kevin Roche, Philip Johnson and John Burgee, have related the hotel more closely to its urban context, as illustrated by Raffle City in Singapore, Lafayette Place in Boston, Centre Credit Lyonnais in Lyons, France, Copley Place in Boston, Marina Square in Singapore, United Nations Plaza in New York City, IDS Center in Minneapolis, Minnesota, and The Crescent, a postmodern proposal in Dallas, Texas.

Tradition and postmodernism

In the Imperial Hotel in Tokyo, Frank Lloyd Wright demonstrated early in the 20th century that hotels must reflect place and tradition, a notion too long unheeded, but now happily adopted in many widely varying examples such as The Bostonian, La Mansion

La Mansion del Rio Hotel, San Antonio, Texas. *By reflecting regional cultural traditions in its architecture, La Mansion del Rio Hotel enhances the city's charming and colorful Riverwalk area.*

del Rio in San Antonio, Texas, Long Wharf Marriott in Boston, and the Inter-Continental Jeddah in Saudi Arabia.

The preference of business and local authorities for international styles over local cultural traditions has fortunately changed. Like all other structures rising in booming Jeddah in the 70s, the Inter-Continental Hotel might also have followed in the path of the International Style. But with the owner's support, architect Harry dePolo of William Tabler Associates and Walter Rutes, then representing Inter-Continental, conceived the design much as Islamic architects might have a century ago, while incorporating the latest technology. Traditional principles that made sense for modern hotels were adopted. For example, arches that overhang the windows provided the sunshading necessary for air conditioning efficiency. A ziggarat form accommodated private terraces needed for the many princely suites: With over 2000 royal members and other affluent visitors, a high percentage of such two-room privately terraced suites were essential. The Royal and Emiri Suites were cantilevered out above the roof because they required greater area than the typical floors and, in Islamic tradition, the roof profile should be a unique form, but not necessarily a dome. This approach led to the early postmodern design for the hotel. During the conceptual phase, Rutes dreamed that on seeing the hotel, the king would feel so much at home that he would move into the Royal Suite. In fact, on completion of the project, the kingdom, impressed by the indigenous architecture, purchased the Inter-Continental as the country's official hotel and conference center. Postmodern eclectic designs often appeal to guests who today increasingly prefer a more residential style, humanly scaled, and with richly decorative detailing.

Lobbies and atriums

Since a hotel's architecture is often obscured and overwhelmed by its dense urban surroundings, the entrance lobbies in downtown hotels must make bold statements and lasting impressions. More than any other element, the lobby quickly sets the hotel's tone and ambience.

Following its reintroduction in the 60s, the colossal atrium became the downtown hotel's most impressive greeting card, often getting out of hand in terms of energy usage, higher construction cost, and repetition. Its appeal has been as much to tourists and sight-seers as sophisticated guests. For example, sitting at Harry's Bar in the highrise atrium of the Westin Bonaventure in Los Angeles, one is impressed by crowds of cheerfully gawking, rate-discounted tour groups.

While vertical atriums are obviously a major attraction at downtown tourist hotels, as well as shopping and mixed-use developments, for some they are reverse symbols of luxury or elegance, often rejected by guests or their lack of warmth and privacy. Hyatt, he chain that built its reputation on such vertical spaces, has lately steered away from using tall atriums in downtown hotels because heir higher costs with little increase in rates have a counterproductive effect on the hotel's viability. After two decades of experience, downtown hotels with comfortably sized horizontal grand spaces decorated in marble, mirror glass, and lustrous metals are perceived o be more upscale, commanding higher room rates than hotels with huge atriums of textured concrete.

But while their benefits to the guest and he hotel may be mixed, their advantages to he city and the visitor are unquestionable. Fascinating to the public, atriums have popularized hotels, while helping merchandize heir restaurants, lounges, and boutiques. They have been most successful when surrounded by large mixed-use developments, interestingly designed and shaped, engineered to avoid energy waste, affordable in construction cost, and matched to the size and rate class of the hotel (preferably over 300 rooms and moderate-to-luxury class).

Atriums have proved highly cost effective n suite hotels, where their efficiency is increased because balcony corridors serve double-room suites. For medium-sized hotels, three- or four-story "horizontal" atriums have also proved effective in ambience and cost. At such hotels as Boston's new complex at Lafayette Place and Sao Paulo's Holiday Inn in Brazil, the vertical atriums have been subdivided by through floors, forming a series of more intimate two-to four-story atriums with guest lounges every few floors.

The landmark atrium at the Hyatt Regency Atlanta is interestingly shaped, well integrated with its surroundings, and comfortably scaled, given its large size. The atrium of the new Marriott Marquis Atlanta is dynamic because of its curved tapering shape. But some other atriums appear boxy, trying more to impress than create comfortable atmospheres, yet in the hands of experienced designers they can project the desired ambience and be optimized for energy usage, acoustics, sun orientation, maintenance of greenery, window cleaning, and otherwise problematic functions.

With or without atriums, the design of large downtown hotels must attract upscale guests at rates to support their typically high development costs. Where they succeed in their objective, such luxury hotels can command $125-a-day rates, returning 40 percent more profit per square foot than modest-rate urban hotels, with their only slightly lower land, construction, and furnishing costs.

In addition, complex circulation patterns can negate the lobby's impact, when a guest cannot readily find the front desk in some hotels. Amid waiting, registration, information, and other functions, the guest should be able to glide quickly from the front desk to the elevator bank and to other major circulation points. Fortunately, of the infinite variety of designs is possible, without having to compromise on efficient circulation.

The tradition of fine artwork in hotel lobbies is happily being revived, for example, in the Henry Moore sculpture commissioned for the lobby of the Seoul Hilton in South Korea. As a sure sign of their positive appeal, hotels such as the Warwick in Houston, the Loews Anatole in Dallas, and the Holiday Inn Crown Plaza chain proudly boasts of their art collections in their ads. Other "memorable lobby experiences" have frequently become the trademark of downtown hotels. For example, the four mallards in the fountain of Memphis, Tennessee's Peabody Hotel have inspired more comment over the years than the hotel itself, with guests cheering along their twice daily waddle to the elevators. Devotees of New York's Inter-Continental (formerly the Barclay) rejoiced when the hotel's colorful parrots were returned to bask in their original glory under the Tiffany skylights in new polished brass cages with embroidered nightshades.

The historic Gran Hotel Cuidad de Mexico of Mexico City still retains its ornate bronze aviaries, although while awaiting restoration, its inhabitants have been stuffed and their chirping dubbed by audio. Also, the fishponds at the Hotel Beijing hold real carp. Other live lobby happenings have ranged from underwater views of pool swimmers at Beirut's former Inter-Continental Phoenicia, designed by Edward Durell Stone, to huge floral displays and multistory waterfalls surrounding the escalators at Boston's Westin Copley Place. But

Hotel Inter-Continental Jeddah, Saudi Arabia. *The 509-room Hotel Inter-Continental Jeddah is set on a podium to conceal its service and parking facilities while the stepped-down structure provides waterviews for all guestrooms, as well as large terraces for the end suites. The entrance drive leads to a traditional arrival court containing reflecting pools, fountains, and planting that is surrounded by graceful shopping arcades leading to the hotel's atrium lobby and tea lounge, Arabian restaurant, cafe, and a nonalcoholic beverage bar. Seating 1,000, a banquet hall and a wedding room, traditionally divided into men's and women's sections, complete the public areas.*

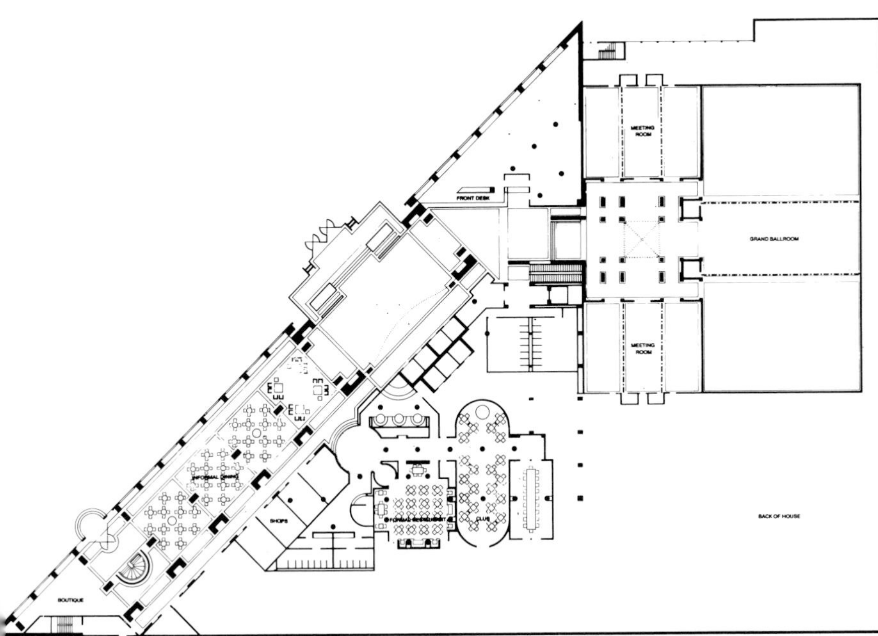

FT AND ABOVE

/arwick Post Oak, Houston, Texas. *Located in ouston's Galleria area, the Warwick Post Oak subtly ɔmbines dark granite paving, pink-gray precast panels, ›flective glass, and stainless steel balcony railings. The 50-room hotel by architect I. M. Pei features an elegant -story atrium in addition to a major ballroom, three ›staurants, two bars, small conference rooms, and retail ›hops. Most of the luxuriously appointed guestrooms, with versized bathrooms and walk-in closets, are arranged ›ong single-loaded corridors, while 50 open onto the ›ndscaped pool and gardens.*

t most fine hotels, lobby decor is primarily to et the mood, with only the *guests themselves* eeded to provide the live action, as best exmplified by the active, exciting lobbies at 'he Plaza in New York or The Plaza Athenae ı Paris.

›ublic facilities

)ue to the lobby's singular importance in owntown hotels and the volume of visitors uring its peak hours at luncheon, cocktail, nd banquet times, lobbies average from 30 o 40 percent larger than at suburban or airort hotels with comparable guestroom caacity. Meeting space is generally 25 percent reater than at suburban or airport hotels, ut considerably less than at convention otels (for further discussion of this, see Chapter 5). Restaurant and lounge areas are imilar to those of suburban and airport otels, although 10 percent less than at reort hotels and 20 percent less than at convention hotels. Retail space is also equivalent o that at suburban or airport hotels, but bout three times the size of that at roadside otels while substantially less than that at reorts or convention hotels. Service areas are lightly larger than at suburban and airport otels and 35 percent greater than at roadside hotels, while 12 percent less than at convention hotels. Detailed space requirements and circulation flow diagrams are in the Design Guide.

Indoor pools and health clubs attract downtown business users as well as guests. When guests are asked if they would stay in a hotel without a pool, most reply negatively. Yet to the question, "Do you use the pool?" the answer is often again negative! Therefore, while pools are used by some, their purpose is primarily to enhance the hotel's status and acceptability. Consequently, unless a major health club membership is desired, the pool need not be large, but must be well designed, preferably with outside views, natural skylighting, and a sun deck.

Guestrooms

Since the average length of stay and number of occupants per room are similar, guestroom sizes in downtown hotels are equivalent to those in suburban and airport hotels. The basic 12.5′ × 18′ (3.8 × 5.5 m) clear room dimension varies only within 10 percent, based on special preferences of owners or operators who believe a slightly larger room will give them a significant competitive advantage. Experience has shown that a foot of width is less important in making the room seem larger than a lighter color or other decorative scheme. For example, in the restoration of New York's Inter-Continental, a mirrored wall was installed in one 11.5-ft (3.5-m) wide room. Most guests felt the room was larger and preferred it to a 12.5-ft wide standard room.

While increased width provides minor additional space between the bed and the dresser, this space does not allow for additional furniture, whereas increased length can provide for an extra chair or sofa bed. Also, increased width adds more cost than length, since it increases structural spans, slab thicknesses, and the exterior facade. Therefore, lengthening the room is less costly and more beneficial to the guest than widening it. A complete facilities and area program for downtown hotels is included in Part 2, Design Guide, as well as typical guestroom floor plans and room layouts.

Trends

Waiting lines at front desks have been eliminated by offering guests preregistration and express checkout service. (For example, Marriott advertises: "At our hotels, checking out is as easy as walking out of your room.") Upper-floor registration for guests in special tower floors has further relieved the wait at the lobby desk. With today's automated express checkin equipment, the trend toward eliminating front desks other than for special information services will continue. The desk of the future will be an island push-button console, providing guests with most of the information they require, including travel and other reservations, show tickets, and so on. Yet special services will still be catered to on a *more personalized basis* at a private desk or office.

Unlike a decade ago, many of the finest restaurants are now in hotels. For example, Marriott advertisements declare that "most people who dine at our restaurants aren't even staying at our hotels." But meals *still* tend to be less fun and more institutionalized than in individually owned restaurants. More varied (including such hybrid cuisines as Italian/Chinese or Japanese/Polynesian), lively, innovative cafes will be introduced, giving interior designers and restaurant concept consultants *greater range for imagination.*

Due to their almost spiritual ambience, atriums will continue to flourish in large complexes, such as the Marriott Marquis in Atlanta (shown on the jacket), providing indoor *public plazas* so needed in the city's central areas.

Increasingly, we go to hotels for activities unrelated to travel, from fashion shows and meetings to health clubs and boutiques, from fine dining to the best pastry or wine shops in town, or for a family weekend away from the suburbs. For instance, L'Hotel Sofitel in Houston, Texas, observes that "some restaurants are so good you want to spend the night." The downtown hotel has become a major factor in our leisure lives, redefining itself into what was earlier called a "happy house," as well as a "destination." As the "medium is the message," so the "*hotel is the trip.*"

3

SUBURBAN HOTELS AND MOTELS

"It's just Minutes from Touchdown to Tee-off"

invites AMFAC at Dallas/Fort Worth Airport in Texas

Over the centuries, caravans, coaches, railroads, cars, and jets have propelled a large share of hotel development. Transportation-oriented hotels were one of the earliest types of lodgings and remain one of the industry's leading growth areas, comprising a quarter of the total hotel rooms worldwide.

The 17th-century *caravansaries*, 18th-century English country inns, and the ever-present Holiday Inn motels of the 1950s fulfilled similar needs as their present-day prototypes. Contemporary airport, roadside and suburban hotels continue to relieve travel fatigue and ennui along today's byways. Their design and technology match advances in the transportation systems they serve as well as increasingly sophisticated customer demands.

Whereas early roadside inns and motels were geared solely to provide "a good night's sleep after a long day's journey," today's hotel caters to continuous patterns of arrivals and departures and wide ranges of recreation and entertainment. Even today's elaborate health clubs, serving air travelers as a remedy for jet lag, are only a forerunner of far more complex health features envisioned in future "spacetels" for treating as yet undetermined effects of weightlessness.

While we have seen in the last chapter how downtown hotels provide essential social and business services for emerging nations that are developing international commerce—the recent phenomenal hotel growth in the Middle East, Africa, Latin America, the Far East, and now, the People's Republic of China—suburban, airport, and roadside hotels play a similar vital role during a later stage of national development. Their social and economic significance is seen in the fact that they exist predominantly in the industrialized countries of North America, Western Europe, and Japan and contribute toward a mature economy with highly developed internal trade, tourism and transportation, a large middle class, and higher living standards. Future demands for suburban and transportation hotels will accelerate dramatically in areas with sustained growth and economic maturity.

THE SUBURBAN HOTEL

Until the last decade, the suburbs were places for small budget motels rather than hotels. Two fundamental trends changed this: (1) increasing problems with downtown areas including congestion, crime, high rents, taxes, and land costs; and (2) corporate decentralization into office parks that followed population migration. This was coupled with a significant shift in public attitudes toward the suburbs. Areas formerly given bad press as "ticky-tacky" in the 60s became chic and popular for living and working in the 80s. This drew business guests and tourists out to the suburbs for much the same reasons as other suburbanites and changed the image that suburban hotels used to have of being like motels and less than deluxe. The Terrace Garden Inn advertises that it is "away from the skyscraper canyons, nestled on green grass, in the midst of 200 of Atlanta's finest stores." Ever sensitive to public taste and frustrated by downtown constraints, hotel developers began "going suburban" to the point where today nearly 70 percent of all hotel growth takes place in the suburbs.

With wide open spaces to work with, architects had a freer hand to generate imaginative designs surrounded by landscaped settings. Due to lower construction and land costs, developers could afford to provide both quality and lower rates in comparison with downtown hotels. The resulting suburban hotels often outclassed their downtown rivals in design, efficiency, and tranquility, although not usually in surrounding excitement. However, new satellite entertainment centers and shopping malls have filled this gap in many locations, such as the Galleria areas in both Houston and Dallas, Texas, so that today a variety of suburban hotels are springing up wherever there are dense concentrations of business or corporate parks, universities, medical centers, and so forth. In the growing North Dallas suburban office area, for example, five major hotels with an aggregate of 2200 rooms opened in 1983. Other markets served by these hotels include health clubs for the surrounding office and residential population. With private restaurants and lounges, these membership clubs have acquired the status of country clubs in many areas and are also used by the hotels as incentives to attract family weekend and package tour business.

One of the most hybrid of all types of hotels, the suburban hotel ranges from the bucolic Sheraton Wayfarer Inn in Manchester, New Hampshire, to the ultra-modern highrise Loews Glenpointe in Teaneck, New Jersey. The advantages they offer in common are better price values—including lower rates, lower food and beverage charges, and free parking—better security, usually free use of health clubs, convenience to suburban offices and airports, and often more public facilities and amenities than downtown hotels of the same rate class. A range of the best designed types are illustrated here and included in the list of hotels in the Appendix.

MARRIOTT BURLINGTON PUBLIC LEVEL

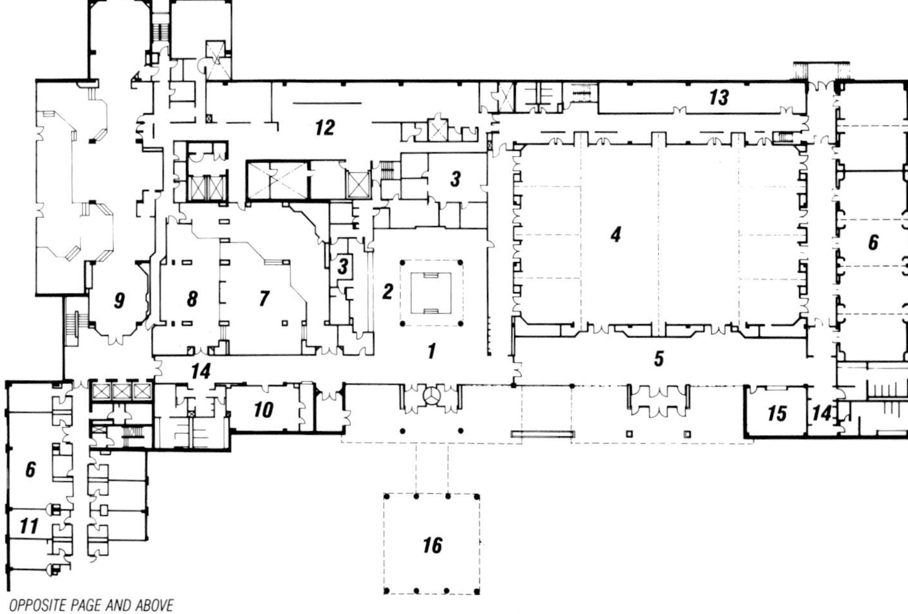

OPPOSITE PAGE AND ABOVE

Burlington Marriott Hotel, Burlington, Massachusetts. *Set on 10 landscaped acres (4 hectares) along Boston's Route 128, the 420-room Burlington Marriott Hotel serves the high-tech industrial and corporate community concentrated along "America's Technology Highway." Its adaptable meeting facilities and other amenities include a large ballroom, two restaurants, an entertainment lounge, and a health club with indoor and outdoor pools, all primarily designed to meet the needs of the area's business visitors. The hotel's brick facade and wrought-iron fencing reflect its New England heritage, while its elegant contemporary porte cochere is specially designed to appeal to its sophisticated high-tech clientele.*

The Marriott illustrates many of the characteristics of typical suburban hotels where, because of larger sites, the public areas are arranged on a single floor surrounded by parking. The highly efficient guestroom "offset slab" configuration allows more capital to be put into extra facilities such as the large nightclub or architectural amenities such as the elegant porte cochere.

Key: ***(1)*** *lobby,* ***(2)*** *registration,* ***(3)*** *administration,* ***(4)*** *ballroom,* ***(5)*** *ballroom foyer,* ***(6)*** *meeting rooms,* ***(7)*** *lounge,* ***(8)*** *theme restaurant,* ***(9)*** *multipurpose restaurant,* ***(10)*** *gift shop,* ***(11)*** *guestrooms,* ***(12)*** *kitchen,* ***(13)*** *storage,* ***(14)*** *toilets,* ***(15)*** *coatroom,* ***(16)*** *porte cochere.*

THE AIRPORT HOTEL

The sonic boom around most airports in this decade has been airport hotels rising out of the ground as typical media ads proclaim: "America's highest flying airport hotel" and other accolades. Every *major city airport* now has a *major airport city* next to it full of new hotels. The largest examples, each approaching 10,000 rooms and hosting most major chains, are Los Angeles, Houston, and Dallas/Ft. Worth, Texas, which now has a 1400-room colossus in its collection. A decade ago, the airport hotel was just another motel near an airport, mostly a place to stay for someone who didn't want to pay downtown rates. As air traffic picked up and major suburban developments moved into airport areas, airport hotels took off into the more rarified atmosphere of atriums and other upscale amenities previously limited to downtown hotels.

With these high-quality facilities, the airport hotel could lure guests with rates lower than those of downtown hotels, because less had been spent on land, and could attract the corporate world that loves to meet at airports. The location was ideal for business guests to fly in from different cities, hold their sessions, and be off in minutes without the hassle of downtown traffic and with savings on cab fares as well.

Once the rules were established, competition began toughening. The quality of the meeting spaces was improved, videotape and teleconferencing capabilities were included, and indoor and outdoor sports facilities were upscaled, aimed straight at the executive business market. But support for *several* airport hotels could only be possible if there was a large corporate community around them.

Another favorable factor has been the development of major restaurant and night life centers near airports such as at the San Antonio, Texas, Airport. This gives the airport hotel a builtin "downtown." Similarly, the Dallas/Ft. Worth Airport is only 30 minutes from both of these cities and near a broad spectrum of sports and tourist attractions, much like a city in itself.

While technical problems such as airport noise have long been resolved by siting hotels away from flight patterns and designing effective soundproofing systems and materials, one potential problem still remains. If airline rates rise substantially or if individuals and businesses cut back on travel, most airport hotels would be put to a severe economic test.

TOP

Sheraton Plaza La Reina, Los Angeles Airport, California. *Confirming the trend toward more business conferences at airports, the 810-room Sheraton Plaza La Reina expanded its meeting space two years after its opening.* *(See also page 58.)*

ABOVE

Holiday Inn Crowne Plaza, Los Angeles Airport, California. *Adding 621 rooms to one of the world's largest hotel complexes, the Holiday Inn Crowne Plaza provides restaurant and lounge capacity for 450 and meeting space for 1000.* *(See also page 58.)*

THE ROADSIDE AND SMALL TOWN HOTEL/MOTEL

When America first began driving in large numbers following World War I, tourists were often offered "free campgrounds" as an inducement to stop and buy gas and groceries. As travel increased, these "field stops" were improved with picnic and water facilities to become 25-cent-per-day "auto camps," soon followed by $1-per-night, canvas-walled "cabin camps." Growing by 1926 to about 2000 roadside "motor courts," the name "motel" was first coined in 1925 by a Californian and generally adopted by the public. By the 1930s, some of the early motels were expanded to more than a hundred rooms, many adopting regional architectural styles such as Spanish colonial in the southwest, log cabin in the northwest, and colonial in New England. They were simple, convenient, and informal—you paid in advance, parked at your door, and left when you pleased without dressing up or tipping. Limited activities included horseshoe pitching or meeting neighboring guests on the lawn.

With the travel boom following World War II, a phenomenal motel expansion began. In one decade, their number doubled and total rooms tripled, compared with virtually no increase in other types of hotels. Major chains entered the market starting with Holiday Inns in 1952, soon followed by Howard Johnson, Hilton, and Sheraton. With about 50,000 hotels by 1960, competition drove out many of the original ma-and-pa operators, and motels—now often called "motor inns"—started to become more elaborate, adding pools, meeting rooms, coffee shops, and several stories. They began spreading worldwide, principally in Europe, and many motor inns became more luxurious to compete with downtown hotels, also adding enclosed pools among other recreation and sports facilities. But although more elaborate, their design typically became boring and repetitive, with little charm or character. For example, one roadside hotel boasted: "North Carolina's grandest drive-in," picturing several large trucks parked in its ballroom—a creative ad, perhaps, but not one likely to promote guest appeal today.

Throughout the 70s and 80s, the former leaders in moderate-range motor inns so upscaled their product that they lost much of their modest-priced customer base. To recapture this group turned off by both the higher prices of the more elaborate inns and the cheap, unimaginative designs of most budget motels, a new wave of well-managed motel chains has unveiled innovative designs combining low rates with a fresher, more sophisticated ambience. These include such rapidly expanding budget hotel companies as La Quinta and Super 8 and more upscale subchains such as Courtyard by Marriott, both demonstrating the lasting vitality of the roadside facility.

Courtyard by Marriott, Atlanta. *The residential theme of the Courtyard-by-Marriott prototype located in Atlanta's perimeter section is enhanced by its gabled roofs, broken facade treatment, and intimately scaled central garden, providing a relaxed activity focus for its oversized guestroom units. A 30-seat restaurant faces the main frontage road, while the cocktail lounge provides a view of the courtyard. Three small conference rooms are included, as well as a game room, vending area, indoor whirlpool, and a swimming pool in the attractively landscaped courtyard which enhances the hotel's contemporary country inn flavor.*

Planning considerations

The successful suburban and transportation-oriented hotel combines its unique personality with a variety of opportunities available in each specific location. As the setting changes and becomes more urbanized, additional elements of the downtown hotel are programmed into the suburban product to create a more competitive hybrid blend. This includes gourmet restaurants, ballrooms, entertainment lounges, and health clubs. Illustrated by the Stouffer's ad: "Much too luxurious to be an airport hotel. Too close not to be," the trend is most prevalent in high-growth decentralized cities such as Los Angeles, Houston, and Dallas where satellite suburban business and entertainment centers tend to flourish. For example, the Park 10 area west of Houston has its first suburban, roadside hotel, the Holiday Inn Crowne Plaza. Its developers expect surrounding growth similar to that in the Galleria area closer to downtown, which during the 70s became Houston's first satellite "city" with several major highrise hotels. In anticipation, the Crowne Plaza has included an atrium and a strong mix of downtown-oriented facilities. By contrast, the suburban roadside properties of the 50s and 60s were not planned for urban expansion and eventually had to be replaced or extensively renovated to relate to changing markets as well as increased land values. The rapidly expanding metroareas at Dallas/Ft. Worth and Los Angeles International Airports exemplify the trend toward locating multichain highrise hotel complexes at key suburban or airport sites. Successful hotel planning not only follows, but promotes future urbanization, creating the potential for new mixed-used development in transitional areas.

Location. While suburban and transportation hotels were traditionally located according to traffic routes, today a large share of their business comes from other directions. Increasingly, downtown business and family travelers choose suburban hotels to avoid extreme traffic congestion, security risks, and higher rates. Competition between downtown and suburban hotels is somewhat analogous to the complementary relationship between the original downtown department stores and their later suburban branches. To further exploit the advantages of suburban locations, hotel developers now relate their properties more closely to regional shopping malls, office parks, entertainment centers, recreation areas, and other important suburban facilities. On this basis, many center-city visitors now feel they are better served by such suburban locations with easy access to both downtown and suburban attractions.

In addition, suburban rates can generally be 15 percent lower, due primarily to more reasonable land values and construction costs. This economic advantage explains the record growth rate and continuing bright potential of this sector. Other factors influencing location are discussed below and summarized in the location factor checklist.

Adaptability to Community. A greater variety of uses are contained within a hotel than in any other type of building. Much like a city itself, embracing not only residential, commercial, entertainment, recreation, office, but even certain industrial uses, well-designed hotels can happily blend compatibly with many different environments and community aspirations. This unique quality has helped spell success for developers even with difficult suburban sites subject to stringent zoning and planning reviews as well as height, density, traffic, parking, and signage restrictions. As the building type with the most mixed uses, hotels are often given special zoning status and consideration for planning variance review and approval. In most situations, much depends on the type of hotel proposed, its design, and environmental treatment. In other words, what is the project going to do to improve the community?

Holiday Inn Crowne Plaza Post Oak, Houston, Texas. *Part of the fast-paced expansion of Houston's satellite Galleria area, the 500-room Holiday Inn Crowne Plaza Post Oak provides restaurant and lounge seating for 600 as well as a health club and glazed pool atrium. The 22-story tower is set at an oblique angle to the West Loop expressway to establish better visibility and to accommodate a longer tower on a constricted site.*

For example, near Miami Airport, a residential community opposed rezoning for a Holiday Inn Crowne Plaza, but changed its mind instantly when presented with a lavishly landscaped, residential-looking midrise design. Near J. F. Kennedy Airport, in New

heraton Meadowlands, New Jersey. *Part of a vast sports complex, drawing over 10 million spectators annually to s national football, basketball, and racing events, the 375-room Sheraton Meadowlands is also designed to capitalize on s location in a fast-growing office and industrial park and its convenient four-mile drive to Manhattan. The 21-story tower oriented perpendicular to the Hudson River so the maximum number of guestrooms have spectacular views of New ork's skyline, while the hotel's height and signage were based on their visibility from Manhattan. An adjoining office wer is also part of the project.*

While sports themes are reflected in the hotel's specialty restaurant, the design of its cafe, entertainment, and lobby unges as well as the 1500-seat meeting complex are primarily oriented toward clientele from the surrounding business ommunity. Included are an 8000-square-foot (743-square-meter) ballroom, three function rooms, five conference rooms, boardroom, and a flexible exhibit hall.

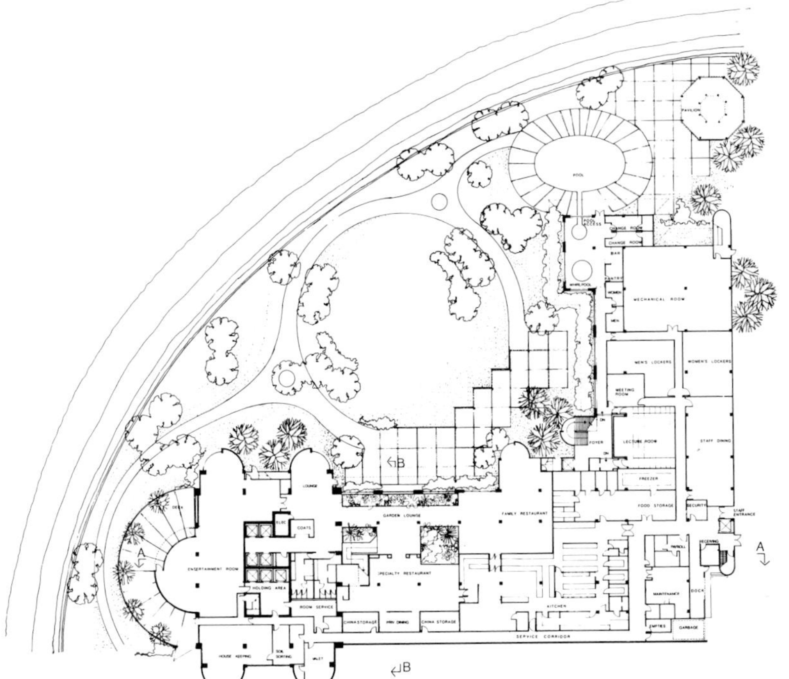

he Mandalay Four Seasons, Las Colinas, Irving, Texas. *Master planned in 1973 between Dallas and Fort Worth, the Las Colinas community encompasses 7000 acres (2833 ectares), half dedicated to open spaces including parks, lakes, and greenbelts as well as varied cultural and recreational amenities. As it was expanded in the 1980s to 12,000 acres 4856 hectares), a virtual city encompassing 9000 residents and 12,000 jobs, its first hotel, the 424-room Mandalay Four Seasons, at 27 stories became its tallest building and a focal oint for the lakefront urban center. The Mandalay offers five restaurants, extensive lounges, meeting and recreation facilities. Feeling that a major hotel provides one of the development's iggest assets along with a central shopping and restaurant complex on Mandalay Canal, one resident expressed "a strong sense of pride to be part of a community so special in terms f planned development." (See also section on planned community developments on page 139.)*

The location factor checklist*

Distance in time from
- ☐ Airport
- ☐ Downtown
- ☐ Entertainment centers
- ☐ Historic sites
- ☐ Industrial parks
- ☐ Interstate highways and intersections
- ☐ Office parks
- ☐ Recreation (parks, beaches, scenic areas, sports facilities)
- ☐ Residential areas
- ☐ Shopping malls
- ☐ Sports stadiums
- ☐ Tourist attractions (theme parks, museums and cultural sights)

Economic factors
- ☐ Competition (existing and proposed hotels, restaurants)
- ☐ Population and business growth trends
- ☐ Land values
- ☐ Construction cost index
- ☐ Energy costs
- ☐ Hotel labor rates
- ☐ Taxes

Environmental factors (*see also the environmental planning checklist in the Appendix*)
- ☐ Character of surrounding neighborhood
- ☐ Security
- ☐ Soil conditions
- ☐ Topography
- ☐ Natural landscaping
- ☐ Drainage
- ☐ Utilities' availability (electricity, gas, water, sewerage)
- ☐ Noise (traffic, airport)
- ☐ Wind direction
- ☐ Climate
- ☐ Environmental impact report (if required)

Expansion potential
- ☐ Site size
- ☐ Availability of adjacent land

Future development trends
- ☐ Area
- ☐ Regional

Political and legal factors
- ☐ Planning and zoning controls
- ☐ Acceptability to the community
- ☐ Easements, restrictions
- ☐ Views

Visibility and roadway access
- ☐ Approach visibility from roadways
- ☐ Accessibility to guest traffic, tour busses
- ☐ Pedestrian access
- ☐ Service access
- ☐ Employee transportation
- ☐ Parking requirements and restrictions

**Rate on a scale from 1 to 10 and compare each item with that of other alternate site locations.*

York City, a neighborhood again opposed a projected Holiday Inn development on the grounds of added traffic congestion. But when confronted with an uninviting airport industrial building as the only other viable prospect, the residents embraced the well-designed hotel as a welcome community asset.

Visibility, Accessibility, and Signage. Because drive-in customers without reservations account for over 15 percent of their occupancy, compared with less than 5 percent for downtown and resort hotels, prominent visibility to travelers from surrounding roads continues to be a feature of successful suburban, airport, and roadside hotels and motels. Potential sites must be evaluated for their natural contours, visibility of building signage, or other alternatives for free-standing signs. For similar reasons, entrance approach patterns providing for ease of auto access and flow for the traveler including adequate deceleration lanes, stacking space, and turning radii are equally essential.

Unfortunately, economic losses due to inadequate access, lack of visibility, or poor signage are still commonplace. For example, a fine new Four Seasons in suburban Houston suffered lower than anticipated occupancies because of its relatively hidden location, difficult for guests and visitors to find, and an otherwise well-designed Marriott in suburban Nashville, Tennessee, with superb visibility, had occupancy losses due to its complex access approach pattern. Proper design emphasis on such concerns significantly benefits both the traveler and the hotel, with prominent, easily readable signage made an interesting design feature, compatible with the architecture and the environment.

The Wyndham Hotel at Greenspoint, Houston, Texas. *With its contemporary gabled roofline and decorative facade reflecting the proportions of a French chateau, the 392-room Wyndham Hotel south of Houston displays an original blend of suburban postmodern design*

The tradition of distinctive signage dates back to the European inns that opened along the Roman road networks serving the newly developed stagecoach transportation system. As hotel owner, Rene Hure, recorded, each inn was known by "the sight of its insignia, painted on a metal plaque, grating its rugged hinges in every wind, signifying the comfort of good lodging and bliss of good cuisine." One can picture the traveler's smile on first

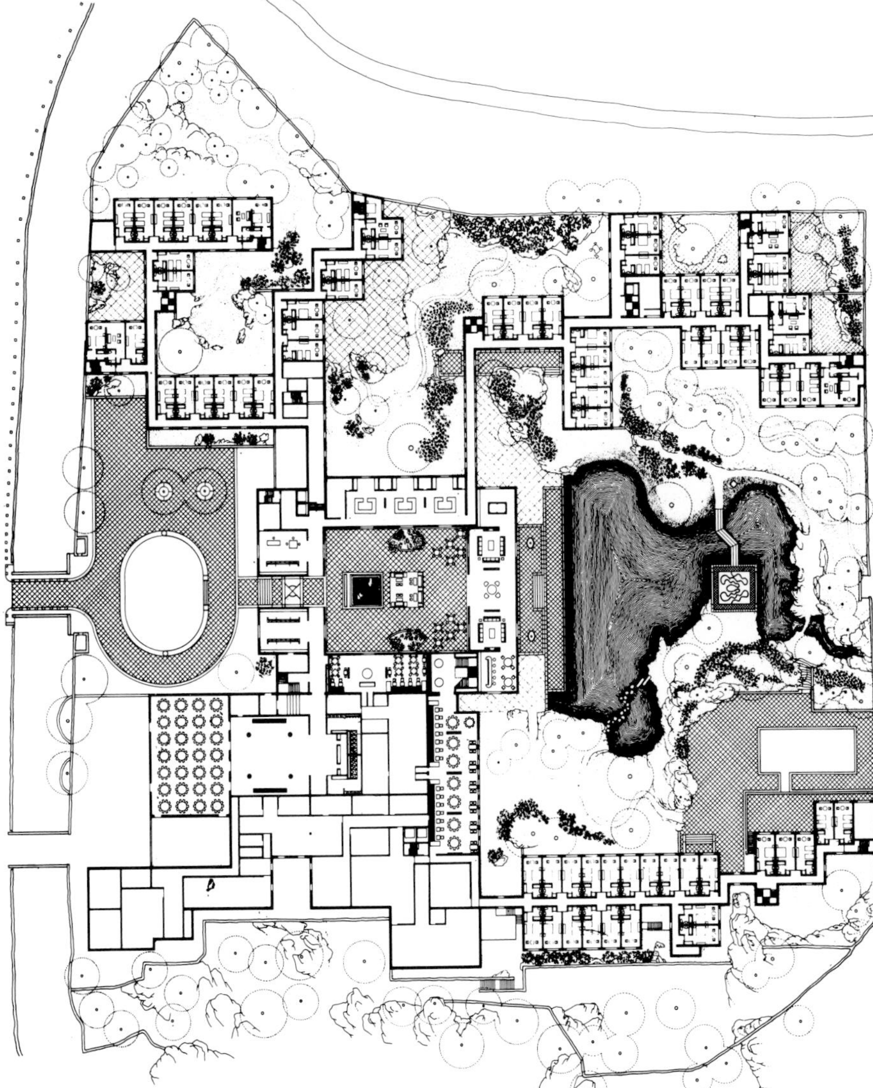

spotting the sign being as bright easily as that of today's weary traveler.

Parking. With almost total reliance on auto access, a suburban location's ability to develop its full potential for occupancy and outside business, including restaurant, lounge, and meeting use, is often governed by its ability to provide adequate on-site parking. (Peak parking needs for guests, visitors, and employees may be established for each hotel based on formula given in Part 2, Design Guide.) For example, after a highly successful opening of a Holiday Inn in suburban Nashville, substantial additional acreage had to be acquired for parking, predictably at a much inflated cost, to support the hotel's actual business demand.

Suburban hotels generally require a minimum of 1.2 cars per room (see the parking requirements matrix in Chapter 17), or about 50 percent more parking than that of the average downtown or resort property. This reflects about 90 percent of guests with cars, including approximately 50 percent with rental cars at airport hotels, 75 percent of employees with cars, and one car for each 2.5 outside customers of food, beverage, and meeting facilities. Parking facilities should be sized to meet peak hour requirements, generally at 8:00 to 10:00 P.M. on a Friday night or on a Saturday night if the hotel has a disco. At these peak hours most guests have returned to the hotel and the restaurants and lounges are operating at full capacity. One of the advantages of mixed-use developments (see Chapter 12) is that some of the parking space assigned to the office buildings can be used by the hotel during such peaks, reducing overall requirements by up to 15 percent. However, peak parking hours for apartments and shopping malls prevent overlapping or significant sharing by a hotel. Planning and design requirements for all types of hotels are detailed in the Design Guide.

Fragrant Hill Hotel, Beijing, Peoples Republic of China. *Nestled in the hills surrounding Beijing, the 325-room Fragrant Hill Hotel was the first of the new wave of hotels being erected in the Peoples Republic of China to serve international guests. The delicate detailing of its facade (patterned after traditional Chinese "half timber" construction) and landscaping pay great respect to its cultural heritage familiar to its architect, I. M. Pei. Guestrooms overlook small courtyards. The units are contained in a series of rectangles zigzagging out from a central building to an old perimeter rock wall that acts as a backdrop for the guestroom courtyards. A skylit formal entry in the central structure leads to an atrium courtyard off which are located major public rooms including a convention center, restaurants, retail shops, an athletic club, as well as indoor and outdoor pools. This new synthesis of East/West defines a "third way" with its typically Western large-scale building and Chinese-inspired spatial organization, movement, color decor, and patterns.*

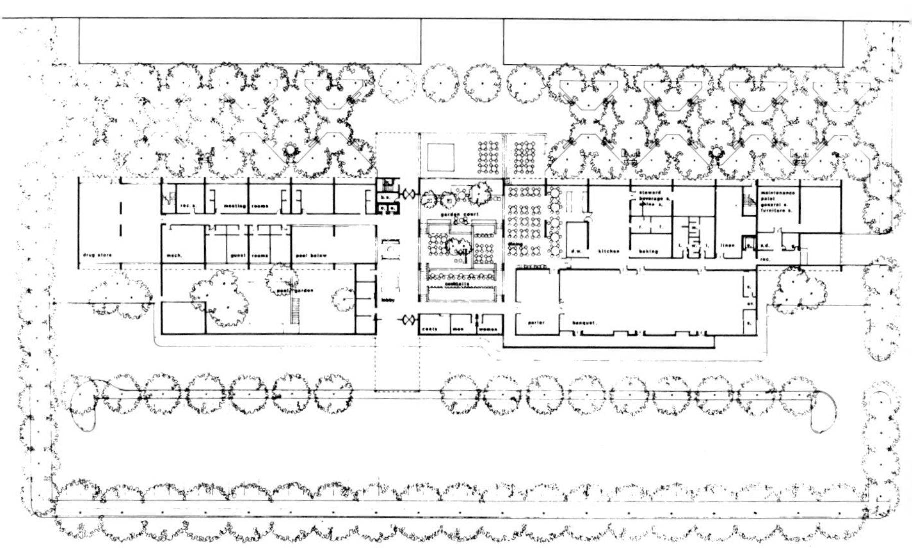

Design considerations

Guestroom sizes for most suburban and airport hotels are generally the standard 12.5′ × 18′ (3.8 × 5.5 m) clear, with insignificant variations of no more than 5 percent in either direction due to minor differences imposed by various chains and/or owners.

While the 12′ × 16′ (3.7 × 4.9 m) room, originally established by Holiday Inns and later increased to 12′ × 18′ (3.7 × 5.5 m) in more upscale markets, became the standard in the motel industry, more variations are being presented to the traveler to choose from on a price-value basis. Successful motel companies such as La Quinta and Skylight have offered larger rooms [from 14′ × 18′ (4.3 × 5.5 m) to 12′ × 24′ (3.7 × 7.3 m)], but not lounges or restaurants (other than vending machines) at rates averaging $30 in prime locations. This has appealed to many guests who want to "put all their money where their room is" and not bother with the amenities normally found in hotels. By contrast, budget chains such as Ibis have maintained food and beverage facilities, but reduced room sizes to 12′ × 14′ (3.7 × 4.3 m). This more segmented market gives people a choice depending on what they want to spend and how they want to spend it and provides an opportunity for smaller entrepreneurs who have unlocked these marketing secrets to be able to compete successfully with the giant chains of the industry.

The hotels illustrated here, as well as the facilities and areas charts in the Design Guide, indicate the extent to which suburban and airport hotels have added amenities approaching downtown hotels. At major airports or regional shopping or office centers hotels' food and beverage facilities and retail areas are equivalent to those of the downtown hotel, while their meeting and function spaces average about 20 percent less and their lobbies and circulation spaces approximately 25 percent less.

Lobbies, circulation space, and retail areas in small town and roadside hotels and motels are generally 50 percent less than those same spaces in suburban and airport hotels. But due to the greater percentage of guests eating breakfast in the hotel, the roadside hotel requires about 5 percent more restaurant space to handle the breakfast peak. Since the restaurant space is not fully used for lunch or dinner, this results in inordinate operating as well as capital costs to provide adequate food and beverage service. But reducing service or lowering standards would risk guest satisfaction. To resolve this dilemma, some roadside hotels have eliminated this service entirely. If there are no restaurants close by, some motels have leased portions of their sites to fast-food chains or free-standing restaurants to provide for guests' convenience as well as to attract sufficient outside business to support the restaurants on their own.

Roadside hotels require about 25 percent less meeting space than that of the average suburban or airport hotel, and their administrative and service areas are about 20 percent less than those of other types of hotels since fewer guest services are generally required. Space standards for small town hotels are similar to those of roadside hotels but

TOP

La Quinta. *One of the first chains to feature larger motel rooms as a tradeoff for omitting all food and beverage facilities, La Quinta also pioneered prefabricated panelized concrete construction, adapting its cost and time savings to the chain's Mexican architectural design theme.*

ABOVE

Hilton Inn, Corning, New York. *Many small towns are building new inns or restoring old hotels to serve local businesses and community functions. After a devastating flood the Corning Glass Works constructed a new 120-room inn as a centerpiece for much needed urban renewal in the town of 15,000. The design features a 3-story atrium containing the inn's lobby bar and restaurant, complete with elegant displays of decorative glass.*

usually with 15 percent more meeting space allowed for groups. Detailed space requirements and circulation flow diagrams are included in the Design Guide.

Due to differences in the size and type of facilities, as well as lower land and construction costs in the suburbs, airport and suburban hotels cost from 10 to 15 percent less to build than the average downtown hotel, while small town and roadside hotels and motels average 30 to 50 percent lower to develop on a cost-per-room basis. The ultimate rate differential among these different types of hotels is almost directly proportional to their differences in development cost. However, by providing a superior design concept, location, or other innovative feature, each hotel attempts to command a premium rate, occupancy, and profitability beyond that which would normally be expected from its development cost. This is what makes winners in the field.

Trends

In the search for new guest-appealing ideas, the selective cross-fertilization of budget motel design with luxury concepts has paid off. In the 50s, large 12′ × 16′ rooms, then a luxury standard, took the motel industry by storm. Incorporating "Holidomes," or recreation atriums, in motels brought success through the 60s and 70s. In the 80s, suite

TOP

Miami Airport Hilton, Florida. *Featuring extensive conference and recreation facilities including boating and water sports, the Miami Airport Hilton has appropriately combined the airport meeting hotel with its Florida vacation milieu.*

ABOVE

Holiday Inn Orlando Airport, Florida. *The highly economical ($40,000 per room total project cost) 302-room Holiday Inn Orlando benefited from several effective cost-saving techniques: (1) separating the guestroom structural and mechanical systems from the public areas; (2) planning the guestroom wings to avoid views of lower level roofs, permitting roof-mounted mechanical units to be used; (3) open planning of the restaurant, lounge, and lobby spaces creating an atrium without adding area to the building; (4) architecturally concealed through-wall air-conditioning; and (5) efficient space layout reducing building area.*

Suburban hotels and motels

ABOVE

Hyatt Regency O'Hare, Chicago. *John Portman's second atrium hotel for Hyatt, ("the classic airport hotel") was recently enlarged from 700 to 1100 rooms because of its great success and the growth of the O'Hare area as a convention destination. The building was kept relatively low to meet the airport requirements; the majority of the guestrooms enclose the square atrium and additional rooms are located in the reflective glass-clad circular towers, forecalling later Portman designs.*

LEFT

Los Angeles International Airport hotel complex. *Due to Los Angeles' widely dispersed growth pattern, over three dozen hotels totaling over 5000 guestrooms have been built at LAX airport. The airport access road, Century Boulevard, passes through the main concentration of hotels, including the Marriott, Hyatt, Hilton, Sheraton, and Holiday Inn Crowne Plaza hotels.* *(See also page 50.)*

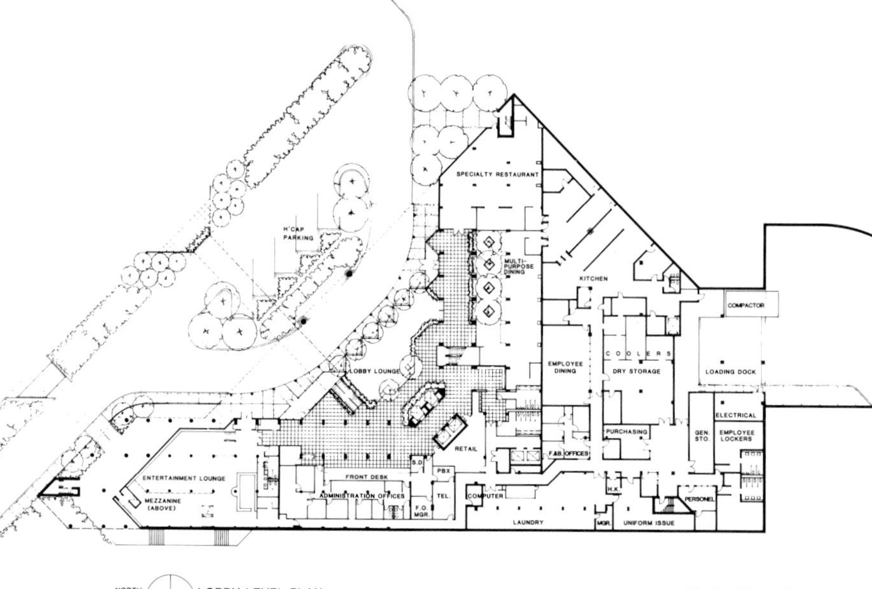

NORTH LOBBY LEVEL PLAN 5 0 10 25 50 100

BELOW

Ramada Renaissance Hotel, Atlanta Airport, Georgia. *The new 505-room Ramada illustrates the efficient one-story layout of the hotel's service space and the convenient clustering of the several food and beverage areas around the atrium lobby. The ballroom and other function space overlook the lobby from the second floor, which also includes a large pool and health spa under a separate free-standing structure.* *(See also photograph, page 13.)*

motels will become the most significant development embraced by price-value–conscious guests, traditionally shunning fancy restaurants or public amenities, but finding large suites irresistible. The cost effectiveness of all-suite construction will make this concept viable for motels (see Chapter 8).

With advances in hotel design, a new generation of improved prototypes has emerged in motels, for instance, Courtyard by Marriott. Large-scale prefabrication of components such as La Quinta relies on and other quick-assembly techniques such as those of Knight's Inn save time and capital. This process will also finally find its way into the moderate and luxury fields where only the surface has been scratched to date.

THE COUNTRY INN

A pure-bred line, directly descended from 18th-century English and European inns, the country inn has enjoyed a strong revival due to its personal charm and intimate scale. For example, Cypress Inn in Carmel-by-the-Sea, California, advertises "all the tradition of the fine inns of the past." With this, a full circle is now completed: from early American inns, to motels, to suburban hotels as elaborate as downtown hotels, to today's inn, proving the resiliency of good old concepts. A decade ago there were only a hundred inns in America, while today there are thousands, including increasingly popular bed-and-breakfast facilities.

Partly a backlash to the "bigger is better" philosophy of most contemporary hotels, this new generation of small, efficient inns has flourished well beyond its origins in New England villages, Southern hamlets, and the rocky Californian coast. Their diversity extends from converted mansions and even lighthouses to new construction using traditional architectural styles. Their owners generally share a love of history, an appreciation of quality, and a common philosophy of personal attention and residential comfort for the guest, an approach which has to some degree happily influenced the design and operation of newer hotels. With their "concierges," "tower floors," and residential-style furnishings, today's hotels have attempted to compensate for their large size in the direction of more personalized service and amenities on which small country inns have long prided themselves.

Planning considerations

Often a historic if not a landmark structure, the inn must maintain a careful relation to the environment, with preservation of the original character of the exterior architecture and natural landscape essential. Interiors are often gutted or remodeled to achieve more functional room layouts, but these must still be compatible in spirit with the original.

Design considerations

Humanist expressions of hospitality and comfort are desired rather than the grand impressions and commercial approaches often followed by other hotel types. A sense of the value of history should be evident at every turn from the recall of architectural styles, detailing, workmanship, and materials to traditional furnishings and artifacts.

This personal approach focuses on the guestroom as the starting point. It must be intimate, warm, and "look like somebody's bedroom," with high design quality of the furnishings even in such modest inns as the New Harmony in Indiana. Period antiques are often used, although not normally of the highest museum quality as in The American Club in Kohler, Wisconsin. Woodburning fireplaces, brass sleigh beds, claw-footed bathtubs as well as built-in hot tubs on terraces are frequently included. Since bedrooms in the older structures are often different sizes and shapes, their individuality is enhanced.

Public areas should be modest and residential. Guests expect designs to evoke a sense of place and regional personality. Research is necessary to identify appropriate eclectic styles. Inns need only a small, usually sit-down reception area, but no lobby; a restaurant, but usually no bar; a sitting/living room with a large woodburning fireplace; and potential conference space. Confirming that the country inn look is in, the new prototype suburban hotels such as Courtyard by Marriott and Hampton Inn have emulated the appearance of inns in their designs.

Systematics, Inc., Little Rock, Arkansas. *The small corporate guest house contains only eight guestrooms (with plans to add eight more) and a public building with a lobby/entertainment area and a restaurant/meeting room. The spacious lounge gains much of its residential character from the handsome natural wood roof trusses and from the simple furnishings and contemporary artifacts.*

Trends

The success of country inns demonstrate the growing desire of many guests for trar quillity, escape from today's technology, and return to the homey old-fashioned values This growth trend will continue to provid opportunities for creative small-scale hot developers. Not since the 50s has the moc est-size individual entrepreneur been able t enter a profitable segment of the hotel indus try, free of prohibitive capital requirements o strong chain competition.

Due to the inn's privacy, relaxed atmc sphere, and reasonable rates, busines groups will increasingly use inns with meetin facilities, as an interesting alternative to th conference center. The country inn's re discovery by a relatively small minority illus trates the healthy possibilities of market seg mentation, in this case reviving a histori hotel type.

ABOVE

The American Club, Kohler, Wisconsin. *Country village character has been carefully preserved in the expansion and conversion of former employee housing into the American Club. In a new wing—8000 square feet (740 square meters) of conference space, and five restaurants seating 600—the inn concept has been broadened to serve more varied functions. Small, comfortable spaces, antique furniture, and artifacts express the ethnic cultures of the region's original settlers.*

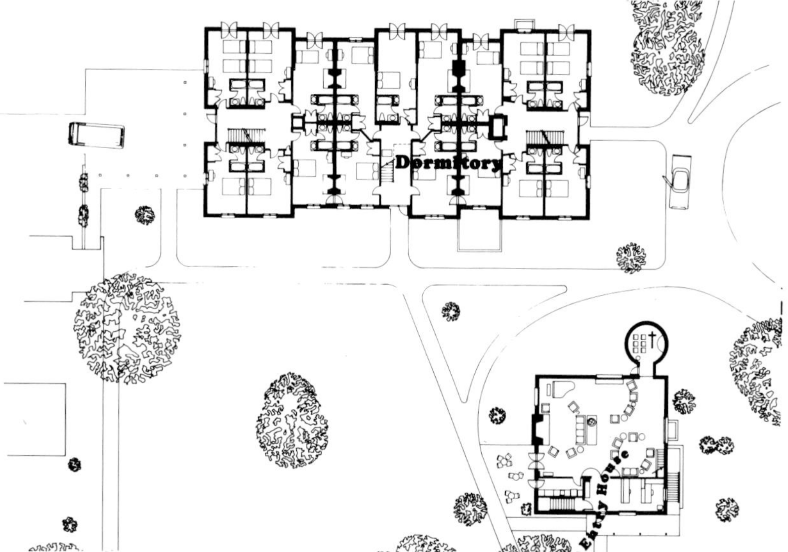

LEFT AND BELOW

The New Harmony Inn, New Harmony, Indiana. *Part of a larger effort to preserve the history of an experimental utopian community, The New Harmony Inn is designed to reinforce the town's existing residential fabric with its brick walls and wood shake roof. The inn consists of a modest entry house for registration, with a lobby that can also be used for meetings, a chapel, and a separate 4-story structure with 45 guestrooms grouped around three entry stairs rather than long corridors.*

4

THE RESORT

"Pool, saunas, jacuzzis, jazzercise classes, tanning center, indoor tennis, disco"

advertises Bolton Valley Ski Resort in Vermont

Among the earliest forms of hotels, resorts trace their lineage to the spas and baths of ancient Greece and Rome, from which they spread through the Roman Empire (see the list of hotel milestones in Chapter 1). Dormant for several centuries, spas were revived during the Renaissance, gradually spreading throughout Europe, where there are over 500 spa resorts today. For example, the town of Bath, England, was founded in Roman times and still flourishes today. The earliest American spas, which were in fact the country's first resorts, were founded in the 1750s including the Greenbrier area in White Sulphur Springs, West Virginia, and the resort town of Saratoga Springs, New York, which reached the height of popularity in the 1850s.

During the early years of the industrial revolution the resort remained the province of the well-to-do. Fashionable hotels such as Mohonk Mountain House in up-state New York and the del Coronado in San Diego, California, prospered in varied scenic mountain and seashore areas. But the 20th-century saw the resort become accessible to the middle class because of steadily rising disposable income and paid vacation time, particularly following World War II. This included dramatic increases in leisure travel by Europeans and Japanese as well as Americans. Resorts experienced a sustained growth boom, eventually evolving like other hotels into more defined categories serving several different types of vacationers, which will be discussed under separate headings below. (A complete list of the entire range of resort hotels is provided in the List of Hotels in the Appendix.)

Beyond type, location is a prime factor distinguishing resorts. In established resort regions such as Hawaii or Palm Springs, California, resort amenities are provided in virtually all hotels. Local environmental considerations determine whether the resorts are lowrise and spread out, such as in Fiji or Majorca, or dense highrise towers as in Rio de Janeiro or Honolulu. In Aruba, for example, to provide the best of both worlds, the government has designated separate highrise and lowrise resort areas, recognizing the need for a choice of ambience to satisfy the different tastes of various types of tourists as well as the objectives of different developers.

This planning philosophy has also been followed in the latest multiresort complexes such as Cancun and Ixtapa, Mexico, where highrise resorts form the backbone of developments, but more tranquil peripheral areas are reserved for vacation villages. The towering hotels are more efficient in handling the masses of tourists on which the viability of these projects is based. With overall densi-

PRECEDING PAGE

Hotel del Coronado, Coronado, California. *When the 339-room Victorian landmark, the Hotel del Coronado, opened in 1888 on the Coronado peninsula of California near the then small port of San Diego, it was regarded as an oasis of culture in the still untamed West, matched only by the city of San Francisco. One of the world's largest wooden structures, with a 60-foot-high (18-meter) pine ceiling spanning its central dining room, it continues to set the precedent for preservation of older hotels, growing to 686 rooms and remaining among the Pacific coast's best known resorts.*

TOP

The Greenbrier, White Sulphur Springs, West Virginia. *Tracing its resort history from the early 1800s, the 650-room Greenbrier, with its impeccably preserved alabaster and green Georgian mansion as a centerpiece, continues to expand on its 6500-acre (2630-hectare) Appalachian Mountain site, accommodating conventions of over 1000 and providing varied sports from bowling to carriage rides, as well as a European-style spa.*

ABOVE

Hilton Head Island, South Carolina. *Covering 42 square miles (109 square kilometers) Hilton Head Island off the South Carolina coast displays vast sea marshes, natural lagoons, and subtropical forests, with sloping sandy beaches lining its oceanside. With its Indian archaeological finds dating back to 3000 B.C. and its plantations begun by British settlers in 1663, the planned resort development was only started in the 1950s. Yet today, the complex hosts over 700,000 resort visitors annually, providing over 2000 types of varied hotel rooms, 4000 condos and villas, and 17 golf courses. Part of the resort community's continued development, the Hilton Head Inter-Continental's postmodern plantation architecture evokes the regions traditions. (See section on the multi resort complex later in this chapter.)*

ties ranging from 3000 to 5000 rooms, the towers conserve open space and views, while the preserved outlying lowrise areas are still available for guests to enjoy.

While most vacation spots, individual or regional, are places you *travel* to, located off the beaten track, new types of "in-city" resorts have also been developed to attract *weekend* vacationers. Located in or close to major cities, often on a lake or beach, and containing elaborate health clubs with indoor and outdoor pools, they function effectively as *partial* resorts, designed to appeal to transient travelers as well as guests preferring convenient, close-by vacations that save time and travel expense.

THE BEACH, GOLF, AND TENNIS RESORT

From the Cote d'Azure to the Gulf of California, Capetown to the Canaries, and Key West to Kauai, most vacationers head for the beach; and seemingly endless beachfronts continue to supply idyllic sites for new and better resorts. Views and swimming are complemented by innovative water sports such as para-sailing, wind surfing, and exploring underwater scuba trails (including schools for certification), as well as imaginative hotel accommodations, keeping the second oldest form of resort, after the health spa, the most popular of all. Major beachfront hotels also provide extensive golf and tennis facilities, matching those of mountain and desert resorts. They emphasize varied sports and fitness facilities and, in many cases, conference centers for business groups. Resort amenities are not lost on the average business traveler who often chooses them wherever available over downtown or suburban hotels. As JP Hotels in Ft. Lauderdale Beach, Florida, advertises: "Business trips are cooler when you stay on the beach."

Groups often select resorts for their business gatherings since their relaxing atmosphere promotes teamwork and more personal contact. "Even when people play a bad round of golf together, it brings them closer," one manager observed. Corporate meeting planners also feel that the resort combines an effective atmosphere for training sales forces, for example, plus a taste of leisure and luxury to motivate them. Resorts go all out to please esthetically through their imaginative designs, lushness, and scenery. Their recreational facilities also give groups a sense of reward after working meetings. For example, Sea Palms Golf and Tennis Resort in Georgia advertises: "Comes with an island and everything else you need to make your next meeting a success." At the same time, resorts are traditionally self-contained, with all facilities and amenities close at hand. This makes it easier to keep groups together for productive meetings, while still giving participants a good time. But the above factors only apply if the resort includes high-quality conference facilities that are foremost to meeting planners. (Note the conference facilities and audiovisual aids checklist in Chapter 6.)

To attract both family and business groups, resorts must provide the greatest possible variety of sports and recreation activities from golf driving ranges to aerobic classes to ensure that *every member* of the group will be satisfied. For example, the Palm Beach Polo and Country Club in Florida uses the following slogan: "America's most sporting resort . . . equestrian center . . . tennis . . . championship golf . . . skeet range . . . croquet lawn . . . carriage driving." (See Chapter 17 for the recreation and fitness facilities checklists.)

Planning considerations

Although closeness to the water is an essential ingredient of the beachfront hotel, environmental controls in most areas with extensive development potential require large setbacks of 200 feet (61 meters) or more from the shoreline. While guestroom balconies and full-height windows help dramatize beach views, water features such as canals and decorative pools enhance the hotel's seashore relationship so as to compensate for separation from the beach, for example, at the Camino Real in Cancun and the Kahala Hilton in Honolulu. Both the Mauna Kea Beach and the Mauna Lani Bay Resorts on the Big Island of Hawaii feature indoor canals with brightly colored reef fish. An octopus provides hours of entertainment for children and adults at the Mauna Lani.

Shaded and landscaped areas should also be provided along the beachfront, relating to water sports facilities, whirlpools, bars, and food service areas. But siting the hotel closer to the shoreline or in a lagoon has proven far more desirable wherever possible, as in such isolated, single-resort settings as Club Med in Cancun and Williams Island in Florida. Hotels built into shoreline bluffs or cliffs are also strikingly effective as at The Tahara in Tahiti and Sheraton Princeville in Kauai, Hawaii.

The Tampa Hilton in Florida shows the importance of guestroom placement in its adver-

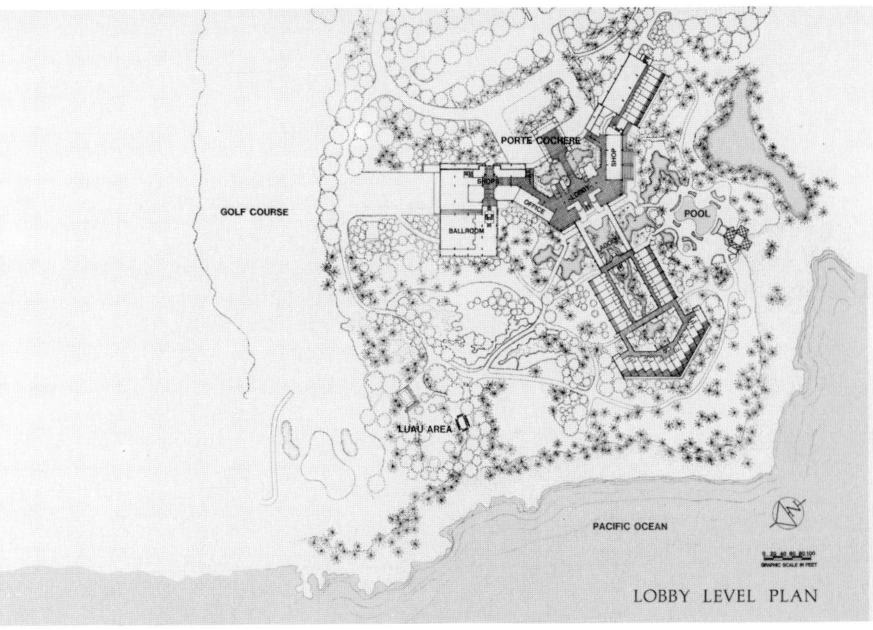

Mauna Lani Bay Hotel, Big Island, Hawaii. *On the unique, lava-formed Kohala coast of Hawaii's Big Island, the 351-room Mauna Lani Bay Hotel is part of a 3200-acre (1296-hectare) preserve, only one-quarter of which is developed as a resort including condominiums, villas, and recreation amenities. Its $9 million golf course is built over natural lava beds, whose ancient fishponds are preserved as water features. The massing of the resort is designed to provide ocean views for nearly all guestrooms, restaurants, and other public spaces. (See also page 5 in Color Portfolio.)*

Mauna Kea Beach Hotel, Kamuela, Hawaii. *Sited on the edge of a coastal lagoon, the Mauna Kea Beach Hotel remains one of the world's finest resort hotels with extensive Polynesian art displayed throughout the public areas and corridors. The residential wings are elevated on stilts to permit the landscaped grounds to flow into interior gardens and courtyards, further enhancing the resort experience.*

tising: "Views with extraordinary rooms." Guestroom wings, if double-loaded (that is, with rooms on both sides of a corridor), must be oriented perpendicular to the beach, assuring that all rooms have at least a 90° view of the shoreline. These can be further enhanced by angling the window wall and/or room toward the view, usually affording the guest a more interesting perspective combining both land and water. While single-loaded wings can provide the guest with 180° views of the beach, their construction costs are about 15 percent higher because they require twice the normal corridor space plus increased building bulk and exterior wall, windows in corridors, and extra air conditioning. Known as "cost guzzlers" they are not only wasteful of energy and land, but require additional staff due to the structure's increased size and length. But a small percentage of single-loaded spaces can often be cost effective, where they provide an economical solution to an otherwise complex site form or building orientation problem.

Atriums with single-loaded balconies can often be justified by luxury resorts, with rates up to $200 a day, such as the $70 million Mauna Lani Bay on the Big Island in Hawaii. With its football-field-long, six-story atrium and surrounding 351 rooms oriented *perpendicular* to the Pacific shoreline, 92 percent of the guestrooms can view the crashing surf.

A 500-room midrise beachfront hotel requires about 10 acres (4 hectares) including swimming pools, landscaping, and parking. But the resort's total land development depends largely on the golf, tennis, and other recreation areas provided. For example, a 10-court tennis center requires another 3 acres (1.2 hectares) and an 18-hole golf course approximately 110 to 160 acres (45 to 65 hectares). (See the recreation checklist in Chapter 17.)

Architect Marcel Breuer once remarked: "The only things people look at are the landscaping and the finish of the building." But while building materials vary in their appeal to taste, *landscaping always brings praise.* This is never more true than at a resort. It also relates the development to its natural environment, whether coastal, mountain, or desert: The Princess in Acapulco, the Stanley Hotel in Vail, Colorado, and Sheraton El Conquistador in Tucson, Arizona, are all fine examples.

Design considerations

For good reason, architects draw on the beauty of the natural landscape as the vital theme for their resort design. Since guests are drawn to their favorite environments, such as the Caribbean for the beach and sunshine or the mountains or rural areas for scenery, these natural attractions are reinforced by the architecture and interiors through color, form, and material. For example, earthy, natural tones and rugged materials are psychologically appropriate in mountain resorts, while teal colors are reminiscent of beach locations. Green interior accents complement a forest setting, while warm desert colors and natural sandstone finishes recall the surroundings of Tucson or Palm Springs.

The area's wide open spaces are often drawn into the resort through atriums, with their large glazed areas and skylights, even furthering the illusion by means of indoor gardens, indigenous trees, water features, light colors, and statuary. Local artwork and decorative motifs can also recall or inform the guest of the area's traditions.

Besides natural and traditional beauty, resorts emphasize luxury. Historically a refuge of the well-to-do, resorts are still expected to be spacious and lavish in amenities and decor. Lobbies should be 30 percent larger than those of suburban or airport hotels and 10 percent greater than those of downtown hotels of comparable size. This reflects the additional time guests spend lounging and socializing in resort lobbies. Since guests enjoy shopping on vacations, 50 percent larger retail space should be provided than in downtown or suburban hotels. Complete space requirements are provided in the Design Guide in Chapter 14, Facilities Programming.

Since both the average length of stay and number of occupants per room is greater in resorts, guestrooms should be at least 10 percent larger. In areas with higher family occupancies such as in Orlando, Florida, near Disney World, the guestroom length should be increased from the standard 18 to 21 feet (5.5 to 6.4 meters) to more easily accommodate additional roll-away beds or cribs. Closets should be at least 4.5 feet (1.4 meters) long, since vacationers pack more clothing and sports equipment. Larger bathrooms are expected, with dressing areas and additional amenities provided in the more luxurious resorts. Balconies at least 5 feet (1.5 meters) deep, furnished with a table, chairs, and at least two chaises, are essential for lounging and sunbathing, as well as enjoying views and relating with the outdoors.

Loew s Paradise Valley Resort, Paradise Valley, Arizona. *Screening the hotel from the surrounding streets to create a walled oasis focuses the guestrooms and public spaces on a series of varied interconnected gardens, courtyards, and pools at the 380-room, 20-acre (8-hectare) Loew s Paradise Valley Resort near Scottsdale, Arizona. Its 275,000 square feet (29,600 square meters) include 30,000 square feet (3230 square meters) of convention facilities, a theater, health club, indoor tennis court, and a 200-seat restaurant and cafe. Yet its faceted block facade, varied recesses, and 1- and 2-story heights blend the large resort with its residential neighbors.*

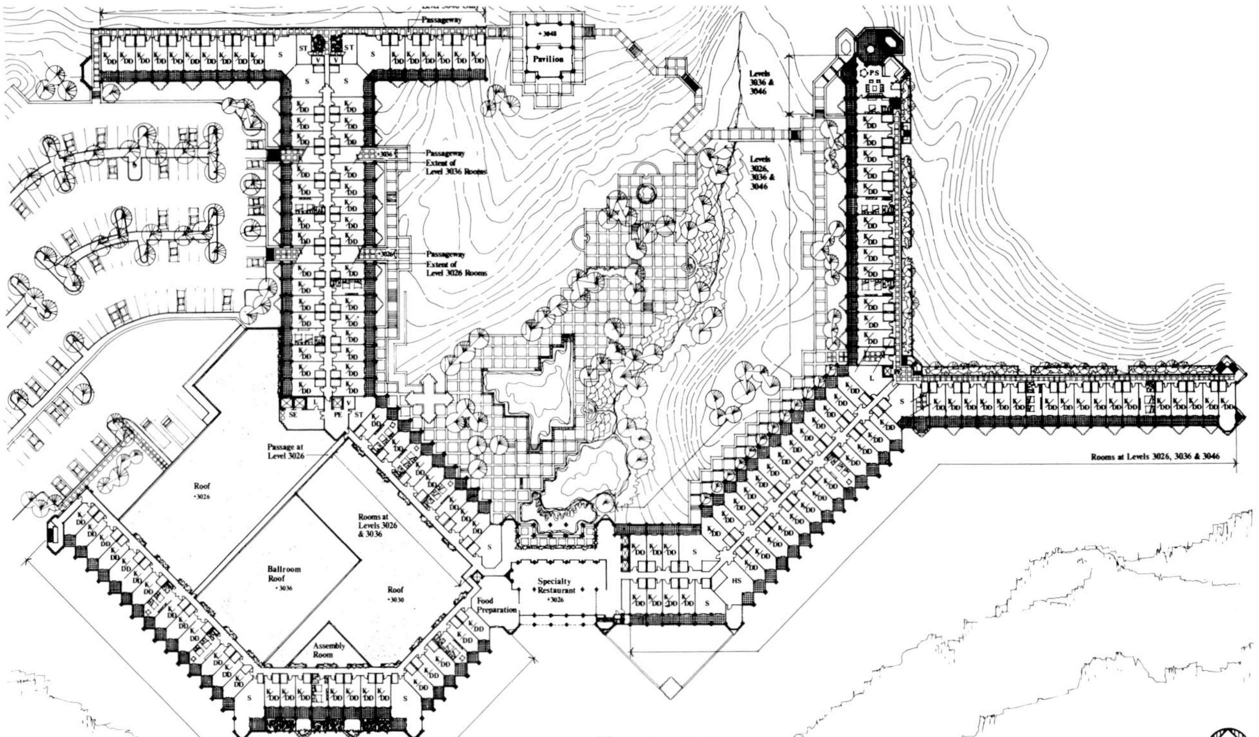

Upper Levels Plan
(Level 3026 Shown)

South Elevation

OPPOSITE PAGE

Loew s Ventana Canyon Resort, Tucson, Arizona. *Sited at the base of an 80-foot (24-meter) natural waterfall, the Loew s Ventana Canyon Resort north of Tucson bridges over the natural watercourses and forms a contoured courtyard for its recreational activities. Its 400 guestrooms, central cafe, sunken lobby lounge, and specialty restaurant are stepped into the hillside, with the convention and ballroom facilities located at the lowest elevation to reduce their bulk. This arrangement affords expansive views of the mountains to the north and the metropolitan skyline to the south. The articulated block facade and vertically ribbed towers blend in color and texture with the site's natural rock formations.*

THIS PAGE

Boca Beach Club Hotel and Cabanas, Boca Raton, Florida. *The Boca Beach Club is the fourth element in the expansive Boca Raton Hotel, complementing the original Mediterranean-style hotel, "The Cloister," a modern tower, and golf course villas. The 212 guestrooms and 147 cabanas of the beach club are carefully sited between the ocean and the intracoastal waterway, permitting most rooms to overlook the beaches, gardens, or pool terraces. (See also color photograph on top of page 5.)*

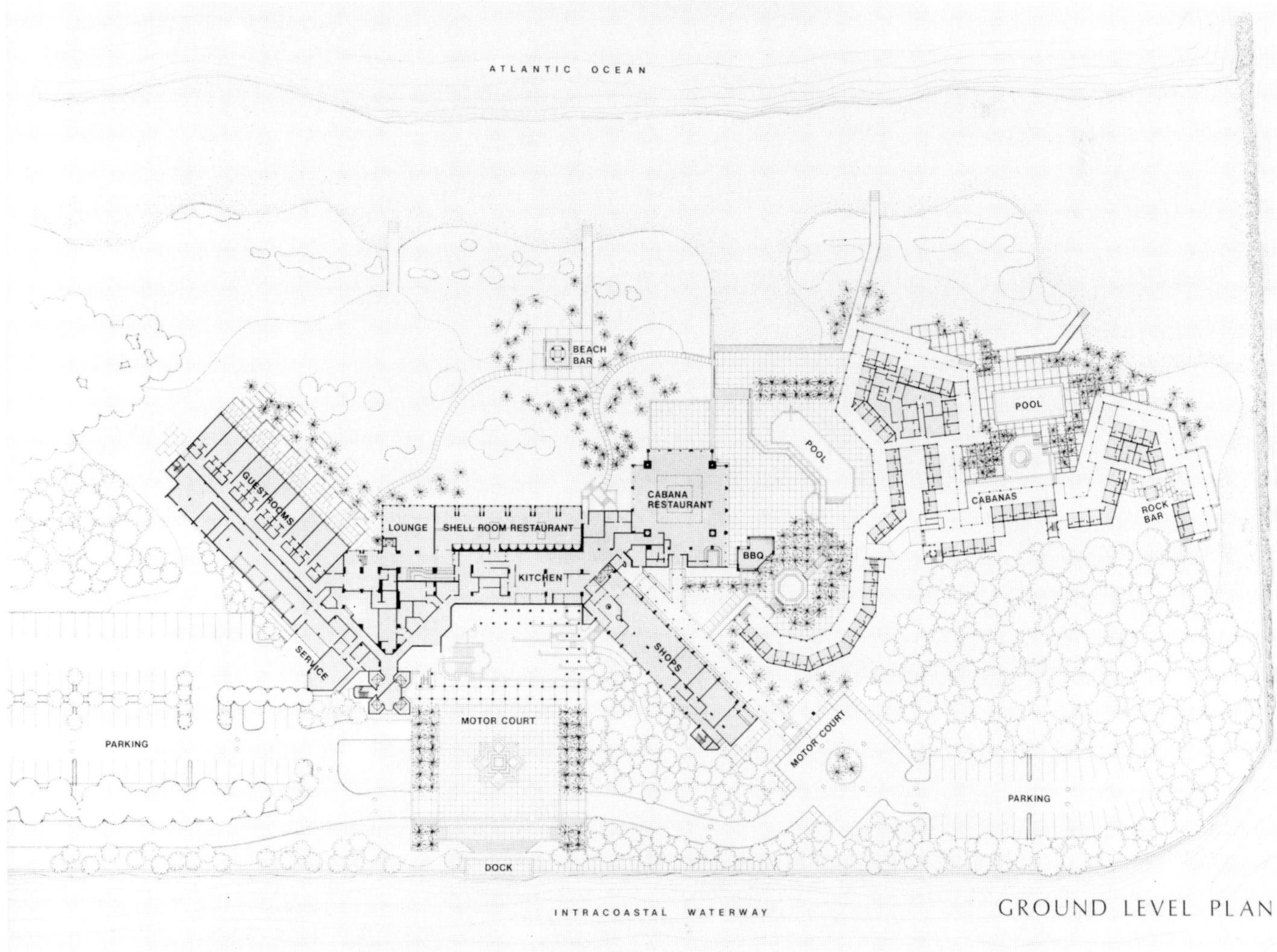

ATLANTIC OCEAN

BEACH BAR

POOL

GUESTROOMS

CABANA RESTAURANT

POOL

CABANAS

ROCK BAR

LOUNGE

SHELL ROOM RESTAURANT

BBQ

KITCHEN

SERVICE

SHOPS

MOTOR COURT

MOTOR COURT

PARKING

PARKING

DOCK

INTRACOASTAL WATERWAY

GROUND LEVEL PLAN

TOP

Las Salinas Sheraton Hotel, Lanzarote, Canary Islands. *The trapezoidal 310-room Las Salinas Sheraton Hotel features terraced guestroom balconies and a lushly landscaped central courtyard, both of which provide welcome relief to the island's rocky terrain. The swimming pool, carved out of the hardened lava flow, creates a unique setting where "art, beauty, and function are truly united," according to architect Fernando Higueras. (See also color photograph on page 12.)*

ABOVE

The Sheraton Princeville, Princeville, Kauai, Hawaii. *Preserving the natural contour of its cliffside site, the Sheraton Princeville is designed on three terraced levels overlooking the Pacific at Pu'upoa Point on the Hawaiian island of Kauai. On 23 acres (9 hectares) adjoining a 27-hole golf course, the 300-room, 350,000-square-foot (32,500-square-meter) resort will include three restaurants, a 7000-square-foot (650-square-meter) ballroom, and 4,000 square feet (372 square meters) of shopping area.*

Full-height glass walls should be provided on the balconies, with doors interlocked so that the cooling system is turned off when they are left open. This prevents condensation and eventually mildew from damaging guestrooms. Some otherwise fine resorts have had this problem, particularly those built of box construction, where coolness in unvented cavity walls has caused continued in-room condensation.

Exterior back-of-house areas, particularly loading docks and service drives, should be concealed by landscaping, retaining walls, and trellises. Truck docks must be roofed and enclosed to prevent unsightly views, noise, and odors. Where visible from upper levels, roofed areas should be terraced and decoratively landscaped to ensure pleasant exterior views from all guestrooms.

No element sets the ambience of the resort more than its pool area. Since guests spend more time there than in any other public space, it affects their overall impression of the resort more than most other elements and provides the same "memorable experience" as the main lobby in the downtown hotel.

Guests expect imaginative shapes, usually emanating jointly from the building and land forms and acting as a transition between them. Fanciful elements such as bridges, islands, grottos, and freeforms help create the desired guest experience as well as decorative backgrounds for their photos, most often taken at the pool. It's shape must provide areas for swimming laps, group play, wading, and, with today's accent on athletics, sports such as water polo. However, diving boards should not be permitted since diving is a prime cause of accidents. The design must also maintain sight lines for lifeguard surveillance of all areas.

A whirlpool at least 8 feet (2.4 meters) in diameter should be located immediately adjacent to the swimming pool, with a second whirlpool near the beach. Pools with spray fountains and related play equipment are designed for resorts with higher family occupancies, but a separate adult pool must be provided in such cases. Children's wading pools should be located close to the main pool for easy surveillance by parents.

Pool design is subject to regional and cultural differences. The Chinese, for example, would consider a separate pool for children an insult to both their children and themselves, since families treasure swimming together at all ages. In some Middle Eastern areas, communal bathing is prohibited in public. Local health and safety regulations also vary. For example, extensive toilet facilities are required in Florida. While ramped pools, allowing bathers to wade in from one end like at a beach, are preferred by guests, they are prohibited in many states due to lack of safeguards against entry by small children.

Pools must be located to obtain maximum sun exposure, but in equatorial climates some shading, such as trellises, must be designed over part of the pool to provide relief. The Inter-Continental in Sharjah along the Arabian Gulf provides a tensile fabric structure over the pool during the day due to the intense sunlight, yet the pool has to be heated at night.

Since even more guests use the pool deck than the pool, chaise space is often inadequate for one of the resorts most popular vacation sports, people watching. More than any other area, the pool deck encourages socializing, and most guests make friends there. Area for at least 1.5 chaises per room should be allowed. Bars are often built into the pool to serve bathers, with snack and marina bars close by, providing food and beverage service to virtually all outdoor areas.

Trends

The luxurious image of resorts keeps evolving through each major hotel boom of this century (for a quick review see the list of hotel milestones in Chapter 1)—from Addison Mizner's Spanish Mediterranean style of the 1920s to Morris Lapidus's glittery Miami Beach *kitsch* of the 1950s to today's postmodern trend toward sophisticated architectural forms reinforced by lavish landscaping, waterscaping, and artifacts, advanced by such leading resort designers as George "Pete" Wimberly of the Hyatt Regency in Maui, Hawaii, Ricardo Legoretta of the Camino Real at Cancun, Mexico, and Edward Killingsworth of the Mauna Lani Bay Hotel on Hawaii's Big Island.

With the steady rise in the number and length of paid vacations and the trend toward earlier retirement, traditional luxurious beach, golf, and tennis resorts will continue to grow; but public preference is shifting toward other forms of resorts discussed in the sections below, emphasizing fitness, informality, personal ownership, boating, skiing, and worldwide sight-seeing, including developments in new, uncharted territories.

TOP

Camino Real, Cancun, Mexico. *With its contemporary pyramidal form rising above a surrounding lagoon, Camino Real's architecture reflects the local Aztec traditions as well as the Yucatan coast's modern multiresort complex. With one meeting room but eight restaurants and lounges and such recreational activities as hydrofoil excursions and parasailing, the resort is oriented toward a variety of vacationers.*

RIGHT

Hyatt Regency Maui, Kaanapali, Hawaii. *Set on 18.5 acres (7.3 hectares) of the Kaanapali Beach Resort complex, the Hyatt Regency Maui is lushly landscaped with Japanese gardens and a network of streams, waterfalls, and imaginatively designed pools, one of its most popular tourist attractions. The $80 million hotel is built around a 70-foot (21-meter) banyan tree in its atrium lobby, also displaying regional art and artifacts valued at over $2 million and an aviary interspersed among a large boutique complex. Its extensive amenities include four restaurants, two lounges, a dinner showroom, and 25,000 square feet (2323 square meters) of meeting space.* *(See also section on the multiresort complex later in this chapter.)*

THE HEALTH SPA

While the original health spa focused mainly on mineral spring-water baths, today's model is founded on elaborate exercising and weight control activity closely supervised by fitness experts (note the fitness facilities checklist in Chapter 17), as well as sports facilities equivalent to beach, golf, and tennis resorts.

Although the word "spa" implies spring water, its specific use and perceived value to health has varied throughout history. Dependence on the theraputic benefits of spa water was much greater prior to the development of modern medicine, with the advent of effective antibiotic medicines gradually changing the emphasis of the health resort in America. Sports and fitness programs replaced mineral bath treatments. Palm Springs, California, for example, originally founded as a mineral spa, has become a world famous sports resort instead.

In today's new health spas, water is used as "the medium, not the medicine." Hydrotherapy, with jet-spray action, warm temperature, buoyancy, and plain tap water, is an important ingredient of exercising and stress-relieving programs as well as treatment of joint and rheumatoid problems. The health spa also acts as a "laboratory" for the whole hotel field, from which innovative programs and equipment are eventually channeled to health clubs in all types of hotels and resorts.

Paradoxically, in contrast with America, old-fashioned spas have enjoyed a resurgence in Europe and Japan. In Dax, France, where mud cures were developed by the Romans, the number of guests has tripled in the past decade. This is partly because Europeans are reimbursed by health programs for their expenses at mineral spas. At Cauterets, a breathtaking scenic site in the French Pyrenees, as in most European spas, sulfur water is inhaled, drunk, and sprayed into every orifice to treat a variety of ailments. At La Bourboule alone, 25,000 asthmatic children take these treatments for two weeks annually. Although spa water has not been scientifically proven to be a permanent healing method, it has brought welcome temporary relief as well as faith and hope to users.

But regardless of the changing fashions in health prescriptions, the spa resort's main virtue of providing psychological environmental treatment is unquestioned. Note the lure of Safety Harbor Spa Resort Hotel and Tennis Club in Tampa Bay, Florida: "Experience a new you, through complete individual pampering." This has long been true from the ancient Baths of Carracalla to modern carefree Palm Springs. In Victorian England, wives suffering from depression or possibly boredom periodically convinced their husbands to send them to Bath, where their recovery was aided by the unrestricted social life for which the spa was noted.

Even authorities who question health spas' therapeutic values still recommend them for personal enjoyment and relaxation due to their pleasant scenery and resort hotel services and accommodations. Many guests select spas because of the choice of special diet menus, with advice by nutritional experts, featured in the spa's restaurants and cafes. In any case, regardless of their style, whether American, European, or Japanese, they will continue to flourish.

Planning considerations

In addition to the health spa buildings, the American spa resort provides hotel and outdoor athletic facilities similar to those at beach, golf, and tennis resorts. But a major feature of health spas is that they primarily serve outside members and visitors as well as their own hotel guests. Therefore, reception facilities, including on-site parking, are generally about double the size required for other resorts.

Since a higher percentage of guests are elderly and many spa guests prefer to take special diet meals in their rooms, efficient circulation is required for easy walking as well as frequent room service. Outdoor terraces and large guestroom balconies are essential for dining and resting. Health spas with room units remote from public facilities report significant guest discomfort and servicing difficulties, for example, when outdoor corridors are subject to wind-driven rain. Therefore, circulation between guestrooms and public facilities should be enclosed wherever possible; otherwise guests may need to be ferried in severe weather between their living units and free-standing restaurants. Golf cart transportation should also be provided for villas or other remote room units.

Design considerations

Since health spas attract more affluent guests than other resorts, guestroom sizes are generally 20 percent larger or are frequently designed as junior suites (see Chapter 16 for a discussion of guestroom types). Other special amenities include card rooms and additional bars, lounges, and cafes at the golf and tennis clubs.

Since about half the health spa use clientele from outside the resort, a separate entrance with its own design motif should be provided as well as convenient enclosed connections to the hotel. Spa reception areas and front desks are as luxurious as hotel lobbies and include a boutique and several seating groups for meeting friends before entering or leaving. After sign-in, storage of valuables, and locker-key formalities, guests proceed to separate and equivalent (almost mirror-image) men's and women's spas.

The World of Palm-Aire, Pampano Beach, Florida. *On 1500 acres (607 hectares), the World of Palm-Aire encompasses three hotels including 205 guestrooms and suites, a 5000-square-foot (538-square-meter) conference center, five golf courses, and a 37-court tennis complex as well as its world-renowned spa. Men's and women's pavilions offer identical fitness facilities such as exercise pools, Roman baths, and Swiss needle showers. Its co-ed exercise area includes a full array of Nautilus equipment, Olympic-sized pool, Parcourse jogging track, and racquetball courts.*

Various healthful sybaritic activities, from tension-relieving massages to progressive-resistance exercising and beauty and fashion consultation, are offered in sumptuous tiled and skylit surroundings, according to individually prescribed three- to ten-day programs supervised by medical, fitness, and other experts. Dressing areas are spacious, carpeted, generously mirrored, and luxurious, with backup areas for storing and issuing robes, slippers, soaps, hair-dryers, and so on. The central wet area containing hot and cold plunges should be atriumlike in design, with full-ceiling retractable skylights and surrounded by whirlpools, saunas, steam baths, and Swiss showers. Also adjoining are the massage rooms and an outdoor massage terrace as well as outdoor whirlpools and an exercise pool for such sports as water polo.

Detailing of finishes and equipment in wet areas is critical, requiring expert consultation. Examples of some nuances often overlooked are that steamrooms should contain a shower and shaving facilities, and their tiled ceilings should be sloped to carry off condensation; terraces for outdoor massages are a popular feature and should not be omitted; and the director's office should be glass paneled and accessible to the central wet area to emphasize personal attention to the guest's activities.

Trends

Due to the influence of health education and the media on maintaining fitness and improving personal appearance, health spas will continue to grow steadily in popularity. The success of the European-style health spa will depend on continued government subsidies. American hotel companies such as Sheraton will continue to enter the European health spa field, influencing its traditional form, while some of the European health practices will be incorporated in American spas. Even traditional European spas such as Vichy, France, have added supervised exercise classes and underwater jet massage facilities catering to the modern spa-goer, while the Greenbrier in West Virginia features a "European-style" spa. But more than other hotel types the development of the health spa varies with different cultures, for example, emphasizing Tai Chi exercises in China, massages in Thailand, shiatzu massaging in Japan, and so on.

Current age demographics auger well for the continued growth of the modern health spa, with its well-equipped hydrotherapy areas for treating joint aches of the aging population. Health spas will continue to attract even greater percentages of women as well as older guests with their elaborate beauty treatment and conditioning facilities. Conference centers will be added to health spas capitalizing on their special appeal to elderly and women's groups.

As guests are introduced to the improved health equipment at spas, they will desire it both at home and on the road. Better programs will be included in all hotel health clubs and new compact equipment incorporated in special "health" guestrooms. Whirlpool tubs, or "environmental climate units," will become standard equipment in guestrooms in many new hotels.

Bonaventure Inter-Continental Hotel and Spa, Fort Lauderdale, Florida. *From its 51-stall riding stable to its 80,000-square-foot (7440-square-meter) World Conference Center, the Bonaventure Inter-Continental Hotel and Spa features a unique array of amenities. The individual guestroom wings, condos, and villas, as well as the hotel's highly rated spa, border its golf courses.*

THE VACATION VILLAGE

Among the boldest and most innovative concepts in hotel history, the vacation village brought to the resort a super-casual atmosphere reflecting the socioeconomic changes of the post-war era. This has to some degree influenced all hotel design, even outside the resort category. Its originator and leading promoter, Club Med, "hotels offer you a room. Club Med offers you an entire village," has set the pace for such developments over the past three decades in virtually every vacation region of the world, but mainly on the three "great global vacation lakes," the Mediterranean, Caribbean, and South Pacific/China Sea. Claiming "an antidote for civilization," "a respite from the frantic pace," and "an avenue to other civilizations," more than any other resort type they capture and even exaggerate the true dictionary meaning of "vacation": a break in routine.

The "break" at a vacation village occurs on several fronts. Location, culture, and design: far away, exotic local themes. Spirit of guests and help: to break down natural reserve and encourage friendliness and group activity. Dress: sparse. Money: beads (at Club Med). Time: no clocks, wake-up alarms, phones, radios, or TVs (at Club Med). Security: no outside door locks. How much further can guests be transported from the reality of their normal work-a-day routines?

But villages have another side. Families have been attracted. In the summer in Europe, 80 percent of village guests are family groups. Club Med has also developed separate family-oriented villages with instruction provided for children in sports, crafts, foreign languages, and computer programming. Accent is also being placed on educational programs for adults. Different villages provide courses in computers, art, sailing, or deep sea fishing, depending on appropriate locations, and with many villages near historic sites, guided tours are featured.

While the original vacation villages of the 50s had tents and guests helped prepare meals, as the concept proved itself, the more well-to-do were attracted. Today, out of approximately a million guests annually, a third earn over $50,000, with acceptance of the village concept growing by the affluent. The more people live in upscale surroundings, evidently the more they want to get away from the modern urban lifestyle to more informal vacation villages.

Planning considerations

The villages' lowrise concepts and ethnic themes are more respectful of local culture and natural environments than many other resorts. Yet during the brief time guests are there, they want to experience pure fantasy. In a sense, *their* reality is kept out simply by emphasizing the *true* environment. Taking a theme park as an example, designers noted that the sight of a highrise building from inside Disneyland spoiled the magical charm for some of the guests. Therefore, more land was acquired at Disney World to prevent such visual distractions. For the same reasons, va-

Club Mediterranee, Cherating, Malaysia. *The first major resort on Malaysia's east coast, the Club Mediteranee Cherating is set on pilings with walls of exotic woods capped by colorful tile roofs. Shaded terraces on all guestroom units provide views of the beach, while the larger structures housing the restaurant, boutique, disco, library, and children's club recall Malaysian palaces.*

cation villages are as hidden as possible, with lateral sight lines laid out to focus guests' views on exotic elements and to screen out distractions.

Long walking distances, normally a source of guests' complaints in spread-out, lowrise hotels, can be made architecturally exciting, enjoyable experiences in the context of a vacation village. For example, after checking-in at the Princess Mediterranean Village in Williams Island, Florida, guests are taken by golf cart on a leisurely architectural tour of the entire village before locating their rooms. Rather than being irritated by the long trek from the lobby to their room, they are impressed by the best features of the resort and have quickly and pleasantly learned where everything is before their vacation even starts.

Turning adversity to advantage, developers have made walking a feature of the village and encouraged it by planning the facilities similiar to the "anchor" stores in shopping malls. For example, if the entrance lobby is at one end, a campanile is designed to create interest at the opposite end, with pools, snack bars, sports and other activity centers also widely spaced. A central plaza is the meeting place and focal point with dual areas, one shaded and trellised for daytime use and another open to the sky for the evenings. By breaking the village into varied courtyards on changing levels, even an 800-room resort can maintain a smaller-scaled, more personal atmosphere.

Design considerations

To further enhance walking experiences, the design needs to provide even more than beautiful vistas, lush indigenous landscaping, and authentic statuary. Since smooth walkways carry urban connotations, surfaces are given varying textures appealing to the tactile senses. For ambient sound, fountains are mounted on walls at turns in walkways or set free-standing in courtyards, accented by refracted light. Outside illumination is provided by wall sconces and path lighting rather than high-intensity floodlights to avoid harsh shadows. Earthy colors are used with bright accents that reflect local decorative themes and artwork. In these idyllic surroundings, guests are made more aware of their senses becoming more responsive to esthetic themes and detailing.

Club Mediterranee Pompadour, Domaine de la Noaille, France. *Featuring an equestrian center, Club Mediterranee Pompadour has meticulously maintained its country village atmosphere. Set on a hillside, its rambling, rustic-roofed farm buildings house restaurants, boutiques, a nightclub, a library, and an art studio. The guestrooms are mainly dispersed behind gabled roofs, providing panoramic mountain views.*

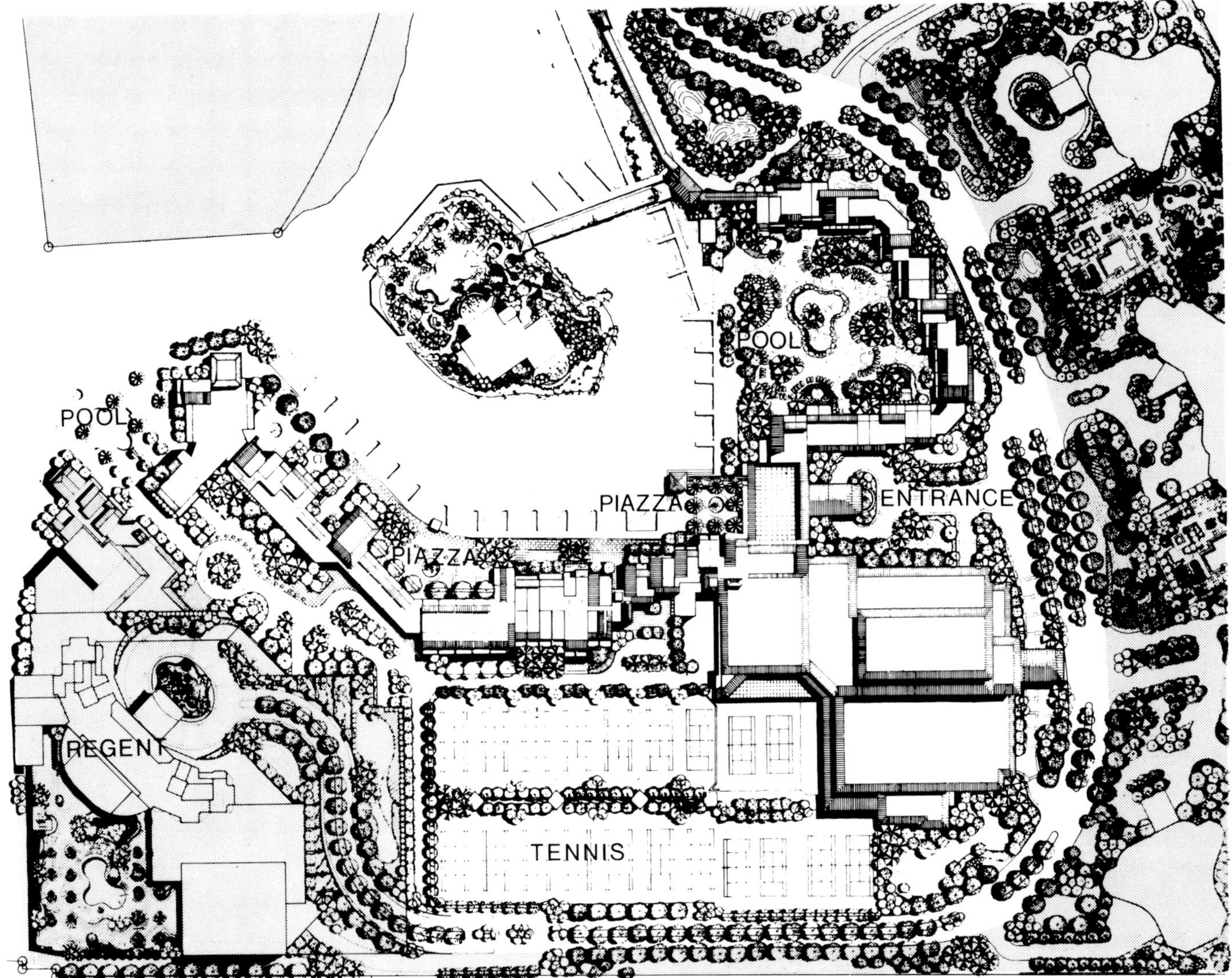

Mediterranean Village, Williams Island, Florida.
Conceived as a luxurious vacation village, the Mediterranean Village on Florida's 80-acre (32-hectare) Williams Island is designed as part of a lively quayside promenade containing a variety of cafes, restaurants, lounges, and boutiques. Set above these are a series of suites, including floor-throughs, skip-stops, and duplexes, designed to emphasize their individuality and waterviews as well as providing convenient access to the entertainment and marina facilities surrounding the village's waterfront.

Trends

The village concept will continue its upscale growth with new luxurious projects featuring larger [16′ × 22′ (4.9 × 6.7 m)] guestrooms and junior suites more comparable in scale with health spas than the modest 12′ × 14′ (3.7 × 4.3 m) sizes in many of today's vacation villages. But even with luxurious rooms, Kona Village in Kona, Hawaii, with rates of up to $180 a day, boasts of its "don't haves," such as "no room phones, TVs, radios, or clocks and no crowds, traffic, buses, or noise," making it truly a place where "less is more."

More "double villages" will be developed, such as the Club Med in Marrakesh that combines a downtown tourist hotel with a remote mountain or beach site reached by daily tour bus for those who prefer balancing daytime natural surroundings with the city nightlife. Conference usage will increase as the business world breaks down its reserve toward the village's uninhibited image.

Since villages are compatible with the environment, they will be able to open in previously "unconquerable" areas of immense potential tourist interest such as Tibet, the Ming Tombs in China, and even on Mt. Everest. Also, schooling facilities in many villages will attract moderate-income family groups, using self-improvement to help justify their vacation expenses.

THE TIMESHARING AND CONDOMINIUM RESORT

Taking its concept from a popular European vacation tradition and its name from the computer industry, timesharing condominiums got their start in the early 60s. Two decades and several unscrupulous projects later, they finally fell under the government regulation they richly deserved. While often overly promoted, timesharing has now matured into a respectable and creative means of financing, along with limited partnerships and other new condo resort funding methods. Timeshare purchasers buy condominum units for one or two weeks per year for some period, often 10 years. In effect they are reserving a private vacation home for a specified time.

Their innovative, inherent advantage and the main reason for long-term success are their built-in high use factor, as compared with other types of resorts. For example, while capital investments are similar, the occupancies of timesharing resorts are generally 20 percent higher than those of other resorts, with the benefits of this efficiency accruing to both developers and users. In other words, the buyer only pays for what he/

she uses while overall business exceeds the competition.

With promotional costs dropping from 50 to 20 percent of sales during the past decade due to greater public acceptance as well as more effective use of national media, timesharing resorts have become better buys. Sales are now motivated primarily because people want to use the resort rather than to gain its relatively minor tax benefits. In addition, a variety of vacation choices have been provided through exchange programs with other timesharing units, which is increasing as the market grows.

A timesharing purchase can be a hedge against the inflationary cost of vacations. For example, if resort rates increase at 10 percent per year, timesharing owners can amortize their purchases in seven years. Note how the Scottsdale/Camelback Resort in Arizona markets its timesharing condo units: "Owning a yearly vacation could be your best corporate move." Not surprisingly, major new timesharing resorts are being added at the rate of over 100 annually.

Planning considerations

Social problems have resulted from mixing timesharing with year-round condo resorts and other housing. Unfortunate losses of needed rental housing units have also occurred due to the conversion of existing apartment structures into timeshare units. Since timeshare owners identify with transient vacationers rather than permanent residents, timesharing resorts should be combined with hotels and separated from primary-home residences or condo communities. Also, neighboring hotels provide the type of restaurants, entertainment, and other amenities sought by timeshare owners.

Condo resorts that are not based on timesharing include both individual living units with resort amenities and resort hotels financed through absentee condo ownership, but operated as hotels. Like timesharing, both methods tap the individual borrowing power of the condo owners who derive tax deductions on interest expenses and real estate depreciation. The site planning requirements and outdoor amenities for timesharing and condo hotel resorts are similar to those

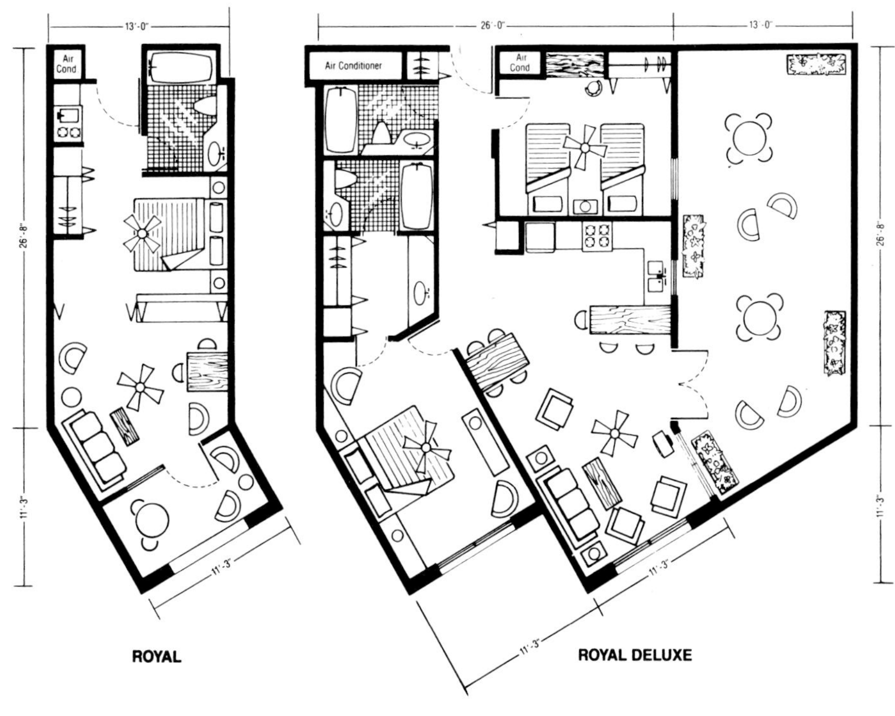

Playa Linda Beach Resort, Aruba, Netherlands Antilles. *Planned in phases with its initial 7-level, stepped-down tower containing 132 timesharing units, ranging from the studios to the two-bedroom suites shown at top, Playa Linda Beach Resort has provisions for three added towers surrounding its raised pool deck with an amenities center overlooking the beach. With the ground floor used for covered parking, all units feature upper-level kitchen/dining areas with balconies angled toward the ocean view.*

for other beach, golf, and tennis resorts, but often with the addition of more individualized townhouse-type units discussed below.

Design considerations

Since prime views are critical to the sale of timesharing and condo units (knowledgeable developers call this "selling the view"), they should be located on beachfronts or marinas and elevated above ground level with public facilities or parking below, such as at Playa Linda Beach Resort in Aruba. Covering over the parking areas also preserves the natural landscape.

Since 70 percent of the timeshare market consists of families with an average household size of 3.5 people who use their unit for up to two weeks annually (as allowed by current U.S. tax laws to maintain their investment tax status), the most typical guestroom unit should be a two-bedroom apartment. Because purchasers are affluent (with $45,000 the median annual income) and sophisticated (with a median of 15.4 years of schooling), their housing standards are high, yet as typical vacationers they expect their unit to contain even more luxurious features than their own home.

Therefore, living/dining areas must be at least 300 square feet (27.9 square meters) in area, luxuriously furnished, and equipped with sofa bed. Food preparation must be made as pleasant as possible, with the kitchen open to the living/dining area and sharing the prime view. Since purchasers want maximum vacation time, quick and easy to use kitchen appliances including a Jenn-Air, Cuisinart, microwave oven, ice maker, and lobster-clam steamer, as well as an outdoor barbecue grill should be furnished. Items such as hoods that recall a standard kitchen should be avoided, since vacationers do not want to be reminded of housework.

The master bedroom should be at least 200 square feet (18.6 square meters) with luxury quality furnishings, while a second bedroom of about 120 square feet (11.1 square meters), usually for children, can be relatively plain. Master bath and dressing rooms of over 100 square feet (9.3 square meters) are expected to have a health spa atmosphere, with a whirlpool tub, separate shower, two-basin vanity, phone, mini-TV, and skylights where possible. Such amenities provide the "sizzle that sells." The second bathroom may be minimal, containing a shower instead of a tub. Closets with mirrored doors in bedrooms and in the living area must be larger than in hotel rooms, but smaller than in residential apartments.

Since timesharing users expect a more impressive entrance than that in a normal hotel room, a 40-square-foot (3.7-square-meter) foyer is recommended. Balconies approaching 100 square feet must be designed and well furnished for frequent, convenient use, with full-width sliding glass panels and access from the master bedroom. To provide a more spacious feeling, ceiling heights should be a minimum of 9 feet (2.7 meters) clear hieght rather than the 8 feet (2.4 meters) normally required in hotels, with sloped ceilings on the top floor. With this additional height, ceiling fans can be provided for comfort, energy savings, and a more residential atmosphere.

This type of unit is the most popular size and the quickest and easiest to sell. It is more efficient to build than smaller units in that its construction cost is lower on a square-foot basis (basic mechanical costs do not increase in proportion to the square footage added), is more favorably priced, and involves proportionately less sales and closing costs compared with a greater number of smaller units. But it is still advisable to include up to 30 percent of one-bedroom units for market flexibility.

Townhouse units should also be included since they add a desirable residential quality to the complex and are strongly in demand. But for hotel servicing purposes, they should be clustered into what are called "fourplexes" or "eightplexes," with central stations in each grouping for housekeeping supplies and equipment. A small percentage of three-bedroom units—not in great demand (up to 10 percent of the market)—should be included in townhouse developments.

With landscaped balconies, irregular facades angled toward the views, and preferably a stepped building form, the timesharing and condo resort, combined with townhouses, appropriately emphasizes the individuality and privacy of its units to a greater extent than other resort hotels.

Trends

As in suite hotels the original developers of timesharing and condo resorts came from the apartment field, acquiring professional hotel management skills as required. With more hotel companies developing timesharing resorts, the field will become more fully integrated into the hotel industry.

Such resorts will continue to provide greater investment advantages than normal hotels. In effect, developers can sell the hotel to many individual investors for about a 20 percent higher price than could be negotiated with a single buyer, at the same time maintaining their interest as managing agent. Even more importantly, they avoid the difficulties and high costs of obtaining institutional financing while also offsetting front-end expenses (including interest on construction loans) through advance sales. Major public underwriting has also been used to fund newer forms of condo and limited partnership ownership.

THE MARINA HOTEL

The marina hotel fills a growing gap in stopover resorts for boaters and convenient vacation centers for water sports enthusiasts. ("Miami's only hotel with a 220-slip marina at its door" boasts Marriott Hotel and Marina in Florida's Biscayne Bay). In addition to becoming a "destination" resort for yachters, a boat-rental facility, and starting out point for sports sailors, the hotel also hosts private boaters from the community who sail over to dine or spend the weekend. Others keep their private boats at the marina, driving over and using the "boatel" for weekend sailing.

Planning considerations

The closest possible integration of the hotel with the marina is desirable for (1) ensuring guest convenience, (2) providing efficient catering service to boats, and (3) dramatizing the resort's theme through its built-in marina views from all guest areas. For food and beverage catering and luggage service to the boats, "golf cart" service is provided.

Marina Facility. While the ultimate size of the marina dock itself depends on the boating market, it should contain for the hotel's purposes at least two boat slips for every five guestrooms, although some provide considerably more; for example, the Bahia Mar Hotel in Ft. Lauderdale, Florida, has 300 guestrooms and a 350-boat marina. The marina facility must include retail shops for boating supplies, fishing and water sports gear, groceries, a clothing boutique, and self-service laundry as well as fuel supply and repair shop. A major overhaul facility may be required if none is available in the area.

The marina administration office must contain navigational facilities and expert personnel to assist guests. Its docks must be equipped with standard boat-servicing outlets for electricity, water supply, and waste, as well as boat maintenance facilities if not available in the vicinity. A private yacht club should be planned adjacent to the hotel where feasible as a desirable visual element and amenity for guests.

Design considerations

The marina hotel is more luxurious than beachfront resorts due to its affluent guests. This should be reflected in 25 percent more

LEFT AND ABOVE

Hotel Inter-Continental Abu Dhabi, United Arab Emirates. *Reflecting the country's seafaring heritage, the 100-slip marina, 452-room Inter-Continental Abu Dhabi provides a social center for the capitol's foreign visitors and residents. Its three public levels contain restaurants, lounges, shops, and an auditorium and are open to a waterfront promenade bordering the marina. Carved screens, decorative tiles, and nonfigurative artwork throughout the interiors reflect traditional Moslem geometric motifs.*

LEFT

Hotel Inter-Continental, San Diego, California. *Featuring a picturesque 450-slip marina berthing hundreds of yachts, the 682-room Hotel Inter-Continental San Diego, itself boat shaped, captures the spirit of the water-oriented California city. Its curved plan also ensures every room an ocean view, while its public spaces and swimming pools are surrounded by a lagoon with rock-enclosed waterslides and falls.*

luxury suites and a higher standard of furnishings throughout. In addition, guestrooms require balconies overlooking the marina.

A second swimming pool should be provided near the dock area for those boat owners and crews staying on their boats. Access to golf and tennis is required to attract other types of vacationers, satisfy all members of a family or group, and provide destination attractions for yachters. Lobbies, restaurants, bars, and lounges, with outdoor terraces, should have prime views toward the marina, opening directly on its main promenade.

Trends

Fulfilling the function of "the common person's" yacht club, marina resorts will continue to grow in number and size as centers for the boating public. But to broaden their occupancy base, they will increasingly add new facilities, services, and amenities and becoming true hybrid resorts such as marina/airport hotels, marina/suite hotels, and marina/conference centers. The new Miami Airport Hilton and Marina, for example, combines its airport location with lushly landscaped grounds, resort recreation facilities, and a lakeside marina.

THE SKI LODGE

Following the development of artificial snow making and easier, safer skiing equipment in the 70s, the number of cross-country and downhill skiers has continued to increase dramatically each season. To meet this increased demand, many ski lodges have matured into full-fledged, year-round resorts offering health clubs, gourmet food, entertainment, and other recreational facilities while still retaining their traditional informality. For instance, Sugarbush Inn in Vermont promises "All the amenities and services of a first class hotel." Since few hotels can survive today on winter-only occupancy, the ski lodge has become a resort for all seasons. By adding the full range of conventional hotel comforts and services as well as indoor pools and tennis, jacuzzis, bike paths, hiking trails, and scenic excursions, the previously rugged lodges have attracted summer tourists and nonskiing winter guests.

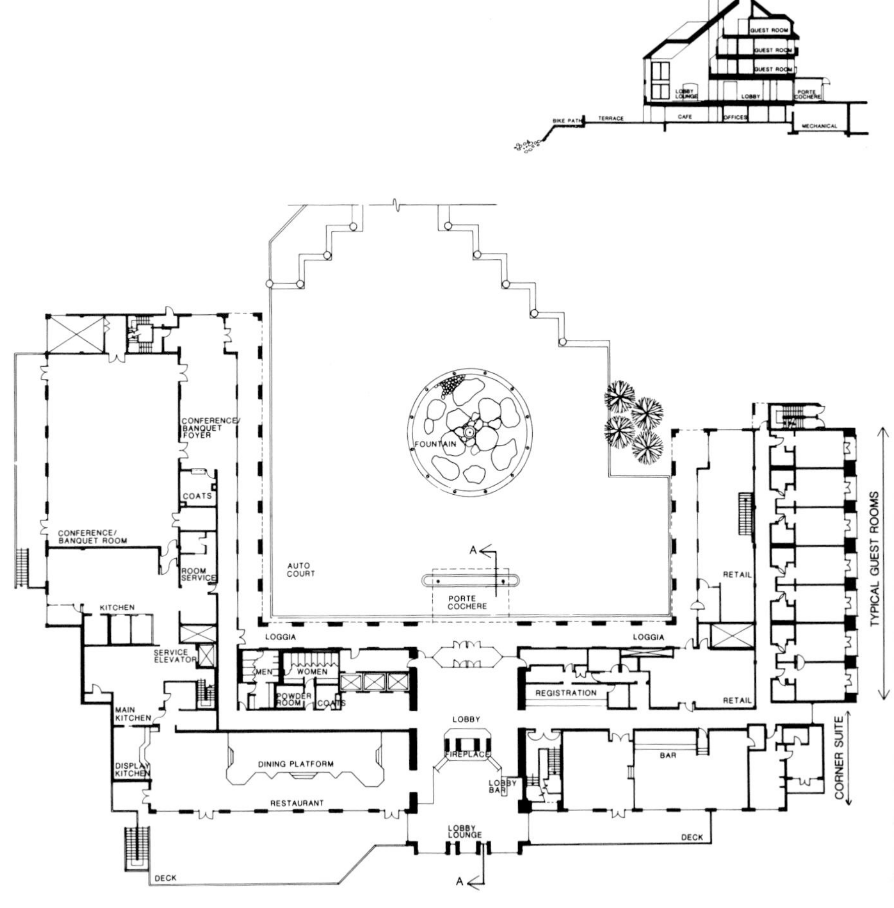

The Westin Hotel, Vail, Colorado. *The Westin Hotel, with its 150 rooms grouped around a central plaza, forms the focal point of a 20-acre (8-hectare) site at the edge of one of the Rocky Mountains' fastest growing resort areas, master planned in the spirit of a northern European village. Retail shops, restaurants, and lounges, indoor athletic facilities, and a conference center are incorporated to attract year-round tourists as well as cater to 250 condo units, some located above the commercial facilities and others clustered along the natural watercourse that cascades through the site to the central plaza.*

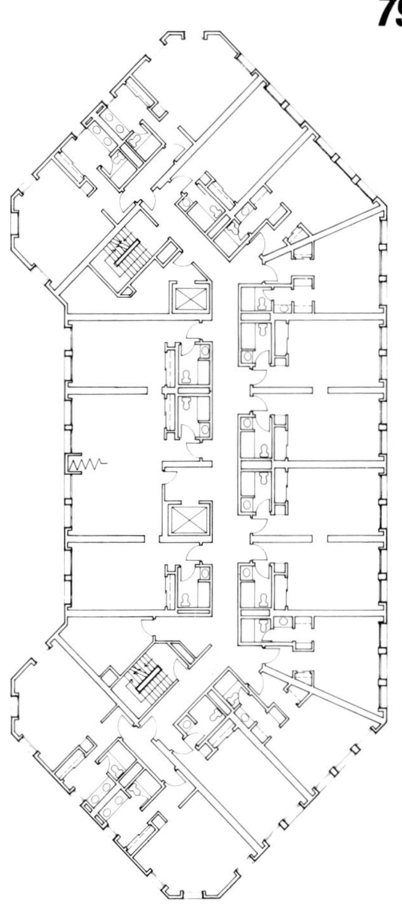

Poste Montane Hotel, Beaver Creek, Colorado. *The 39-room Poste Montane Hotel blends into its wooded setting much like the small Alpine ski lodge. The two lower levels contain restaurants, lounges, and shops, above which are three guestroom floors, the topmost with garret ceilings adding to the lodge's warmth and charm.*

Planning considerations

Due to concerns about natural preservation in rapidly expanding ski areas, strict environmental and planning controls have been exercised over new developments. At the same time, even larger ski resorts have been needed to satisfy the increased demand as well as to justify the high costs of gaining environmental approvals. However, large-scale developments can be planned to blend with the natural landscape and, through phased development, be better timed to meet actual demand.

The Westin Hotel in Vail, Colorado, for example, was developed as part of a 20-acre (8-hectare) site including condos and a "village square" with extensive retail, entertainment, and service facilities. A future conference center is also planned as a means of generating additional year-round resort business. The Poste Montane in Beaver Creek, Colorado, while representing a smaller ski lodge, was also part of an overall master plan including five other lodges of various sizes.

Since most guests travel by air to reach the larger ski resorts, lodges should be located within an hour's drive of major airports and close to a commuter airport. While the majority of guests arrive by van, taxi, or tour bus, up to 40 percent drive or rent cars at the airport. Due to snow conditions, parking garages are generally provided, preferably built into the natural terrain to maintain a low profile. However, in large resorts, extensive unrestricted surface parking can become a serious eyesore and should be avoided.

Like the conference center, the vacation village, and the country inn, the ski lodge does not need high visibility and should avoid extensive signage that would intrude on the natural landscape. As guests arrive, skis are checked in outside the lodge and routed directly to a central ski storage area; a special outside "ski elevator" between the entrance drive and ski storage area can be used for this purpose. The ski lodge is often built into a hill with its ski facilities, including storage, service, and ski shop areas, located on a lower level directly accessible to the ski runout and remount area behind the lodge. A 200- to 300-foot (61- to 91-meter) wide area at the base of the chair/lift should be large enough to accommodate waiting lines, assembling classes, and resting and lounging on sun decks.

The main ski slopes are preferably located on the north side of the mountain to assure maximum accumulation of a hardpack snow base. The ski lodge can therefore be oriented so that most guestrooms have both maximum southern exposure to the sun and views of the skislope. While balconies and roof terraces are as popular at ski lodges as they are at beach resorts, they are more costly to construct due to snow loads and the greater waterproofing protection required. Guests prefer upper-floor rooms with panoramic views. Wherever possible rooms with dormer windows and sloped ceilings should be designed into ski lodges, since it has been proven that such features are highly desired psychologically.

Design considerations

Fireplaces are expected in the main public areas and are desirable in as many guestrooms as possible. However, the number of fireplaces is usually limited by environmental controls on smoke pollution, which may restrict them to corner suites on all floors.

Double glazing is required for increased comfort during the winter. At 5000 feet (1524 meters) air conditioning is generally omitted due to comfortable summer temperatures. Often mini-refrigerators are offered in guestrooms, since skiers become dehydrated and need to quench their thirst. Showers in each room should be considered as a convenience for skiers who overwhelmingly prefer them to tub baths.

Durable materials must be used throughout the interiors, since skiers in boots tend to abuse them. Hard-surface stone flooring should be used at the entrance lobby due to heavy boot traffic and dampness. However, for acoustical reasons dense carpet is required in other public areas to dampen the sound of boots.

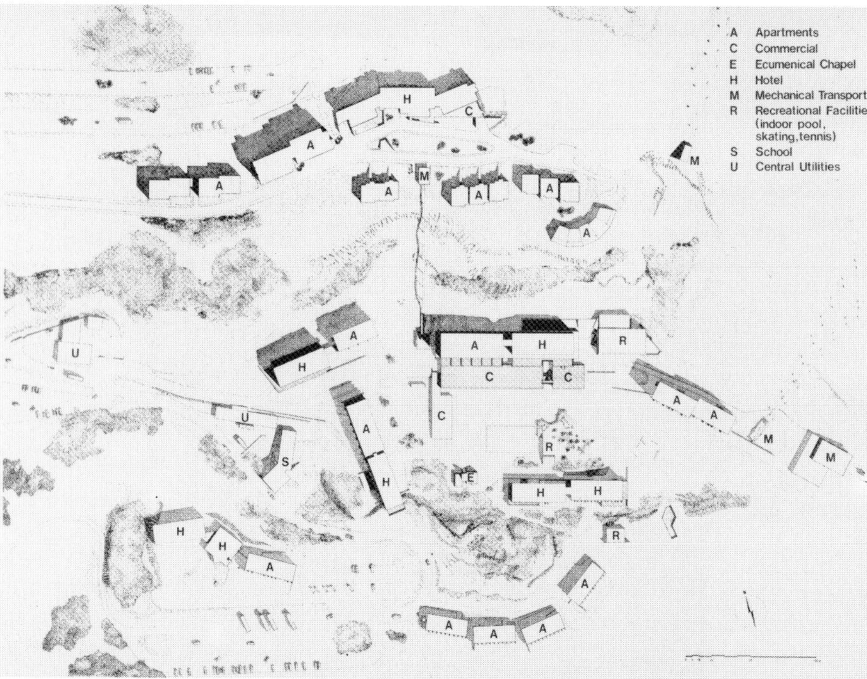

The bar and lounge areas should be designed to play up the unique social mix that occurs at ski lodges. The main cocktail lounge is used primarily by more affluent, middle-aged guests. It requires a fireplace, comfortable furnishings, a mountain view, and a piano. Another bar is needed nearby to provide a hangout for the younger, more raucous skiers. It needs a dance floor and disco music. No exterior view is required. The blending together of the two different groups contributes to the ski lodge's its unique atmosphere.

While lunch is at most a light snack, dinner at ski lodges is considered an important social occasion for discussing the day's activities and reenergizing with gourmet food. Restaurants require exterior views, with outdoor decks for daytime use and raised interior levels to enhance the view. A mix is required of an upscale restaurant for the older, more affluent skiers and a cafe for the younger set, with a self-service indoor/outdoor snack bar for daytime service.

Trends

Continued fitness consciousness, new computerized ski-learning techniques, and improvements in all types of ski equipment will accelerate growth of ski lodges. Summer resort amenities will be added, and more viable sites will be selected based on their year-round appeal. All-suite ski lodges will be developed to better accommodate longer stays and increasing family demand for summer vacations.

Conference center facilities will be added to ski lodges to stimulate out-of-season use. Environmental concerns will be satisfied by underground parking and clustering ski lodges in dense developments to better preserve major open spaces.

It's projected that huge cable-supported transluscent fabric structures will permit safe all-weather, year-round, day/night skiing in a few major worldwide locations; and the land can accommodate heavy development, multi-resort communities of up to 5000 rooms, with ski lodges and villages of 1000 rooms, will be built before the end of the century. This will be particularly appealing to older skiers, because such communities will extend their skiing years, and it will also enlarge the overall skiing population, thereby counteracting the otherwise negative age demographics affecting future lodge development.

Flaine, France. *Contrasting delicate wooden balconies against massive concrete backgrounds, master Bauhaus architect Marcel Breuer blended the international style into an Alpine setting in this ski lodge complex at Flaine in France.*

THE TOURIST/SIGHT-SEEING RESORT

Related as closely as possible to the tourist attractions they serve, tourist/sight-seeing resorts vary as much in theme as in their different sites. While Disney World's Contemporary and Polynesian Hotels are closely woven into an overall concept, approaches vary at other such resorts. The guest house at the natural-walled city of Petra in Jordan, several lodges in the midst of wild game parks in Kenya, and a charming in-town hotel blended into the hillside of a Goan fishing village on the Indian Ocean illustrate diverse design solutions to the specific objectives and opportunities of each tourist site. Major hotels in world-famous tourist attraction centers such as Cian, Giza, Kathmando, Kwielien, Kyoto, or Luxor are designed primarily to facilitate visits to their sacred shrines, antiquities, and scenic wonders.

Planning considerations

While the tourist/sight-seeing resort is located preferably as close as possible to its featured attraction, environmental separation from the resort is often required due to the nature of the site. In such cases, special transportation systems such as car-trains or monorails, used so effectively at Disney World, should be considered to prevent excessive auto and bus traffic from detracting from guests' enjoyment of the site. Wherever possible, newly developed sites should be planned with provisions for potential hotel development.

The design character of the resort should respect the tourist site and its environment. For example, hotels located in historic districts, such as the Royal Sonesta in New Orleans, Louisiana's French Quarter and the Mills House Holiday Inn in Charleston, South Carolina, adopted traditional designs to blend with the community and thereby enhance the

ABOVE

Contemporary Hotel, Walt Disney World, Orlando, Florida. *Demonstrating the trend toward providing convenient guest transportation between hotels and the tourist attractions they serve, the 1050-room Contemporary Hotel features a monorail station within its atrium lobby. (See also page 209).*

RIGHT

Al Ain Inter-Continental Hotel, Abu Dhabi, United Arab Emirates. *Out of respect for its neighbors, the 9-story Inter-Continental Hotel in Al Ain (a tourist site in the Abu Dhabi desert bordering on mountainous Oman) steps down gently toward the community's oasis, which is integrated with the hotel's pool area. Often visited by the royal family and their foreign guests, the terraced balconies of the 265-room resort provide shaded views for all guestrooms, while patterns of Arabic calligraphy, pottery, and tile are reflected throughout its restaurants, lounges, and interior spaces.*

guests' experience. The Mills House went as far as to duplicate the exterior design of the building that originally stood on the site. In Egypt a royal hunting manor was adapted by the Oberoi Meenah House to accommodate visitors to the Pyramids at Giza.

With their smaller scales, the tourist/sightseeing resorts at Petra, an ancient Jordanian city walled in by natural rock, Goa on the Indian coast, and Agra at the Taj Mahal in India were able to blend with their landscapes as well as the local cultural idiom. Surrounded by an oasis, the Inter-Continental Al Ain in Abu Dhabi in the United Arab Emirates used extensive landscaping and a step-down building form to harmonize with the natural surroundings.

But at such major international tourist sites as Kyoto, hotels and resorts must cater to an ever-growing volume of visitors and tour groups, requiring extensive traffic-handling facilities for buses and rental cars as well as parking and taxi service for guests taking their own tours. As their popularity increases to avoid congestion, well-integrated people-mover systems are essential between tourist attractions and their nearby resorts.

Adaptive reuse of a variety of existing buildings provides the most appropriate environmental solution for such tour cities as Florence, where scores of traditional villas and townhouses have been restored to provide tourist accommodations respectful of the adjacent historic and museum sites. In Qufo, one of China's most historic cities, guests have been permitted to stay in Confucius's restored mansion, rather than change the area's atmosphere with a new hotel.

Design considerations

Lobbies must be 20 percent larger than at other types of resorts having the same

ABOVE

The Mena House Oberoi, Giza, Egypt. *Sharing the base of a plateau with the Pyramids and Sphinx, the hotel Mena House Oberoi is set on an oasis of 40 acres (16 hectares) of rolling lawns and ornamental gardens. Originally a royal hunting lodge, it features authentic Pharaonic design motifs throughout its deluxe guestrooms, gourmet restaurant, and other public spaces, blending with its historic site.*

LEFT

The Petra Forum Hotel, Wadi Mousa, Jordan. *Serving visitors to the ancient natural walled city, the 80-room Petra Forum Hotel is designed to intrude as little as possible on its spectacular 300-foot high (91-meter) red-rocked tourist site with its nearby carved monuments steeped in 9000 years of history. Built of local sandstone, the hotel is terraced to follow the rugged terrain, providing panoramic views. A restaurant and archaeological exhibit center are also blended into Petra's rugged formations, with guest transportation through a 1-mile (1.6-kilometer) entrance passage provided by camel or horse. (See also page 4 in Color Portfolio.).*

number of guestrooms primarily to handle tour groups, much like convention hotels. This includes space for sight-seeing reservation desks and for assemblying tours. Restaurants should be 20 percent larger, with buffet service provided for groups to allow maximum time for their sight-seeing excursions.

While retail areas remain similar to those at other resorts, they should be devoted primarily to local crafts bought as souvenirs. Since guests often collect paintings on such trips, an art gallery is also appropriate. Interesting retail displays are essential since they become a major element of the decor.

Trends

Inspired by Disney World's example, closer integration will be provided between resorts and theme park developments in Japan and the Middle East as well as at new American sites. Challenges to relate the latest technology with local traditions will be presented in such sensitive regions of potential mass tourism as Cian, Kwielien, and Soochow in China and Luxor and Aswan in Egypt. While China's initial expansion of sight-seeing hotels will first serve millions of new international visitors, a second wave of resorts will be needed in the next decade for its own growing middle class. Such hotels associated with historic sites and educational theme parks will prove vastly popular given the emphasis in Chinese culture on history and education of the young.

No corner of the planet, from the high-altitude scenery of Nepal to the penguin-packed ice flows of Antarctica is ultimately immune from tourism. From watching Galapagos tortoises to Texas whooping cranes, there is no end to the possibilities of naturalistic as well as historic sight-seeing. Current experience in blending small resorts with tourist sites will put designers to the test in increasingly delicate locations now undergoing international tourist expansion such as Tibet.

Royal Orleans, New Orleans, Louisiana. *The traditional 356-room hotel, delicately laced with wrought-iron balconies, preserves the historic environment while conveniently located in the heart of the French Quarter only one block from Bourbon Street.*

THE MULTIRESORT COMPLEX

Mega-developments continue to open virgin territories to tourism. Their huge scale is needed to justify government funding of airports, highways, and other vital services in the social and physical infrastructure. The 40-square-mile (103-square-kilometer) Hilton Head Island Resort on the eastern shore of South Carolina ("for years an undiscovered paradise. Now one of the world's premier resort communities" advertises Sea Pines Plantation there), the Kaanapali region of Maui, and the Bernadin development on the Adriatic Coast of Yugoslavia provide models of cooperation among government, private developers, and, in one case, the World Bank.

In the space of a decade, the Mexican National Tourist Agency, FONATUR, has launched two major regional hotel developments, with others to follow. Cancun, less than a decade ago a barren coastal strip on the tip of Mexico's Yucatan peninsula, now offers over a dozen major resorts, a conference center, and related tourist shopping and entertainment features. Ixtapa, on the Pacific 150 miles (241 kilometers) south of Acapulco, which was cut out of jungle a few years ago, already contains 9 major resorts out of the 13 planned, including a Sheraton, Holiday Inn, Camino Real, and El Presidente.

Such projects typically consist of broad landscaped avenues paralleling the beach, lined with widely spaced modern hotels, and a marina. Ixtapa wraps around a bay surrounded by hills, with a shopping plaza and golf course provided across the avenue from the ring of beachfront hotels. Both complexes offer a quieter outlying beach area a few miles from the main hotels for future vacation village development including a Club Med. Just as a freeway from Mexico City opened Acapulco to a tourist boom in the 50s, a similar radial highway is expected to set off the same scenario for Ixtapa in the 80s. Likewise, in the Baja region a new airport at Jose del Cabo has set the stage for the development over the next decade of 4500 hotel rooms, golf courses, hundreds of homes and apartments, and a new city of 40,000.

Planning considerations

Exploratory studies required to launch developments of this scale involve teams of social, economic, transportation, marine, geological, ecological, meteorological, agronomic, anthropological, and other experts. For each of several potential sites varying data on climate, wind, tides, currents, quality of sand, sources of fresh water, power supply, sewage disposal, and a myriad of other environmental concerns are investigated and evaluated by computer. At the same time, the natural beauty of the landscape is considered (see the environmental planning checklist in the Appendix). A beachfront strip several square miles in area is selected for development and a master plan is prepared to locate a major new airport, plan hundreds of miles of roads, and prepare for population growth of 50,000 people needed to service industries stimulated by the 10,000-tourist population, all controlled to safeguard against overbuilding and potential damage to the environment.

Social and political problems frequently affect the eventual development of large multiresort sites. In Ixtapa, while creating foreign exchange credit and employment were the main objectives, the administration was understandably sensitive to media charges that public funds would be used to create "gilded ghettos for gringos." Therefore a moderately priced, government-sponsored vacation center geared to middle-class Mexican families was carefully included in a satellite development a few miles away. These lowrise budget hotels, containing basic bunk beds, rent for $10 per day.

Another problem was the potential gentrification of a nearby colorful fishing village, Ixtapa's chief tourist attraction, now featuring restaurants and nightlife as well as a town center for the expanding service population. This must be balanced by further government subsidies to improve social services, with moderate-cost housing to enhance the quality of life of the local population.

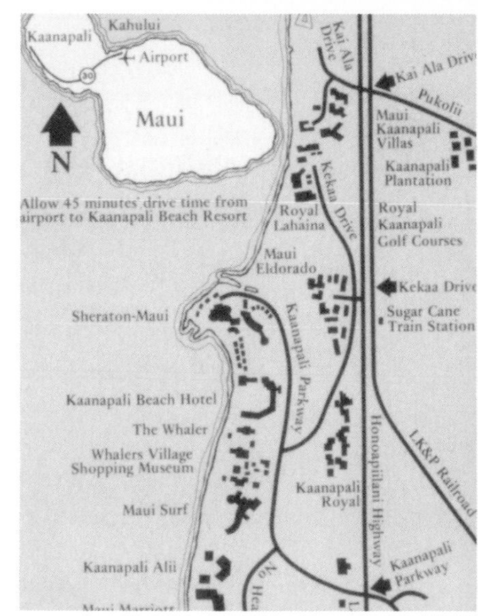

Kaanapali Beach Resort, Maui, Hawaii. *Covering 1200 acres (486 hectares), Kaanapali Beach Resort was originally master planned in 1959 around the concept of a self-contained resort city where "the tourist can stay without ever having to leave the resort." It has since grown to 12 luxury resort hotels and condominiums comprising 5000 rental units surrounded by recreation amenities including twin 18-hole golf courses, 3 miles (5 kilometers) of beaches, and 40 tennis courts as well as its own shopping complex, passenger train system, and a unique whaling museum. While the hotels are individually operated by such chains as Marriott, Sheraton, and Hyatt Regency, an architectural review committee ensures that each new development conforms to the highest environmental design standards. The overall developers install and maintain the infrastructure including the transit systems, walkways, and landscaping that features extensive botanical gardens.* *(See also page 69.)*

Regional tourist sites

The larger the resort, the more it must depend on local points of interest to help attract tourists. Tours of historic Charleston and Savannah are high on the agenda of vacationers at the Hilton Head Resort complex. The cloud-piercing peak of Haleakala is the most favorite tour of visitors to Maui. But since more points of interest were needed, a Whaling Museum was created in the heart of the Kaanapali complex.

One of the reasons for selecting Cancun for tourist development, which was more important than its powdery white sand, "best snorkeling in the Caribbean," and 240 days per year of pure sunshine, was its proximity to the Mayan ruins of Tulum and Chichen Itza. Offering boat excursions to ancient island settlements, the Cancun complex provides three escape-days from its modern resort core to more stimulating activities for the mind and spirit. As essential as gaming and glittering nightlife is to Las Vegas, attractive tourist excursions help make multiresort complexes viable, addressing guests' educational interests, particularly of families, and the need for breaks even in a sybaritic vacation.

Ixtapa, Mexico. *Master planned on 6 miles (10 kilometers) of Mexico's Pacific beaches near the picturesque fishing village of Zihautanejo, Ixtapa, has grown within a few short years to include over 3800 rooms in 10 major hotels including chains such as Camino Real and Sheraton, a vacation village, and a Robert Trent Jones–designed golf course as well as budget accommodations and housing for local employees. Due to the popularity of its multi-resort developments such as Cancun and Ixtapa, the Mexican tourist development agency has also planned the expansion of Loreto and Los Cabos on the Baja Peninsula, a few hundred miles from California, to include over 2000 additional hotel rooms and related amenities, anticipating 50,000 annual visitors by 1990.*

Trends

The potential of multiresort complexes is strongest in areas of unique natural or historic interest also favored by sunny climate and convenient transportation. Within three hours of several major U.S. population centers, Mexico is fertile ground for more new resort regions. Brazil will follow with its more interesting historic areas, such as Salvadore 300 miles (483 kilometers) north of Rio which has the essential qualifications: excellent climate, historic sites, and a beautiful beachfront ready for resort development adjacent to a new convention center.

Outside the Union of South Africa, large territorial complexes have opened, featuring resorts and casino motels. When supersonic travel eventually arrives, Tasmania, Kilimanjaro, and the Mombassa coast of Kenya will become promising areas for resort complexes. Subject to political changes and stability, other regions with natural advantages are Angola (the up-and-coming "Brazil" of Africa), Lake Victoria in Uganda, and the Turkish Mediterranean coast near the historic sites of Perge and Side.

As this type of resort proves its appeal and efficiency, other nations beside Mexico will find multiresort complexes an irresistible means of stimulating needed development, employment, and international exchange.

ABOVE

Cancun, Mexico. *Cancun, once an uninhabited jungle area on Mexico's northeast Caribbean coast, was selected by the government as the ideal location for a new major resort due to the quality of its sand beaches and surrounding waters, nearby historic sites, and relative closeness to U.S. population centers. Expanding from two hotels in 1974 to 25 a decade later, the large complex now offers a wide variety of recreation, dining, shopping, and nightlife entertainment, as well as centralized convention facilities.*

LEFT

Porto Carras Resort, Sithonia, Greece. *A complete 250-acre (101-hectare) community, Porto Carras Resort in northern Greece accommodates 4500 tourists and many of the resort's 5000 employees. The $75 million complex offers a 19-acre (8-hectare) marina and yacht club, championship golf course, pools, tennis courts, riding stables, a museum, and amphitheatre, as well as a casino, disco, and full complement of restaurants and lounges. Varied in type but unified by a contemporary Mediterranean architectural motif, the hotel structures include two midrise beach units with 1900 beds, a luxury tower for 1000 guests, a 200-unit village inn, and clusters of hillside bungalows accommodating 800.*

5 CONVENTION HOTELS

"Where meetings become working vacations"

points out The Broadmoor in Colorado Springs, Colorado

The French philosopher De Tocqueville, the first to identify America's appetite for group participation, would not be disappointed by the mass meeting activity held in today's convention-oriented hotels and conference centers. Each year, over 100 million guests stay at hotels while attending conferences, and that group keeps increasing at the rate of about 8 percent annually. Specialized forms of hotels catering primarily to meetings now account for over an eighth of total hotel rooms worldwide. As the Sheraton Waikiki in Hawaii advertises: ". . . make it a convention they'll never forget."

The convention hotel features meeting spaces and related facilities specially designed and equipped to serve the large group, including exhibit halls for trade shows, group registration and administrative areas, and, depending on the hotel's overall size and market, banquet rooms seating from 500 to 5000 and guestrooms accommodating from 300 to 3000. The convention hotel's smaller counterpart, the conference center (see Chapter 6), caters to the limited size group whose requirements vary from 30 to 300 guestrooms. While the convention hotel, large conference center, conference center, and mini-conference retreat vary in usage, they are distinguished by the quantity of guestrooms they contain—limited by the maximum group size they can accommodate, as shown in the table on page 88—and are further differentiated by the nature of the meetings and types of groups they serve.

While the convention hotel can accommodate varied meetings of all sizes, it focuses primarily on larger groups, whereas the conference center provides a more intimate atmosphere often preferred by smaller- and medium-size groups. A large convention hotel today requires a minimum of 1000 rooms committed to the convention, without which large groups may not consider a hotel. In planning the facility another 200 to 400 rooms must be added to avoid turning away transient travelers during peak convention periods.

Many older convention hotels, unable to expand, have been outgrown by today's larger conventions. Increasingly higher average attendance at conventions and trade shows often spills over into several hotels centered about a "lead" convention hotel. This has created opportunities for larger-capacity meeting and exhibit halls in such lead hotels, more comparable in scope with civic centers and municipal auditoriums.

Convention hotels and civic centers compliment each other by strengthening a city's ability to attract large-group conventions.

Categories of convention hotels and conference centers

TYPE OF HOTEL	MAXIMUM GROUP SIZE ACCOMMODATED IN HOTEL*	NO. OF GUESTROOMS
Large convention hotel	3000 guests	800 to 2000
Convention hotel	1200 guests	300 to 799
Large conference center	450 guests	150 to 299
Small conference center	255 guests	30 to 149
Mini-conference retreat	45 guests	10 to 29

Assumes full capacity with one-half the rooms at double occupancy.

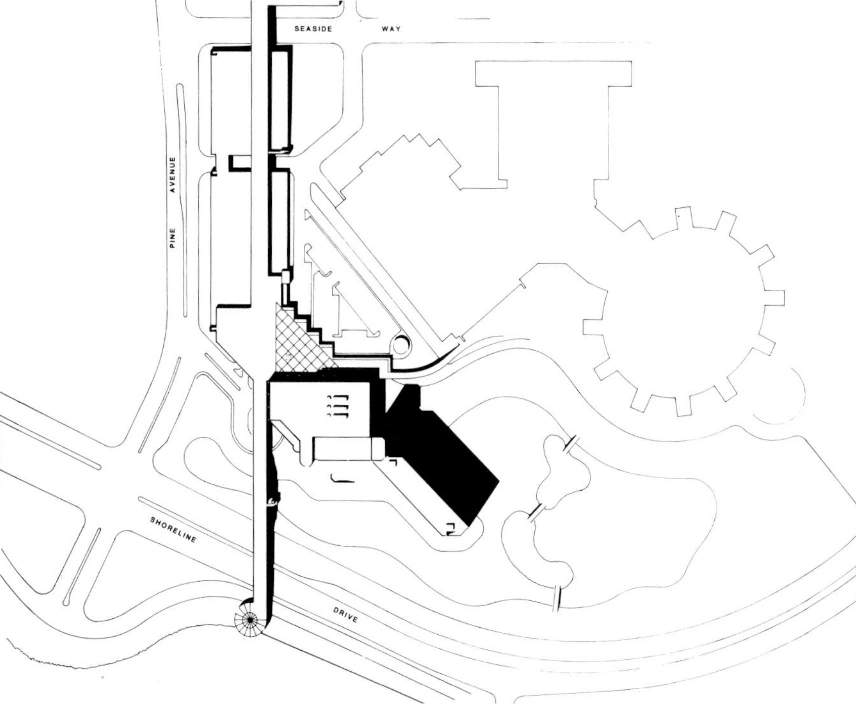

Moreover, without sufficient hotels nearby, civic centers have proven to be financial disappointments. For example, Memphis, Tennessee's extensive Convention Center, built in the 70s with no major adjacent hotels, operated far below its forecasts. To make their center successful in the 80s, the city encouraged private development of a connecting hotel on adjacent city-owned land, using available state aid and Industrial Revenue Bonds. Similar planning and financing techniques for integrating future civic center developments with private hotels have been initiated in cities such as Chattanooga, Tennessee, and St. Petersburg, Florida, to avoid the problems experienced in other localities.

The lack of coordinated planning between government-sponsored convention centers and private hotel developments became apparent during the 70s in cities ranging from Lausanne, Switzerland, to Monrovia, Liberia, where additional adjacent hotels are still needed for these developments to acheive their full potential. Benefiting from such unfortunate examples, the trend in master planning for new civic centers is to provide for surrounding hotels containing facilities complementary to those in the civic center. Long Beach, California's Hyatt Regency is one of several hotels wisely planned by the city immediately adjacent to its convention arena, theater, and exhibit hall. Hotels, such as the Crowne Plaza Holiday Inn adjoining New Orleans's Rivergate Convention Center, provide relatively smaller meeting spaces, with the intention of maintaining a symbiotic relationship with the convention center, to both facilities' profit.

By contrast, today's self-contained convention hotels have added huge new meeting and exhibit facilities, allowing them to compete

PRECEDING PAGE

Atlanta Marriott Marquis, Atlanta, Georgia. *The 1675-room Marriott Marquis (also pictured on the jacket o this book) impressively curves and tapers from its podium to the entertainment facilities on its roof. In addition to 10 food and beverage outlets, the hotel contributes a 3000-person ballroom, 43 meeting rooms, and 40,000 square feet (3,720 square meters) of exhibition space to the 11-building Peachtree Center complex.*

LEFT

Hyatt Regency Hotel, Long Beach, California. *Conveniently adjoining the Long Beach Convention Center, the 542-room Hyatt Regency Hotel provides needed accommodations for conventioneers. Sited on the shoreline, it is also designed to provide waterviews and benefit from the nearby water-related attractions. Linked to downtown by a 1/4-mile long (.4-kilometer) boardwalk, the hotel's surrounding lagoons and recreation decks provide a water/park atmosphere for its restaurants and lounges, including convenient access to the marina and water sports. Supplementing the convention center, 17,200 square feet (1600 square meters) of meeting space, including a ballroom of 10,000 square feet (929 square meters) are provided.*

with civic centers for the expanding convention market. For example, Orlando's well-designed convention center has not generated the activity expected due to the absence of adjacent hotels and the strong competition offered by several large new convention hotels in the area (see Chapter 11, The Mega-Hotel). Given equivalent space, most large groups would prefer to hold their meetings, functions, and exhibits within a single hotel rather than use convention centers because of the added convenience of having all their activities under one roof. (See the List of Hotels in the Appendix for representative convention hotels.)

The Sheraton Premiere Hotel, Universal City, California. *Adjoining the movie studio and entertainment center at Universal City, California, the $74 million, 455-room Sheraton Premiere Hotel provides a 16,000-square-foot (1486-square-meter) ballroom, tiered amphitheatre, luxurious boardroom, press room, and eight meeting rooms to serve conventions and conferences. Three 40-foot-high (12-meter) completely glazed pavilions house the lobby, a 250-seat grand cafe, 120-seat cocktail lounge, and 86-seat gourmet restaurant that change their airy, garden-like atmosphere by day to a glittering, mirrored ambience by night. The pavilions focus on a landscaped court, the hotel's main entrance motif.*

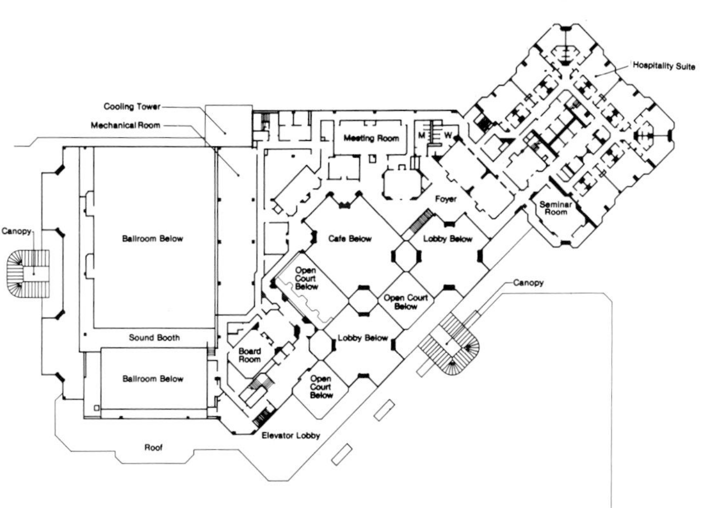

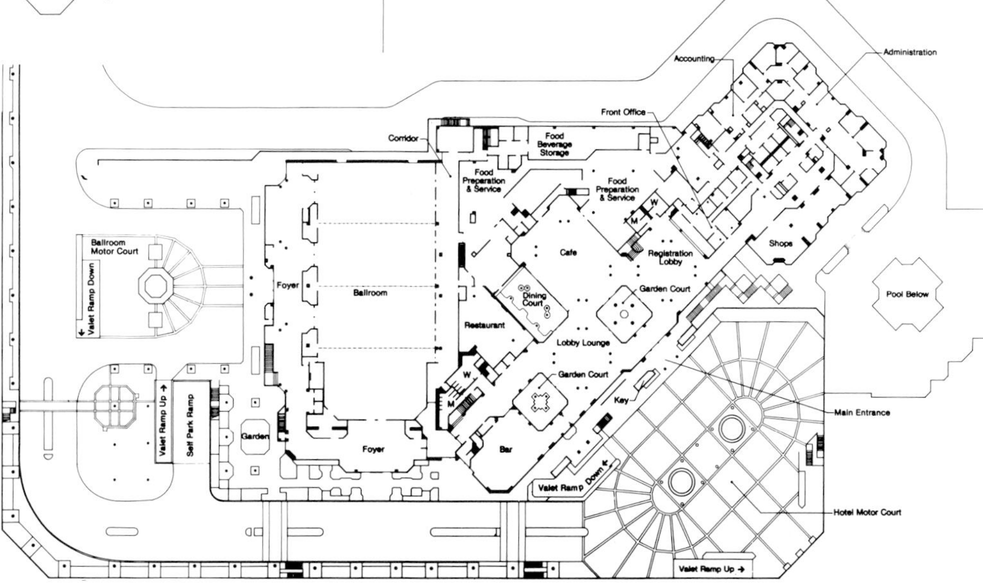

PLANNING CONSIDERATIONS

Since 70 percent of meeting attendees arrive by plane, cities with well-developed air transportation are preferred as major convention sites, emphasizing the importance of convenient air travel in selecting locations for convention hotels. For similar reasons, new suburban sites close to airports, such as the Four Seasons Mandalay near the Dallas/Ft. Worth Airport in Texas, have proven as viable a direction for new growth as continuing the expansion of traditional downtown sites, such as the Marriott Marquis in Atlanta, or established convention resorts, such as the Greenbrier in West Virginia.

Based on the projected growth of the convention market, it would not be inconsistent to include 150,000 square feet (13,900 square meters) of meeting and exhibit space in major downtown convention hotels—divided about 40 percent for exhibit space, 40 percent for main and junior ballrooms, and 20 percent for meeting rooms. Such areas are already provided by the Hilton and Hyatt Regency Chicago and Sheraton Washington. Strategies of each chain are to spread their networks of large convention facilities to every major city. Only in this manner can they hope to establish and hold repeat clients, providing them with the variety of locations they desire years in advance. For instance, the Sheraton-Twin Towers in Orlando, Florida, advertises "75,000 square feet of meeting and exhibit space, one of its strongest features."

Downtown land sites large enough to support these types of hotels are rare. For example, early design studies of a typical 50,000-square-feet (4645-square-meter) block in Chicago indicated that although the zoning permitted a 1200-room hotel tower, there was not sufficient land left over to accommodate the required 35,000-square-feet (3250-square-meter) clearspan ballroom. A larger 100,000-square-feet (9290-square-meter) block proved viable for both a tower and office building, providing the lower three levels were used for shopping. But this would force the ballroom and exhibit hall to an upper level where the problems of servicing large exhibitions would be prohibitive.

In San Francisco, the expansion of an existing convention hotel received zoning approval, but the clearspan banquet rooms needed at the base of the new tower made the project structurally unfeasible. Unlike office or apartment structures, today's convention hotels are increasingly difficult to build on downtown sites. To solve this problem, an innovative structural system was devised for The Carlton, a Westin Hotel in Johannesburg, South Africa. The tower is supported by diagonal structural framing, which is spread over the lower floor meeting and banquet areas.

Even so, to conserve land on downtown sites, function rooms are generally stacked vertically on three or more levels, complicating the design of the public areas and requiring complex food servicing systems as, for example, at the New York Hilton and the Sheraton New Orleans. Some of the original convention hotels, such as the Willard in Washington, D.C., and the St. Regis in New York, were able to provide clearspans for their ballrooms by placing them on the roofs. This approach was structurally efficient, and

The Carlton, Carlton Center, Johannesburg, Union of South Africa. *By transferring the structural loads from its guestroom tower in "spread-eagle" fashion over its lower floors, The Carlton, a Westin Hotel, was able to accommodate large convention and meeting spaces within a limited downtown site.*

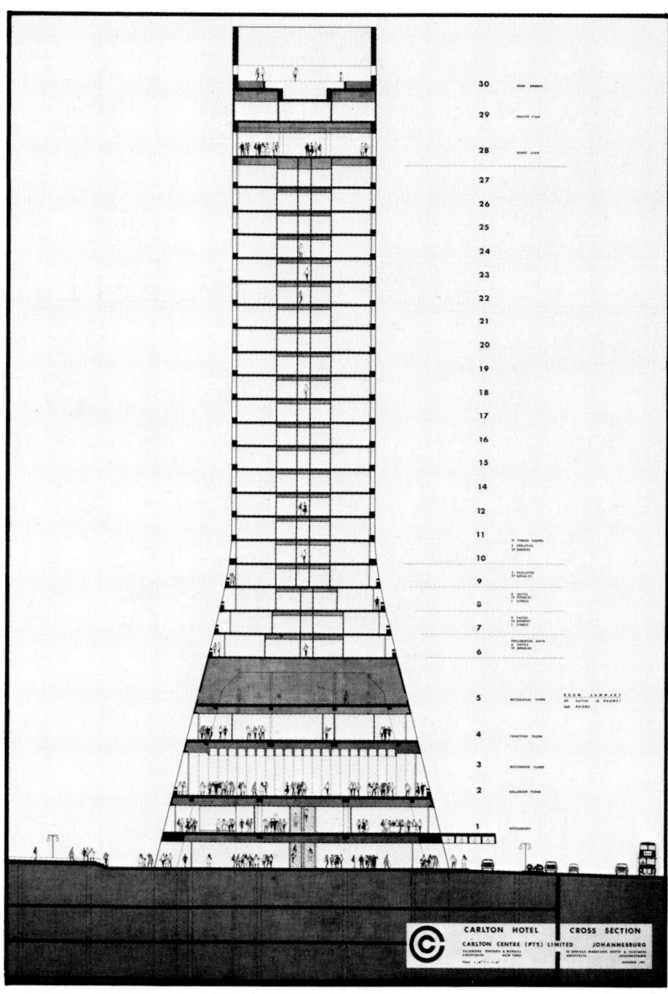

the rooftop ballrooms it produced are still much admired for their dramatic views. But with the increased capacities of today's meeting and banquet facilities and the extensive elevators and fire stairs that are now required, this solution is no longer practical.

Cities are wisely considering special zoning or other means of assembling larger sites needed to satisfy the demand for major new convention-related hotels.

Even in suburban or resort areas (for further discussion of convention resorts, see Chapter 4), the site plan is still primarily influenced by the convention hotel's most significant feature, its huge clearspan ballrooms, banquet halls, and function areas. For an 800-room convention hotel, large land sites, averaging from 3 to 10 acres (1.2 to 4.1 hectares) [depending on whether garage or surface parking is provided] are required to accommodate its massive meeting halls and extensive recreation areas.

A separate entrance drive is required for the meeting area, with curb dropoff space for four buses. Trucks must be able to unload exhibits directly into the ballrooms and exhibit halls as well as at nearby hotel loading docks. Car-size freight elevators are required to service upper- or lower-floor convention spaces. Additional parking must be included for outside visitors attending convention functions (for further discussion of this see the Design Guide). Generous landscaping and water features are essential to soften the appearance of the building complex and parking areas.

DESIGN CONSIDERATIONS

Since convention hotels involve greater mass circulation by guests as well as outside visitors attending meetings, their lobby areas may be as much as double the size of suburban or airport hotels of comparable guestroom capacity and about 30 percent larger than those of downtown hotels or resorts. Because of the greater number of outside visitors they require 10 to 15 percent larger restaurant and bar lounge capacity. Fifty percent more shopping facilities are required than at downtown, suburban, or airport hotels, or about the same amount as at resorts.

Meeting and function facilities must be about double that of airport and suburban hotels and a third more than at downtown or resort hotels. Due to meeting sales and coordination services, 15 percent more administration area is required than at downtown or resort hotels and 25 percent more office space than in suburban or airport hotels.

Back-of-house service areas and employees' facilities need to be about 12.5 percent greater than in downtown or resort hotels of the same number of rooms and 15 percent above that of suburban or airport types. This increase is primarily due to greater servicing requirements for the more extensive banquet and meeting facilities as well as the larger restaurants and lounges. Complete data on required facilities and areas are given in the Design Guide.

The interrelationship of the key convention spaces must encourage the flow of attendees, mainly between the ballroom and the exhibit hall and between the ballroom and the breakout rooms (for smaller meetings). If any of these elements is on a different floor, escalator service and a visual connection between their preassembly areas is required.

Franklin Plaza, Philadelphia. *Designed for conventions, the 800-room Franklin Plaza provides over 50,000 square feet (4645 square meters) of well-planned meeting and exhibition space, its focal point being a 2000-seat ballroom with preassembly areas accommodating 1400 overlooking the atrium lobby.*

The Registry Hotel, North Dallas, Texas. *The 570-room Registry Hotel caters to its corporate and residential community with extensive convention and social facilities normally found in a 1,000-room hotel. It features a 25,400-square-foot (2360-square-meter) main ballroom, 20,000 square feet (1858 square meters) of reception and exhibition space, a junior ballroom, two boardrooms, and 13 additional meeting rooms as well as four lounges, four restaurants, and a 700-seat showroom.*

Convention hotels require the latest in audiovisual technology including teleconferencing facilities, projection booths and equipment, sound systems, provisions for simultaneous translation in international locations, flexible lighting and dimming facilities for different types of function room use, movable stages, daises, dance floors, and sound-proof movable partitions (folding into concealed pockets) to subdivide function rooms into flexible sizes. Sliding chalk boards, continuous map and chart rails, tack and pin-up surfaces, movable podiums and lecterns are required in conference, breakout, and board rooms. (See the conference facilities' audiovisual checklist in Chapter 6). One thousand square feet (93 square meters) is considered the most practical size for a typical meeting room permitting flexibility for large or small breakout sessions with either conference table or theater-style seating.

Ceiling heights in ballrooms and meeting spaces must be designed to accommodate projection sight lines for audiovisual presentations as well as a spacious appearance. The minimum height for a ballroom of 10,000 square feet (929 square meters) is 16 feet (4.9 meters), while 20 feet (6.1 meters) is required in a room over 15,000 square feet (1390 square meters). Audiovisual experts frequently assist in laying out all meeting spaces and provisions for equipment (for further discussion see the section on consultants in Chapter 24).

Lighting is one of the prime factors in providing comfort in meeting rooms. A combination of fluorescent for reading and writing and incandescent for softer ambience, with dimming systems, is required. Often track lighting is added for free-standing presentations or displays along walls.

Due to the growth in the number and size of business associations and trade shows, exhibit halls from 20,000 to 50,000 square feet (1860 to 4650 square meters) are in demand. Clearspans are not essential in exhibit spaces. For economy of structure and site use, clearspan ballrooms are often placed above the exhibit areas, which contain columns approximately 40 feet (12.2 meters) on center, with power outlets for servicing displays. Escalator service must be provided so that the attendees can circulate directly between upper floor banquet and meeting rooms and the exhibits below, a type of design generally referred to as "forced flow" by meeting planners. This arrangement also facilitates direct truck service to the exhibit floor—a critical factor, since the cost and time of unloading and setting up exhibits is a major consideration in selecting the hotel, also affecting the turn-around time for use of the exhibit space by other groups. Storage space must be provided for furniture and equipment equivalent to 10 percent of the meeting and function areas as described in the Design Guide.

TRENDS

Without additional convention hotels containing meeting and exhibit spaces of from 150,000 to 200,000 square feet (13,940 to 18,580 square meters), cities such as New York and Chicago will lose conventions and trade shows to such areas as Atlanta, Boston, Montreal, Nashville, Orlando, Toronto, and Washington, D.C. Government assistance in assembling the required convention hotel sites or creating space for convention districts, using techniques such as landfill and acquisition of air rights over railroad yards, is needed if various cities are to remain competitive. Sites are also required for additional hotels to be connected directly to civic centers.

Downtown entertainment centers, such as the redeveloped seaport areas in Boston and Baltimore, while attracting tourists and hotel business, also help draw conventions. In Atlanta, which has excellent convention hotels but lacks downtown entertainment, the Rouse Company is now considering remedies for the former Atlanta "underground" area.

Teleconferencing capabilities in convention hotels will create opportunities for even larger group attendance, with meetings held simultaneously in different regions, thereby also saving travel costs. Continued growth in the popularity of business and cultural meetings and the demand for their expansion are demonstrated by the priority given over the past decade to construction of highly ambitious convention, trade, and exhibition centers in developing Third World nations from Riyadh, Saudi Arabia, to Nairobi, Kenya, Lagos, Nigeria, to Doha, Qatar, and Belgrade, Yugoslavia, to Salvador, Brazil, as well as the continued promotion of convention centers and hotels by almost every major city throughout the industrialized world.

Dohā Sheraton Hotel, Doha, Qatar. *Sited on 100 acres (41 hectares) of landfill bordering on the Arabian Gulf, the $150 million, 442-room Doha Sheraton Qatar provides convention and conference facilities for international meetings as well as a focus for social activity in the capital city of 200,000. The 16-story, pyramidal-shaped structure, its dramatic tapering atrium illuminated by a skylight at its apex, integrates advanced technology with traditional climatic forms. The atrium provides an effective outdoorlike but fully air-conditioned gathering place with pools and large trees—a true oasis in a torrid climate. It also includes restaurant and lounge areas and views of the Gulf from its interior observation deck. Among the recreation facilities is a six-lane bowling alley, a popular feature in Middle East hotels. Islamic design motifs are incorporated throughout the hotel's decor, maintaining the country's deeply rooted culture in the face of its rapid rise to a major oil producer. Accommodating 700, its ballroom and a triangular 650-seat auditorium provide the latest in audiovisual systems including simultaneous translation into seven languages, closed circuit TV to all guestrooms and satellite transmission capability.*

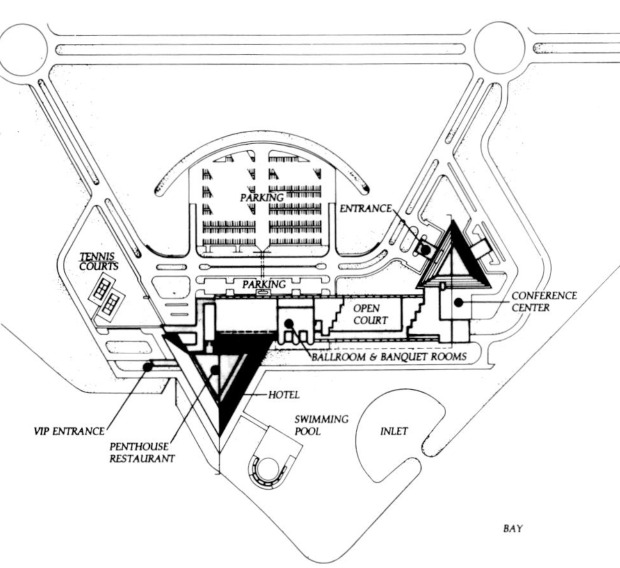
PARKING
ENTRANCE
TENNIS COURTS
PARKING
CONFERENCE CENTER
OPEN COURT
BALLROOM & BANQUET ROOMS
HOTEL
VIP ENTRANCE
PENTHOUSE RESTAURANT
SWIMMING POOL
INLET
BAY

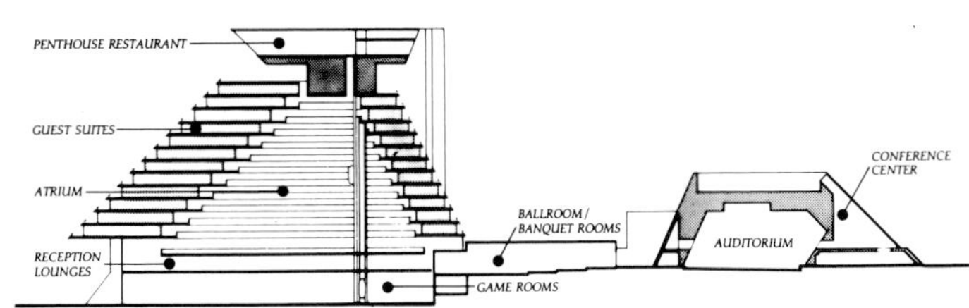
PENTHOUSE RESTAURANT
GUEST SUITES
ATRIUM
RECEPTION LOUNGES
BALLROOM / BANQUET ROOMS
GAME ROOMS
CONFERENCE CENTER
AUDITORIUM

6

The Conference Center

"When your organization requires a meeting of the minds rather than a mass meeting . . . rooms for groups of 10 to 90"

offers the midtown Hotel Inter-Continental in New York City

Beginning in the 60s with educational conference centers such as Columbia University's Arden House and corporate meeting centers such as General Electric's executive conference facility in Crotonville, New York, the conference center emerged as a new business tool for management and development of human resources. It provided a distraction-free atmosphere conducive to learning, training, and problem solving that was better than any ordinary office or hotel setting. Today, corporate, professional, and trade groups actively encourage their personnel to use conference centers to assure more productive meetings.

This also signals a fundamental shift in the continuing education of managers away from business schools that react too slowly to changing market conditions to conference centers where individual company needs can be met more quickly. Advancing from Asilomar, the first experimental center set up on the California coast in 1913 to run meetings for the YMCA, to about fifteen centers all in the Northeast United States a decade ago, there are now several hundred worldwide servicing over a million meetings annually.

The conference center caters to smaller groups seeking quieter, more intimate businesslike surroundings than are generally found at convention hotels. Many conference centers prefer to remain compact for greater privacy, averaging between 75 and 125 guestrooms, with 300 guestrooms considered the limit for large executive conference centers. Groups larger than this are better served by convention hotels (see Chapter 5), while the small mini-conference retreats handle an increasing demand, often by high-level executive groups desiring even greater privacy and confidentiality. Many mini-conference centers were conversions from large residences or country inns. While meeting facilities were added at first primarily to grapple with problems of midweek and wintertime lags in business, owners soon found their inns could thrive by doubling as intimate conference retreats. (See the List of Hotels in the Appendix for a review of typical conference centers.)

Size differences for various types of conference centers, from 10 to 300 guestrooms, and comparisons to convention hotels are indicated in Chapter 5. They are also further subdivided by use, as shown in the table above.

Planning Considerations

Sites providing a sense of privacy and separation from surrounding development are essential, but they must be convenient to

Categories of conference centers

TYPE OF HOTEL	USERS
Executive conference center	Mainly for corporate meetings, but open to all.
Corporate conference center	Owned by a single corporation, but open to others on a limited basis.
Resort conference center	Serves vacationers as well as corporate clientele.
University and other nonprofit facility	Mainly for educational and nonprofit organizations, but open to others on a limited basis.

OPPOSITE PAGE AND BELOW

Arrowwood of Westchester, Rye Brook, New York. *The 276-room Arrowwood of Westchester conference center is sited on 114 rolling wooded acres (46 hectares) outside New York City. Its 5-story cedar-shake building with its modern country-estate look provides 35 audiovisual equipped meeting rooms including a 500-seat auditorium, 120-seat amphitheater, nine large conference rooms, and several variously sized breakout rooms, some conveniently placed in the guestroom wings. A dining room, four banquet rooms, a public restaurant, and lounge/pub cater to attendees and private guests. At the center's hub is the spacious ramped atrium space surrounded by a complete health club.*

airports and preferably within an hour's drive of suburban or downtown business centers. Settings with rolling topography and natural landscaping are preferred to soften the building forms and completely screen parking areas from view. However, parking can in fact be more remote, since conference guests will rarely use their cars during their stay.

Unlike other hotels, conference centers should be concealed from surrounding roads to foster privacy and concentration; and since building signage is unnecessary it should be avoided with only a small directional sign at the entrance drive. The large conference center, with its visible outdoor recreation activities, should project somewhat the ambience of a country club, while the small conference center and mini-retreat need to cultivate a more residential flavor resembling a mansion or parklike estate.

Terraces need to be provided for outdoor meetings, along with paths and jogging trails for exercising and relaxing. Site planning should be informal, creating a feeling of relaxation and privacy, while avoiding distracting features or surroundings and giving sponsoring organizations maximum control over their meeting's attendees. Recreation breaks and a fresh natural environment are important, "freeing the spirit for creative production," according to one psychologist.

DESIGN CONSIDERATIONS

Every element should be directed toward creating a total learning environment for the serious meeting, as at Arrowwood—"where the meeting is the message"—advertised as "a true executive conference center" in Rye, New York. Designed for studying, guestrooms require desks large enough for holding study materials or for small groups to study together, a wall-mounted marker-board that can be concealed during nonstudy periods, closed circuit TV, provisions for computer terminals, and both desk and bedside telephones. Ten percent of the guestrooms should have foldup wall beds so those rooms can be used for study groups.

LEFT

Scanticon-Princeton, Princeton, New Jersey. *The executive conference center is designed to fit its 25-acre (10-hectare) wooded site with the meeting facilities, dining rooms and lounges, and guestrooms in three distinct sections. The 26 state-of-the-art conference rooms are the focus of the center, which features, in addition, audiovisual control booths for each room, a production studio, simultaneous translation, and professional conference planning services.*

BELOW

Minaki Lodge, Minaki, Ontario, Canada. *With indigenous architecture related to its scenic mountain lake setting, the 120-room Minaki Lodge typifies the private secluded atmosphere preferred by conferees. In addition to complete audiovisual facilities, it provides extensive recreation amenities designed to serve executive groups year round as well as tourists drawn to the area during the vacation season. Built in 1914 by the Canadian National Railway and now a national landmark, the lodge was totally renovated in 1982.*

The conference center provides the happy medium between businesslike and luxurious atmospheres. For example, a golf course must be available nearby for relaxation, but it should be only nine holes so it's not too distracting. Since relaxation is conducive to learning and exercise breaks are often provided between sessions, the conference center must include a health club with a fully equipped exercise room, whirlpool, sauna, and steam bath, as well as indoor swimming, racquetball, squash, and tennis in the large conference center. The complete range of amenities is only appropriate for the large conference center since (1) the economics of the small conference center with under 150 guestrooms will not support them and (2) meetings by larger groups are generally longer, necessitating a greater variety of recreation activities. The greatest number of meetings attracted by the small conference center are of 20 to 30 attendees for one or two days, whereas the large conference center often caters to groups of 100 to 300 staying from three to five days. To maximize the use of extensive health club and sports facilities during the summer (generally the low season for business conferences) centers have increasingly become part-time resorts, offering attractively priced weekend packages for vacationers.

Restaurants and lounges in the large conference center usually include a buffet-style dining room, a more formal restaurant for dinner and lunch, a cocktail lounge, and an entertainment facility. In addition to a conventional atrium or lobby, a separate landscaped and skylit space should be provided as a crossroads area at the intersection of the main circulation corridors. An updated professional version of the student commons, it stimulates random contacts between attendees passing among seminars, guestrooms, meals, and recreation breaks.

Meeting rooms include classrooms and conference rooms for 30 to 70, breakout rooms for 10 to 15, boardrooms for 15 to 20, an amphitheater for 100 to 150, and banquet rooms for 60 to 400. Meeting facilities should be specially equipped and detailed to increase concentration levels, ease understanding and remembering information, and reduce fatigue by using the most comfortable seating, lighting, acoustics, and amenities.

A night club should be included for hard-working conferees to "get away from it all without getting too far." Equipped with a sound system and full stage, it is also ideal for presenting business shows. Other special service amenities include attractive coffee-break lounges with island counters blending in with the lobby decor and concealed pantries conveniently dispersed throughout the conference sections. Business services should feature in-house print shops, photo labs, and graphics studios for making name tags, issuing meeting minutes, duplicating slides, or designing company reports, ads, or logos. A complete facilities program is included in the Design Guide with the required study, lecture, learning, and related aids listed in the accompanying checklist.

TRENDS

With continuing education in ever-increasing doses and managers destined to spend half of their time being trained, retrained, or training others in new and better ways to do the job, conference centers will exceed their present 8 percent annual growth rate. As the business community relies on them more, they will become larger and more conveniently located, even in the heart of downtown areas, however, keeping their intimate scale and relaxed, yet serious atmosphere. Former convention hotels, ideally located, but too small to compete for today's larger meetings, will be transformed into such new downtown conference centers.

Conference facilities in corporate offices will increasingly be replaced by outside centers that, due to their specialization, will be better equipped, better run, and more efficiently organized and used than typical office meeting areas; in addition they will more conveniently provide for such amenities as coffeebreaks, lunches, social, and exercise breaks. Conference centers will also be linked by teleconferencing networks, encouraging more frequent use of this medium to reduce excessive business travel at the same time increasing businesses' dependence on them.

Study, lecture, learning, and audiovisual aids checklist

Monitor meeting rooms simultaneously; channel programs to attendees' rooms
- ☐ Closed circuit TV system

Study aids in guestrooms
- ☐ TV monitors
- ☐ Computer terminals
- ☐ Large desks
- ☐ Marker-boards
- ☐ Extra desk phone

Lecture aids in classrooms, conference and breakout rooms
- ☐ Overhead, slide, and movie projectors
- ☐ Projection rooms, screens
- ☐ Podiums, lecterns, portable platforms
- ☐ Controlled projection, controlled audio, dissolve units, automatic programmers
- ☐ Variable lighting

Learning aids in classrooms, conference and breakout rooms
- ☐ Sliding marker-boards
- ☐ Map rails, chart rails
- ☐ Tack and pin-up walls
- ☐ Flip charts, blackboards, easels

Lecture and learning aids in amphitheater
- ☐ Front and rear projection
- ☐ Dual- and multi-image screens
- ☐ Ceiling-mounted TV monitors
- ☐ Program sound
- ☐ Voice amplification
- ☐ Audience participation and audio tape record/playback, video cassette playback
- ☐ Projection TV
- ☐ Multi-lingual translation system and available translators, every other seat with microphone, each seat with headset and control panel
- ☐ Stage, podiums, lecterns

Presentation aids in ballroom, banquet rooms
- ☐ Multimedia front and rear projection
- ☐ Flexible staging, power grids, and audiovisual distribution

General learning, audiovisual, presentation, and business communications facilities and amenities
- ☐ Satellite video teleconferencing system (one-way or open channel for two-way communication)
- ☐ Mobile TV production units
- ☐ Video roleplay systems
- ☐ Remote TV camera pickup and distribution
- ☐ Telephone conferencing
- ☐ Quotron machine (round the clock, worldwide stocks and commodities)
- ☐ In-house print shops, photo labs, and graphics studios
- ☐ In-house technicians to operate equipment and engineers to repair it if back-up is not available
- ☐ Shapes and materials of rooms designed for excellent acoustics
- ☐ Variable lighting designed for reading, writing, and general ambience
- ☐ Comfortable ("18-hour chairs") seating
- ☐ Coffee-break lounge areas provided near conference rooms
- ☐ Exercise breaks provided in health club

RESIDENTIAL AND CONDOMINIUM HOTELS

"A residential dwelling with all the amenities of a luxury hotel"

informs the United Nations Plaza Tower in New York City

While the early transient hotels always attracted some permanent residents, the concept of foresaking house and home for more carefree hotel living reached its peak of fashion during the hotel boom of the roaring 20s. Affluent groups, celebrities, artists, and others who savored hotel services and could afford them on a full-time basis moved in. Hotels welcomed permanent guests ensuring their occupancy. Also, prestigious residents enhanced their image.

Lower rates brought on by the depression of the 1930s made hotel living even more popular. With tourist and business travel at a low, more hotels decided to convert to residential status. The Waldorf-Astoria, completed in the midst of the depression, decided to open one of its two towers as a residential hotel (later converted in the 60s to the first hotel based on the concept of "luxury towers within a hotel"). In New York, other prominent residential hotels of the 20s include Hotel des Artistes, Ansonia, Volney, and Alrae. Chicago boasted the St. Clair, the Croyden, and the Eastgate, while many other major hotels such as Boston's Statler became primarily residential in the depression years.

In the hotel boom of the mid-70s, the major chains vied to acquire such older well-known downtown hotels as New York's Pierre, Sherry Netherland, Barbizon, and Delmonico, attempting to vacate them for renovation. But these hotels contained so many long-term tenants, understandably unwilling to give up their lifestyles or attractive leases that the deals fell through. In the case of the Pierre, the residents actually purchased the building, hiring Trust House Forte to manage the transient hotel portion. Later transformed into a minimum condominium hotel under Four Seasons management, the Pierre adapted its residential lineage to new hotel trends.

Other examples of current hotels still maintaining many long-term residents are New York's Regent Mayfair, home of the famous Le Cirque Restaurant; the Lombardy, also noted for its chic Laurent Restaurant; the Carleton, which houses the elegant La Follie disco-restaurant; the Ritz Towers; and the Chelsea Hotel, legendary as a haven for artists and writers. As noted, the original hotel dining rooms, not needed in residential hotels, have often made their mark as fine independent restaurants.

Emerging primarily in larger U.S. cities, this type of hotel housed mainly affluent residents desiring the luxury of hotel services. The trend was further supported by a depression-driven abundance of available hotel rooms. But as the demand for transient

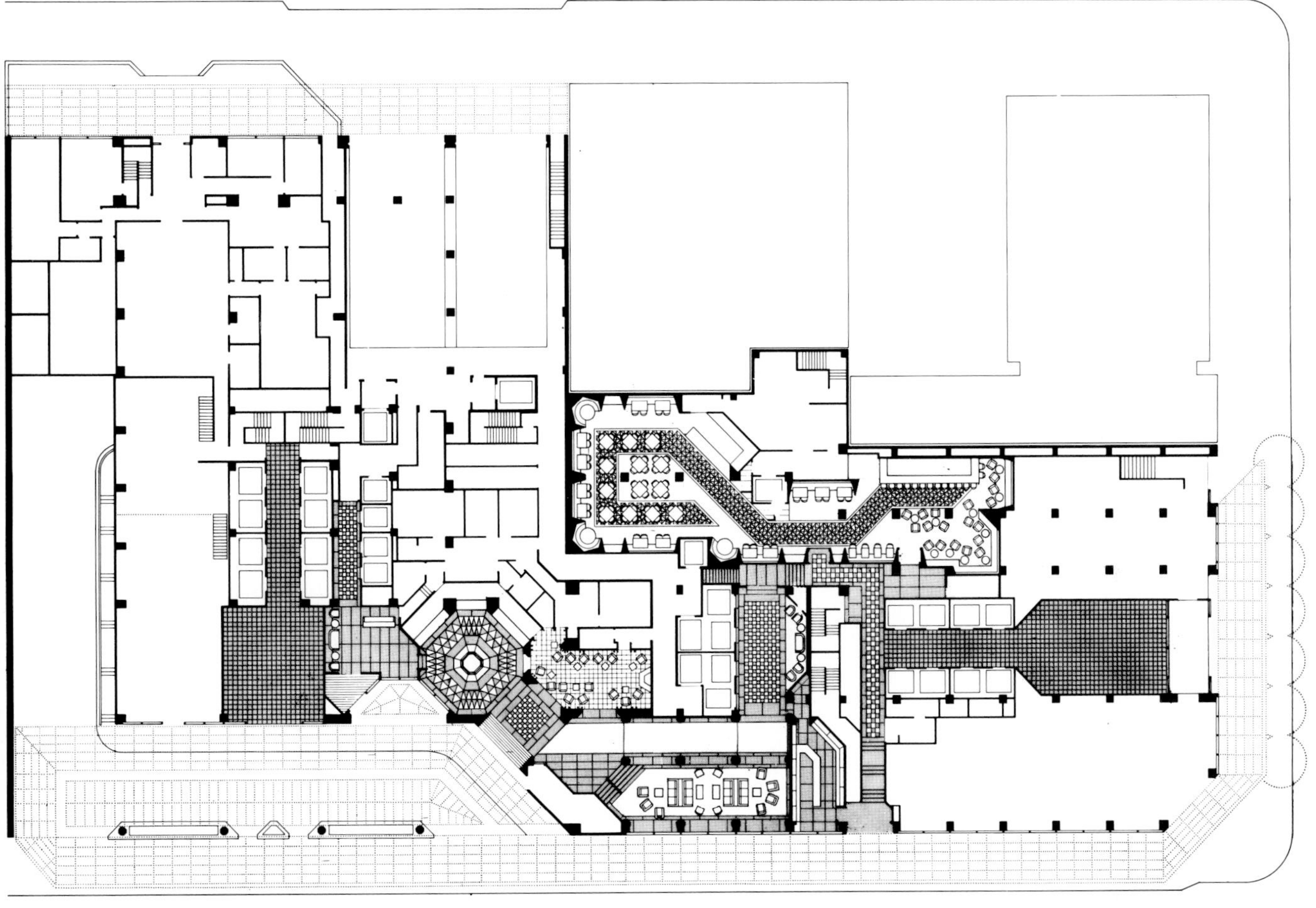

OPPOSITE PAGE AND ABOVE

United Nations Plaza Tower Hotel, New York, New York. *The 290-room United Nations Plaza Hotel, built in 1976, and the new 115-apartment United Nations Plaza Tower completed in 1984 share a central porte cochere, reception lobby, and restaurant and lounge facilities at street level. (See also page 14 in Color Portfolio.)*

hotels returned in the postwar era and luxury condominiums offering hotel-style services appeared, the residential hotel declined, transformed into the condominium hotel and suite hotel of the 80s. It provided an important link in the evolution of transient hotels to today's new condo and "all-suite" concepts (see tree diagram of hotel types in Chapter 1). It also helped maintain the residential flavor in hotel design, contributing to the present revival of the residential style in hotel interiors. (For a selected group of residential and condo hotels, see the list of hotels in the Appendix.)

PLANNING CONSIDERATIONS

Located in highrise residential areas adjacent to central business districts, the original residential hotels differed from their traditional downtown neighbors by their larger suites and limited amenities. Since many of the suites contained kitchenettes, restaurants were not essential for residents. Room service was often provided by privately leased restaurants, catering primarily to an outside clientele rather than hotel guests. Residential hotels provided a small reception desk, 24-hour concierge, and maid service, just as luxury condos do today. Meeting and banquet space was not needed.

New York's zoning ordinance still maintains a separate use category for such hotels, allowed in highrise residential zones, providing that 20 percent of the suites have kitchenettes and any restaurants or lounges are entered only through the hotel lobby. By meeting these requirements, one of the city's most luxurious hotels, the Regency, could be developed on an upper Park Avenue residential site.

With the sharp rise in hotel rates and continuing tax shelters and financing advantages of condominium ownership, the need for residential hotels is being more economically served by full-service condos and condo hotels. A growing number of luxury condos such as New York's Trump Tower, Olympic Tower, and the Atrium, offer more elaborate services than many downtown hotels including reception desks, concierge and message service, bellmen, valet parking, maids, porters, health clubs, restaurant clubs, lounges, and boutiques, as well as convenient downtown locations. Based on similar financial advantages, the downtown condo hotel has begun to parallel the development of the condo resort in vacation areas.

DESIGN CONSIDERATIONS

The current form of condominium hotel, pioneered in 1982 by Boston's Ritz-Carlton and later followed by New York's United Nations Plaza and Boston's Four Seasons, consists of approximately 100 residential units attached to a luxury hotel. Starting tenuously at the Ritz, where the connection between the hotel and condo tower is limited to room service and maid service, the concept is becoming bolder and more unified as it matures. For example, the condo and hotel towers have been closely linked by a central lobby and porte cochere at the United Nations Plaza, while at the Four Seasons the condo hotel has been fully integrated into a single structure. This configuration favors the condo units with upper-floor views of the Boston Public Gardens, while the health club and pool are located at a middle floor accessible to both hotel guests and condo residents.

Four Seasons Place and Four Seasons Hotel, Boston, Massachusetts. *Facing Boston's Public Garden, the Four Seasons Place condominium offers 100 residences atop the luxurious, 290-room Four Seasons Hotel. With its upper eight floors serviced by a private elevator bank rising from a special entrance lobby, the condominium joins the hotel at the eighth floor swimming pool/spa, with room service, maid service, laundry, valet, concierge and other hotel amenities available around the clock to its residents.*

TRENDS

Rather than fading away, the residential hotel of the 20s and 30s has changed its ownership and image to the condo hotel and other more profitable residential variations. Where residential demand is strong, hotels will continue to devote some of their floors to condo units. For example, New York's Marriott Essex House has converted 150 of its upper-level suites to condominiums with views of Central Park at prices ranging from $200,000 to $1,000,000. Originally apartments, then converted to a hotel, and reconverted to condominium units, the structure demonstrates the growing interchangeability between residential and hotel use.

New hotels have continued to promote a residential atmosphere, such as Brock Residence Inn, a suite hotel discussed in Chapter 8, while condo apartments have increasingly adopted hotel amenities, such as the Atrium in New York City. With hotel rooms becoming more like apartments, considering the trend toward suite hotels and timesharing units, and condos offering more hotel services and amenities, residential and hotel criteria are continuing to merge. Also, hotel management has become increasingly involved in the condo field. Symbolizing this trend, the concierge, originally the manager of an apartment house, has become an indispensable fixture of the modern hotel.

Like the residential hotel, this new hotel type offers many options to its residents from luxurious hotel services and amenities to convenient guestrooms for their visitors. But most importantly, its financial structure will prove attractive to both residents and hotel owners for the following reasons: (1) the developers can help finance the hotel from the sale of the condos avoiding direct interest charges, including that during construction if the units are presold; (2) condo owners can take advantage of normal personal tax write-offs for interest and real estate taxes or depreciation of rental property; and (3) the hotel can manage the condo portion more efficiently for the owners while gaining additional revenue for the hotel company.

Condo buyers will be allowed to custom design their units—for example, converting units on two floors into duplexes during the design phase. They will find the combination of direct access to the hotel and its amenities, yet with private entrance lobby and elevators serving their condo units, irresistible. The hotel will also have the flexibility to change its mix between hotel rooms and condos as future economic conditions dictate.

8

THE SUITE HOTEL

"Luxurious suites with your own kitchen for the price of a hotel room"

advertises Seacoast Towers Apartment Hotel in Miami

Not every innovation comes out of rational market research. Some fine ideas are stumbled on by accident. The suite hotel concept was discovered during the recession of the 70s when unsold condominiums were rented in desperation as suites. They were expected to appeal mainly to long-term guests such as relocated families seeking more spacious accommodations than those offered by ordinary hotels. But with a living/dining/kitchenette area plus a private bedroom, not surprisingly these economically priced suites attracted all types of travelers, even overnight walkins knowing a good buy when they saw one.

Some of the original condo developers motivated by their "suite success" launched major chains such as Guest Quarters, featuring highrise, conventional double-loaded "side-to-side" suites, an arrangement generally more adaptable to tight urban sites, and Granada Royale, offering midrise hotels with "back-to-back" suites, their suite living rooms facing balcony corridors surrounding a large skylit, landscaped atrium and only their bedrooms having exterior windows. The midrise atrium concept also made the best use of spreadout suburban sites. Based on a plan conceptually designed by Walter Rutes, Holiday Inns developed a more daring triangular-shaped atrium concept and created a subsidiary chain, Embassy Suites, before acquiring the Granada Royale chain.

In addition, the advent of the all-suite hotel has allowed new developers to enter the luxury market for which suite hotels, with their larger room units, are ideal. Examples include the Windsor Court in New Orleans, Louisiana, and La Reserve in White Plains, New York, featuring only large, lavishly appointed suites. Restored hotels such as The Hermitage in Nashville, Tennessee, and the Croydon in Chicago have also adopted the all-suite concept, turning adversity to advantage by combining smaller rooms into luxurious suites more compatible with their original construction. Suite hotels have also proven successful at airports, demonstrated by the Royce Hotel at West Palm Beach Airport (which claims to be "the newest in suite hotels") and the Marina City Club Resort Hotel near Los Angeles Airport (which advertises "enormous suites . . . just 7 minutes from LAX").

The Regent on Williams Island, Florida, also illustrates the dovetailing of the suite concept with resorts, since both cater to longer-staying guests and family groups typically seeking larger, more residential accommodations. Brock Residence Inn ("more than a room . . . a residence") offers duplex suites with fireplaces. Days Lodge, a division of

Days Inn, and other budget chains have also launched suite roadside motels.

Thus, in less than a decade, the suite hotel has tested most major markets and rate classes including downtown, suburban, airport, resort, restoration, luxury, medium-price, and budget categories. Since most suite hotels are thriving, *the single guestroom may go down as the most unimaginative concept in hotel history*. For years, many sophisticated travelers have preferred small inexpensive suites to larger single rooms. But until the 80s, there was no economical method of satisfying this demand.

Now, given the proven efficiencies and practical advantages of suites, the single room seems a relatively primitive concept by comparison. For virtually the same price, suites provide sufficient space for receiving guests, holding business meetings, entertaining, dining, watching TV, phoning, or working in the living room while maintaining privacy for those sleeping or relaxing in the bedroom. With relatively minor cost tradeoffs made possible by the economically designed all-suite hotel, the question has become not *whether* to build them, but what *kind* of suite layouts will become the most popular for various types of guests. (For a sampling of hotels in this category, see the List of Hotels in the Appendix.)

PLANNING AND DESIGN CONSIDERATIONS

The most effective type of suite layout must be integrated with the most efficient building plan, often influenced by the planning constraints of the site. Since the suite unit is larger and more complex than the single room, its layout has a much greater impact on the ultimate building form. For example, while a back-to-back, single-loaded suite facing an atrium may provide the most desired unit, the overall building may not fit economically on a downtown site zoned and priced for high rise towers. Conversely, the requirements of a highrise site may influence the design of the typical suite, for example, requiring double-loaded corridors with side-to-side suite units. The suite hotel, therefore, requires more detailed site evaluation to ensure accommodation of the suite unit layouts.

Facilities and area programs for suite hotels are included in Part 2, Design Guide, while their unique aspects are discussed below and their general requirements included in related chapters on downtown, suburban, and resort hotels, in Part 1.

Suite units

Being able to offer the many advantages of two rooms for virtually the same rate as one has been achieved in the all-suite hotel through optimization of building area and economy of mechanical equipment. Since the two-room suite still has a single bathroom and, with the back-to-back layout, only one air conditioning unit with a single control, its mechanical costs are comparable with those of standard hotels. Also, since bathrooms and wet bars are located back-to-back, each mechanical shaft serves four rooms, or two suites, with little increase in exterior wall for the additional rooms. Therefore, while the typical suite is only 40 percent greater in area than the single room [475 square feet (44 square meters) versus 340 square feet (31.6 square meters)], the square foot cost of such area is only 25 percent more. The most expensive elements, such as the mechanical equipment and perimeter walls, are almost unchanged.

Compared with a standard king-size room with a hideabed sofa, the two-room suite requires only a few additions, the most expensive being an extra TV. Other compensating savings are in the reduced public and service areas discussed below.

The typical suite unit consists of a separate bedroom, bathroom, living/dining room with a wet bar, and occasionally kitchenette. But few guests use the kitchenette, which requires extra space, expensive equipment, and related mechanical costs. Therefore, except for larger two- and three-bedroom units, which are designed for longer-term relocated families, such as those featured by Brock Residence Inn in a number of areas, the kitchenette has not proved cost effective. It has generally been replaced by a wet bar, with a counter sink, glass cabinet, mini-refrigerator, and coffee maker, normally built into a wall unit or credenza in the dining area close to the plumbing riser for economy. Other than for relocation units or resort condos, kitchenettes have often displeased guests because they make the living room appear smaller and

TOP

Typical Back-to-Back Suite Plan. *The cost economy of this back-to-back suite lies in the fact that it requires only 13 feet (4 meters) of exterior wall and corridor and one air-conditioning unit. Other savings are due to the following factors: (1) one plumbing stack serves two suites; (2) the increase in floor area over a single room is inexpensive to build; and (3) a relatively minor amount of additional furniture is required.*

ABOVE

La Reserve Hotel, White Plains, New York. *A hotel of luxurious suites in White Plains, New York, La Reserve illustrates the high caliber of the new suite hotels.*

PRECEDING PAGE

Brock Residence Inn, Oklahoma City, Oklahoma. *Exemplifying the prototype suite hotels specially catering to longer-staying business guests and relocated families, the Brock Residence Inn features 2-story, gabled-roofed residential units, some bilevel, with fireplaces, private entrances, and balconies overlooking landscaped courtyards. The accent is on the amenities within the suite itself rather than on elaborate lobbies, lounges, restaurants, or room service. Registration is taken care of at an entry gatehouse.*

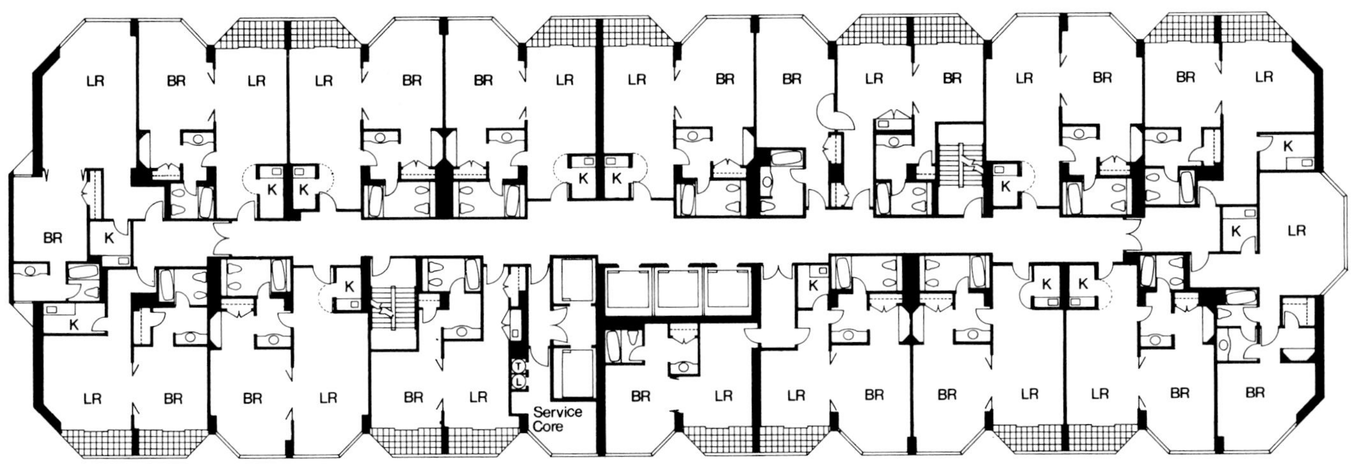

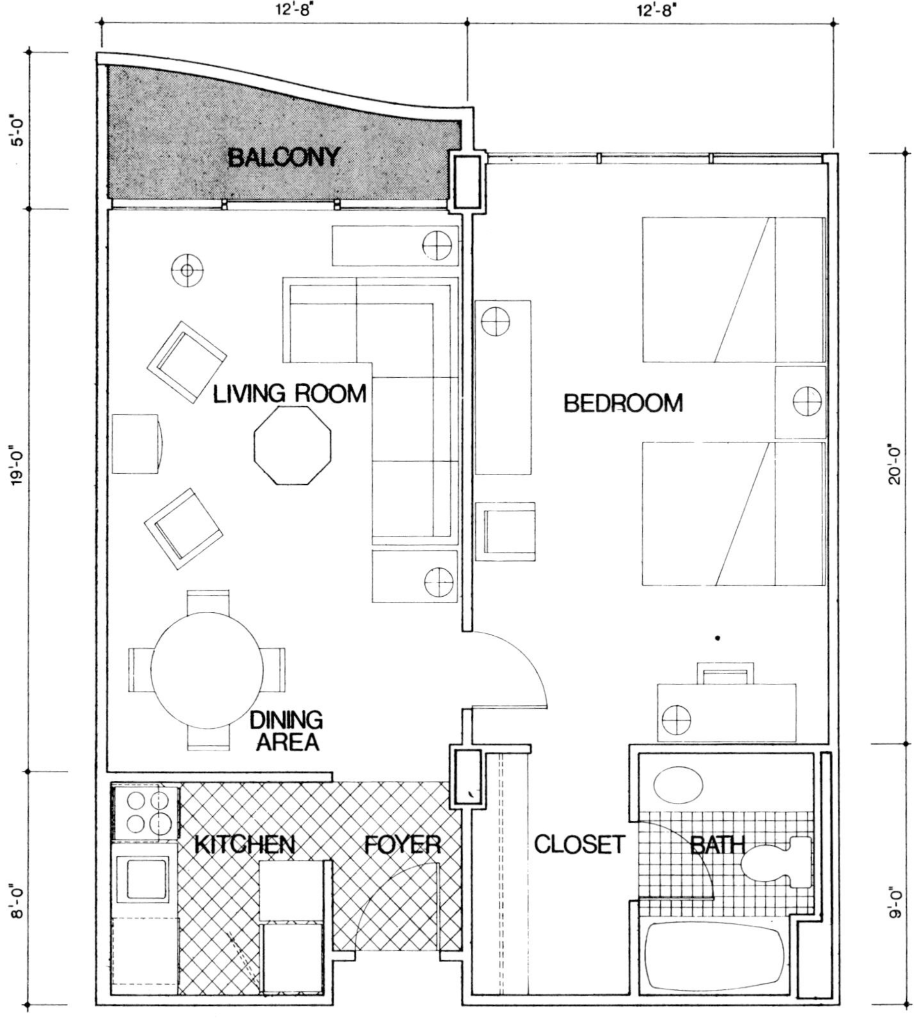

less luxurious and they remind guests of housework. A hideabed sofa and 4-foot (1.2-meter) round table seating four are essential in the living/dining room to accommodate families.

Suites facing an atrium should provide a large window, appropriately draped for privacy and double glazed for soundproofing. Although some codes allow interior living rooms not used for sleeping to be built without such windows, this approach does not satisfy guests. Rooms with atrium views have proven popular and are considered safe in emergencies, with fire walls along the atrium and exterior windows in the bedrooms. Sprinklers are required on each side of the atrium wall or one-hour fire-rated glass. Living room windows have often been subdivided for a more residential look, with the mullions enclosed between the double glass for easy cleaning.

Suite bedrooms can be smaller than single guestrooms since, with their adjacent living/dining rooms, they do not require a desk or second chair, and with a hideabed sofa in the living room, they generally do not require more than one bed. But bathrooms, closets, and drawer space should be 20 percent larger for suites than for single rooms. In minimum-size suites, bedrooms are 12.5′ × 13.5′ (3.8 × 4.1 m) and living/dining rooms

TOP

Windsor Court Hotel, New Orleans, Louisiana. *On a 1-acre (.4-hectare) downtown site, the $28 million, 23-story Windsor Court Hotel provides 332 luxurious suites with bay windows and balconies. The deluxe all-suite hotel is entered through a landscaped drive-in courtyard. A mezzanine overlooking the lobby includes a gourmet restaurant, lounge, ballroom, and meeting rooms with a function terrace, a rooftop pool above the hotel's 4-story garage.*

LEFT

Guest Quarters, Tampa, Florida. *A new prototype of one of the earliest all-suite chains, the upscale, 15-story Guest Quarters hotel includes 225 suites with kitchens and dressing rooms as well as a full range of public amenities.*

12.5′ × 16′ (3.8 × 4.9 m), while in luxury suites, bedrooms are a minimum of 12.5′ × 18′ (3.8 × 5.5 m) and living/dining rooms 14′ × 18′ (4.3 × 5.5 m). Balconies are required in resorts and luxury suites. Area standards for different types of suite units are summarized as in the accompanying table.

Typical suite floors

In suite floor plans, the single-loaded back-to-back plans and the double-loaded side-to-side plans occupy virtually the same area since in both cases each *bay* of corridor serves two *rooms*. The atrium plan applied to a suite hotel therefore becomes twice as efficient as when used in a standard hotel since its balcony corridors serve twice as many rooms.

The triangular plan has proven more efficient in area compared with other building shapes, with a greater proportion of perimeter space devoted to suites and the central atrium reduced to minimal size required for natural lighting and windows in suite living rooms. The triangular atrium is interesting in form and more intimately scaled, while providing ample lounge seating at the ground level and creating a festive indoor/outdoor ambience.

Since 200 feet (61 meters) is the maximum allowable distance between stairs in any atrium hotel, the optimum traingular plan can be extended to 400 feet (122 meters) of corridor serving a maximum of 40 suites per floor. This floor plan can be served by two stairs located at each of the base corners, with the elevator bank at the triangle's apex conveniently near the lobby. While in some atrium hotels the elevators have been split into two banks on either side of the atrium, this reduces their efficiency by 30 percent, causing extra waiting time.

Several optional program variations are available in the above plan such that (1) single rooms can be added at the corners and connected to typical suites to form three-room suites; (2) larger luxury suites can also be formed; (3) the atrium can be enlarged to increase the number of suites per floor; and (4) additional restaurant or meeting spaces can be provided by expanding the ground floor beyond the guestroom tower. While seven stories and approximately 200 units has proven to be an optimum size for structural systems and elevators as well as for management efficiency and marketing of the property, additional floors can be added, as required to accommodate high demand factors or to dilute premium last costs with the number of atrium elevators increased accordingly.

Public areas

The atrium acquaints guests with the hotel's amenities, all clearly visible from the lobby and the glass elevators. Much like a well-planned shopping mall, the basic design shape helps merchandize the amenities. Any promotional signs in the elevator cabs would be redundant in such a hotel, and other in-hotel advertising is almost unnecessary. Guests are invited by their living room views to enjoy the amenities in and around the atrium.

While the naturally landscaped atrium is ideal for a lobby bar, lounging, and breakfast dining, more privacy is required for the restaurant and bar alongside but not directly under the high-ceilinged area. Several well-equipped meeting and board rooms are also required; these should be located on the ground floor with direct service from the kitchen and using of a portion of the atrium as a prefunction area.

While access to the indoor pool should be close to the atrium, the pool itself as well as other sports activities should not be located in the atrium, where they would change the hotel's tone.

Service areas

The emergence of the all-suite concept has permitted a fresh look at the effectiveness of a hotel's operating areas and staffing. Although twice the number of rooms, the number of *units* remains approximately 200, still an efficient size for close personnel management. When layouts and service circulation are simplified and condensed, they improve employee morale and productivity and reduce total building area as they have in the new suite hotels.

Suite unit area standards (in square feet and square meters)*

AREA	MODERATE	UPSCALE	DELUXE
Living/dining room	200 (18.6)	220 (20.4)	260 (24.1)
Wet bar/Kitchenette	20 (1.9)	55 (5.1)	90 (8.4)
Bathroom	45 (4.2)	60 (5.6)	70 (6.5)
Foyer/dressing area	25 (2.3)	30 (2.8)	35 (3.2)
Closet	10 (.9)	15 (1.4)	20 (1.9)
Bedroom	175 (16.2)	210 (19.5)	225 (20.9)
TOTAL	475 (44.1)	590 (54.8)	700 (65.0)
Balcony	—	20 (1.8)	50 (4.6)

*Gross areas include partitions and chases.

Embassy Suites, Overland Park, Kansas. *Embassy Suites in Overland Park, Kansas, is the initial prototype of an all-suite chain owned by Holiday Inns, with several more properties under construction. The concept was based on the cost efficiency of back-to-back suites combined in a triangular atrium configuration that optimizes circulation space, elevators, mechanical and electrical systems, and the relation of back-of-house services to the public areas, while maximizing the visual impact of the public facilities. This permits the suites to be priced at rates similar to those of single-room hotels. The 200-suite or larger prototype includes a restaurant and lounge in the atrium, and five boardrooms nearby. To preserve the quiet, upscale ambience of the atrium, the pool and health club are located in a separate area.*

TRENDS

The public has been impressed with the freshness of the all-suite concept and the distinctive prototypes that have appeared. Improvements will continue in this relatively new and maturing hotel type. The living/dining room will be further developed to accommodate a flexible variety of features such as computers, business equipment, exercising machines, folding wall beds, and housekeeping facilities for the convenience of business groups, families, and other guests.

Suites will continue to gain popularity among business women, who prefer to have their beds out of sight during in-room meetings. The elderly will also respond to the advantages of suites since they generally spend more time in their hotel rooms.

By the end of the century, it is estimated that a considerable proportion of single rooms will be converted to suites. Furthermore, a tremendous spurt in new hotel construction can be forecast in order to replenish the reduced room supply caused by conversion to suites.

Just as Club Med is identified with vacation villages and Harrah's with casino hotels the tendency to establish separate chains of suite hotels will continue. Out-competing single-room hotels, suite hotel facilities and space requirements will vary according to subtypes such as downtown, suburban, airport, luxury, resort, residential, and, in seeming contradiction, a suite *motel*. Designed for price/value-conscious guests mainly interested in good basic room units but without many other amenities, this could become the most innovative suite type of all.

9

The Super-Luxury Hotel

"It stands there like a dream"

reads an advertisement for the Hotel Danieli in Venice

There is a level of luxury and class to which only a handful of uniquely styled, impeccably managed, small hotels can aspire. The most prestigious major chains such as Four Seasons, Regent, Mandarin, and Inter-Continental may come tantalizingly close, but even they can rarely match the ultra-charm and poshness of the world's most exclusive closely managed hotels. Noted for their pampering service and unstinting privacy, these hotels are often sought out by the super-rich and famous, from royalty to movie stars.

As the royal court once indicated the wealth and culture of a nation, super-luxury hotels often symbolize the highest aspirations of a society. Both the best hotels of the world's capitals and the luxurious guest houses maintained for foreign dignitaries by governments such as the People's Republic of China are designed to put a nation's best foot forward to visiting diplomats, business executives, and cultural leaders.

Located in some of the major cosmopolitan cities and a few of the most chic resort areas, truly super-luxury hotels are more rare than five-star restaurants. Their room rates average over $200 a night, with suites ranging from $350 to $700. But the valet will return a pressed suit in less than 30 minutes and the concierge will shop for a guest who has forgotten to pack the essential black tie or provide a stenographer for dictation at midnight.

Often identified with a personality who is its owner, well known by the affluent, the titled, and celebrities, a personal style is also cultivated by the managers and staff. For example, the maid at L'Hotel in Paris is usually invited for breakfast by one of the world's leading matinee idols whom she mothers while he stays at the hotel. But the leading force on which the virtues of the hotel depend is its concierge. Ever-resourceful as well as multilingual, the concierge can get anything from a gift-wrapped breakfast in bed to an elaborate stereo system for a famous conductor, and he or she must keep a detailed dossier on the peculiarities and tastes of all repeat guests.

Besides its location, price, small size, personal management, luxurious facilities, highest standards of service and individual personality, the super-luxury hotel uniquely indulges the guest's fantasy of living in his or her own private palace. (For a representative list of such hotels, see the Appendix.)

Planning Considerations

Often deriving their character from historic restoration, urban super-luxury hotels such as Campton Place in San Francisco are usually located near luxury shopping, theater, and entertainment centers. However, the Mansion on Turtle Creek in Dallas and the Remington in Houston, among the newly constructed super-luxury structures, selected suburban locations close to luxury stores on the edge of an exclusive residential area.

Since most guests prefer privacy, porte cocheres should be relatively inconspicuous, with valet parking. Some hotels such as L'Ermitage in Los Angeles furnish complimentary chauffeur service. In suburban areas, where entrance drives are provided, they should be enclosed courts or thoroughly screened with landscaping to assure as much privacy as possible. Exterior signage should be kept small and subdued.

DESIGN CONSIDERATIONS

Entrance lobbies should be elegantly small and fully residential in character, with registration generally held at private desks. Traffic in the lobby will be minimal due to the rapid service and familiar clientele. The Remington also has provided a living room and private outdoor terrace off the lobby for quiet lounging. Quality artwork is expected throughout the public areas, best exemplified by the Diego Velázquez in the lobby of the Westgate in San Diego, California.

The gourmet restaurant is an essential ingredient of the super-luxury hotel often, as at Campton Place, boasting an internationally renowned chef. The restaurant should seat no more than 80, with an adjoining cozy bar for about 30. If the hotel exceeds 150 rooms, a brasserie is also required. Decor must be exquisite, including such treatment as coffered ceilings, wood and beveled mirror paneling, floral displays, and extensive landscaping. The most elegant china, silver, and crystal are expected; for example, Wedgwood china service is used at Campton Place. A vintage wine cellar is a must.

Other than a distinguished board room and a few well-appointed private meeting rooms seating about 75, super-luxury hotels vary in additional facilities. In the Remington, a ballroom/banquet room seating 500 is also provided, as well as a business center offering secretarial, translation, and communications facilities. While indoor pools are required in resorts and in new super-luxury construction, they have been omitted in downtown restorations. But an outdoor roof garden, sun deck, and sauna must be provided as a minimum.

To project a luxury image, exteriors should be marble or granite, with full balconies for all rooms and lavishly landscaped terraces and courtyards at the public levels.

Guestrooms

While room sizes are generally large—14.5′ × 22′ (4.4 × 6.7 m) at new hotels, such as the Remington—room sizes are often average at restorations due to existing conditions. But the rooms must be richly and elegantly appointed, with fine mouldings, decorative doors, and detailing throughout. Campton Place furnishes a Louis XVI writing desk and a Henredon armoire in all guestrooms; the Remington features canopied beds in its suites; and L'Hotel provides valuable antiques handed down from famous personalities such as Mistinguette's bed in one room and Oscar Wilde memorabilia in another.

OPPOSITE PAGE, ABOVE, AND PAGE 108

The Remington on Post Oak Park, Houston, Texas. *Integrating grandeur and intimacy, the spaces of the 248-room Remington are replete with paintings and artifacts inviting individual discovery, furniture groupings arranged for private conversation, and backgrounds of discretely dark oak paneling. Signaling the renaissance of super-luxury hotels, the understated contemporary architecture recalls the proportions of 19th-century English manor houses.*

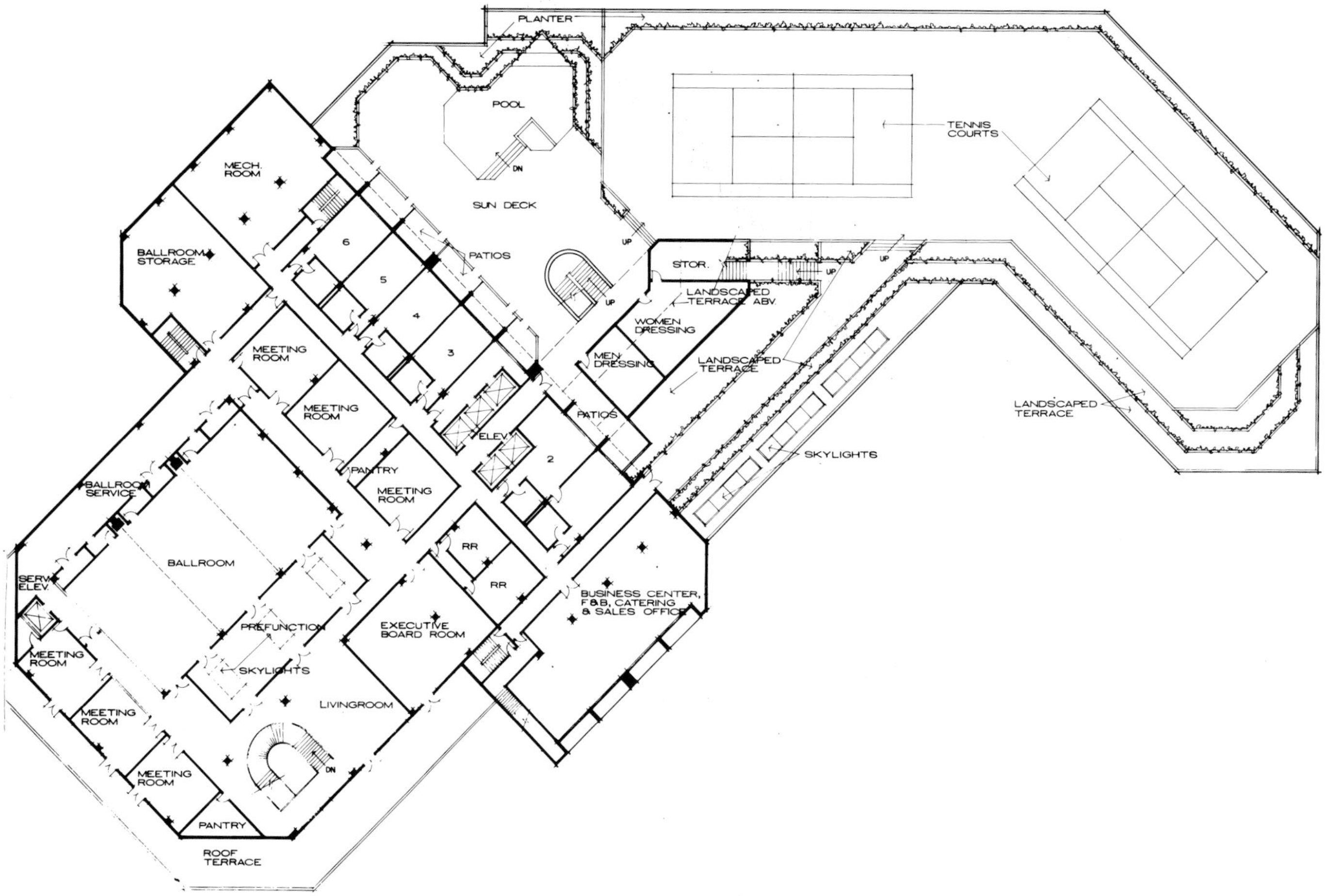

Bathrooms should have marble floors, walls, and vanities, double lavatories, decorative fittings, whirlpool tubs, and bidets. Accessories should include lighted shaving mirrors and towel warmers.

TRENDS

One would hope that this type of hotel proliferates as a sign of a more prosperous economy. Having proved helpful in creating the super-luxury atmosphere, further restorations will be developed in several cities where high-luxury demand exists but the supply is

OPPOSITE PAGE

Campton Place, San Francisco, California. *Restored from two older downtown San Francisco structures, the Campton Place features a renowned gourmet restaurant, French period furniture in its guestrooms and public areas, a residentially scaled lobby. (See also pages 10 and 11 in Color Portfolio.)*

Key: ***(1)*** *lobby,* ***(2)*** *registration,* ***(3)*** *administration,* ***(4)*** *cocktail lounge,* ***(5)*** *restaurant,* ***(6)*** *kitchen,* ***(7)*** *storage,* ***(8)*** *toilets,* ***(9)*** *guestrooms,* ***(10)*** *open.*

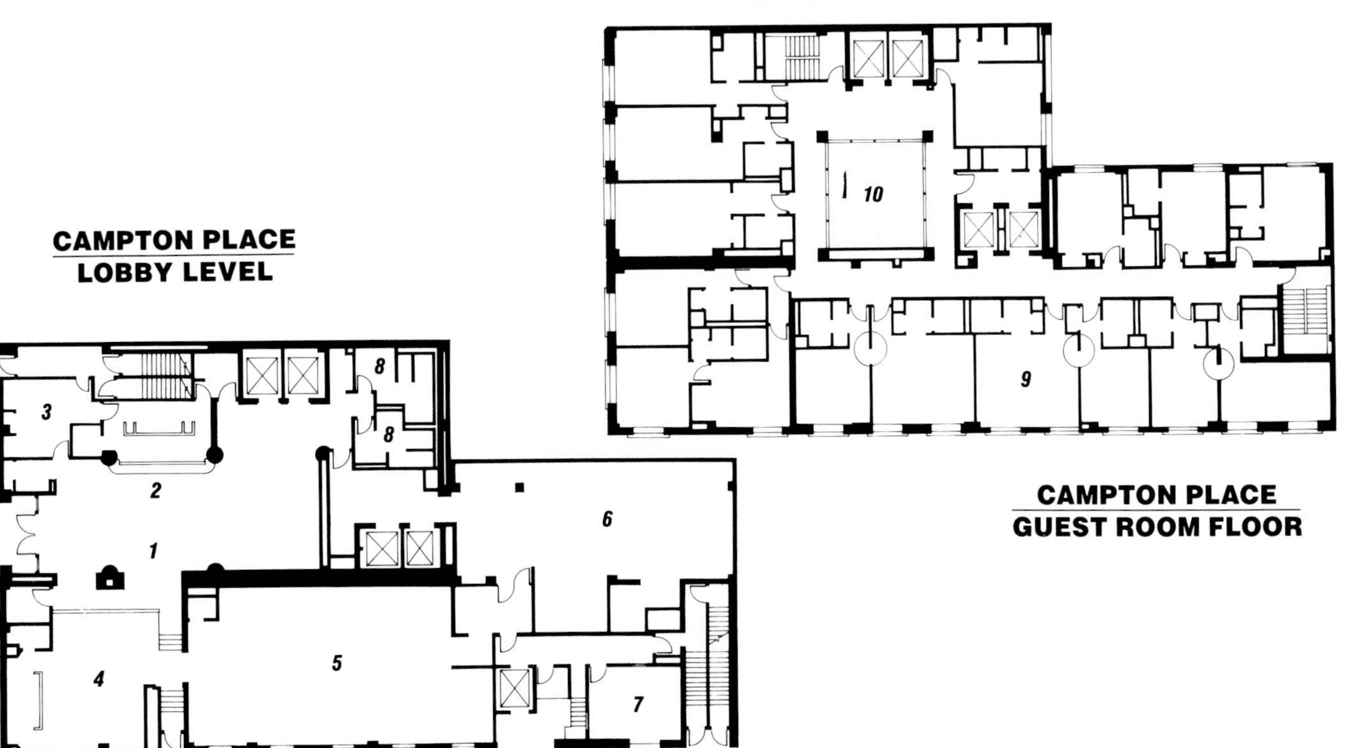

CAMPTON PLACE
LOBBY LEVEL

CAMPTON PLACE
GUEST ROOM FLOOR

near nil. They will continue to be spearheaded by devoted hoteliers such as Campton Place President William F. Wilkinson since this area of individual entrepreneurship has not yet proven profitable for the large chains.

Hoteliers from the legendary Cesar Ritz, founder of the exclusive chain, to the innovative Rene Hatt, developer of the Nova Park Élysée in Paris, have dreamed of creating a major chain to attract the super-luxury guest. But capturing the oldest unbranded sector of the market has proven elusive for a large hotel chain. A theoretical blueprint for a widely publicized 50-hotel, $2 billion joint venture, including a prototype design and construction cost forecast, was proposed in 1982 to the W. B. Johnson Co. Holiday Inns suggested a concept of super-luxury service that had to be shelved due to a major obstacle foreseen by Johnson—the excessive startup costs and time required to train the thousands of highly qualified staffers who would be needed to provide the concept's most essential ingredient—superior personalized service. With this central problem still unresolved, the potential partners in this visionary scheme went their separate ways: Johnson to acquiring and revitalizing the Ritz-Carlton chain and Holiday Inns settling for its less ambitious but upscale Crowne Plaza subchain. Perhaps the larger hotel companies await a breakthrough in robotics to provide the degree of service required by the super-luxury hotel. (With hotels fully computerized today, can this development be far behind?) With properly programmed robots, even a budget chain might attempt to operate a future Hotel Danieli!

The super-luxury hotel will continue to compete with the separate luxury tower in larger hotels. With its closely run small size, experienced staff, and single high standard throughout the hotel, the super-luxury concept will keep its lead in quality and personal service. As Wilkinson says: "When you have some guests who are considered VIPs and others who are not, they will get treated differently, while we are only concerned with one class of service." But the increased competition between these two different luxury concepts will serve to benefit both the guest and the industry.

Grand Bay Hotel, Coconut Grove, Miami, Florida. *The 204-room Grand Bay Hotel lavished $30.5 million on perfecting its intimate and luxurious quality. With private terraces integrated into its 13-story, stepped-down form, each room with bay views, a 4000-square-foot (372-square-meter) ballroom with a function terrace, a grand cafe with outdoor dining, museum-piece artifacts in its lobby, bilevel penthouse suites, and a Regine's disco, the super-luxury hotel projects a varied, lively, and sophisticated ambience.*

10

UPDATING THE EXISTING HOTEL

"A symbol of London's elegance and sophistication since 1889"

says The Savoy

Far exceeding new hotel construction, upgrading of existing hotels and expansion, restoration, and conversion of other buildings to hotels has become a multibillion-dollar industry. Not only are extensive periodic renovations considered a necessary way of life to keep hotels refreshed and marketable, but major restorations of fine hotels and the adaptive reuse of a variety of building types to hotels have continued to attract the imagination of the public as well as the investor.

Periodic redecoration and *renovations* are essential for hotels to stay competitive. After a hotel gains popularity, *additions* often are needed to satisfy increased guest demand and maximize return. Also, *restorations* of older hotels have continued to increase in popularity due to the public's renewed interest in traditional values, preservation, and psychological relief from modern technology.

THE RENOVATION

With growth in the existing hotel inventory, renovation has now become the industry's leading construction and design activity. Typically, within about six years after the opening of a fine new hotel, it needs refurbishing or renovation. Worn out by guest use around the clock day in and day out, its interiors have also become outmoded by the latest fashions of its competitors. These factors, combined with increasing expectations of freshness and innovative design of furnishings and decor, contribute to the rapid obsolescence of the hotel.

For these reasons, hotels must continually renovate or they will decline and eventually fail. In this respect, some hotels are doomed to failure, much like corporations being dismantled for their assets. By avoiding expenditures required to keep the hotel in fully updated shape, the owner continues to milk revenues as well as the tax depreciation write-offs for as many years as possible. Eventually, a new owner may be found, willing to invest in upgrading the deteriorating physical plant in order to reverse its downward trend and give new life to its public image. If the hotel's location has remained good or become even better, which is often the case, remodeling can be an even more viable investment than new construction for the following reasons:

1. Acquisition and renovation normally cost less than new construction.
2. Renovation can be completed sooner than new construction thereby reducing financing costs. And the hotel can be kept open by completing the remodeling in phases.
3. The existing hotel is usually better known and often has a more convenient location than

UPDATING THE EXISTING HOTEL

PRECEDING PAGE AND THIS PAGE

Grand Hyatt, New York, New York. *The former Commodore Hotel, gutted and fully rebuilt as Hyatt's first entry into New York City, connected to Grand Central Terminal, one of the earliest mixed-use complexes (see Chapter 12), containing the usual open lobby, restaurants, lounges, and shops. The 20,000-square-foot (1858-square-meter) ballroom was completely refurbished and new conference and banquet rooms established on the mezzanine levels overlooking the lobby. Many of the smallest guestrooms were eliminated or combined to reduce the hotel to 1400 units. The hotel's most dramatic feature is its "thrust bar," cantilevered out over the 42nd Street sidewalk, creating views to the east and west and establishing a dynamic presence for the hotel.*

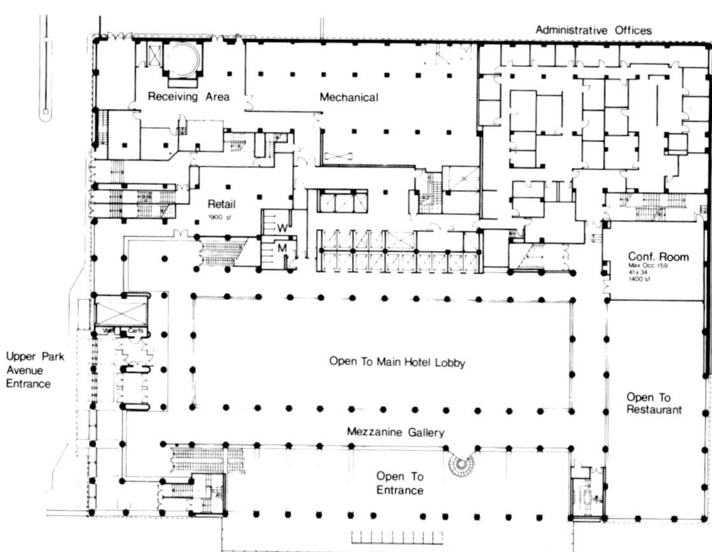

Mezzanine

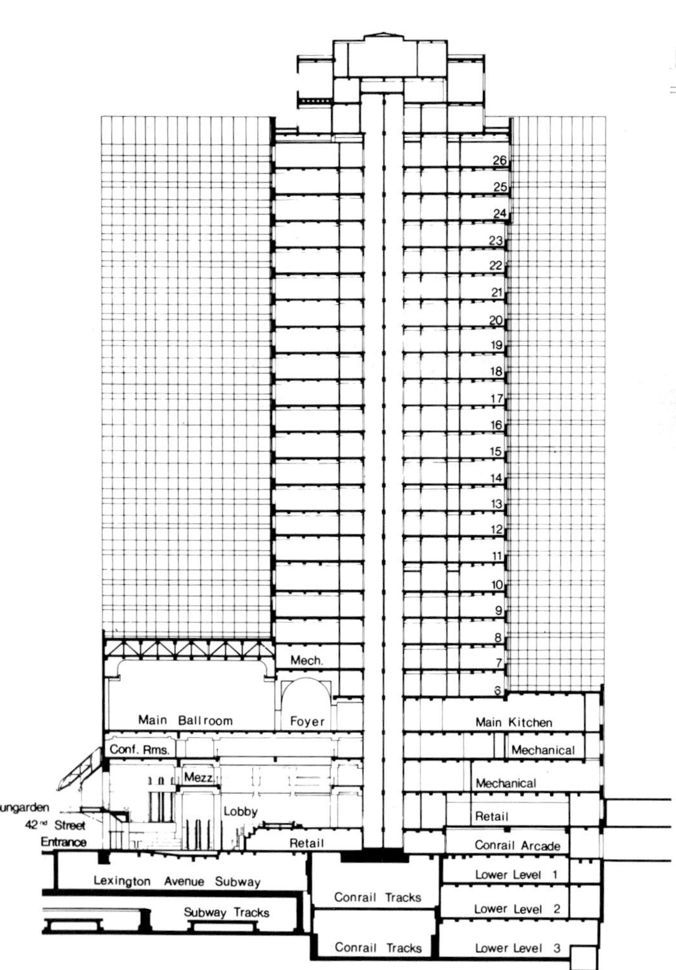

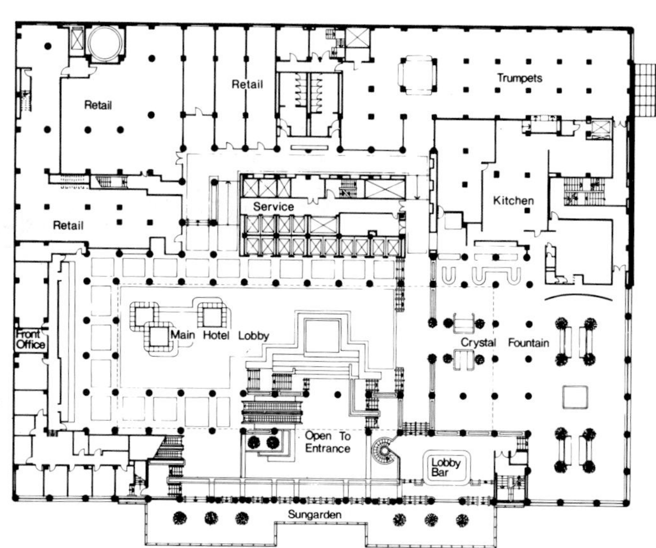

Hotel Lobby

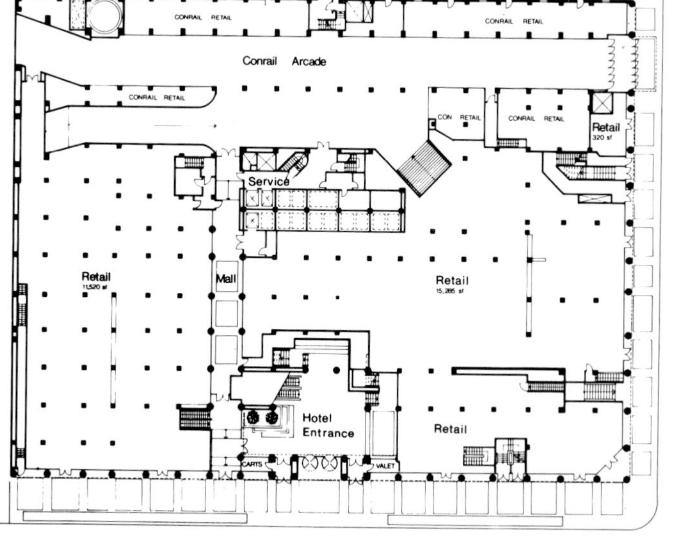

Street Level

Ramada Renaissance, Geneva, Switzerland. *Upgrading an existing moderate-scale inn in Geneva to a Ramada Renaissance Hotel included completely refurbishing 220 rooms and suites and gutting and redesigning its public areas. A larger, more flexible 110-seat restaurant with central buffet service, plus à la carte dining in its surrounding salons, was designed with flexibility to serve all three meals, replacing a previous single-purpose dining room. Adjoining the upgraded hotel lobby pictured here, a 45-seat cafe was provided as a further amenity, replacing previous meeting rooms.*

The ages of famous hotels

HOTELS OVER 100 YEARS

Three Kings Hotel, Basle, Switzerland
Cour St. Georges, Ghent, Belgium
Hotel Krone, Solothurn, Switzerland
Hotel d'Angleterre, Copenhagen, Denmark (now an Inter-Continental)
The Continental, Paris (now an Inter-Continental)
Hotel des Trois Couronnes, Vevey, Switzerland
St. Louis Hotel, New Orleans, Louisiana
The Chelsea Hotel, New York City
The Cincinnatian in Ohio
Mohonk Mountain House, New Paltz, New York
Grand Hotel, Point Clear, Alabama
Grand Hotel, Mackinac Island, Michigan
Hotel Del Monte, Monterey, California
The Capital Hotel, Little Rock, Arkansas
Teller House, Central City, Colorado

HOTELS OVER 75 YEARS

The Savoy, London
The Broadmoor, Colorado Springs, Colorado
The Palace Hotel, San Francisco (now a Sheraton)
The Brown Palace, Denver, Colorado
Hotel Del Coronado, San Diego, California
Claridges, London
The Connaught, London
The Copley Square Hotel, Boston
The Willard, Washington, D.C.
The Plaza, New York (now a Westin)
The Ritz, London
The Hotel Taj Mahal, Bombay, India (now an Inter-Continental)
The Hermitage, Nashville, Tennessee (now a Park Suite Hotel)
The Bellevue-Stratford, Philadelphia, Pennsylvania (now a Westin)
The St. Regis, New York (now a Sheraton)
The Seelbach, Louisville, Kentucky
The Jefferson, Richmond, Virginia

any alternate new site (for example, "The brand new hotel at the grand old address" is the advertising slogan of the Capital Hilton in Washington, D.C.).

4. Investment tax credits of up to 25% are available for renovation of older buildings.

Once the hotel has been renovated and reopened, it begins a new cycle, and in about 6 more years, it needs not only a second renovation, but by this time it also needs a *major overhaul*. In addition to the usual problem of fatigue, much of its equipment has now become obsolete and needs replacement. Its systems, such as computers and life safety devices, may no longer be state of the art, and new features currently demanded by the consumer and offered by competing hotels must be added (see the existing hotel checklist later in this chapter).

The potential lifespan of a hotel, if it is properly maintained, now runs about a century. Several major hotels have already celebrated their 100th anniversaries, while a few, such as the Hotel d'Angleterre in Copenhagen, Denmark, are approaching their 200th. Within the next decade, other famous hotels will reach their centennial, while several have already passed their 75th birthdays, as noted in the accompanying list of ages of famous hotels. Among the oldest European inns still functioning as hotels are the 75-room Three Kings Hotel in Basle, Switzerland, the 83-room Cour St. Georges in Ghent, Belgium, and the 40-room Hotel Krone in Solothurn, Switzerland. The ages of these unique historic lodgings are 958, 756, and 501 years old, respectively!

Many hotel developers and operators traditionally have done an admirable job of renovation and preservation, usually beyond that of other commercial buildings. Moreover, they have increasingly applied their restoration know-how to the adaptive reuse of buildings into lodging facilities. The renovation cycle includes the three stages of hotel refurbishing beginning with decorative upgrading and leading, after decades, to a total renovation.

Most developers prefer to follow the renovation route for at least a significant portion of their company's growth. They seek out new acquisition projects that may also come with undeveloped or adjacent land available for additions to the hotel where it is justified by market demand (see the section on The Addition below). About 15 percent of the growth of most major hotel companies is based on the acquisition of older properties. Combined with the routine renovation cycle, affecting all hotels, the total dollar volume of remodeling work continues to exceed new construction by a wide and increasing margin, as more hotels open and begin on the renovation cycle.

*The existing hotel checklist**

MECHANICAL SYSTEMS
- ☐ **Heating, Ventilating, and Air Conditioning Systems (see also Energy Conservation)**
- ☐ Temperature and humidity control
- ☐ Fresh air and odor control
- ☐ Mechanical noise and vibration control

Life Safety Systems (see Chapter 21, Special Systems)
- ☐ Sprinklers, standpipes, hose racks, fire extinguishers
- ☐ Smoke detection, fire alarm, voice annunciation, command post
- ☐ Emergency power generator, lighting, fire pumps, elevators
- ☐ Kitchen hood protection (dry foam), computer room (halon)
- ☐ Smokeproof exit stairs (pressurization, ventilated vestibules)
- ☐ Fire-resistive walls around guestrooms (1-hour), stairs and between floors (2-hours), fire-rated doors, closers

Energy Conservation
- ☐ Computerized energy management systems
- ☐ Heat recovery systems (kitchen and laundry hot water and exhaust)
- ☐ Air purifying systems (exhaust recirculation)
- ☐ Insulating windows (double and solar glazing)
- ☐ Life cycle energy analysis

Vertical Transportation Systems
- ☐ Passenger
- ☐ Service and freight elevators
- ☐ Escalators
- ☐ Conveyors

Telephone and Communications Systems (see Chapter 21, Special Systems)
- ☐ Computerized least-cost routing, accounting, wake-up call, and so on
- ☐ House phones, public phones, telex service, master TV antenna

Light Dimmers
- ☐ Meeting and banquet spaces
- ☐ Restaurants
- ☐ Lounges
- ☐ Lobbies

MANAGEMENT SYSTEMS

Computerized Hotel Management Systems (see Chapter 21, Special Systems)
- ☐ Room status, guest histories
- ☐ Accounting, auditing, inventories
- ☐ Word processing
- ☐ Billing, point-of-sale charging
- ☐ Automatic bar systems
- ☐ Reservations

Security Systems (see Chapter 21, Special Systems)
- ☐ Card-locking systems, door peepholes
- ☐ TV surveillance of entrances, service dock, elevators, escalators
- ☐ Alarms for exit stairs, cashier
- ☐ Cashier's vault, safe deposit boxes (front desk)
- ☐ In-room vaults

Entertainment Systems
- ☐ In-room movies
- ☐ Satellite TV, AM/FM
- ☐ Bedside control
- ☐ Master antenna

Front Desk Equipment (see Computerized Hotel Management Systems above)
- ☐ Safe deposit vaults
- ☐ Cashier's vaults
- ☐ Time stamps

Health Clubs (see Chapter 17 the Fitness Facilities Checklist)
- ☐ Exercise equipment
- ☐ Sauna, steambath, and so on
- ☐ Pool and whirlpool

Bathroom Accessories
- ☐ Pulsating shower heads
- ☐ Lighted shaving mirrors
- ☐ Towel warmers
- ☐ Shoe polishers
- ☐ Whirlpools and steambaths

Audiovisual systems (see the audiovisual aids checklist in Chapter 6)
- ☐ Projection
- ☐ Sound
- ☐ Translation

Automatic Doors
- ☐ Entrance
- ☐ Revolving
- ☐ Service and kitchen

Movable Partitions
- ☐ Meeting Spaces
- ☐ Ballroom

Soundproofing
- ☐ Guestrooms
- ☐ Meeting spaces

Repair Shops and Equipment
- ☐ Carpentry
- ☐ Plumbing
- ☐ Electrical
- ☐ TV

Parking Systems
- ☐ Automatic entrances
- ☐ Directional signs

General
- ☐ Interior fixed decor
- ☐ Signage
- ☐ Interior furnishings
- ☐ Kitchen and bar equipment
- ☐ Laundry and dry cleaning equipment, laundry chute
- ☐ Waste disposal systems, compactor

**Rate the existing condition of each item on a scale from 0 to 3, estimating the cost of new additions or upgradings as required to meet current standards.*

ABOVE

Sheraton O'Hare Airport Hotel, Chicago, Illinois. *Transforming a 21-year-old inn into the Sheraton O'Hare Airport Hotel was accomplished under a $15 million renovation program including the complete redesign of its public areas and refurbishing of its 468 guestrooms. Two restaurants and two lounges with 590 seats were redone at an average cost of $1200 per seat including the remodeling of the kitchens and bars.*

LEFT

Sheraton Savannah, Georgia. *The $5.5 million renovation of the 210-room Sheraton Savannah transformed a tired, 36-year-old seaside resort into a first-class executive conference center. Major impact was accomplished with relatively minimal costs in the restaurant at $600 per seat and in the lobby at $30 per square foot, including new furniture, fixtures, and finishes.*

Renovation cycle of the existing hotel

STAGE	COST/ROOM (APPROX.)	SCOPE
6-year refurbishment	$5,000–10,000	Replacing fabrics, carpets, most furniture, vinyl wall covering, repainting.
12-year major overhaul	$20,000–30,000	Repeating above plus upgrading systems and equipment (e.g., computers, life safety, kitchen, laundry).
50-year "gut-job" renovation and/or restoration	$50,000+	Repeating all the above plus changes in partitions, areas and circulation, and exterior renovation and/or restoration.

THE ADDITION

Like renovation, additions to a hotel can be extremely cost effective for many reasons:

1. Adding rooms costs less on a cost-per-room basis than building from scratch, providing the public, back-of-house, and core areas and utilities can be used or expanded efficiently.
2. The hotel can continue to operate during construction of the addition.
3. The added rooms capitalize on the existing hotel's already well-known location.

The accompanying hotel addition checklist highlights required planning and design considerations.

Hotel addition checklist

Evaluate Capacity of Existing Areas to Accommodate Added Traffic:

- ☐ Entrance drives and parking
- ☐ Lobby and front desk
- ☐ Food and beverage outlets
- ☐ Guest circulation (including elevators)
- ☐ Service circulation (including elevators)
- ☐ Kitchen, laundry, loading dock, employees' facilities

Obtain Data on Existing Conditions:

- ☐ As-built drawings
- ☐ Site surveys including existing utilities and landscaping
- ☐ Legal and zoning restrictions
- ☐ Soil tests
- ☐ Detailed inspection of existing structural and mechanical conditions to coordinate with proposed new construction and avoid possible damage to existing installations

Evaluate Engineering Systems to Be Used:

- ☐ Connections to existing structure and foundations
- ☐ Structural constraints of site
- ☐ Energy analysis including existing mechanical and electrical systems and capacity of plant and utilities services

Re-evaluate Renovation Needs of Existing Hotel in Terms of Matching Higher Standards of New Addition:

- ☐ Architectural upgrading of the exterior (for example, entrance canopy, balconies, facade materials, windows, roof treatment, signage, paving, landscaping)
- ☐ Interior upgrading (furniture, furnishings, finishes, decor, lighting, graphics)
- ☐ Life safety, security, communications, audiovisual, and computerized hotel management systems (see Chapter 21, Special Systems)

ABOVE

Ritz-Carlton, Boston, Massachusetts. *The 1920-vintage Ritz-Carlton hotel overlooking the Boston Public Gardens was expanded with the addition of a second brick and granite wing containing luxurious condominiums, entered from Commonwealth Avenue, and elegant conference and banquet rooms with their own entrance. (See also Chapter 7, Residential and Condominium Hotels.)*

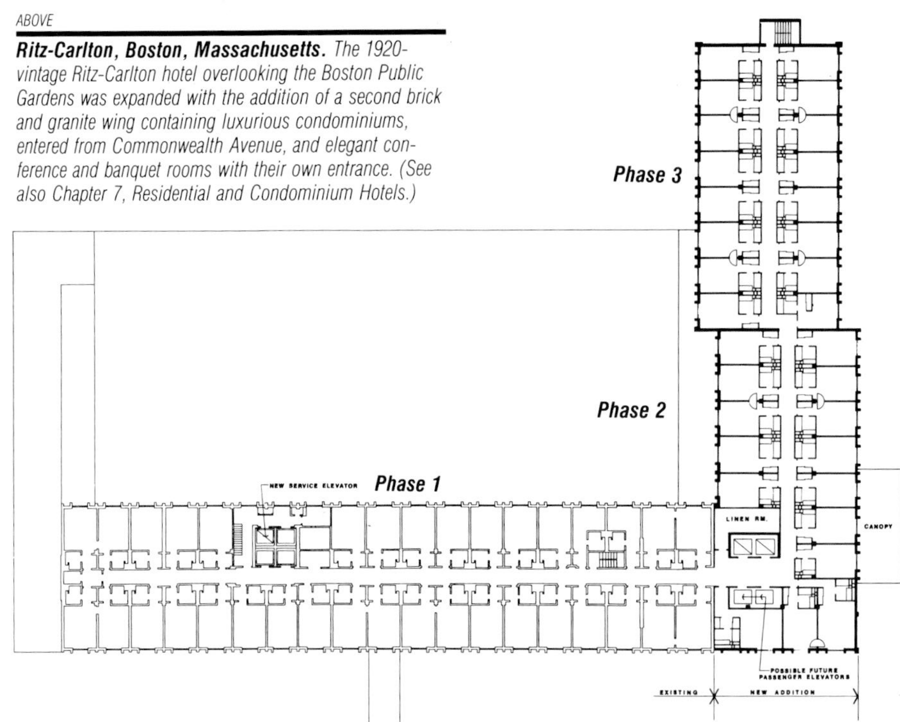

RIGHT

Hotel Inter-Continental Lusaka, Zambia. *Master planning the site for maximum expansion, a 96-room addition was designed for the 7-story, 210-room Hotel Inter-Continental in the capital of Zambia. Plans were also made for a second 96-room addition that included provisions for expanding the new elevator bank at a later date.*

The Restoration

Given increasing impetus by public concern for historic preservation, hotel restorations have been enthusiastically welcomed by travelers, becoming one of the industry's most vital areas of development worldwide. After momentum was gained in the early 70s with such noted successes as Inter-Continental's pioneer and painstaking restorations of the Hotel Continental on Rue de Rivoli in Paris and the Taj Mahal Hotel overlooking the harbor in Bombay, India, few cities still remain without their landmark hotels having been restored. In addition to conserving resources and appealing to guests and the community, well-executed restoration projects, particularly of hotels prominent in the city's business, political, and social life, help record the community's history for future generations. From the Bellevue-Stratford in Philadelphia, Pennsylvania, to the Galvez in Galveston, Texas, fascination with old hotels has never been stronger and more beneficial to developers and the city.

In addition to financial success, the preservation of a historic hotel has an enormous impact on the community. Many of these sometimes abandoned structures are located in economically depressed innercity areas, still not recovered from the post–World War II exodus to the suburbs. For example, in Memphis, Tennessee, the revitalization of downtown can be timed from the restoration and reopening of its famous Peabody Hotel in the 80s. After a 20-year hiatus, it again became the center of the community, attracting suburbanites back to its ballrooms and roof garden for their social and business functions and spearheading a new spirit of significance and activity for the surrounding downtown area.

Hotel restorations need not be limited to buildings of landmark architectural merit. Through imaginative "restoration," ordinary older hotels can be transformed to an even more elegant ambience than in their heyday, giving the illusion of being returned to a former luxury that they actually never possessed. In this manner, significant improvements can be made to the original product, both technically and esthetically. The Halloran House in New York, for example, is a far cry from the undistinguished hotel that it replaced.

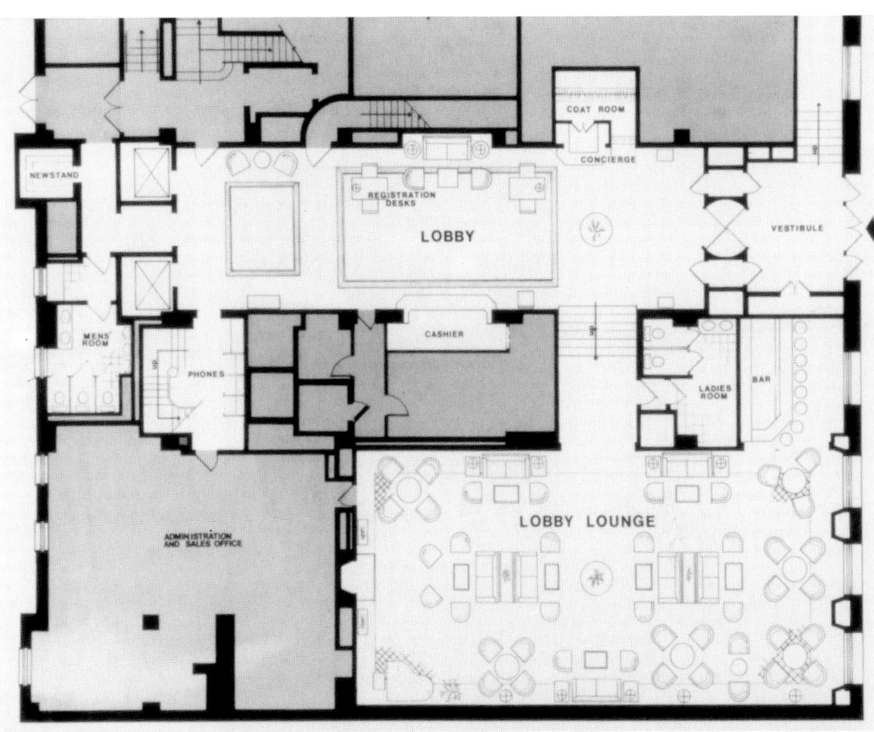

Mayfair Regent, Chicago. *The 216-room Mayfair Regent, located on Chicago's fashionable Lake Shore Drive, features an elegant lobby lounge decorated with hand-painted Chinese murals where English high tea is served daily. The lobby has a highly residential character; guests register at a pair of antique desks set on Oriental carpets rather than in the commercial setting of newer hotels. (See also color photograph on page 7.)*

ABOVE

Hotel Willard Inter-Continental, Washington, D.C. *The 14-story Willard, opened in 1901 as Washington's preeminent hotel and abandoned in the mid-1970s as obsolete, is undergoing a $70 million restoration. With its lobby meticulously refurbished and the original front desk retained as a conciergerie, the chandeliered Peacock Alley returned as an arcade for new boutiques, and the 100-seat mirrored Crystal Room preserved as one of the city's premiere restaurants, the hotel's return to its former grandeur is assured. Complete new mechanical and life safety systems and a new elevator bank serve its 394 guestrooms, which have over 100 different sizes and designs.*

RIGHT

Mayfair Regent, New York. *The Mayfair Regent of New York, located on the Upper East Side amongst elegant apartments and condominiums, features luxurious service that attracts discriminating guests. The lobby lounge, reminiscent of the grand salons of European hotels, compliments the gourmet restaurant by offering breakfast, afternoon tea, and cocktails. It also doubles as the reception space for L'Orangerie, the hotel's principal banquet room.* *(See also color photograph on page 6.)*

OPPOSITE PAGE

Four Seasons Olympic Hotel, Seattle, Washington. *Painstaking detail was taken to preserve the 1924 Italian-Renaissance architecture of the restored Four Seasons Olympic Hotel, including new techniques used to refurbish its stone facade, wood-framed Palladian windows, and carved oak columns in the lobby. Luxurious features were also added to create a more intimate residential atmosphere, rather than continue to compete with the larger new convention properties nearby. For example, by reducing the number of rooms from 756 to 451, their sizes were nearly doubled, with half becoming suites.*

Guestroom sizes varied greatly among the older hotels. Those built for the luxury market such as the restored Barclay in New York, now the Inter-Continental, had larger rooms sufficient for today's normal standards, while others built as "salesmen's" hotels had a smaller room module, with tiny or sometimes remote bathrooms. The latter type involves a far more costly "gut job," necessitating the removal of most partitions and mechanical chases, while in the luxurious older buildings more of the existing construction can be retained. Therefore, converting less than first-class buildings to current competitive standards requires more extensive modifications. Nevertheless, so long as the capital costs of the restored hotel do not exceed the cost of a new hotel, such restorations will be viable, given the present public preference and popularity of restored hotels. Besides, since many of the older hotels were built with great skill, they usually function as well as new hotels after complete renovation and technical upgrading.

RIGHT

Adolphus Hotel, Dallas, Texas. *The $45 million renovation and expansion of the landmark Adolphus Hotel included restoration of the original 1912 structure and architectural integration of more recent additions with a new facade. The interior refurbishing reduced the number of rooms from 800 to 440 oversized guestrooms averaging 500 square feet (46 square meters). Throughout the hotel rare art and antiques are displayed; paintings, chandeliers, tapestries, carved mantelpieces, clocks, and decorative accessories create a marvelous experience for the guest.*

BELOW

The Netherland Plaza, an Omni/Dunfey Hotel, Cincinnati, Ohio. *Opened in 1931, the Netherland Plaza, now an Omni/Dunfey Hotel, was restored to its original French Art Deco splendor, including its sparkling 500-seat Hall of Mirrors that rivals its Versailles model.*

OPPOSITE PAGE

The Inter-Continental Paris. *Opened in 1878, its 5-story facade inspired by the controlled architecture of Paris' Rue de Rivoli and Place Vendome, and one of the earliest mixed-use complexes (see Chapter 12), the 500-room Continental Hotel was sensitively restored in 1968 as the Inter-Continental Paris. One of the early major hotel preservations, its Napoleon Ballroom ceiling frescos are considered a national treasure. (See also page 3 in Color Portfolio.)*

ADAPTIVE REUSE

Restoration of older hotels has become so popular that buildings available to be restored are in short supply. Therefore, developers have increasingly turned to conversions of existing structures, sometimes with landmark status, that have outlived their previous use, be they banks, railway terminals, palaces, or more modest structures such as apartments, dormitories, or fire stations. For instance, Meridien Hotels boasts of its conversion of the Federal Reserve Bank ("a treasured Boston landmark") and Marriott proudly advertises its extensive upgrading of a former pirate's lair in Barbados ("it's not just a castle . . . it's a kingdom").

That ingenuity continues to be the soul of adaptive reuse is supported by the fact that in 1841 a harem in downtown Cairo, Egypt, was turned into one of the world's most famous hotels, Shepheards, giving recycling an early, rousing start. However, prior to the 70s, conversions to major hotels were rare, although there are notable exceptions. The stained-glass, domed atrium in the Gran Hotel in Mexco City on historic Zokalo Square was originally built as a department store; Cortez's Palace near Taxco, Mexico, was converted to the noted Villa Vista Hermosa Hotel in the 50s, and European tourists continue to enjoy the hundreds of castles, summer palaces, mansions, and chateaux transformed for many years into delightful vacation hotels. Built as a summer palace for the Portuguese royal family, the Palace Hotel in Bussaco, for example, was converted into a hotel as far back as 1909, but the pace of conversions of such chateau, castles, abbeys, manors, and so on quickened in the tourist boom of the 70s.

In the past two decades, adaptive reuse has proven a fertile field for development, inspiring almost infinite inventiveness (see the table on adaptive reuse examples of structures converted to hotels). Examples range from Guy Louis de Bourgeron's conversion of a college dormitory at L'Ecole des Beaux Arts to one of Paris's most successful super-luxury hotels, L'Hotel, to Hilton's conversion of grain silos in Akron, Ohio, and Sheraton's adaptation of a fire station to form part of its hotel in Greensboro, North Carolina. Also included are the recycling of an office building and a bank, as well as the conversion of the Paris-Match building to that city's most unique new luxury hotel, the Nova-Park Élysée. (For a more complete review of adaptive reuse projects, see the list of hotels in the Appendix.)

The accompanying existing hotel checklist highlights services, amenities, and hotel

Adaptive reuse: examples of structures converted to hotels

TYPE STRUCTURE CONVERTED FROM	HOTEL CONVERSION
COMMERCIAL	
Bank	Meridien Hotel, Boston, Massachusetts
Department store or retail shop	Gran Hotel Cuidad de Mexico City, Mexico City Planters Inn, Charleston, South Carolina
Office building	Hyatt Regency, Buffalo, New York Nova Park Élysees, Paris Landmark Hotel, San Antonio, Texas The Capital Hotel, Little Rock, Arkansas
Parking garage	Bookshire Hotel, Baltimore, Maryland
PUBLIC	
City hall	Best Western Hotel De Ville, Binghamton, New York
Customs house	Hotel (proposal announced), Boston
Fire station	Sheraton Greensboro, North Carolina Hilton, Columbus, Georgia
Immigration building	Hotel (proposal), Ellis Island, New York
Lighthouse	East Brother Lighthouse Inn, Port Richmond, California
Police station	Hotel (proposal), New York City
Railway terminal	Hilton at Lackawanna Station, Scranton, Pennsylvania Choo Choo Hilton, Chattanooga, Tennessee Omni/Dunphy, St. Louis, Missouri
Treasury building	Inter-Continental Sydney, Australia
RESIDENTIAL	
Apartment house	Stanford Court Hotel, San Francisco Marriott Essex House, New York Tremont Hotel, Baltimore, Maryland Park Suite Hotel, Kansas City, Missouri Sheraton Winnipeg, Canada
Company housing	American Club, Kohler, Wisconsin
Dormitory	L'Hotel, Paris
Farmhouse	Inn at Chester, Chester, Connecticut
Harem	Shepheards Hotel, Cairo, Egypt
Hunting lodge	Oberoi Mena House, Giza, Egypt
Palace	Marriott Cairo, Egypt Palace Hotel, Bussaco, Portugal Villa d'Este, Lake Como, Italy Jaipur Lake Palace, Jaipur, India Villa Vista Hermosa, Mexico (Cortez's palace)
Private home	Helmsley Palace, New York City (partial) Hotel Qufo, China (Confucius's home) Hotel D'Angleterre Inter-Continental, Copenhagen, Denmark Holiday Inn Chateau Le Moyne, New Orleans, Louisiana Roxborough Hotel, Ottawa, Canada Queen Victoria Inn, Cape May, New Jersey Numerous bed-and-breakfast inns
RELIGIOUS	
Church	Hilton International Budapest, Hungary
Convent	El Convento Hotel, San Juan, Puerto Rico
Monastery	Geneva-on-the-Lake, Geneva, New York
Priory	Hotel at Bath, England
OTHER	
Castle	Chateau de Creissels, France (built 801) Chateau de Meyrargues, France (built 970) Numerous castle hotels throughout Europe
Grain silos	Hilton Quaker Square, Akron, Ohio
Granary	Copenhagen Admiral Hotel, Copenhagen, Denmark
Pirate hideaway	Marriott Sam Lord Castle, Barbados, West Indies
Ship	Queen Mary, Long Beach, California
Stable	Conference center (proposed), Tarrytown, New York

technical systems generally requiring replacement or improvement in renovated or restored structures and which will continue to need upgrading as technological improvements emerge.

Planning and design considerations

Since renovations, additions, restorations, and adaptive reuse projects vary with the type of existing hotel, their planning and design criteria will depend on the material discussed in related Chapters in Part 1 and Part 2, Design Guide. However, since existing conditions require frequent departures from standard space programs and special effects can be achieved through compromise and ingenuity, the existing hotel becomes a "type" of its own. Also, as noted, restorations in and of themselves enjoy a unique guest following.

Hotel restorations frequently require new entrance drives, parking, and truck service docks where such facilities do not already exist. But cooperation has often been obtained from local authorities to permit the use of valet parking at nearby garages, add special decorative treatment of porte cochere paving and curbing, and revise traffic lanes to accommodate guest arrival traffic and service loading.

Hotels should be planned for a minimum of 50 percent expansion wherever possible, and additional land should be acquired to permit possible future horizontal expansion of the guestroom floors as well as ground level public areas. Where sufficient land is not available, the expansion wing can be planned over a parking area, with a garage structure to be built for expanded parking.

In suburban or resort sites where sufficient land is available, a lowrise expansion wing enhancing the original architectural massing has often been added. Designing for vertical expansion is usually impractical for the following reasons: (1) the excessive construction disturbance, noise, and vibration would interfere with guests' comfort in the existing hotel; (2) the necessity of raising the elevator machinery and other mechanical facilities to accommodate the added floors would interrupt the operation of the existing hotel during the expansion; and (3) the extra capital cost of oversizing the foundations and structural supports for the additional floors in the initial phase is often unfeasible.

Suburban and roadside hotels have often been expanded by creating atriums in courtyards or areas adjacent to guestrooms often surrounding them with additional lowrise wings. Designed with indoor pools and recreation facilities as well as cafes and lounges, these skylit domed and landscaped spaces have added visual excitement, increased revenue-producing activities, and balanced midweek business occupancy by attracting family guests on weekends.

In addition to periodic interior remodeling, architectural upgrading has been required to remove the dated look of many 50s and 60s hotels. Guests judge the state of the interiors by the architecture; that is, hotels that look about 10 to 15 years old are often assumed to have dated, tired furnishings and decor. To many, a "folded-plate" structural roof, upturned canopy, or similar cliche of the 60s reads as clearly as a sign saying "interiors outdated." Such motifs have had to be replaced with less faddish designs. Simplified designs such as undercutting the building to form an integral rather than an applied canopy have proven less apt to become outmoded, while well-designed landscaping has provided the most timeless and universally appealing exterior treatment.

Cairo Marriott Hotel, Cairo, Egypt. *The 1869 Egyptian palace is the centerpiece of the Cairo Marriott Hotel, containing two 20-story towers and low garden wings of guestrooms. The grand salons facing the Nile—originally built for the opening of the Suez Canal—were converted to a series of ornate mosaic-tiled lounges, restaurants, and loggia. The remains of various ornamental iron porches were consolidated to create a new "golden portico" at the entrance, the only major change to the palace's exterior.*

Much older buildings, if well maintained, feature more intricate interior detailing, one of the factors drawing guests to restorations. With guests most concerned with interior style and comfort, one of architecture's major roles in renovations, as well as new construction, is to psychologically set the stage for the hotel's interiors.

RIGHT AND BELOW

Hotel Nova-Park Élysées, Paris, France. *Transforming Paris-Match magazine's office building by restoring its handsome Second Empire facade and that of an adjoining building, the Hotel Nova-Park Élysées created 73 living units, including 61 individually themed suites (Suite Thousand and One Nights, Garden Suite, and Royal Suite), four restaurants, three lounges, a nightclub, and disco in Paris' Triangle d'Or near the Champs Élysées. With 152,200 square feet (14,150 square meters) of space, it also includes an elaborate fitness club, business service and conference center, and 70-car underground garage. To a far greater degree than most hotels, its design appeals to guests' fantasies through its exotic decor. This psychological approach is the basis of today's more varied guestroom designs and increasing diversity in hotel types. (See also pages 1-2 in Color Portfolio.)*

OPPOSITE PAGE

Hotel Meridien Boston, Massachusetts. *Adapting Boston's Federal Reserve Bank to become the luxurious Hotel Meridien Boston added new-found glory to a venerable 1922 Renaissance Revival (shown at far right) model of Rome's Palazzo della Cancellaria. Intensive use was made of such bank functions as the large vaults that became kitchens. To ensure the hotel's viability, three floors of guestrooms were added under a contemporary mansard roof, combining the old and the new in a manner not inconsistent with the building's surrounding urban context. The sloped roof also adds an interesting garret look preferred by guests.*

Hyatt Regency Buffalo, Buffalo, New York. *The largest conversion of an office building to a hotel, the Hyatt Regency Buffalo combines a complete renovation of the 1923 Genesee Building with a new guestroom wing and atrium structure. The original cast-iron facade has been restored to form one edge of the new lobby—where the original marble and bronze portal defines the entrance to the entertainment lounge. Also in the original building, the penthouse suites were designed to take advantage of the 14-foot (4-meter) arched windows with views of downtown and Lake Erie. As counterpoint to the Genesee Building, the atrium trusses enclose a contemporary lobby and mezzanine bar.*

Trends

The pace of renovations will accelerate to match the numerous innovative features offered by competitive new hotels. Where this is impractical, existing hotels will be modified to the specialized types for which they are best suited. For example, older transient hotels with smaller rooms will be converted to suite hotels. Older convention hotels, lacking sufficient banquet or exhibit space to meet today's competition, will be transformed into conference centers with upgraded audiovisual facilities, focusing on small business groups rather than conventions.

Downtown hotels will offer conference center floors such as at Chicago's Palmer House and Towers, in which guestrooms

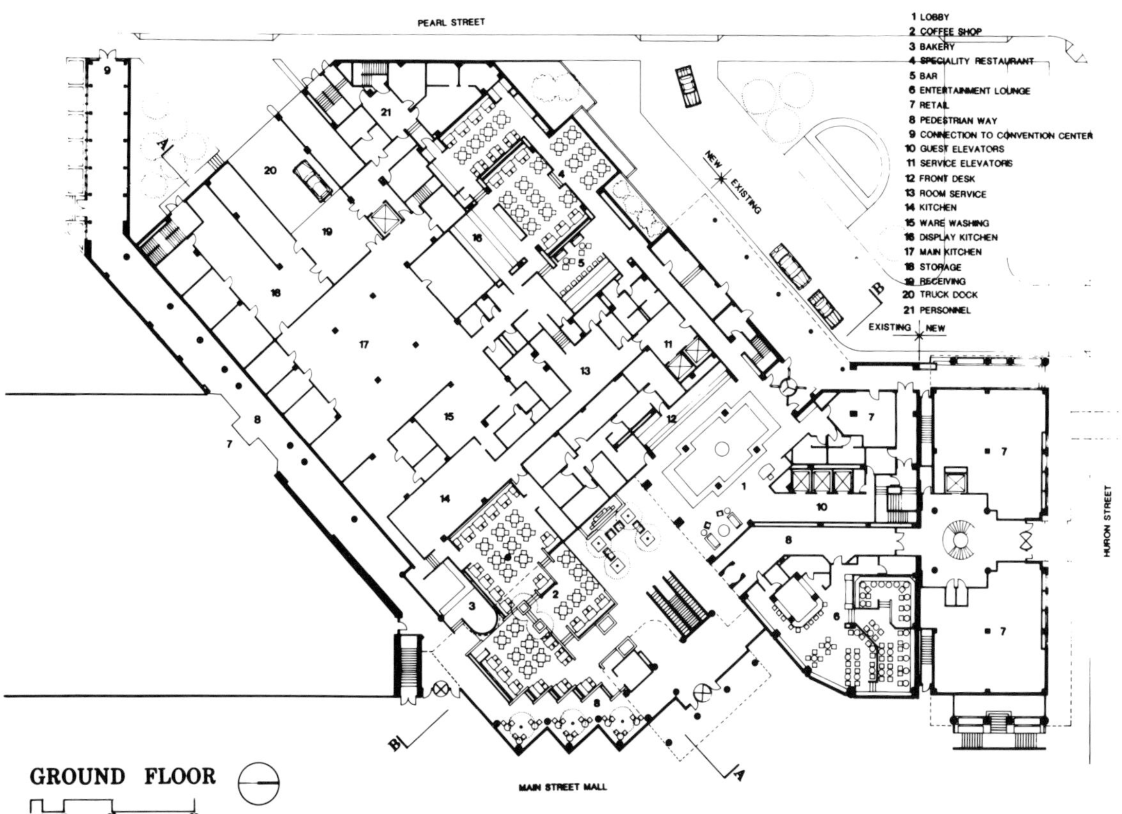

PEARL STREET
1 LOBBY
2 COFFEE SHOP
3 BAKERY
4 SPECIALITY RESTAURANT
5 BAR
6 ENTERTAINMENT LOUNGE
7 RETAIL
8 PEDESTRIAN WAY
9 CONNECTION TO CONVENTION CENTER
10 GUEST ELEVATORS
11 SERVICE ELEVATORS
12 FRONT DESK
13 ROOM SERVICE
14 KITCHEN
15 WARE WASHING
16 DISPLAY KITCHEN
17 MAIN KITCHEN
18 STORAGE
19 RECEIVING
20 TRUCK DOCK
21 PERSONNEL
NEW
EXISTING
EXISTING
NEW
HURON STREET
MAIN STREET MALL
GROUND FLOOR

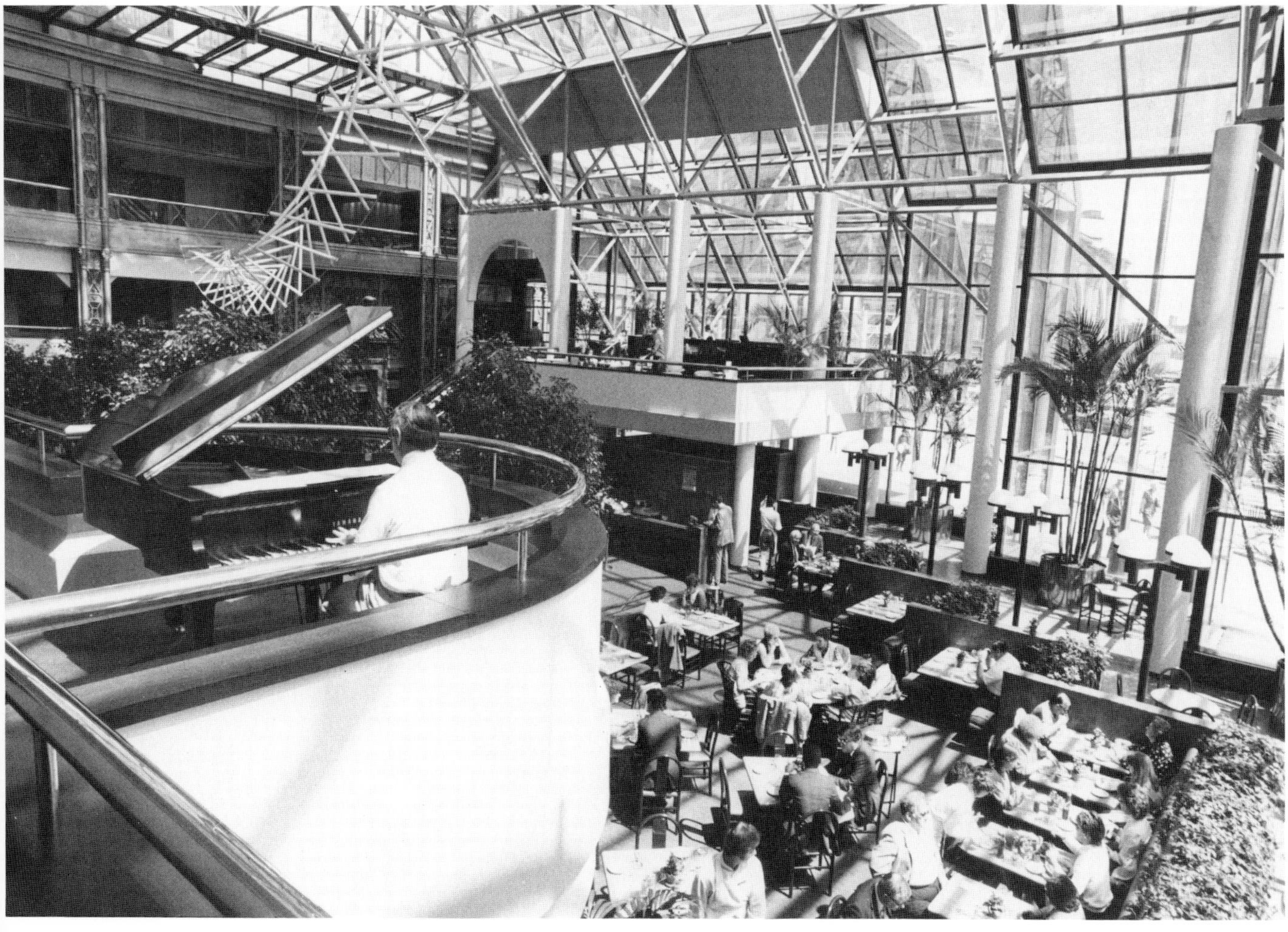

were converted to audiovisual meeting rooms surrounding a reception lobby and coffeebreak lounge. Business center floors will also be created, with guestrooms that convert to dual-use offices by day, furnished with executive desks, files, and extra phones; with an answering service in the company's name; secretarial, translation, messenger, and beeper-call services; as well as computers, audiovisual equipment, quotron, and viewdata equipment for business information and business reference libraries.

Most hotels will need to be reequipped with more advanced automatic front desk systems, the latest in-room entertainment equipment, and business aids, including personal computers and teleconferencing capability. Considerable retro-fitting will be required to install more efficient life safety, security, and energy management systems as they become cost effective (see Chapter 21, Special Systems).

Restaurants will be redone to feature more inventive hybrid cuisine concepts, such as displaying food preparation, which makes hotel dining more fun, and accenting more intimate and private seating arrangements. As existing hotels invest more extensively in upgrading their basic systems and public spaces, guestroom additions will become increasingly cost effective, wherever possible. Improvement of the leisure and meeting facilities in guestrooms will be emphasized in renovations, while their residential character and postmodern flavor will also be enhanced. Full-wall mirroring will be used to enlarge the smaller rooms in older hotels, while new whirlpool/steam baths will upgrade their bathrooms to meet the competition of new hotels.

The popularity of restorations will be further enhanced by the historical references now used in the postmodern design trend. But with few hotels left to be restored, other types of structures will be sought; for example, smaller apartment houses will be adapted to small downtown hotels and suburban estates to country inns and conference retreats. Such developments will continue to create business opportunities and more individualized management responsibilities in the hotel field, a healthy sign offsetting the reverse trend to bigness in most other industries.

The Hilton at Lackawanna Station, Scranton, Pennsylvania. *A 1908 French Renaissance train station in Scranton was reopened 75 years later as The Hilton at Lackawanna Station. Preserving its historic hub of an earlier heyday, the station's high-vaulted waiting room was adapted as the hotel's lobby and public area, while its remaining six stories were converted to 150 guestrooms.*

11 THE MEGA-HOTEL

"Once in a while we even impress ourselves"

proudly admits the Hyatt Regency Grand Cypress in Orlando, Florida

Following a decade of rapid hotel expansion in Orlando, Florida, including Disney's own family-oriented hotels featuring innovations such as built-in monorail service, the area's tourist development accelerated to a point where hotels of even greater size and variety were called for. As one of the world's leading vacation destinations, it takes only a slight upward turn in the worldwide economy, disposable income, or vacation time to trigger demand for thousands of additional hotel rooms in Orlando.

Never has a greater opportunity been presented for planning hotels so imaginatively and grandly. Designers, developers, and hotel companies are meeting the challenge in the 80s with a new wave of well-designed hotels and tourist attractions. In fact the term "mega-hotel" was coined by the Marriott Orlando. In the process, America is continuing its leadership in the leisure-time industry, now becoming more noted for its innovative amusement parks and hotels than for its automobiles. The story is significant for similar future developments.

Little more than a decade ago, Orlando was just another Florida town. Until recently (let's call it "stage one") new hotel development serviced the growing tourist/sight-seeing market, following the fortunes of Disney World and other new attractions. But today ("stage two") hotels are designed as *destination resorts* and *convention centers* as well as *centers for sight-seers* and *business travelers*. The major coverage of these four different markets defines the mega-hotel. (Casino hotels discussed in Chapter 13 approach mega-hotel status where they also serve as destination resorts and convention hotels.) Stage-two expansion still capitalizes on stage one's not insignificant advantages—the world's largest array of such sight-seeing features as several family theme parks, wild animal displays, and nature preserves, such as Discovery Island. Combined with a pleasant climate and setting, a well-designed international airport, and convenient local transit systems (monorails, tour boats, and so on), with *nothing else quite like it*, the "Vacation Kingdom of the World" has become greater than the sum of its parts.

With attendance at Disney World, EPCOT Center, Sea World, and Busch Gardens, among others, exceeding expectations, additional tourist attractions surrounded by hotel sites were planned (for example, Universal City and Agriplex). The unique form of hotel created for this further transformation contains all the features of a tourist and convention center and family and sports resort rolled into one. A wide range of facilities was de-

PRECEDING PAGE

The Orlando Marriott Resort, Orlando, Florida. *Stepping down 28 floors to its 8-story atrium, the 1500-room Orlando Marriott Resort is designed to cater to four main types of guests. (1) family wings are near activity areas and parking; (2) tower suites are for business travelers; (3) tour groups are housed near the main entrance; and (4) locations close to sports facilities are for vacationers. As a destination resort, the hotel offers indoor and outdoor pools, a spa and extensive trails, water features and landscaping spread over its 193 acres (78 hectares). The site also includes 200 split-level condos bordering on a golf and tennis complex as well as over 80,000 square feet (7432 square meters) of meeting, banquet, and exhibit space to attract conventions.*

RIGHT

Headquarters Hotel, Orlando, Florida. *Across from the Orange County Convention Center in Orlando, the 27-story Headquarters Hotel provides 57,900 square feet (5379 square meters) of convention space including a 23,500-square foot (2183-square meter) ballroom, four restaurants, extensive recreation, and other amenities individually designed to cater to the mega-hotel's varied clientele.*

BELOW

Hyatt Regency Grand Cypress, Orlando, Florida. *Centerpiece of the 730-acre (295-hectare) Grand Cypress Resort near Walt Disney World, the $110 million, 750-room Hyatt Regency Grand Cypress hotel caters to vacationers, convention-goers, families sightseeing the area's many attractions, and business travelers. The last are lured by the hotel's upper-floor Regency Club featuring upgraded guestrooms as well as three Presidential Suites, two of them bilevel penthouses. Convention space encompasses 57,000 square feet (5295 square meters) including a 25,000-square-foot (2322-square-meter) ballroom, and 21,000 square feet (1950 square meters) of exhibit space. As a vacation destination, the resort offers a prime golf course, 21-acre (8.5-hectare) lake, and a half-acre (.2-hectare) pool with waterfalls, grottoes, and a gourmet restaurant on its central island. "Our guests come for other reasons than Disney, although they might bring the kids along for that," said one staffer.*

Leading the arriving guests to their first look at the great 18-story atrium in the stepped T-shaped tower, a wide garden avenue rises through lush planting and waterfalls to a huge trellised entrance court. Artwork valued at $1 million is displayed indoors and out. An internal transit system adapted from early 1900 European trolley cars provides tours of the grounds' planned shopping and entertainment features as well as 600 villas, 5 miles (8 kilometers) of riding trails and nature walks through a 55-acre (22-hectare) conservation area were developed with the advice of the Audubon Society.

signed to appeal to several different types of tourists such as business and convention groups, children, teens, and golf and tennis vacationers. While convention goers attended meetings, their families could be treated to Orlando's many sight-seeing attractions, as well as the special in-hotel features oriented toward children and spouses. This unusually broad mix of facilities has encouraged many business travelers to stretch their trips into family vacations. By cultivating a more diversified market, the multipurpose mega-hotel now commands a higher and more diversified occupancy and is therefore considered a safer investment. Due to its economy of scale, it has also proven efficient to operate.

Continuing the trend set by Hyatt, Marriott, Sheraton, and a new hotel called Headquarters have also developed mega-designs combining large convention centers and family vacation resorts with luxurious facilities designed to serve Orlando's fast growing high-tech industrial community. The different facilities provided for each type of customer are visually expressed in the building's design: a family-oriented wing surrounding a large swimming pool; a game and recreation center for teen and subteen activities; convention and meeting centers seating up to 5000 with football-field-sized exhibit halls; special tower sections designed to attract business guests; various ethnic food, specialty, and self-service restaurants appealing to family, teen, and business guests; and major health and recreation features for vacationers of all types. (Note the listing of such hotels in the Appendix.)

Planning considerations

Mega-hotels of 1000 to 1500 rooms, with the extensive convention facilities and amenities discussed above, are uniquely outside urban areas. With sites of 50 acres (22 hectares) or more, comprehensive environmental studies are needed to deal with a list of community concerns ranging from flood control to archeology (see the environmental checklist in the Appendix). They are also required to establish the project's cost and feasibility as well as to obtain governmental approvals.

In the case of Disney World, EPCOT Center, and other major attractions, several hotel sites were planned as part of their overall development and were therefore taken into account by the initial environmental studies. This avoided piecemeal planning later on and simplified the rapid development of hotels integrated with tourist attractions that used predetermined systems and standards for transportation, municipal utilities, landscaping, building massing, and density. An additional year's lead time would have been required for planning a mega-hotel on a new site not previously approved for hotel use and lacking the necessary advance studies. Planned hotel groupings such as those created at Disney World and EPCOT Center proved far more attractive to the public than normal roadside strip developments and have therefore shown higher than average occupancy rates.

Compared with other hotels and resorts, the mega-hotel requires a greater number of entrance approaches for its different functional elements and varied types of guests and services. Separate drives are needed for the main lobby, convention hall, exhibit area, tour group entrance, and several sports centers. Additional exterior entrances are preferable for the entertainment lounge and restaurants and for remote guestroom wings. Special truck service access is necessary directly into the exhibit area. Access by at least three approach roads is required into the site to provide adequate car queuing space. Planners should provide for a minimum of 1.5 cars and .01 tour buses per room.

Because of the hotel's resort character, huge size, and extensive parking areas, unusual amounts of landscape treatment are needed, for which a budget approaching $2 million would not be inappropriate. One or two lakes, needed to retain surface drainage, as well as such other water features as falls, moats, and decorative streams, are normally created as visual amenities. They provide the main views from restaurants, lounges and guestrooms. Two swimming pools, one specially designed for children with a water slide or other features, plus .01 tennis courts per room and an 18-hole golf course (where the hotel is not adjacent to an existing one) are needed as basic minimum outdoor amenities (see Chapter 17 for the recreation checklist).

Hotels of this scale often include their own special transit systems (for example, open cart trains, decorative trolleys, and electric golf carts) to provide convenient access to tourist sites and recreation facilities and to enhance the guest's experience.

Design considerations

While mega-hotels appear to run counter to the trend toward more specialized single-purpose hotels, the new concept succeeds because of "in-hotel segmentation"—clear recognition of the needs of different types of guests so each feels the hotel is oriented toward his or her interests. For example, the hotel may provide the latest in children's-activity pools in a landscaped courtyard surrounded by the family wing of guestrooms and also in a separate area, a more quiet, relaxed pool area, accessible to the tower floors, with a landscaped view and fully equipped health club. Each group benefits.

As in the above example, the design must provide for reasonable *separation* of the activities of each group (that is, the convention complex, exhibit hall, towers floors, teen center, children's game rooms, adult health club), much like the mix of a city, while at the same time *combining* functions where appropriate (for example, food fair, outdoor barbecue, lounges, shopping). The atrium, further enlivened by moving water, changing daylight, lush plants, and sculpture, is the "city square" where the mega-hotel's varied mix of guests come together for liveliness and color.

The larger mega-hotels provide a "youth hotel" for families, with nursery play areas, a "kinder-care" center with one dormitory bed per 100 rooms (which has proven to be safer and more efficient than hiring in-room babysitters), and a teen-age classroom with computerized educational games. Large rooms—[minimum 13′ × 21′ (4 × 6.4 m)]—are required to allow for rollaways and cribs needed to accommodate families. The elevator capacity must be increased by 10 percent due to the greater number of occupants (3.4) per room, the higher use of passenger elevators by children, and the greater demand for room service by families on vacation.

To attract business travelers, the towers rooms, serviced by a private elevator bank, must be a minimum of 13′ × 21′ plus balconies [compared with 13′ × 18′ (4 × 5.5 m) for standard guestrooms]. The towers guest is also provided with concierge service, a rooftop lounge, and outdoor terrace (for continental breakfasts, cocktails, and private use by towers guests). Due to the hotel's large scale, all guestroom floors should provide upper-floor atriums, which integrate daylighting with their elevator lobbies.

The design of convention and resort elements are discussed in earlier chapters, while a summary facilities program for the mega-hotel is included in the Design Guide.

Trends

While mega-hotels represent a new peak in evolving hotel design, the demand for them will only apply in *regions* attracting several major markets. Because of their resort attributes and proximity to established business and convention centers as well as sightseeing attractions, other sites for potential development include, San Diego, California, Honolulu, Hawaii, and Singapore.

12

MIXED-USE DEVELOPMENTS

"Imagine a place so well conceived that every need is fulfilled"

boasts the Mandalay Four Seasons of Las Colinas, a new planned community near Dallas/ Ft. Worth, Texas

Each element of the mixed-use complex, including its hotel, office building, condominiums and shopping mall, benefits from integration with a larger, more prestigious project. With its higher visibility and more ambitious overall planning concept, the impact of the entire development is far greater than the sum of its parts. In addition to its more efficient methods of land use, assembly, construction, and financing, the mixed-use complex encourages innovative design, often overriding outdated zoning regulations, improving traffic circulation patterns, and initiating planning variances beneficial to both the community and the developer.

Louis XIV conceived the first major coordinated commercial complex, the Place Vendome, with its classic facades unifying its shops, offices, apartments, and hotels, including Paris' Ritz. But it took the hotel boom of the 1920s almost two centuries later for New York's Grand Central Terminal to revive the mixed-use concept with the railroad's ramps, shopping, and restaurant arcades interconnecting with several nearby hotels.

E. M. Statler, pioneer developer of the modern hotel, erected the first major hotel/ office building, now the Boston Park Plaza, on a full block in 1927. But for the next three decades, mixed-use developments from New York's Rockefeller Center in the 30s to Montreal's Place Ville St. Marie in the 50s omitted hotels due to the prevailing oversupply of rooms, a mark of the boom-and-bust cycle of the 20s.

When room demand finally returned in the 60s, hotels again became essential elements in such pioneer mixed-use complexes as Boston's Prudential Center, containing a 1500-room twin tower Sheraton; Carleton Center in Johannesburg, South Africa, with its 700-room Westin Hotel; and Place Bonaventure in Montreal including a 400-room Hilton. These key projects set the pace for downtown revitalization by attracting both regional and international clientele to their large convention facilities, office structures, and impressive malls and by providing the latest in recreation and entertainment amenities for the city. The Prudential development, the largest complex of its kind up to that time, included a 5000-seat civic auditorium and popular visitors' observation center atop its office building as well as two apartment towers and a 3000-car underground garage. Due to competition from other nearby developments such as Copley Place, as well as to better support the increased number of hotel rooms, the Prudential complex is now planning to vastly increase its commercial, office, and convention and exhibition facilities.

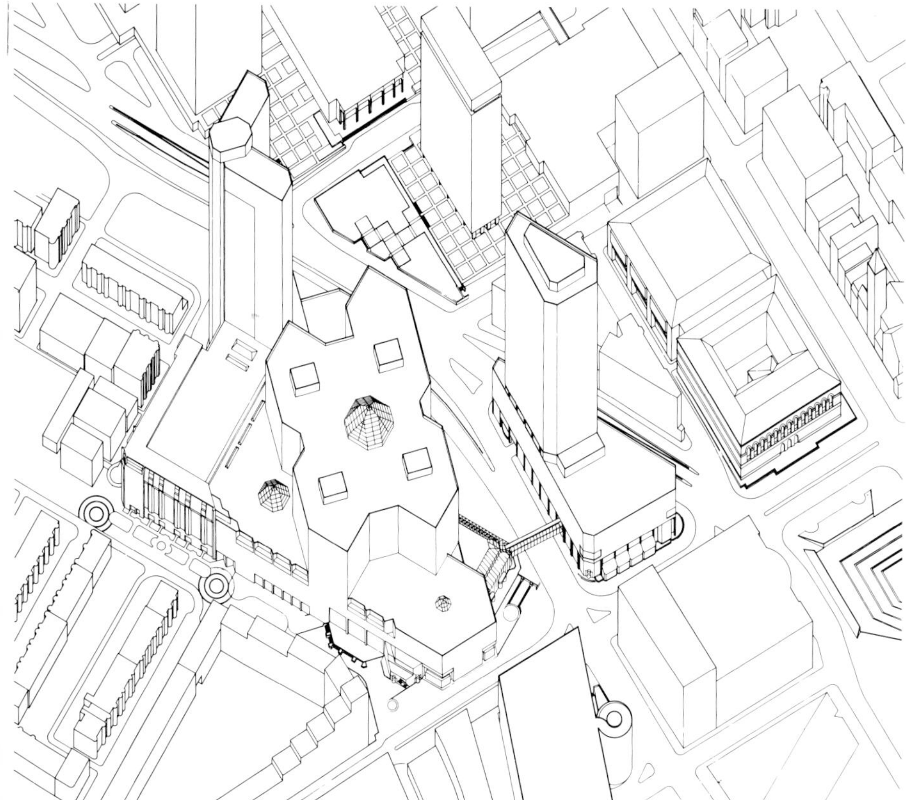

Copley Place, Boston, Massachusetts. *The $500 million Copley Place complex includes two major hotels—the 804-room Westin and the 1139-room Marriott [together offering 90,000 square feet (8361 square meters) of meeting and convention space]—plus four office buildings, a shopping center, a nine-cinema complex, 100 apartments, and parking for 1400 cars. Its focal point is a 4-story skylit atrium with radiating shopping arcades linking all the building's elements and connecting to parking, commuter trains, and rapid transit facilities.*

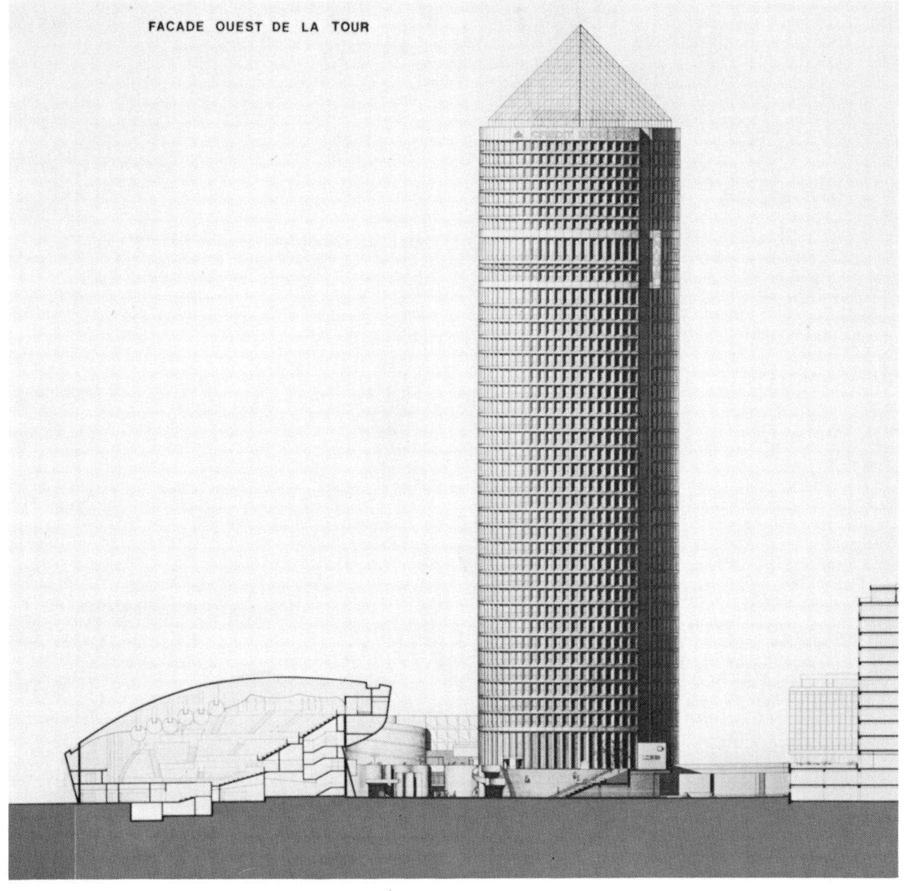

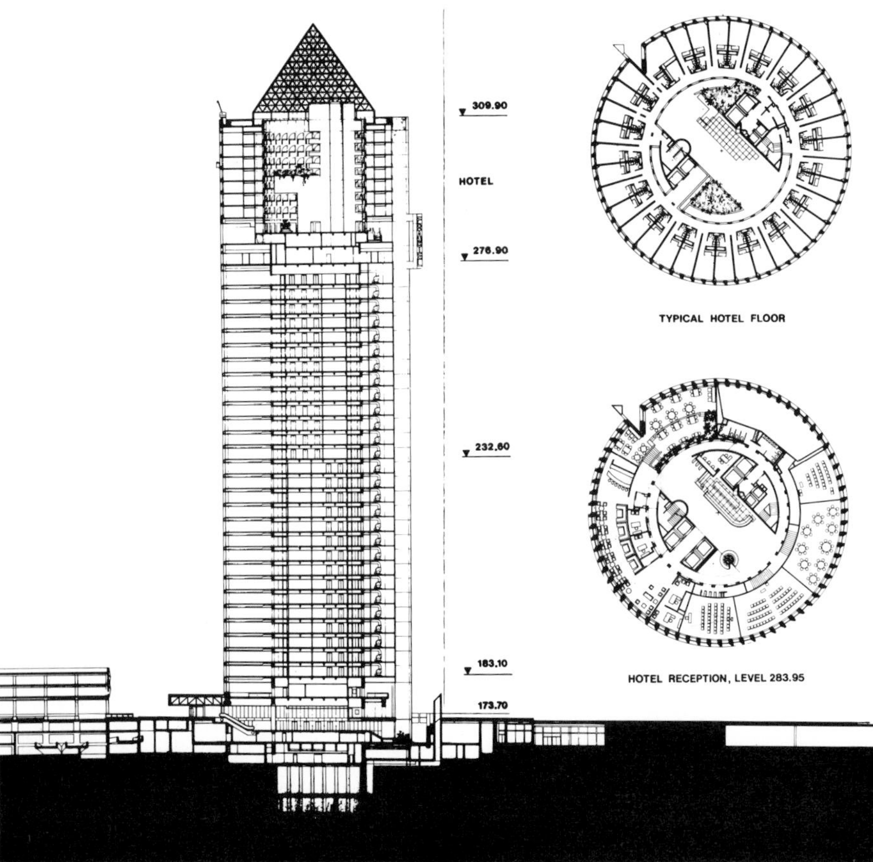

Credit Lyonnais Center, Lyon, France. *The Gothic strains of architect Araldo Cossutta's designs, such as his buttresses and castlelike interiors at Boston's Long Wharf Marriott Hotel, are also evident in his turretlike treatment of the Credit Lyonnais Center ingeniously integrating a ring-shaped Francotel hotel atop the cylindrical office building. (See also page 16 in Color Portfolio.)*

In the 70s, such complexes spread to most major cities including Embarcadero Center in San Francisco and Renaissance Center in Detroit, where their huge atriums are the focus of hotel/office/shopping centers, the trademark of their architect and co-developer John Portman; Water Tower Place in Chicago, with its Ritz-Carleton Hotel topping a multistory shopping mall; and the United Nations Plaza in New York, combining its Hyatt hotel, condo, and office building in a sleek composition that minimizes its bulk in relation to the surrounding community. Portman's *grand atriums*, Loebl-Schlossman-Hackl's *vertical complex* at Water Tower Place, and Kevin Roche's *compact towers* for the United Nations Plaza, each has proven to be an economically as well as architecturally valid solution to mixed use. Other vertically stacked variations include Araldo Cossutta's cylindrical Francotel Hotel atop the Credit Lyonnaise offices in Lyon, France, and Romaldo Giurgola's Lafayette Place Hotel topping Jordan Marsh's shopping mall in downtown Boston.

But a new generation of mixed-use designs has emerged with I. M. Pei's towering Raffles City and John Portman's Marina Square, both providing a focal point for rapidly expanding Singapore, as well as The Architects Collaborative's Copley Place in Boston, blending with its community and connecting with the two-decades-old Prudential complex. These newest developments contain even higher ratios of hotel space, justified in Singapore by the city's phenomenal business growth and in Boston by the expansion of its convention center.

Similar to locating major department stores at the opposite ends of a shopping mall, Copley Place is anchored by its two large hotels. In addition to a combined total of 2000 guestrooms, their exciting restaurants, lobbies, and lounges invite the public in at each end via escalators to an upper-deck concourse leading through a multilevel shopping mall with 100 boutiques including Tiffany's, Gucci, and St. Laurent, 10 restaurants, and a Neiman-Marcus department store.

A second major trend in multiuse and planned community development is exemplified by Lincoln Properties' 178-acre (72-hectare) Harbour Island community in Tampa and the Koll Company's 96- and 124-acre (39-

and 50-hectare) developments in California's Irvine area. While such concentrated downtown locations as Raffles City and Copley Place are considered mixed-use complexes, spreadout suburban sites with large residential and recreational areas such as Harbour Island and Irvine are more appropriately termed "planned community developments." When such developments are resort oriented, such as at Hilton Head in South Carolina, Kaanapali in Maui, or Cancun in Mexico, they are considered "multiresort complexes" as were discussed in Chapter 4.

Offering a taste of the future in a category all its own, Las Colinas, Texas, a 10,000-acre (4050-hectare) planned city, has an urban core of highrise buildings along its lakefront as well as a planned 112-acre (45-hectare) mixed-use area containing a variety of hotels.

Due to the importance of mixed-use complexes to the overall community, their planning has attracted such leading designers as Pei, Roche, Johnson/Burgee, Giurgola, Portman, Cossutta, Welton, Becket, Ehrenkrantz, Hillier, Morris/Aubrey, and The Architects Collaborative.

A representative grouping of such complexes is provided in the list of hotels in the Appendix.

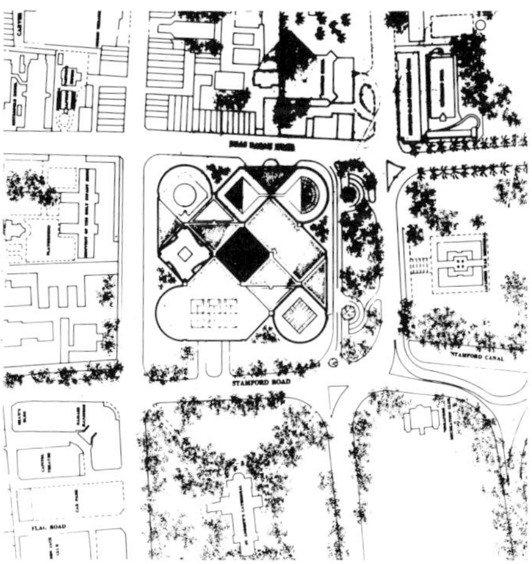

ABOVE RIGHT

Marina Square, Singapore. *The Portman-designed mixed-use complex, within walking distance to many of Singapore's tourist attractions, includes three major hotels as well as restaurants, cinemas, shopping, office, and recreational facilities. Each of the world-class hotels (Marina Mandarin, Oriental, and Pan Pacific) is focused around a major atrium space and, together, form one of the premiere international convention complexes.*

ABOVE AND RIGHT

Raffles City, Singapore. *Taking its name from the venerable Raffles Hotel bordering its downtown Singapore site, the new Raffles City complex contains two major hotels, the 71-story Westin Stamford, and the 42-story Westin Plaza, as well as an office tower connected by a 7-story podium with extensive shops, restaurants, and cafes. Its rooftop restaurant offers panoramic views from Asia's tallest structure and the world's tallest hotel.*

PLANNING CONSIDERATIONS

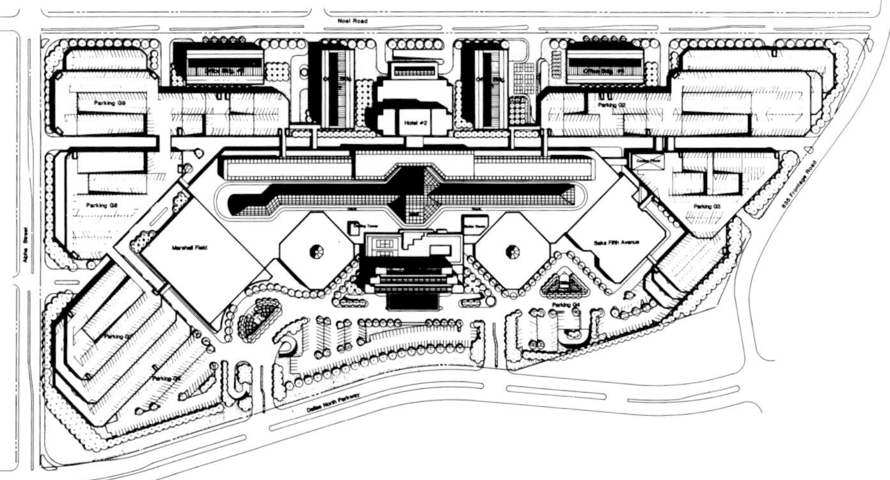

Galleria, Dallas, Texas. *The centerpiece and formalized entrance to Dallas's 43-acre (17-hectare) Galleria, the 440-room Westin Hotel Galleria offers complete meeting and entertainment facilities for local and international travelers, including four restaurants and two ballrooms accommodating groups of 1500. Much like its earlier counterpart at Houston's Galleria, the hotel structure is architecturally integrated with the adjoining 200-shop mall and features extensive recreation amenities including a jogging track and ice-skating rink.*

Started during the "shopping mall culture" of the 60s, the public's infatuation with malls even outstripped their love for hotels. Therefore it was natural for both functions to be wedded in the 70s in such pioneer developments as the Houston Galleria, where the hotels supplied potential shoppers while the malls provided hotel guests with a wealth of extra amenities. Also, business offices in the Galleria attracted corporate travelers, while the entertainment and dining opportunities within the mall drew much-desired weekend guests. Conventioneers and executives brought their families on business trips to enjoy the Galleria's array of shops and recreational facilities, while many tourists were drawn to the hotel-in-mall concept, providing instant activity for their vacations.

Other complementary advantages of such mixed-use developments include: (1) combined health clubs for hotel guests and community members, with athletic facilities often located on the mall's roof; (2) the combined comfort and security of an enclosed mall; and (3) the combined efficiency of a central energy plant serving the entire complex. Hotels have therefore been added by many regional mall developers where there is sufficient business demand in the area to support them.

Since the peak business hours of shopping malls and hotels overlap, separate additional parking is needed to accommodate both functions. A specific parking area should be set aside for hotel use to ensure space for its guests. With underground garages, a separate shuttle elevator between the garage and the lobby is preferable for security purposes, rather than extending the central elevator bank directly to the garage levels. To simplify traffic, the service entrances should be combined for all facilities in the complex and located underground on tight urban sites.

While the cost per square foot of office buildings, shopping centers, apartments, and hotels varies within 15 percent, the financial returns on a square-foot basis are often 25 percent higher for offices and malls than for apartments or hotels. Yet the latter are considered safer long-term investments, because they are less subject to rental market fluctuations. Also, hotels often act as catalysts, promoting other more lucrative surrounding development, and are as essential as residences for a balanced community. For this reason, incentives are often provided for developers to include hotels and apartments in their complexes. As well as tax abatement, communities have considered offering zoning bonuses of added office space in return for including more hotel rooms and residential units in a mixed-use or planned community development.

As much as a hotel's success is based on the right mix of facilities, a complex's viability hinges on the *optimum combination of uses* it offers. How many hotels and the type and extent of other uses can be gleaned from market and feasibility data. Such analysis permits a more rational evaluation of *overall* profitability rather than of each component by itself. For example, while the hotel has a lower rate of return than the office building, its presence increases the desirability of the offices and their rental rate, raising the *average* rate of return for the total complex. Mixed-use investments are also considered safer and more insulated against market fluctuations of any one component. For example, during a period of temporary oversupply and decline in office rentals, the development's shopping revenues and hotel rates can be maintained or even increased, thereby continuing to carry the total project.

After the facilities programming, the choice of *design concept*, whether vertical, horizontal, atrium-oriented, anchored by department stores or hotels, or tied in with adjacent complexes and transit facilities, is influenced by specific site parameters, opportunities, and a sensitivity analysis of the community. Typically, boldness, determination, and imagination by a dedicated group of developers and community leaders are needed to spearhead projects of such size and complexity, requiring extensive government and citizens' approvals, huge capital commitments, and a decade of planning and construction. In high-density urban areas, even assembling a few acres well served by rapid transit and in the path of commercial growth is often a miraculous accomplishment.

RIGHT

The Crescent, Dallas, Texas. *Combining three office towers of 1.25 million square feet (116,130 square meters), a retail mall, and a 228-room hotel on a 10-acre (4-hectare) site in Dallas' revitalized Oak Lawn area, The Crescent complex links the older downtown to the new arts district and its museum and symphony hall. Recalling the French influence in Texas architecture of the late 1800s, mansard roofs, rusticated stonework, and wrought-iron porticos mark this as one of the postmodern movement's strongest statements and the first applied to a major hotel–office complex.*

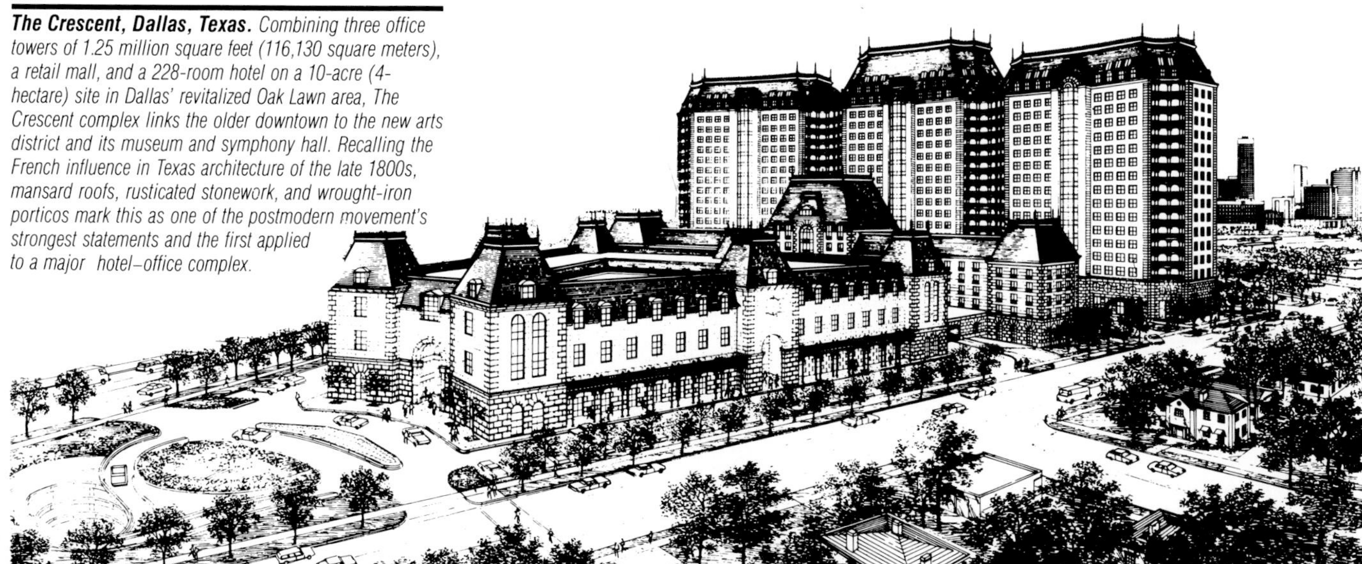

ABOVE

Cityplace, Dallas, Texas. *Cityplace near Dallas is planned as a self-contained community providing for the development of all types of uses including hotels.*

RIGHT

Koll Center, Irvine, California. *Located on a 46-acre (19-hectare) tract in the heart of Irvine's fast-growing business and financial community midway between Los Angeles and San Diego, the Koll Center Irvine comprises 1.3 million square feet (120,775 square meters) of highrise offices as well as the 500-room Irvine Marriott Hotel and other restaurants and amenities. Serving the complex's business occupants, the hotel includes 20,000 square feet (1858 square meters) of conference and meeting space as well as two restaurants, a lounge, lobby and poolside bars, and indoor-outdoor health club with extensive plazas, landscaping, and water features to unite its diverse elements. A second similar project, Koll Center Newport, has also been developed in the nearby Newport Beach/Irvine area featuring a Hyatt Regency Hotel surrounded by an office park with extensive on-site recreational amenities.*

Mixed-use complexes

The site of Boston's Copley Place was a blighted tangle of intersecting turnpikes, a gaping, unattractive void in the urban fabric. Based entirely on unique leased air rights above railway lines and Turnpike Authority cloverleafs, the design was subjected to more than 50 citizens' review hearings, with over 30 civic and neighborhood associations participating. The massing was changed and housing added at the request of the community, even though the project displaced no existing residences. But such democratic processes resulted in the neighborhood being pleased and in a better urban design.

In addition to covering over the expressways, the design's stepped massing, low along Copley Square and approaching the scale of the Prudential Building at its other extreme, was integrated well with its surroundings. The "fortress" syndrome of other blank-walled, raised-plaza complexes was avoided by large glassed openings at the street level, further enlivened by shops, street landscaping, pedestrian bridges, and escalators. The elegance of the hotel lobbies, with their fine marble finishes carried throughout the shopping areas between the two hotels, as well as the mall's mix of high-fashion boutiques, have conferred a "classy" ambience on Copley Place.

Its prime competitor, Lafayette Place, a "vertical" complex located in the heart of Boston's crowded shopping district has done much to help the city upgrade a portion of its downtown area, which borders on a porno area called the "combat zone." Attached to a new pedestrian mall and connected to its surrounding department stores, the complex has added almost twice as many stores as Copley Place, centering around an outdoor public plaza in which fashion shows, concerts, art exhibits, and festivals are routinely scheduled.

The hotel's tower as originally conceived was about 40 stories high with all single-loaded corridors surrounding its triangular

ABOVE

Copley Place, Boston, Massachusetts. *By covering over a blighted tangle of expressways, this hotel/office/shopping complex restored the urban fabric of Boston's Back Bay.*

RIGHT

Lafayette Place, Boston, Massachusetts. *In the center of Boston's downtown retail district, the $140 million Lafayette Place complex combines 300,000 square feet (27,870 square meters) of retail and restaurant space on three levels with an elegant 21-story hotel surrounding a public open-air plaza as its focal point, featuring year-round special entertainment events, and a 1055-car garage. Complementing New England's largest shopping center, the hotel contains two restaurants and lounges as well as extensive conference, ballroom, and health club facilities.*

atrium, but the height was eventually reduced to 21 stories for greater efficiency and viability, with a partial double-loaded wing leading into the atrium. Both the Copley and Lafayette complexes complement each other well by serving different income levels and sections of the city, while continuing Boston's tradition of renewal through development of advanced hotel types.

Planned community developments

Across a narrow channel from downtown Tampa, Florida, Harbour Island, a community of 4500 residences, 1,200,000 square feet (111,484 square meters) of shopping and office space, and three hotel conference centers, has been planned over a 10-year period. By the transformation of barren land, dredged from Tampa Bay in the 19th century, into landscaped plazas, waterwalks, marinas, and an outdoor amphitheater, the new community, connected to Tampa by bridges and a monorail, provides a much-needed focal point for the nation's third fastest growing city.

The mix of facilities and their esthetic qualities were subject to one of the most thorough environmental and marketing studies ever undertaken, involving over 20 separate consultants (see the environmental checklist in the Appendix) as well as interviews and polls of local groups on their preferred style of design. As a result, the architecture relates in scale to the existing downtown buildings, but projects old world charm through the use of brick, copper roofs, and stone-paved plazas, design components common in the Tampa area. The small shops and restaurants featuring varied cuisine and outdoor dining with water views will maintain a relaxing festival atmosphere for residents and visitors, providing an ideal setting for the tourist, business, and conference hotels included in the development.

Harbour Island, Tampa, Florida. *Sited on a 178-acre (72-hectare) island in Florida's Tampa Bay, the Harbour Island development, master planned for 14,000 residents, includes a 9-story, 210,000-square-foot (19,510-square-meter) office building, a 100,000-square-foot (9290-square-meter) retail complex, and a 300-room hotel in the first phase. Condominiums, a conference center, a 500-room hotel, and over a million square feet (92,903 square meters) of office space will follow in the second phase. All building elements will be tied together with extensive plazas, water features, bridges, and an elevated people-mover system, as well as entertainment and recreation amenities along the island's natural shoreline. As one of the fastest-growing cities in the United States, Tampa will, in the next three years, add 50 percent to its retail and office space and more than double its hotel and convention facilities. As a large, planned complex close to the downtown area, the Harbour Island development will create a much-needed urban focus for the now sprawling Tampa community.*

The medical hotel complex

The advent of advanced medical services at the beginning of the century was accompanied by such mixed-use developments as the Kahler Hotel, built in 1907, as an extension of the Mayo Clinic in Rochester, Minnesota. Part convalescent hotel and hospital unit, it contained an upper-floor surgical and obstetrical suite and nursing school. More elaborate examples were developed through the 20s, culminating in another combined 600-bed structure including a transient hotel, convalescent unit, and hospital adjoining the clinic.

While such mixed-use medical hotels continued through the 40s, this unique concept declined in the post-war era primarily due to government-subsidized hospital development. Today's more recent major medical hotels—such as the 450-room Cleveland Clinic Foundation's Clinic Inn; the 16-story Queeny Tower at St. Louis, Missouri's Barnes Hospital, containing three floors of guestrooms and a restaurant, bar, and pool atop the hospital; and the 400-room Houston Marriott at the Texas Medical Center—cater largely to patients under examination and are specially equipped to provide nursing service, preexam preparation, and diet meals.

Representing the return of a similar concept, the new Wyndham Hotel at Travis Centre in Houston, Texas, has been combined with a medical office building. Moreover, with medical clinics expanding their aerobic activities, including cardiovascular and other special exercising programs requiring longer client visits and closer ties to hotels for guest convenience, renewed interest in hospital-related hotel complexes has emerged. For example, the Scripps Clinic in San Diego is planning a new competition-designed 50,000-square-feet (4645-square-meter) Aerobic Center, connected to a Sheraton Hotel, on a site designated by the city. Suite hotels, connected by bridges to medical centers, are also being planned today for the convenience of patients preferring to remain with their families during periods of prolonged examination and treatment.

Ecumed Orlando, Florida. *Planned as an international center for the medical field, Ecumed in Florida contains extensive office and convention space as well as hotel rooms.*

Moscow World Trade Center, Moscow, U.S.S.R. *The Moscow World Trade Center was developed to handle the Union of Soviet Socialist Republics' surge of international trade and foreign business visitors in the late 1970s. Overlooking the Moscow River, the complex is fully integrated for those who desire to live and work there. In addition to its 600-room international hotel, it includes a special residential hotel that at 625 units is the largest of its kind. Tied to the two hotels by a 9-story landscaped atrium are 325,000 square feet (30,195 square meters) of office space, a meeting and convention center, theater, shopping and recreation facilities, restaurants, and a computer center.*

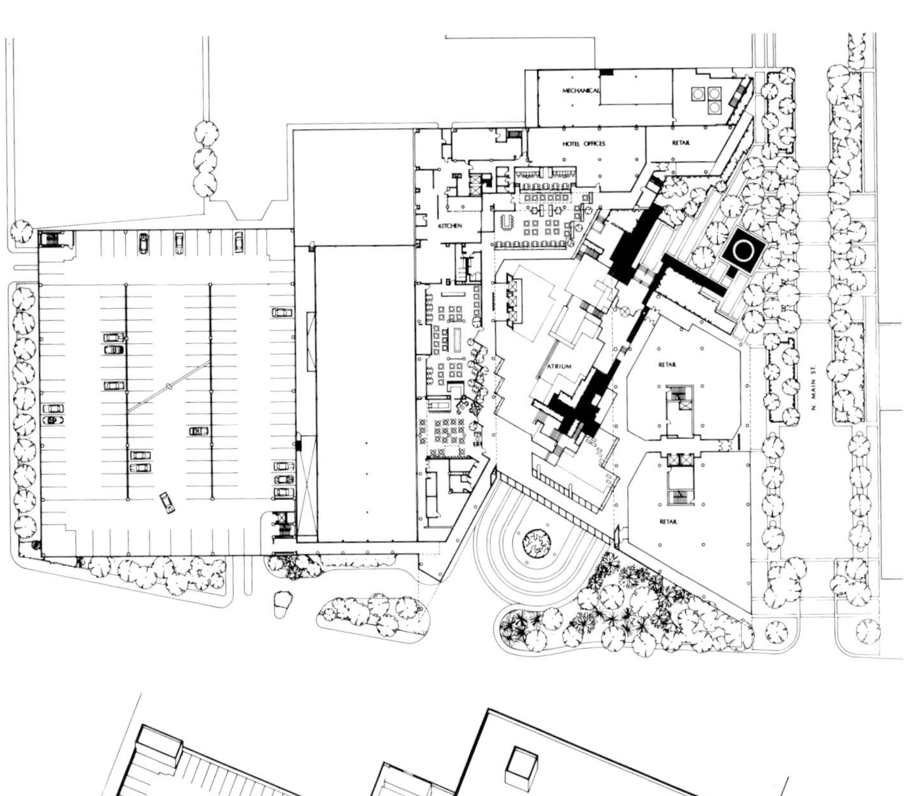

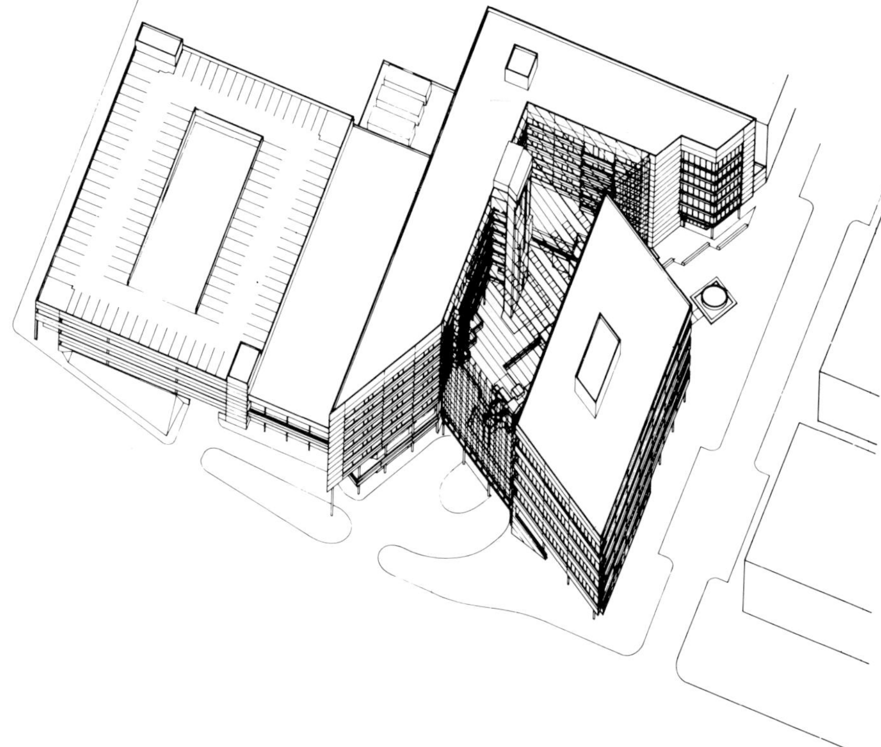

DESIGN CONSIDERATIONS

To reinforce the complex's overall theme, hotel lobbies should be treated compatibly as extensions of their connecting malls and atriums. Attracting more visitors than conventional hotels and requiring greater circulation space to serve their increased number of boutiques and bar/lounge capacities, lobbies should be 20 percent larger than those of other downtown hotels with comparable guestroom capacity. Hotel restaurants and lounges should have entrances directly on the mall where possible, with open cafes on the center's atriums. Their restaurant and bar seating should be 30 percent more than in conventional downtown or suburban hotels, reflecting the greater built-in demand for lunch and dinner, drawing from the center's retail, entertainment, and office areas.

While health clubs should be designed to attract members from the surrounding office and residential community, they must be connected directly to the hotel for the convenience of guests. To exploit opportunities for revenue created by the number of shoppers in the complex, lobby retail shops should preferably be 100 percent greater than in other downtown or suburban hotels. But if lack of space dictates that no retail space can be provided in the hotel, the mall can adequately serve guest convenience shopping.

In vertical complexes, hotel lobbies should ideally be located at the ground floor, rather than on an upper level, to better identify the entrance and create a more welcome feeling for the guest at the street level as well as to efficiently handle registration and baggage. But where lack of ground-floor space necessitates upper-floor "sky lobbies," a well-defined street entrance-level lobby with a concierge desk, adequate shuttle elevators and escalator service, and a grander and more comfortable upper lobby become essential.

Greenville Commons, Greenville, South Carolina. *The mixed-use office, hotel, and parking structure is designed around an 8-story skylit atrium. The double-loaded corridors of the Hyatt Regency Hotel provide a highly efficient guestroom floor plan, while the public facilities are designed in an open plan with the lounges and restaurants sharing the excitement of the atrium space.*

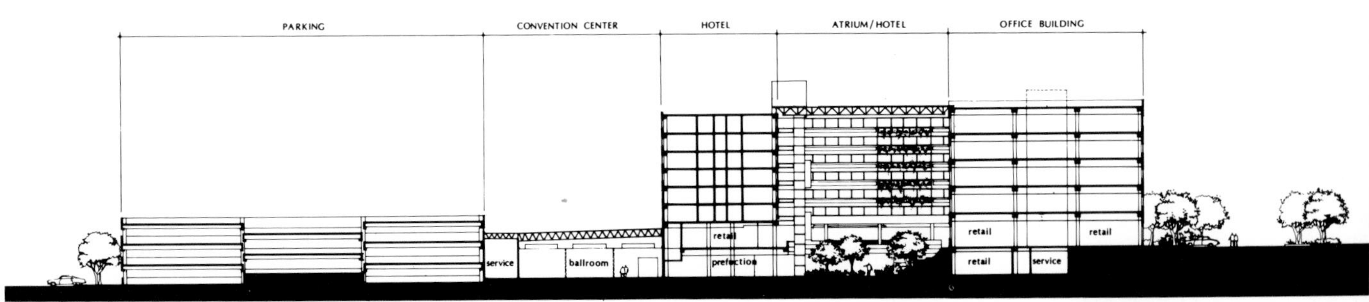

TRENDS

Hotel/shopping malls will continue to proliferate, growing into such mega-complexes as the Copley Place–Prudential Center in Boston and the Millender–Renaissance Center in Detroit. Linked by pedestrian bridges, skyways, and monorails to other business centers and tourist attractions, including seaport districts and historic sites, some city areas are being reshaped in the image of Norman Bel Geddes' once visionary Futurama.

Improved hotel design will continue to be stimulated by planned environments such as Harbour Island, Irvine, and Las Colinas. Due to overcongestion, existing city growth will stabilize, with more development being channeled to new satellite communities, particularly in overpopulated Asian, African, and Latin American regions. New hotels will increasingly be associated with both mixed-use renewal complexes and totally planned communities serving new population growth. Through such projects, hotels will be better positioned to serve the specific needs of the medical center, the commercial and office complex, and the planned residential community.

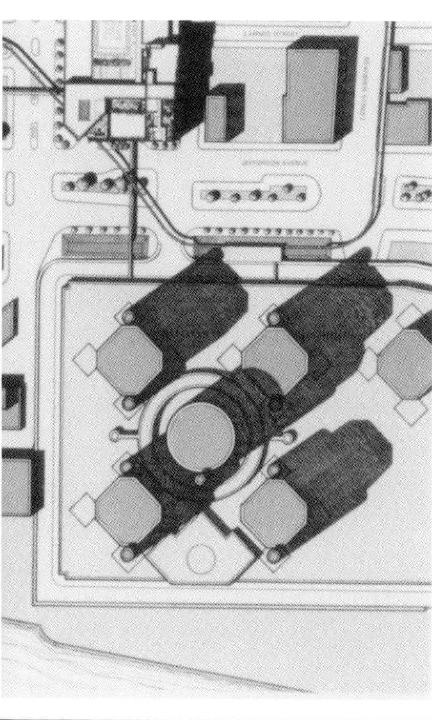

Renaissance Center and Millender Center, Detroit, Michigan. *The two massive mixed-use complexes are sited on adjoining parcels in the heart of Detroit. The 1970s Renaissance Center (right in site plan) combines a 1400-room Westin Hotel, the center element, with over 3 million square feet (280,000 square meters) of office and commercial space in the four lower towers and podium. The two-square-block Millender Center adds a 20-story, 260-room Omni/Dunfey hotel, as well as apartment, office, and commercial space, linked together with skyways and a monorail system to the downtown areas.*

13 THE CASINO HOTEL

"Stage extravaganzas"

entices MGM Grand Hotel in Reno, Nevada

Due to gaming revenues, the casino hotel can offer deluxe accommodations at more competitive rates than other hotels, thereby attracting not only gaming customers but many other types of guests as well. In fact, their elaborate entertainment and resort facilities act as a magnet for international tourists and conventions. This trend became evident in Las Vegas in the 1950s, where the casino hotel was first developed, and later was used to promote tourist travel in the Caribbean. Gaming in hotels has since spread to several countries including one small African nation whose economy is supported almost entirely by its casino hotel revenues.

Most European-style casinos, from London to Deauville, France, Nairobi, Kenya, to Marrakesh, Morocco, and Monaco to the island of Macau off Hong Kong, were traditionally separated from hotels. While the Broadmoor in Colorado Springs, Colorado, briefly experimented with gaming at the turn of the century, it wasn't until 1947 that the first successful casino hotel, the Flamingo, was built in Las Vegas. Its owner was reputed to be a notorious underworld figure. From this dubious start gaming eventually developed into one of the most profitable segments of the U.S. hotel industry. Tighter government supervision along with the entry of major hotel companies into the field eventually proved cleansing to the gaming industry, with Holiday Inns emerging in the 80s as the worldwide leader.

Some of the established hotel companies, feeling increasing competition from casino hotels in certain regions, decided they had better enter the gaming field or perish, while others continued to remain aloof or wait for the right opportunities. Holiday Inns, represented by its subsidiary, Harrah's, in all four major gaming areas in the United States—Reno, Lake Tahoe, and Las Vegas in Nevada, and Atlantic City, New Jersey—and Hilton Hotels and Ramada Inn are among those diversified hotel chains that now depend on their gaming divisions for a major share of profits as well as for investment funds to help develop other nongaming hotels. While companies such as Resorts International, Caesar's, and Golden Nugget specialize in gaming, they are planning more conventional hotels to help promote package tours for their casino hotels. Continuing such trends toward integrating the gaming and hotel industries, Marriott and Sheraton, traditionally reticent about gaming in the United States, have expressed interest in casino hotels overseas, while Inter-Continental, which has not yet developed casino hotels in the United States, operates several in Africa.

Various African and South American countries encourage gaming to attract international tourists, while casino hotels in a dozen Caribbean islands from Antigua to Guadaloupe cater to the growing U.S. market. Like Las Vegas in the 50s, Atlantic City in the 80s has developed approximately three new casino hotels a year. This impressive array of luxury hotels, condominiums, and related shopping and entertainment features has, not surprisingly, created worldwide attention. Where and when new gaming areas will emerge is unpredictable. But in appropriate locations, casino hotel districts continue to generate considerable tourist travel and related economic growth. (For a selected listing see the Appendix.)

PLANNING CONSIDERATIONS

As demonstrated by Atlantic City's example, casino hotels can be used to create opportunities for urban revitalization of economically depressed areas. To assure more diversified economic growth and encourage related types of tourist development, only deluxe casino hotels with at least 500 rooms were permitted as a means of attracting family vacation and convention travelers in addition to gaming guests. Other strict regulations enforced on owners and operators were designed to ensure that the casino hotels would be free of underworld elements.

But there were other inherent dangers in too rapid, haphazard growth. Not fully anticipated or addressed in Atlantic City were the problems of congestion and inflationary pressures seriously affecting local residents due to the sudden concentration of casino hotels. With potential gaming profits so great, cooperation with owners should be possible on future developments to help fund improvements needed by the city to absorb the new construction. Such methods have been used in cities like San Francisco where downtown hotels contributed to the rehabilitation of neighborhoods in return for special zoning approvals. As another example, in Aruba, a casino license was granted in return for the owner's agreeing to add a recreation park as part of the casino hotel for the use of both local residents and tourists.

To disperse too dense development and provide a choice of different types of resort environments, Atlantic City wisely encouraged two distinct casino hotel districts: the traditional "glittery" boardwalk zone and a new outlying marina area. While the second area is developing its resort character, most boardwalk hotels while successful have failed to date to revive the city's original visual fabric and live frontage concept. Instead of stepping their massive towers back and lining the boardwalk with retail and entertainment areas, they have, unfortunately, turned solid walls on this historic opportunity.

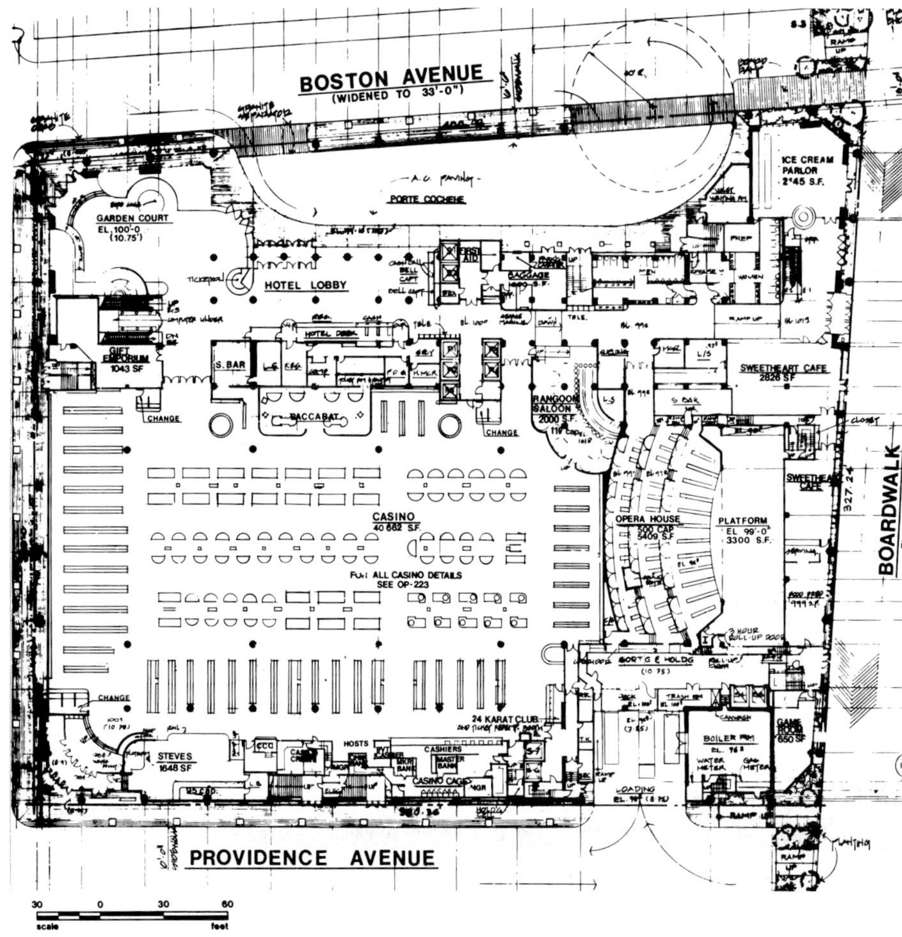

OPPOSITE PAGE AND ABOVE

Golden Nugget, Atlantic City, New Jersey. *With its casino winning $263 million in one year and its earnings approaching $14 per square foot of area per day, the $160 million Golden Nugget ranks as the most successful of all hotel casinos, attracting the most affluent gaming public. While offering the opulent decor pictured here in lavish complimentary suites and restaurants to lure its high-rollers, the hotel also serves as a model of back-of-house efficiency with its four restaurants arranged so that all can be serviced by a single central kitchen. (See also page 9 in Color Portfolio.)*

Another important planning consideration is the substantial bus volume caused by daily tour groups, which are a vital part of the casino hotel's business. To solve this, special intracity traffic control systems and bus marshaling yards are run jointly by the city and the hotels. Bus schedules are filed daily by each hotel so buses' arrival, stacking, waiting, and holding patterns can be centrally coordinated by the city. Some hotels such as the Golden Nugget have even set up their own bus companies to better serve their needs while earning additional revenue from "hauling guests to the blackjack table."

A typical casino hotel, with a gaming area of 25,000 square feet (2320 square meters), requires an entrance drive with curb dropoff space to accommodate a minimum of five tour buses, or a ratio of one bus per 5,000 square feet (465 square meters) of gaming area. The typical one-day tour group arrives late in the morning for a six-hour stay. A special buffet dining room must be provided to cater a meal for such groups, and the dining space must be convenient to the gaming area. If on a different level, it must be serviced by escalator, since quick and efficient flow assures maximum time at the gaming tables.

European-style hotel casinos are often semidetached or free-standing buildings, such as the Inter-Continentals in Kinshossa, Zaire, and Lusaka, Zambia, and are connected to the hotel by covered walkways. This is in accordance with local custom and because certain government institutions funding hotels prohibit casinos inside the hotel structure. Some governments that promote casino hotels to attract tourists and provide local employment in the casinos prohibit or limit play by their own citizens. In Ecuador, for example, separate entrances must be provided for local residents to control and limit their visits.

Since most guests are drawn by the *fantasy* of gaming, they expect the casinos to have glittering interior designs and symbols of fantasy on the exterior. Huge, often flashing building signs and extravagant, brightly lit entrance canopies are the rule. Their design challenges the imagination. In one design proposal for Harrah's in Atlantic City, for example, the Cambridge Seven created the illusion of a "waterfall of light" cascading over the entire building facade instead of signage.

DESIGN CONSIDERATIONS

Since many in-hotel amenities are designed primarily to promote the gaming operation, casino hotels must provide a much higher proportion of nonrevenue-producing space than any other type of hotel. This includes elaborate "high-roller" suites furnished free to large-stake players, "star" suites maintained for "big name" attractions entertaining at the hotel, and "hold" tables permanently reserved in restaurants for quick service to high-rollers so they can spend maximum time on the gaming floor. For example, the main complimentary suite at Harrah's boardwalk casino contains 2400 square feet (223 square meters), including a living room with grand piano, library, two bedrooms, and a private elevator. The extent of luxurious, complimentary accommodations depends on the level of gaming customers each casino hotel attracts. This ranges from the Golden Nugget in Atlantic City that draws many higher-rollers to the Holiday Inn Riverboat in Las Vegas that is more geared to the moderate gaming guest.

But in spite of their architectural imagery as glittering, glitzy Xanadus essential to attract high-rollers, the building plans are a model of functional efficiency designed to cut costs behind the scenes. For example, the Golden Nugget, the most luxurious hotel in

ABOVE

Proposal for Harrah's North Boardwalk site in Atlantic City, New Jersey. *An early design study for Harrah's Hotel and Casino on a North Boardwalk site, with shops and entertainment along the Boardwalk frontage and stepped tower set back from the beach, recalled the city's traditional resort fabric.*

LEFT

Harrah's at Trump Plaza, Atlantic City, New Jersey. *The angular-shaped, 39-story Harrah's at Trump Plaza ensures ocean views for its guestrooms, while its 7-story podium contains an entrance atrium displaying Harrah's priceless antique auto collection. Adjacent to the convention center, the boardwalk hotel is connected by escalators to the 60,000-square-foot (5575-square-meter) casino on the third level, housing 123 gaming tables and 1734 slot machines. With 4000 on staff, the complex's 1.5 million square feet (139,355 square meters) include seven restaurants, a 750-seat showroom, extensive convention and meeting space, and a health club with indoor swimming and outdoor tennis. Skywalks are planned to the adjoining Convention Center and nearby transit hub.* *(See also page 8 in Color Portfolio.)*

Atlantic City, is so planned that only one kitchen serves all four restaurants, a model of efficiency for any hotel.

The hotel casino

No other type of building contains a greater amount of unrecorded currency than a large casino hotel. Two million dollars in cash plus $6 million in negotiable chips is not uncommon. This influences various aspects of the design. A maximum security "money path" must be provided to and from the cashier's "cage" on the gaming floor. All cash and chips from the gaming tables are deposited at the cage, and access to the cage is protected by a "man-trap" vestibule. Due to the complexity of its design and security provisions, a single cage is generally preferred regardless of the size of the gaming floor. Coins from the slot machines are transported by electric carts. For this reason, floors must be designed for 300-pound (136-kilogram) live load, or with three times the strength of normal public assembly spaces.

The money path leads from the cage to "hard and soft count rooms." Machines are used for counting, except in some areas such as Atlantic City, where soft currency is required to be counted manually on transparent lucite tables under TV surveillance. The money then proceeds to a special "money truck loading dock." Since this is usually on another level, a separate "money" elevator must be provided with a 5,000-pound (2270-kilogram) load capacity, observed by TV surveillance cameras and operated from the cage.

No other building contains security monitoring systems equal to a casino. Called the "live peek" in Atlantic City and the "eye in the sky" in Las Vegas, the system of pan-and-tilt cameras concealed by glazed ceiling bubbles is monitored by security guards in special screening rooms. It also records the gaming action at each table on time-stamped video tape. Films can be closely reexamined if any complaints or other suspicions of cheating arise. The tables are also watched directly by security guards on catwalks provided above one-way mirror-glass ceilings. In addition, the layout of the gaming tables is carefully designed to facilitate surveillance of the dealers and players by nonuniformed security guards, or "floaters," generally positioned at the ends of each line of tables. Smaller European-style casino hotels are often less security conscious, omitting TV surveillance and preferring a more casual arrangement of tables rather than the straight-line layout favored by American-style gaming operators for ease of dealer and player surveillance. Gaming tables in large casinos are generally laid out in groups of up to 12, with each group centered about a supervisor, or "pit boss."

Overall security is usually maintained jointly by a government agency and the management, with control offices located at the cage and overhead TV monitor station. Since they have authority to detain suspects, a security cell must be provided on the premises. Dealers are generally on 40-minute shifts and must be provided with men's and women's lounges, dressing facilities, and a self-contained private dining room adjacent to the gaming area.

The number and type of games varies with the location. But in an American hotel casino, a ratio of about five black jack tables to each roulette and craps table is average. One baccarat and one high-stakes black jack table should be provided, with others added at a ratio of about 1 for every 50 other gaming tables. While black jack and roulette tables may be combined in any grouping, the other game tables are located in separate groups. In addition, separate areas are required for one big six wheel-type game, with others added at a ratio of about 1 for every 120 gaming tables. Based on the above ratios, the area required for the gaming floor will average approximately 250 square feet (23.2 square meters) per table.

Hotel casinos planned with more widely spaced table layouts have with few exceptions proven less inviting to gaming customers who generally prefer a more crowded atmosphere. As a rule, not only is it more pleasing to the guest to keep the space tight but it also saves area and construction cost while increasing the "win-per-square-foot ratio," a significant measure of a casino hotel's success. (For example, the most successful hotel casinos win close to $14 per square foot per day.)

In European-style hotel casinos the ratio of types of games changes, with the number of roulette and baccarat tables generally doubling and craps games cut by half. In some areas such as Las Vegas, additional space must also be provided for poker tables, keno, bingo, and sports book betting operations.

Since some guests prefer to play slot machines alongside the gaming floor and others prefer them in separate areas, they are usually located about evenly in both places. A coin cashier's cage is required for about every 50 machines. Slot machine areas should have low ceilings not exceeding 10 feet (3 meters) to accentuate the sound of coins when the machines hit, whereas the gaming table area may have higher ceilings of 15 to 20 feet (4.6 to 6 meters) depending on the room size and proportion. Carousels with circular groups of slot machines are increasingly popular, occupying about 20 square feet (1.9 square meters) per machine as opposed to 10 square feet (1.9 square meters) for conventional lineal layouts.

Amenities and entertainment facilities

Bar/lounges should be integrated directly with the gaming floor to enhance the ambience of both areas and stimulate business from one to the other. This also simplifies bar service to the gaming tables. Restaurants should also be convenient to the gaming area and, if on a different level, accessible by escalator, with good visibility from the gaming and entrance lobbies. Cafes and buffet dining areas should be open to the main public spaces, with entrances to the signature and specialty restaurants directly on the main lobbies and circulation concourses. Elaborate dinner shows and famous entertainers are expected in large-scale casino hotels. But due to the high cost of entertainers, major showrooms are usually impractical for small- or medium-size casino hotels. Those with gaming areas under 10,000 square feet (929 square meters) generally provide cabaret entertainment lounges rather than more costly dinner showrooms.

Convention facilities

A New York hotelier's nightmare would be that the Atlantic City complex of casino hotels becomes such a powerful magnet it begins to draw away New York's convention business. Because casino hotel districts become vacation spots and entertainment centers with near-by air service, they make ideal convention centers. Usually clustered together, they are convenient for large groups spilling over into two or more hotels. With the addition of more new casino hotels and increased meeting and exhibit capacity, the "casino capital" of the East Coast may also become a "convention capital" of America.

Guestrooms

Casino hotel rooms are larger and more luxuriously furnished than those in most suburban or downtown hotels with typical clear room dimensions ranging from 13′ × 18′ (4 × 5.5 m) to 14.5′ × 20′ (4.4 × 6.1 m). This reflects both the ability of the hotel to offer greater luxury through the support of gaming revenues and the effort to attract resort and convention business as well as the more affluent gaming guest. In-room security vaults should be provided in casino hotels, although safe deposit boxes will also be required at the hotel cashier's counter at a ratio of about one for every three guestrooms.

TRENDS

Casino hotels will increase in size to 1500 rooms to provide greater efficiency and attract larger convention groups. Meeting space of 50,000 square feet (4645 square meters) will be common, with gaming areas exceeding that. Recreation facilities will be further expanded to cater to the resort and convention business.

In-room electronic gaming will be developed and programmed into the guestrooms via closed circuit TV and potential two-way TV gaming shows may be channeled into other noncasino hotels. Gaming tournaments by expert players will draw live audiences, furthering expansion of casino hotels.

To reduce travel time and relieve urban congestion, both helicopter and hydrofoil commuter systems to Atlantic City will be developed, using people-movers from transfer terminals to casino hotel and convention areas. Most gaming hotels will develop "feeder hotels" in major cities to promote package tours to New York/Atlantic City or San Francisco/Lake Tahoe, thereby completing the merger of the gaming and hotel fields.

Harrah's Marina Hotel Casino, Atlantic City, New Jersey. *In addition to its 46,000-square-foot (4275-square-meter) casino, Harrah's boasts convention and meeting spaces, a theater, varied restaurants, lounges and shops, and a children's and teen center all linked together by a 3-story, space-framed, skylit atrium. Differing from Las Vegas and more in keeping with Atlantic City's traditions, the design emphasizes expansive views of the bay and an on-site lagoon seen from the hotel's public spaces and its 12-story guestroom tower.*

LEGEND OF SPACES

NUMBER	AREA	SPACE
102	80	BELLMAN
103	472	FRONT DESK
104	72	VAULT
105	374	BAGGAGE ROOM
106	88	RECEIVING OFFICE
106-A	720	RECEIVING
106-B	97	ELEVATOR EQUIPMENT
107	246	TIMEKEEPER
108	253	RESERVATIONS
109	121	CASHIER WORK AREA
110	230	MAIL AND INFORMATION
111	85	FRONT OFFICE MANAGER
112	660	TRASH HANDLING
113	5536	COFFEE SHOP
114	1580	KITCHEN
115	255	WOMEN'S TOILET
116	238	MEN'S TOILET
117	392	STAGE STORAGE
118	128	BAR STORAGE
119	160	TICKET OFFICE
120	624	STAGE SHOP
121	11171	SHOW LOUNGE
122	142	SERVICE BAR
123	330	GREEN ROOM
124	275	STAGE MANAGER OFFICE
125	4085	FOOD BAZAAR
126	3700	SHOPS
127	240	AIRLINE/RENTAL AGENTS
128	264	TELEPHONES
129	3377	LOBBY LOUNGE/BAR
130	7350	CONCOURSE (25% = 1837)
131	710	MEN'S TOILET
132	680	WOMEN'S TOILET
133	45	JANITOR
134	400	BAND PLATFORM
135	2421	BAR
135-A	80	ICE
135-B	395	SERVICE BAR
136	42662	CASINO
137	1575	BAR
138	98	BAR STORAGE
139	1122	SLOT REPAIR
140	260	SERVICE BAR
141		SHIFT MANAGER
142	95	STATE EMPLOYEE
143	313	SERVICE BAR & STORAGE
144	121	CAGE MANAGER
145	25	TOILET
146	1432	CREDIT OFFICE
147	556	SOFT COUNT
148	25	TOILET
149	70	VAULT
150	88	EMPLOYEES BANK
151	88	MAIN BANK
152	100	SECURITY
153	1063	HARD COUNT
154	50	STORAGE
◯		BAR CLASSIFICATION

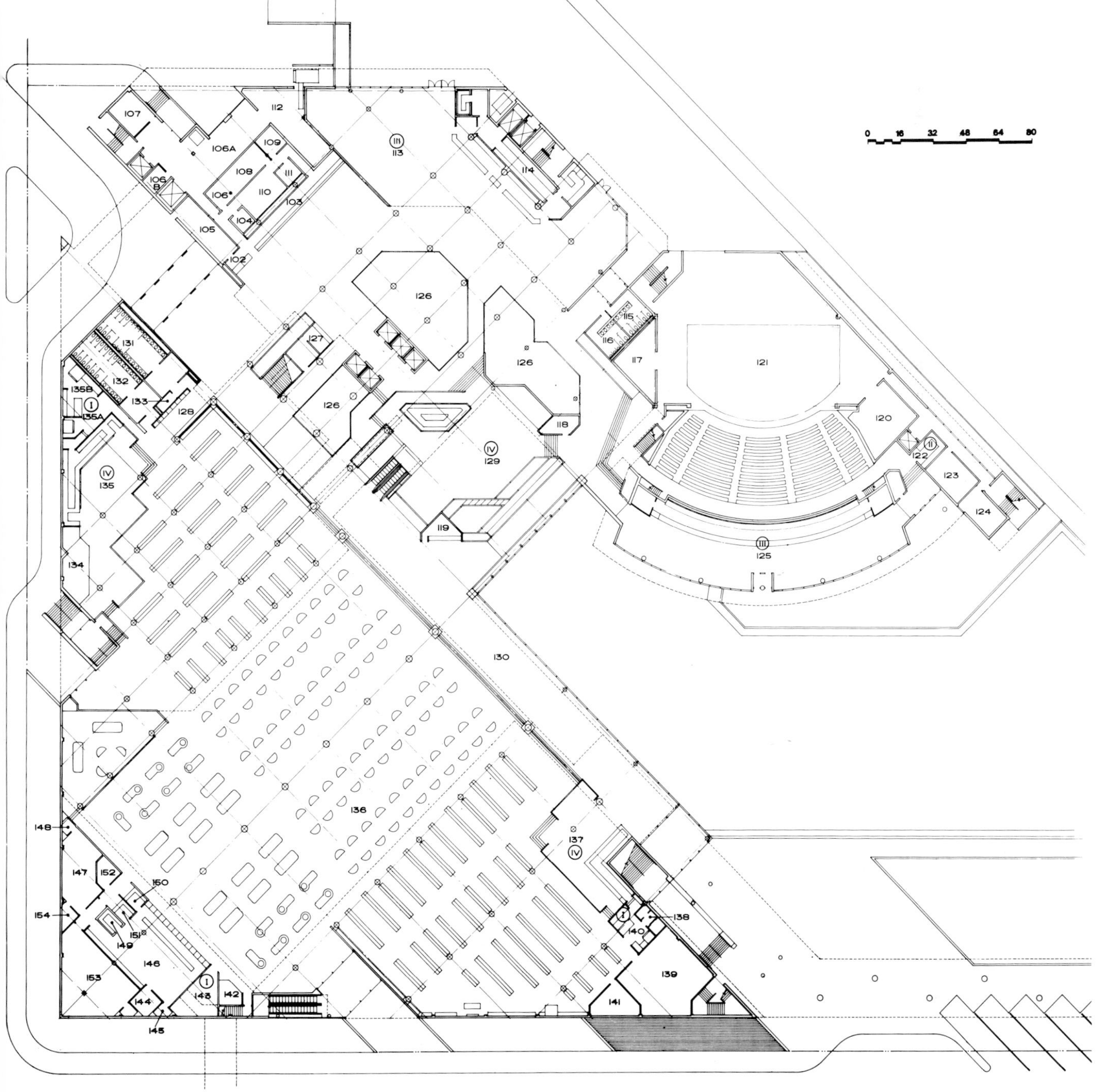

Part 2
DESIGN GUIDE

Hotels are a particularly complex and difficult building type. The Design Guide will focus on the program, planning, and design issues critical to a successful hotel and, in addition, will highlight the types of operational and financial decisions that affect and influence the architectural and interior design. In the following chapter, the guide includes a discussion of the many aspects of the predesign documentation that are not limited to space requirements. Later chapters cover planning standards for guestroom, public, administration, and back-of-house areas, as well as a discussion of construction and special building systems important in hotel properties.

14 FACILITIES PROGRAMMING

"If one is to put a hotel in an overbuilt area, he must have a different mousetrap — either a highly systemized, economy-level project, or the very finest and most luxurious one."

Dale Keller

The programming phase of hotel development is especially important because of the highly competitive nature of the hotel business. The predesign documentation for a new project or for a major expansion or repositioning of a hotel must fully describe and define both the space needs and the operational requirements. Without such information, the architect and design consultants are not able to fine tune standard rule of thumb numbers or to create a unique hotel for a precise market. Much of this documentation is required to obtain a lender's package to finance hotel.

Complete facilities programming is much more than a list of the space requirements; it must also address a variety of needs: location, market demand, competition, quality level, operational features, restaurant concepts, staffing, budget, and so forth. Feasibility consultants generally recommend a mix of certain facilities, but the hotel management company, working with the owner and architect, develop the final program. For hotels of 200 rooms and more or for those aimed at special markets, the market and program material shown on opposite page are needed.

ANALYZING PROJECT FEASIBILITY

A first step in the development of a new or expanded hotel is the preparation of a market study and financial projections. The first part analyzes the demand for lodging within particular market segments and compares these with the existing supply of hotel facilities. The projections forecast revenues and operating expenses for five or more years, based on estimates of inflation and competition. See Chapter 22 for more on feasibility.

At many properties, particular opportunities exist for attracting additional revenue-generating business to the hotel guestrooms; restaurants, lounges, and entertainment areas; meeting and banquet rooms; or retail and recreational facilities. A thorough market study will identify these possibilities as well as define a myriad of needs within these spaces, such as the guestroom mix, special food themes, audiovisual requirements, or health club preferences.

The need for such a study may be most obvious in mixed-use developments, where it is paramount that the hotel recognize the demands that the offices, shops, sports arena, or other uses will place on the facilities. The Omni Hotel in Miami, for instance, is part of one of the largest shopping developments in the southeast, and it capitalizes on foreign tourists to increase demand for rooms as well as for its food and beverage business. The hotel was, in fact, designed for this particular market. At the Sheraton-Park Central in

Market and program material needed for 200-room hotel

FEASIBILITY STUDY	
☐ **Market analysis**	Analysis of economic conditions, demand for hotel services, and present supply of hotels.
☐ **Competitors' survey**	Analysis of competing facilities, services, amenities, and price.
☐ **Site analysis**	Evaluation of local environment and of particular parcel for suitability to hotel (see location factor checklist in Chapter 3).
☐ **Financial projections**	Forecast of income and operating expenses for 5 to 10 years.
PROJECT DEFINITION	
☐ **Statement of purpose**	Concise paragraph integrating market, site, and facilities.
☐ **List of revenue-producing areas**	Summary list of guestroom types, food and beverage outlets, meeting and banquet rooms, retail, recreation, and parking.
SPACE PROGRAM	
☐ **Space allocation program**	Detailed list of space requirements for all areas.
DESCRIPTION OF OPERATIONS	
☐ **Description of operations**	Explanation of operational procedures and functions including flow diagrams.
☐ **Food and beverage (F&B) program**	Definition of the concept or theme for each F&B area.
☐ **Staffing guide**	Listing of personnel requirements by department.
PROJECT BUDGET	
☐ **Outline budget**	Categorization of costs including construction, furnishings and equipment, development costs, financing, land, and preopening expenses (see capital cost outline in Chapter 24).

Dallas, Texas, the fast-growing and affluent North Dallas office and residential districts influenced the developers to add not only additional restaurants and lounges but also a 40,000 square foot (3700 square meter) health club to the hotel.

Local characteristics may dictate the elimination of particular facilities or services as well. The Back Bay Hilton in Boston, located next to the area's largest convention hotel and city auditorium, offers small meeting and banquet areas, but does not contain any major convention space of its own. In cities such as New Orleans, Louisiana, hotels often provide the bare minimum in restaurant space because of the reputation of and competition from renowned local restaurants. Thus, it is imperative that hotel developers and architects understand the influence of the hotel's location and primary markets on the mix of facilities and on their design.

A second issue is equally important: The initial program and the ensuing design must recognize that the market seldom remains constant. The need for hotel facilities is likely to change, often substantially, over relatively short periods. As a result, the project should include components that increase its flexibility or its ability to adapt to a changing or growing market. Forward-looking developers seek a design that permits the expansion of the original hotel, perhaps by building a second guestroom tower, by extending a new wing, or by constructing additional convention space or health club facilities. Each of these alternatives for growth and change should be identified in the program and should be considered thoroughly during the conceptual design.

DEFINING THE PROJECT

With so many designers and consultants at work on major hotel projects, a consensus on the goals and objectives of the development is essential: What market is it supposed to attract? What class and what type of hotel might it be? What services and amenities should it provide? Which public functions should be emphasized? Therefore, it is helpful to prepare a concise definition of the project to identify these issues, to outline the primary public facilities, and to provide a gross estimate of the size of the project. The box below illustrates the type of statement that clearly defines the project's intent.

> The facility is to be a deluxe, highrise, convention/resort hotel of 500 rooms. The complex, located in a residential, commercial, and "clean" industrial suburb of Detroit, should be designed to accommodate convention groups, the commercial traveler visiting local corporate headquarters or research facilities for stays of comparatively short duration, and should also attract the "weekend vacationer" in a major urban area with extremes of climate. Public facilities should cater to the suburban population, to business groups associated with industries in the area, and to local, state, and regional civic, business, and professional organizations.
>
> Statement of Facilities Requirements, The Sheraton Corp.

The second part of the preliminary definition of a new or expanded hotel project is a summary of the principal public facilities. Before the developer and his team can move on to the program and later design phases, they need a precise list of the revenue-producing areas, those on which the support and service areas are based. This list forms the core of the expanded space program. For example, even a cursory listing of the restaurant and banquet requirements influences the size and design requirements of the kitchen, food storage, and employee locker areas. As the developer focuses on the projections for operating income and expenses, the designers refine their summary list of major facilities to better meet the project objectives. This enumeration should include:

Guestrooms
- ☐ Number of room "keys" (separate rental units)
- ☐ Number of room bays (total equivalent room modules)
- ☐ Typical room and suite dimensions

Lobby and public areas
- ☐ Architectural image
- ☐ Amount of retail shop space

Food and beverage
- ☐ Capacity of each restaurant
- ☐ Capacity of each lounge
- ☐ Quality level and theme for each

Function space
- ☐ Dimensions of the ballroom
- ☐ Amount of meeting and banquet space

Other
- ☐ Need for exhibition space
- ☐ Amount of recreation facilities
- ☐ Parking requirements

OPPOSITE PAGE

Sheraton Washington, Washington, D.C. *The totally renovated and enlarged convention hotel, its ballroom and meeting complex in a low wing beside the guestrooms, sits on the edge of Washington amidst acres of landscaped grounds.*

Typical figures for early estimates

	MOTOR INN*	COMMERCIAL*	CONVENTION*	SUPER-LUXURY
Number of guestrooms	150	300	600	250
Net guestroom area	310 (29)	330 (31)	330 (31)	400 (37)
Gross guestroom area	420 (39)	460 (43)	480 (45)	580 (54)
Total guestroom area	63,000 (5,860)	138,000 (12,835)	288,000 (26,785)	145,000 (13,485)
Guestroom percentage	80	75	70	75
Total project area	78,750 (7,325)	184,000 (17,110)	412,000 (38,315)	192,500 (17,900)
Total area/room	525 (49)	615 (57)	685 (64)	770 (72)

**Area figures in square feet (square meters) exclude parking and recreational facilities.*

The early estimates of project size generally are little more than the application of basic rules of thumb—common guestroom dimensions and gross project area per room—coupled with the experience of architects, developers, and management company staff; yet they establish a necessary order of magnitude for the hotel. Until a more detailed program is established, this gross approximation of project size is the critical basis for all cost estimates. In the detailed program examples later in this chapter, the area requirements vary tremendously depending on the type, quality level, and architectural configuration of the hotel. Early estimates are based on such numbers as shown above.

ALLOCATING PROGRAM AREAS

The development of the architectural space program does not occur at one time nor does it result in a static document. The early definition establishes an approximate total area for the project; later, the architect develops a space list at the beginning of the schematic design and refines a more detailed program during the preliminary and the design development phases. Because the technical services staffs of the major hotel-operating companies have the experience to react quickly and accurately to requests for programmatic information, comprehensive programs frequently are not prepared. Instead, the detailed planning and space-use information is transmitted through a comprehensive chain-developed *Design Guide* or bit-by-bit during the ensuing design phases as the architect requires more specific technical information. But, with computer programs now available (such as Strategic Hotel Area Program Estimate and Evaluation—SHAPEE), detailed area information can be issued early and can be easily updated during the design phases.

The preliminary program permits the architect to begin the schematic studies for the project. Usually, the management company staff prepare the list based on their own standards as well as on their experience with similar projects and on the market information provided in the feasibility report. They analyze the broad guidelines established in the earlier estimates to see whether the estimates still accurately reflect the size, class, and hotel type of the project. The staff then expand these guidelines to include a list of the principal guestrooms, and public, administrative, and service areas.

Often, the mix of food and beverage outlets or the balance between a large ballroom and the smaller meeting and banquet rooms will be modified to reflect the operator's knowledge of a local market or to exploit the management company's development strategies. Thus, an operator's programming and planning expertise should influence the project at the earliest date.

The space list prepared by the operating company begins to set the framework for a clear understanding of the facilities and of the type of image the hotel wants to project to the public. The operating company identifies the mix of guestrooms and suites; defines the specific dining rooms, lounges, and function areas; details the amount of administrative office space; and allocates area to service functions—kitchens, receiving, storage, employee areas, laundry, housekeeping, engineering, and maintenance spaces. A program checklist with approximate areas for three sizes of hotels appears on pages 155–156.

Operating companies issue their programming material in a variety of forms. Holiday Inns has developed extremely detailed space programs for different size hotels at each typical hotel location (downtown, suburban, airport). These programs specify precise area requirements. For example, the lobby program includes public seating, bellman stand, luggage storage, house and public phones, elevators, and stairs. Hyatt Hotels, on the other hand, although it provides a moderately detailed list of the functional areas and their space requirements, simply states that the lobby should be a "function of the architectural design, of ample space and character appropriate to its function of welcoming guests and serving as a popular meeting place."

These two approaches illustrate the differing development strategies of the two management companies. One is known worldwide for its tight and efficient control of the building program, which permits the construction of competitive hotels at prices far below many of their competitors. The other is famous for its spectacular architectural and interior design, which, over the past two decades, has set the standard for the largest commercial and convention hotels.

The use of experienced architects and consultants from within the industry is most helpful to fine tune those areas that diverge from the standard prototypes. In the table on pages 156–157, details are given of how dramatically the space requirements for hotels with similar numbers of rooms can vary.

Therefore, a precise program depends on understanding the interconnection between a variety of planning and design aspects of hotels. It is clear that the net guestroom area is a major determinant of project size; it is less obvious that the eventual choice of a particular configuration for the guestroom structure can change the net-to-gross factor from about .35 in the most efficient plan to over .55 in the least efficient.

Developing a clear project statement may help to define some of the quality, facilities, and architectural alternatives that are basic to establishing an accurate program. The following factors, many of which are undetermined until the schematic design phase is complete, greatly influence the space requirements for hotels and resorts.

- ☐ Architectural configuration (see Chapter 15)
- ☐ Number of floors
- ☐ Location of food and beverage outlets (may require various satellite kitchens)
- ☐ Location of the ballroom (may require pantry; also establishes column-free zone that affects guestroom tower placement)
- ☐ Availability of basement space
- ☐ Ratio of land to gross building area (affects stacking of public areas, duplication of circulation and lobbies, and need for parking structure)

Detailed hotel program checklist

SPACE*	SIZE OF HOTEL (NUMBER OF ROOMS) 200	500	1000
Guestrooms (number of rooms)			
☐ King (43%)	86	215	430
☐ Double-doubles (50%)	199	250	500
☐ Handicapped (2%)	4	10	20
☐ Suites (5%)	10	25	50
☐ Manager's apartment			
☐ Corridor			
Support:			
☐ Elevators			
☐ Linen storage			
☐ Vending, ice			
Lobby (square feet)			
☐ Flow area	2000	4000	7000
☐ Seating	200	500	1000
☐ Retail	100	800	2000
☐ Assistant manager	0	100	100
Support:			
☐ Bellman station	50	50	50
☐ Telephones			
☐ Toilets			
Food and beverage outlets (square feet)			
☐ Coffee shop	2400	3500	4400
☐ Specialty restaurant	0	2800	0
☐ Theme restaurant	0	0	4000
☐ Rooftop restaurant	0	0	3000
☐ Deli	0	0	750
☐ Snack bar	0	0	0
☐ Cocktail lounge	1600	1920	2400
☐ Lobby bar	800	2000	2000
☐ Entertainment lounge	0	3150	0
☐ Nightclub	0	0	5000
☐ Pool bar	0	0	450
Support:			
☐ Performers' dressing rooms	0	0	250
☐ Bar storage	75	100	100
☐ Toilets, coats, telephones			
Function areas (square feet)			
☐ Ballroom	3500	8000	20000
☐ Ballroom foyer	900	2000	5000
☐ Junior ballroom	0	4000	1200
☐ Junior ballroom foyer	0	1000	300
☐ Banquet rooms	0	2400	6000
☐ Meeting rooms	1200	2400	6000
☐ Boardroom	0	600	1200
☐ Lecture theater	0	1200	1500
☐ Exhibit hall	0	0	15000
Support:			
☐ Function room storage	500	2500	5000
☐ Audiovisual equipment storage	0	100	200
☐ Convention registration	0	0	200
☐ Projection booth	0	250	400
☐ Translation booth	0	0	0
☐ Banquet captain's office	0	100	200
☐ Toilets, coats, telephones			
Administration (square feet)			
Front office			
☐ Front desk	160	250	420
☐ Front office manager	120	120	120
☐ Assistant manager	0	120	120
☐ Credit manager	100	100	100
☐ Director of rooms	0	150	150
☐ Reception/secretary	100	100	100
☐ Reservations area	80	200	250
☐ Reservations manager	0	120	120
☐ Telephone operators	80	150	200
☐ Fire control room	80	120	120
☐ Bellman storage	150	200	300
☐ Safe deposit boxes	30	60	60
☐ General cashier	0	120	120

SPACE*	SIZE OF HOTEL (NUMBER OF ROOMS) 200	500	1000
☐ Count room	125	150	200
☐ Work area/mail	40	100	150
☐ Storage	40	80	120
Executive office			
☐ Reception/waiting	200	250	300
☐ General manager	150	200	250
☐ Executive assistant manager	0	180	180
☐ Resident manager	0	0	180
☐ Food and beverage manager	120	150	175
☐ Secretary	100	150	200
☐ Conference room	0	200	250
☐ Copying and storage	40	100	100
Sales and catering			
☐ Reception/waiting	150	200	300
☐ Director of sales	150	150	200
☐ Sales representatives	0	330	550
☐ Director of public relations	0	150	150
☐ Secretary	0	225	375
☐ Catering manager	0	150	200
☐ Banquet manager	0	150	175
☐ Banquet representatives	0	100	200
☐ Function book room	0	80	100
☐ Beverage manager	0	120	120
☐ Convention services	0	120	240
☐ Secretary	0	150	225
☐ Copying and storage	50	150	200
Accounting			
☐ Reception/waiting	0	100	100
☐ Controller	120	150	180
☐ Assistant controller/auditor	0	100	100
☐ Accounting work area	150	600	800
☐ Payroll manager	120	120	150
☐ Secretary	0	100	100
☐ Copying and storage	100	200	300
☐ Computer room	0	100	150
☐ Dead files	100	125	175
Food preparation (square feet)			
☐ Main kitchen	2000	9000	13000
☐ Banquet pantry	0	1200	2000
☐ Coffee shop pantry	0	0	0
☐ Specialty restaurant pantry	0	1200	1200
☐ Bake shop	0	850	1000
☐ Room service area	75	300	500
☐ Chef's office	100	120	120
☐ Dry food storage	300	1000	1800
☐ Refrigerated food storage	200	800	1200
☐ Beverage storage	150	500	1000
☐ Refrigerated beverage storage	100	250	400
☐ China, silver, glass storage	200	500	1000
☐ Food controller office	100	120	120
☐ Toilets	100	150	150
Receiving and storage (square feet)			
☐ Loading dock	200	400	800
☐ Receiving area	250	500	1200
☐ Receiving office	120	150	150
☐ Purchasing office	120	175	200
☐ Locked storage	125	175	200
☐ Empty bottle storage	100	125	150
☐ Trash holding area	150	200	250
☐ Refrigerated garbage	80	100	120
☐ Can wash	100	120	120
☐ Compactor	150	200	200
☐ Grounds equipment storage	200	300	400
☐ General storage	1000	2000	4000
Employee areas (square feet)			
Personnel			
☐ Timekeeper	100	120	120
☐ Security	0	120	120
☐ Personnel/reception	120	150	200
☐ Personnel manager	120	140	160

Detailed hotel program checklist (continued)

SPACE*	SIZE OF HOTEL (NUMBER OF ROOMS) 200	500	1000
☐ Assistant personnel manager	0	120	120
☐ Interview room	100	100	200
☐ Training room	0	225	250
☐ Files and storage	50	80	100
☐ First aid	80	100	150
Employee facilities			
☐ Men's lockers/toilets	400	900	1700
☐ Women's lockers/toilets	400	1200	2300
☐ Banquet staff lockers	0	400	600
☐ Employee cafeteria	400	1000	1800
Laundry and housekeeping (square			
Laundry			
☐ Soiled linen room	100	150	250
☐ Laundry	1000	2500	4000
☐ Laundry supervisor	0	100	120
☐ Valet laundry	100	150	200
☐ Supplies storage	50	125	175
Housekeeping			
☐ Housekeeper	100	125	150
☐ Assistant housekeeper	0	100	120
☐ Secretary	0	100	100
☐ Linen storage	500	1500	3000
☐ Uniform issue/storage	250	500	800
☐ Supplies storage	0	100	200
☐ Lost and found	100	150	200
☐ Sewing room	0	100	200
Engineering (square feet)			
☐ Engineer	100	125	150
☐ Assistant engineer	0	100	100
☐ Secretarial	0	100	100
☐ Carpentry shop	0	200	250
☐ Plumbing shop	0	200	250
☐ Electrical shop	0	200	250
☐ Paint shop	100	200	250
☐ TV repair shop	100	150	200
☐ Key shop	60	80	100
☐ Energy management computer	0	120	120
☐ Engineering storeroom	300	800	1000
Mechanical areas (square feet)			
☐ Mechanical plant	1200	3000	6000
☐ Transformer room	150	1000	1500
☐ Emergency generator	0	300	500
☐ Meter room	50	100	150
☐ Fire pumps	0	100	200
☐ Electrical switchboard	200	750	1000
☐ Elevator machine room	100	400	800
☐ Telephone equipment room	100	500	800
Recreation (square feet)			
☐ Swimming pool	800	1200	1500
☐ Pool including deck	2000	3000	4000
☐ Whirlpool	0	100	200
☐ Lockers, toilets, sauna	300	500	1000
☐ Exercise room	0	500	800
☐ Game room	300	300	500
☐ Manager's office	0	100	200
☐ Attendant	0	80	100
☐ Equipment storage	100	250	400
☐ Pool pump/filter	100	200	200
☐ Racquetball/squash	0	1200	2400
☐ Golf/tennis club	0	0	0
☐ Children's playroom	0	0	500

**The program for the public or front-of-house hotel areas depends to a great extent on the issues discussed in the first half of this book: location, hotel type, market segment, quality level, type of ownership, and architectural configuration. Nevertheless, it is possible to outline the types of spaces and the approximate area requirements for different-size hotels with the caution that these numbers are averages and must be adjusted for each particular hotel or resort project.*

Space requirements by hotel type

	BUDGET INN		MOTOR INN		CONFERENCE CENTER	
Guestrooms						
Number of guestrooms		150		150		250
Bays (including suites)		150		152		255
Net area (sq ft)		250		310		325
Gross factor		.15		.35		.40
Guestrooms total (sq ft)		**43,125 (82.5%)**		**63,612 (77.2%)**		**116,025 (67.2%)**
(sq m)		**4,011**		**5,916**		**10,790**
Public area	Seats	Area	Seats	Area	Seats	Area
Lobby		600 (1.1%)		1,200 (1.5%)		2,500 (1.4%)
Food and beverage						
Cafe	100	1500	120	1800		0
Restaurant		0		0	225	4050
Restaurant		0		0		0
Cocktail lounge	50	750	75	1,125		0
Lobby bar		0		0	75	1500
Entertainment lounge		0		0	150	2,550
Total		**2,250 (4.3%)**		**2,925 (3.5%)**		**8,100 (4.7%)**
Meeting & banquet						
Ballroom		0	300	3,000	550	6,050
Ballroom foyer		0		600		1,815
Meeting/banquet		0	75	900	750	11,250
Total				**4,500 (5.5%)**		**19,115 (11.1%)**
Exhibition/casino						
Gross factor		.15		.15		.20
Public area total (sq ft)		**3,278 (6.3%)**		**9,919 (12.0%)**		**36,658 (20.6%)**
(sq m)		**305**		**922**		**3,316**
Administration						
Front office		300		450		875
Executive offices		0		300		625
Sales and catering		0		300		1,250
Accounting		150		150		500
Total		**450**		**1,200**		**3,250**
Gross factor		.15		.18		.20
Administration total (sq ft)		**518 (1.0%)**		**1,416 (1.7%)**		**3,900 (2.3%)**
(sq m)		**48**		**132**		**363**
Service area						
Food preparation						
Main kitchen		750		1,140		2,675
Banquet kitchen		0		0		0
Food/beverage storage		150		342		803
Total		**900**		**1,482**		**3,478**
Receiving/storage						
Receiving/trash		330		446		772
General storage		300		300		500
Total		**630**		**746**		**1,272**
Employee areas						
Personnel		0		0		750
Employee lockers		600		678		1,285
Employee dining		300		339		643
Total		**900**		**1,017**		**2,678**
Laundry/housekeeping						
Laundry		900		1,056		2,070
Housekeeping		450		528		1,035
Total		**1,350**		**1,584**		**3,105**
Engineering/mechanical						
Engineering office/shop		300		450		1,250
Mechanical		600		1,200		2,500
Total		**900**		**1,650**		**3,750**
Gross factor		.15		.15		.20
Service area total (sq ft)		**5,382 (10.3%)**		**7,451 (9.0%)**		**17,138 (9.9%)**
(sq m)		**501**		**693**		**1,594**
Total area (sq ft)		**52,302**		**82,398**		**172,721**
(sq m)		**4,864**		**7,663**		**16,063**
Area/room (sq ft)		**349**		**549**		**691**
(sq m)		**32**		**51**		**64**
Recreation						
Swimming pool and deck		0		2,500		2,500
Health club		0		300		2,000
Golf/tennis club		0		0		0
Recreation total		**0**		**2,800**		**4,500**
				260		419

ALL SUITE	SUPER LUXURY	SUBURBAN	RESORT	CONVENTION	LARGE CONVENTION	CASINO	MEGA-HOTEL
250	250	350	350	500	1,000	1,000	1,500
250	270	357	364	515	1,030	1,050	1,600
450	400	330	350	330	330	330	330
.50	.45	.40	.45	.45	.45	.50	.50
168,750 (82.3%)	**156,600 (78.0%)**	**164,934 (69.8%)**	**184,730 (73.6%)**	**246,428 (68.5%)**	**492,855 (68.1%)**	**519,750 (68.0%)**	**792,000 (69.1%)**
15,694	**14,564**	**15,339**	**17,180**	**22,918**	**45,836**	**48,337**	**73,656**

Seats	Area	Seats	Area	Seats	Area	Seats	Area	Seats	Area	Seats	Area	Seats	Area	Seats	Area
	2,500 (1.2%)		2,500 (1.2%)		3,150 (1.3%)		3,500 (1.4%)		4,500 (1.3%)		9,000 (1.2%)		11,000 (1.4%)		20,000 (1.7%)
	0		0	180	3,060	180	3,060	220	3,740	275	4,675	500	9,000	550	9,350
150	2,700	150	3,300	120	2,280	120	2,400	150	2,850	200	3,800	200	4,000	250	4,750
	0		0		0		0		0	150	3,300	120	2,880	150	3,300
	0	100	1,700		0		0	120	1,920	150	2,400	250	4,500	150	2,400
75	1,500	50	1,000	75	1,500	60	1,200	100	2,000	100	2,000	150	3,000	175	3,500
	0		0	150	2,550	200	3,600	175	3,150	250	4,500	350	3,000	300	5,400
	4,200 (2.0%)		**6,000 (3.0%)**		**9,390 (4.0%)**		**10,260 (4.1%)**		**13,660 (3.8%)**		**20,675 (2.9%)**		**29,680 (3.9%)**		**28,700 (2.5%)**
375	4,125	325	3,575	700	7,000	455	4,550	1150	11,500	2500	25,000	1500	15,000	3750	37,500
	1,238		1,073		2,100		1,365		3,450		7,500		4,500		11,250
200	2,400	250	3,750	525	6,300	280	3,360	1150	13,800	2500	30,000	1000	12,000	3750	45,000
	7,763 (3.8%)		**8,398 (4.2%)**		**15,400 (6.5%)**		**9,275 (3.7%)**		**28,750 (8.0%)**		**62,500 (8.6%)**		**31,500 (4.1%)**		**93,750 (8.2%)**
											25,000 (3.5%)		**50,000 (6.5%)**		**28,125 (2.5%)**

ALL SUITE	SUPER LUXURY	SUBURBAN	RESORT	CONVENTION	LARGE CONVENTION	CASINO	MEGA-HOTEL
.25	.25	.25	.25	.25	.25	.25	.25
18,078 (8.8%)	**21,122 (10.5%)**	**34,925 (14.8%)**	**28,794 (11.5%)**	**58,638 (16.3%)**	**146,469 (20.2%)**	**152,725 (20.0%)**	**213,219 (18.6%)**
1,681	**1,964**	**3,248**	**2,678**	**5,453**	**13,622**	**14,203**	**19,829**
875	1,000	1,400	1,400	2,000	2,800	3,200	4,200
625	875	875	1,050	1,250	2,000	2,000	2,700
750	1,000	1,400	1,050	2,000	2,800	2,400	4,200
500	500	1,050	1,050	1,500	2,100	4,500	3,150
2,750	**3,375**	**4,725**	**4,550**	**6,750**	**9,700**	**12,100**	**14,250**
.20	.20	.20	.20	.25	.25	.25	.25
3,300 (1.6%)	**4,050 (2.0%)**	**5,670 (2.4%)**	**5,460 (2.2%)**	**8,438 (2.3%)**	**12,125 (1.7%)**	15,125 (2.0%)	17,813 (1.6%)
307	**377**	**527**	**508**	**785**	**1,128**	**1,407**	**1,657**
1,885	2,705	4,612	3,570	8,037	12,194	10,814	18,225
0	0	703	458	1,265	3,300	1,620	8,250
566	812	1,329	1,208	2,326	3,099	2,487	5,295
2,451	**3,517**	**6,643**	**5,236**	**11,628**	**18,593**	**14,921**	**31,770**
618	953	1,346	1,397	2,244	2,859	2,492	4,042
500	750	1,050	1,400	2,000	4,000	5,000	7,500
1,118	**1,703**	**2,396**	**2,797**	**4,244**	**6,859**	**7,492**	**11,542**
750	875	875	1,050	1,000	2,000	3,000	3,000
1,127	1,562	2,203	2,121	3,259	4,439	6,704	6,645
564	781	881	954	1,304	1,776	2,681	2,658
2,441	**3,217**	**3,959**	**4,125**	**5,563**	**8,214**	**12,385**	**12,303**
1,754	2,082	2,839	3,000	3,911	5,548	5,204	9,056
877	1,249	1,704	1,800	2,347	3,329	3,122	6,339
2,631	**3,331**	**4,543**	**4,799**	**6,258**	**8,878**	**8,326**	**15,396**
1,250	1,500	1,750	3,500	2,000	3,500	3,500	5,250
2,500	2,500	5,250	5,250	7,500	12,000	15,000	22,500
3,750	**4,000**	**7,000**	**8,750**	**9,500**	**15,500**	**18,500**	**27,750**
.20	.20	.25	.25	.25	.25	.25	.25
14,867 (7.3%)	**18,922 (9.4%)**	**30,677 (13.0%)**	**32,134 (12.8%)**	**46,490 (12.9%)**	**72,554 (10.0%)**	**77,029 (10.1%)**	**123,450 (10.8%)**
1,383	**1,760**	**2,853**	**2,989**	**4,324**	**6,748**	**7,164**	**11,481**
204,996	**200,694**	**236,206**	**251,118**	**359,993**	**724,003**	**764,629**	**1,146,482**
19,065	**18,665**	**21,967**	**23,354**	**33,479**	**67,332**	**71,111**	**106,623**
820	**803**	**675**	**717**	**720**	**724**	**765**	**764**
76	**75**	**63**	**67**	**67**	**67**	**71**	**71**
1,800	0	3,000	4,000	2,000	2,000	3,000	5,000
1,200	1,200	1,600	2,000	1,600	2,400	3,000	2,800
0	0	0	3,000	0	0	0	4,000
3,000	**1,200**	**4,600**	**9,000**	**3,600**	**4,400**	**6,000**	**11,800**
279	112	428	837	335	409	558	1,097

Space Requirements by Hotel Type: Area per Room. *The chart illustrates how hotel space needs vary from budget inns to all-suite and super-luxury hotels, the latter requiring more than twice as much area per room as the former. The figures at the bottom list the area per room for each of the major functional categories in the previous table. For example, a motor inn requires about 549 square feet (51 square meters) for each guestroom; of this total, 22 square feet (2 square meters) per room are devoted to restaurants and lounges and 10 square feet (.9 square meters) to kitchens.*

Scope of some necessary decisions

GUEST SERVICES	
☐ **Parking**	Valet, self-park?
☐ **Luggage handling**	By guest or bellman, public or service elevator?
☐ **Front desk procedures**	Computers, room status, credit, safe deposit?
☐ **Guestroom food service**	Hours, menu, cart, or tray?
☐ **Restaurant service**	Hours, types of service, outdoor?
☐ **Recreation**	Hours, open to public, children, safety, lockers?
☐ **Guestroom communication**	Phone, cable TV, message systems, wake-up?
☐ **Guestroom amenities**	Turndown, extra linen, butler?
☐ **Guest security**	Key system, fire evacuation procedures?
STAFF OPERATIONS	
☐ **Employee entrance**	Timekeeper, security?
☐ **Employee uniforms**	Issuing, laundering?
☐ **Employee facilities**	Cafeteria, lounge, recreation, housing?
☐ **Staff communications**	Paging, housekeeping systems?
☐ **Data processing**	Reservations, accounting, phones?
☐ **Accounting/controls**	F&B control, drop safe, closed circuit TV (CCTV)?
☐ **Food preparation**	Central/decentralized?
MATERIAL HANDLING	
☐ **Receiving area**	Separate receiving from trash, control, purchasing?
☐ **Laundry**	In-house, guest laundry, hours?
☐ **Trash and garbage**	Holding, refrigeration, compaction, glass, can wash?
☐ **Vertical circulation**	Stocking of linen, rooftop restaurant, trash/linen chutes?

DESCRIBING THE OPERATIONS

The facilities program is incomplete until the hotel operations, as well as the basic space requirements, are fully defined and described. Usually developed by the hotel operator, the description of the operations includes various checklists of guest services, staff functions, and material handling in addition to schematic diagrams that show the designer which spaces must be adjacent to each other. Because services vary greatly from property to property, the complexity and the importance of their description also differ.

Among the most challenging aspects of hotel design is the necessity to develop a plan that accommodates both the great variety of guest markets and the operational requirements of the hotel. These are often in conflict, and the cost of providing for every need is likely to be prohibitive. Architects and operators have to make countless value judgments, for example, about whether the hotel will cater primarily to individuals or to groups, the relative prominence of the several restaurants and lounges, or the need for direct food service to the secondary meeting rooms.

For the most part, the key planning objective is to group public functions around the lobby, to position service functions around the receiving area, and to cluster food outlets and function rooms around the kitchen. You will see in the following chapters more detailed organizational diagrams that describe the functional areas in hotels and resorts.

Many operating decisions are changing because of the increased automation and computerization of the hotel industry. The labor-intensive nature of the industry forces hotel management to establish creative new procedures and systems to reduce the necessity for repetitive staff work while they maintain a quality level of service. The checklist above outlines the scope of some necessary decisions.

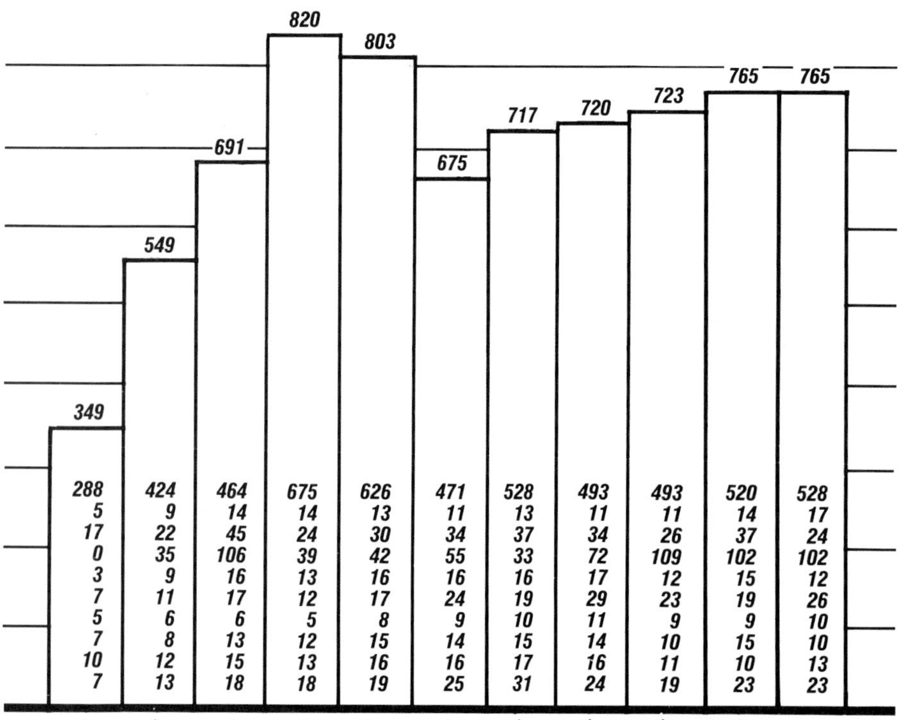

	BUDGET INN	MOTOR INN	CONFERENCE CENTER	ALL-SUITE	SUPER-LUXURY	SUBURBAN	RESORT	CONVENTION 500 rooms	CONVENTION 1000 rooms	CASINO	MEGA-HOTEL
	349	549	691	820	803	675	717	720	723	765	765
GUESTROOMS	288	424	464	675	626	471	528	493	493	520	528
LOBBY	5	9	14	14	13	11	13	11	11	14	17
FOOD & BEVERAGE	17	22	45	24	30	34	37	34	26	37	24
MEETING & BANQUET	0	35	106	39	42	55	33	72	109	102	102
ADMINISTRATION	3	9	16	13	16	16	16	17	12	15	12
FOOD PREPARATION	7	11	17	12	17	24	19	29	23	19	26
RECEIVING & STORAGE	5	6	6	5	8	9	10	11	9	9	10
EMPLOYEE AREAS	7	8	13	12	15	14	15	14	10	15	10
LAUNDRY/HOUSEKEEPING	10	12	15	13	16	16	17	16	11	10	13
ENGINEERING	7	13	18	18	19	25	31	24	19	23	23

Space Requirements by Hotel Type: Area per Room. *The chart illustrates how hotel space needs vary from budget inns to all-suite and super-luxury hotels, the latter requiring more than twice as much area per room than does the inn. The table at the base lists the area per room for each of the major functional categories in the previous table.*

One area that directly affects the guests' perception of the entire hotel is the food and beverage operation. The operator or a qualified restaurant consultant must provide highly detailed descriptions of each individual restaurant and lounge so that the architect, interior designer, and kitchen planner can together develop a unified design and operation. The description of the food and beverage concept should detail every aspect of the operation, including capacity, floor area, name and graphics, menu, theme, hours, staffing, special equipment, uniforms, and table service requirements. These elements will be more fully described in the discussion of planning hotel restaurants and lounges in Chapter 17.

The description of the hotel operations should also include a complete staffing program. The number of employees and their assignments affect the space requirements in three primary areas: administrative offices, employee lockers and toilets, and employee cafeteria. In resorts and some international hotels, staff housing may even be required. In addition, the staffing program dictates the need or desirability for different systems and equipment in the numerous office and back-of-house areas.

PREPARING THE PROJECT BUDGET

A final part of the facilities program is the preparation of an outline budget (see accompanying table). Because total project cost varies enormously—from $25,000 to over $150,000 per guestroom—strict budget control throughout the entire design and construction process is critical. Budgeting is made more difficult by the common practice in hotel work of using separate architectural and interior design firms. Therefore, the developer must define precisely the design and budget responsibilities of the architect, interior designer, and other consultants, for example, differentiating between the general construction budget and the furniture, fixtures, and equipment (FF&E) budget.

In addition, the entire FF&E category, with which the architect and many developers often are unfamiliar, frequently approaches 30 percent of the general construction budget. While the fact that both the FF&E and preopening budgets are usually left to the hotel operator to establish reinforces the cooperative effort, it leaves the developer with a sense of less control over the budgeting effort. The extraordinary amounts of non-construction dollars required to equip and open a hotel emphasizes the need to establish budget controls at the outset.

Project outline budget

BUDGET CATEGORY	PERCENT	INCLUDES
General construction	60–65	Building, sitework, general conditions
Furniture, fixtures, and equipment	14–16	
Hotel interiors		Guestrooms, public areas, administrative offices, signage
Equipment		Kitchen, bar equipment, and back-of-house (front office equipment, carts, vehicles, lockers, copiers)
Expendables		Linen, china, glassware, housekeeping equipment and uniforms
Special systems		Telephones, computers, TV antenna, sound, security, special audio/visual
Development costs	7–10	
Architectural/engineering fees		All engineering, landscaping
Design consultant fees		Interiors, kitchens
Purchasing fee		
Financing fee		
Developer's fee		
Project field staff		
Insurance during construction		
Taxes		
Legal, permits, surveys		
Interest during construction	8–10	
Preopening expense and working capital	3–4	Training, preopening payroll, office, advertising and promotion, opening ceremonies
Land	not included	
Total	100	

The project budget is jointly assembled by the design and development team. The architect establishes the construction budget based on the space program, schematic design, and the outline specifications; the developer and hotel operator usually compare it to their experience with similar projects. The furniture, fixtures, and equipment budget is prepared by the hotel operator, although the interior designer may be asked to propose an interiors budget to meet the project objectives. The development costs and financing expenses are estimated by the project developer in consultation with the hotel operator and other consultants. The preopening budget is established by the operator. See Chapter 24 for a detailed capital cost outline.

15 THE GUESTROOM FLOOR

"A hotel is a place where the 14th floor is the 13th floor in disguise."

Shelley Berman

The planning of the typical guestroom floor presents some of the greatest challenges in hotel design. Because it represents between 65 and 85 percent of the total hotel area, any savings in the design of a single floor is multiplied many times. Therefore, a major planning goal should be to maximize the amount of salable guestroom space and keep to a minimum the circulation and supporting areas.

In addition, there are other planning objectives. The building should be oriented and the plan configuration selected not only to enhance views but to reduce future energy expenses for heating and air conditioning. The building shape should reflect the need to minimize the impact of lateral wind loading on the structure. The organization and layout of each floor should take into account the need to reduce as much as possible the walking distances for both the guest and the housekeeping staff. Also, to better accommodate possible future expansion, the architect should consider how the guestroom floor can be extended, how the structure can be increased in height, or how additional towers can be phased as demand for rooms increases (see checklist on opposite page).

The program requirements for the guestroom floors are relatively few: a designated number of guestrooms or suites, guest and service elevators conveniently located, exit stairways that meet the building code, adequate linen storage and vending areas, and small electrical and phone equipment rooms.

The analysis of alternate plan configurations for the guestroom structure is one of the earliest design studies for a hotel. These plan types range in shape from long, double-loaded corridor plans, to compact vertical towers, to flamboyant atrium structures—each with a myriad of variations. Lowrise motor inns generally are planned with a double-loaded corridor and may be shaped into L, T, □, or other patterns. Highrise buildings may follow similar shapes, can be terraced into pyramidlike forms, or can be placed against a large lobby space so that some of the rooms look into the hotel interior. The tower plan, where the guestrooms surround a central core, can be rectangular, circular, or practically any shape. And the atrium configuration, originally a basic rectangular plan, has taken on numerous complex shapes in more recent designs. These various configurations are illustrated with selected plans throughout this chapter.

What is the most appropriate configuration for the guestrooms? In densely populated urban areas, the limited amount of site area and the proposed arrangement of public and support spaces on the lower floors are the most critical considerations. Two principal conditions, the preferred location of the guest and service elevators and the column-free ballroom, frequently dictate both the guestrooms' position on the site and the shape of the guestroom structure.

At resort properties, the opposite is true: Internal functional organization of the hotel elements is secondary to the careful design of the buildings to fit their setting and to provide views of the scenery. At airport sites, height limitations often dictate the choice of a specific plan, one which packages the rooms into a relatively low and spread-out structure.

While the choice of a plan type is the result of a balanced consideration of site, environment, and space requirements, the architect must realize that a particular configuration will shape the economies of the project—construction cost and energy expense primarily—and the more subtle aspects of guest satisfaction. The most economical design may not provide the best design solution. Thus, a less efficient plan type may offer more variety in room types, a more interesting spatial sequence, shorter walking distances, and other advantages that affect the guest's perception of the value of the hotel experience.

The designer and developer should include the following planning and architectural considerations in their analysis and eventual selection of a plan configuration for a particular hotel.

PLANNING EFFICIENCY: MAXIMUM GUESTROOM AREA

In order for the operator to realize profits, the design team must maximize the percentage of floor area devoted to guestrooms and keep to a minimum the amount of circulation and service space (service elevator lobby, linen storage, chutes, and vending). Although esthetic issues cannot be ignored, a simple comparison among alternate plans of the percentage of space allocated to revenue-producing guestrooms leads to the selection of more efficient solutions (see accompanying table on page 162).

Analyses of scores of different tower plans show that some configurations yield more efficient solutions than other types. The choice of one configuration over another can mean a saving of 20 percent in gross area of the guest room tower and of nearly 15 percent in the total building. For example, the three principal plan alternatives—the double-loaded slab, the rectangular tower, and the atrium—using the same net guestroom dimensions, will vary from 460 to 575 gross square feet (43 to 53 square meters) per room.

The study also indicates the effect of subsequent minor decisions on the efficiency of the plan—standard groupings of pairs of guestrooms, double- or single-loaded circulation, grouping of public and service elevators, and efficient access to end or corner rooms (the most difficult planning problem in certain configurations). Because guestrooms account for such a major part of the total hotel area, the designer should establish a series of quantitative benchmarks for the efficient design of the guestroom floors.

The relative efficiency of typical hotel floors can be compared most directly by calculating the percentage of the total floor area devoted to guestrooms. This varies from below 60 percent in an inefficient atrium plan to more than 75 percent in the most tightly designed double-loaded slab. Clearly, the higher this percentage the more options are available to the developer and the architect: Additional guestrooms can be built; larger rooms can be provided for the same capital investment; the quality of the furnishings or of particular building systems can be improved; other functional areas of the hotel can be enlarged; or the total construction and project cost can be substantially reduced.

The following sections contain a description, for each of the basic guestroom configurations, of the planning decisions that have the most influence on creating an economical plan. In some plans, it is the number of rooms per floor, in others it is the location of the elevator core, whereas in others the shape of the building is most critical. In general, the most efficient configurations are those where circulation space is kept to a minimum, that is, in structures with either double-loaded corridors or compact center-core towers.

SLAB PLANS

The "slab" configuration includes those plans that are primarily horizontal, including both single- and double-loaded corridor schemes (see accompanying plans). The planning variables are few; they are concerned primarily with the shape (straight or L-shaped), the layout of the core, and the location of the fire stairs. The architect must answer the following questions:

- ☐ **Corridor loading:** Given site conditions, are any single-loaded rooms appropriate?
- ☐ **Shape:** Which particular shape (straight, "offset," L, "knuckle," courtyard, or other configurations) best meets site and building constraints?
- ☐ **Core location:** Should the public and the service cores be combined or separated and where in the tower should they be positioned?
- ☐ **Core layout:** What is the best way to organize public and service elevators, linen storage, chutes, and vending?
- ☐ **Stair location:** Where should the fire stairs be located?

The high degree of efficiency of the slab plan is based primarily on the double loading of the corridors; single-loaded schemes require 4 to 6 percent more floor area for the same number of rooms. For example, only where external factors, a narrow site dimension, or spectacular views suggest single-loading should it be considered.

While slab plans as a category are the most efficient, experienced hotel architects and management company staff have found approaches to further tighten plan layouts. Configurations that bury the elevator and service cores in interior corners have several advantages. They slightly reduce the non-guestroom area, substantially reduce the amount of building perimeter, and increase the oppor-

Guestroom floor planning objectives

ORIENTATION/SITING

- ☐ Consider solar gain; generally N/S preferable to E/W exposures.
- ☐ Analyze wind loading.
- ☐ Study the potential for guestroom views.
- ☐ Site the structure to be visible from the road.
- ☐ Assess the relative visual impact and construction cost of various guestroom plan configurations.

FLOOR LAYOUT

- ☐ Organize plan so that guestrooms occupy at least 70 percent of gross floor area.
- ☐ Locate elevators and stairs at interior locations rather than on exterior wall.
- ☐ Develop corridor plan to facilitate guest circulation.
- ☐ Provide elevator lobby in middle third of structure.
- ☐ Locate vending near public elevators.
- ☐ Provide service elevator, linen storage, and chutes in central location.
- ☐ Plan corridor width at 5′ (1.5 m) minimum, 5′6″ (1.6 m) preferred.
- ☐ Plan guestroom distance to exit stairs at 150 ft maximum (if fully sprinklered) or as directed by local code.
- ☐ Design guestrooms back to back for plumbing economies.
- ☐ Locate handicapped guestrooms on lower floors and near elevators.

The design of the guestroom floors, which often represents three-quarters or more of the total hotel, is critical to the efficiency of any project. Planning objectives, which help the architect assess the relative success of any particular design concept, include the points in the checklist.

OPPOSITE PAGE

Pavilion Inter-Continental Hotel, Singapore. *The Pavilion Hotel illustrates many features of a John Portman–designed atrium, his first outside the U.S.: planter-filled balcony railings, glass elevators, water features, and open restaurants and lobby seating areas.*

Guestroom floor analysis

TOWER CONFIGURATION	ROOMS/FLOOR	DIMENSIONS, FT (M)	GUESTROOM (%)	CORRIDOR, SQ FT (SQ M)	PERIMETER × ROOM WIDTH	COMMENTS
Single-loaded slab 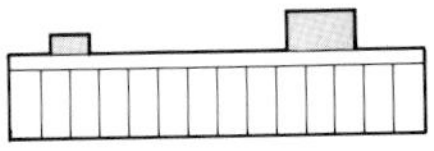	Varies 12–30+	32 × any length (10)	65	80 (7.5)	2.2–2.4	Some economy in that vertical core can be absolute minimum—not affected by room bays.
Double-loaded slab 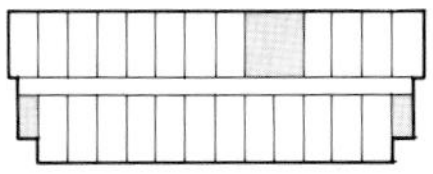	Varies 16–40+	60 × any length (18)	70	45 (4.2)	1.6–1.8	200 ft (61 m) plus dead-end corridor for two stair scheme; can be turned into L or T.
Offset slab 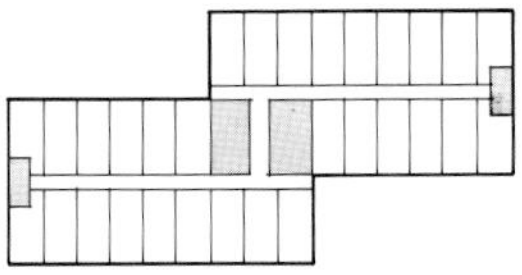	Varies 24–40+	80 × any length (24)	72	50 (4.6)	1.4–1.6	Core is buried, creating lower perimeter factor; higher corridor because of elevator lobby; also other shapes.
Rectangular tower 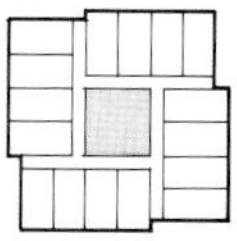	16–24	110 × 110 (34 × 34)	65	60 (5.6)	1.5–1.7	Planning problems focus on access to corner rooms; fewer rooms/floor make it difficult to plan core.
Circular tower 	16–24	90–130 diameter (27–40)	67	45–65 (4.2–6)	1.05	Smaller diameter for 16 rooms per floor; larger for 24 rooms; corridor area varies tremendously; perimeter of 16–19 ft (4.9–5.8 m)
Triangular tower 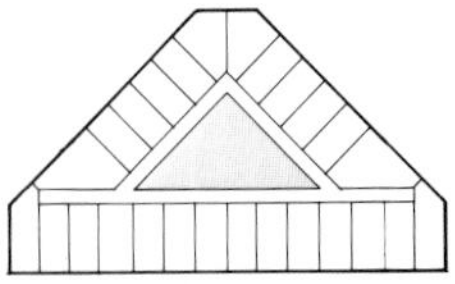	24–30	Varies	64	65–85	1.4–1.8	Central core inefficient because of triangular shape; corner rooms easier to plan than with square shape.
Atrium 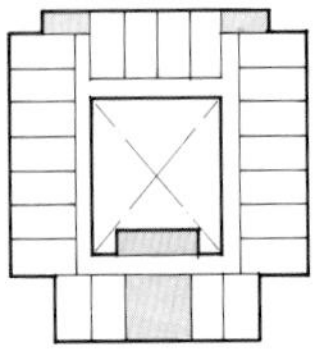	24+	90+ (27)	62	95 (8.8)	1.6–1.8	Open volume creates spectacular space, open corridor balconies, opportunity for glass elevators; requires careful engineering for HVAC, especially smoke evacuation; can be shaped into irregular configurations.

Each guestroom floor configuration has certain characteristics which affect its potential planning efficiency. The table shows the basic building dimensions, the usual percentage of floor area devoted to guestrooms, the amount of area per room needed for corridors, and a "perimeter factor," a multiple of the room width required for the exterior wall. For example, the table shows that double-loaded slabs (and the "offset slab" modification) are the most efficient in terms of guestroom area percentage and that the atrium plans are the least economical in providing guestroom space.

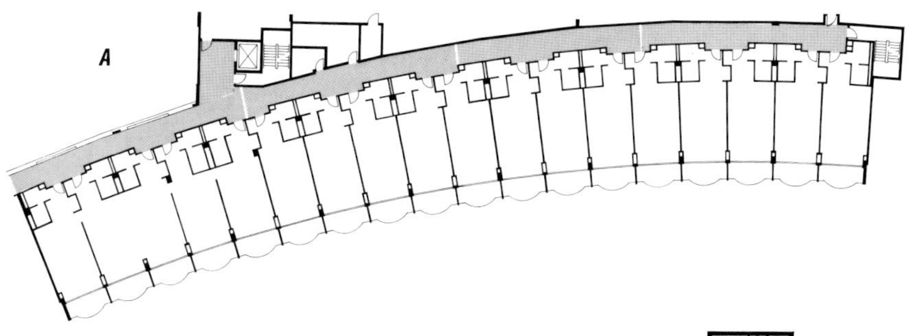

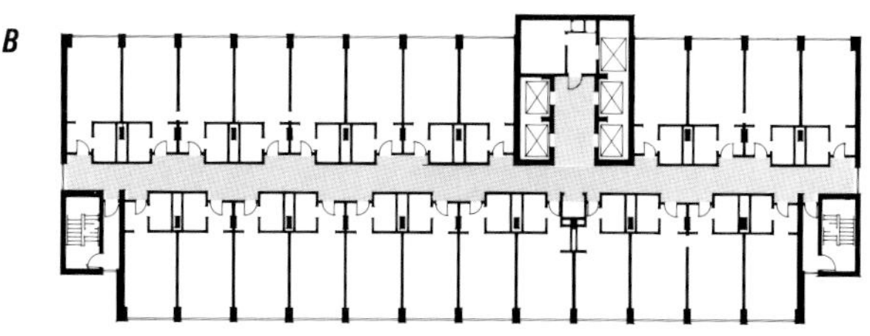

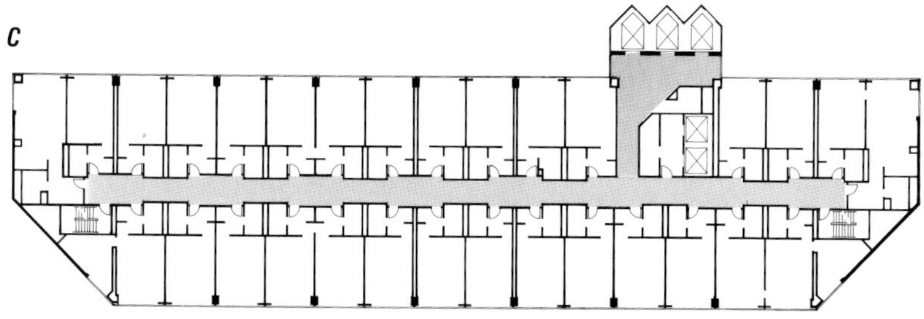

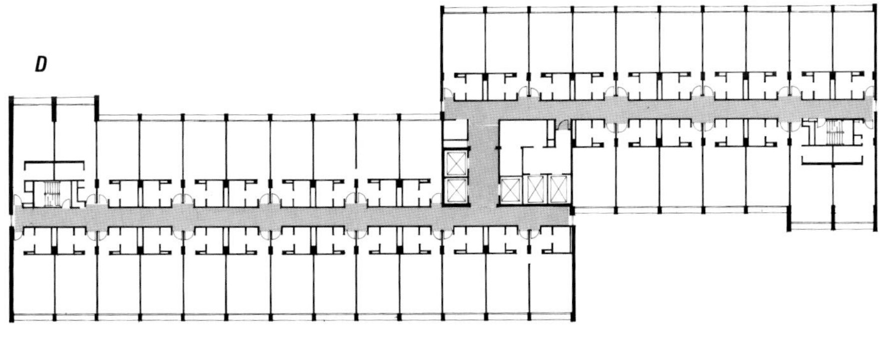

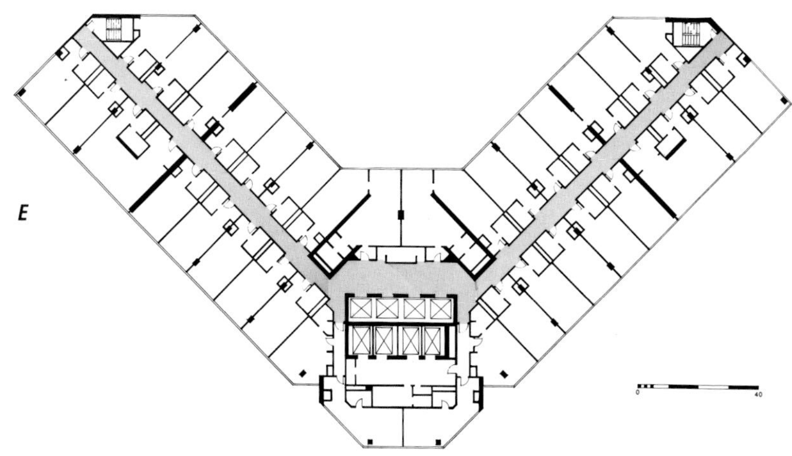

SLAB CONFIGURATIONS

A. SINGLE-LOADED PLAN *(Alameda Plaza Hotel, Kansas City, MO): Plan represents typical single-loaded design with elevators and stairs unrelated to guestroom structure.*

B. DOUBLE-LOADED PLAN *(Sheraton Hartford, Hartford, CT): Layout illustrates economical elevator core with service area "behind" the public elevators.*

C. DOUBLE-LOADED PLAN *(Hyatt Regency Flint, Flint, MI): Design features elevators pulled out of the tower; stairs in bathroom zone at suite.*

D. DOUBLE-LOADED OFFSET SLAB *(Westin Hotel, Tulsa, OK): The core, equivalent of three guestrooms, is positioned in center of offset; stairs accommodated by extending end rooms.*

E. DOUBLE-LOADED L SLAB *(Boston Marriott Hotel/ Copley Place, Boston, MA): Layout includes elevators buried at corner of L shape creating economies similar to offset arrangement.*

tunities for creating architecturally interesting buildings. The "offset slab" plan, for example, is especially economical because the public and service cores are combined and, in addition, because no guestrooms are displaced from the building perimeter. The "knuckle" configuration, which bends at angles, creates interestingly shaped elevator lobbies, provides compact service areas, and breaks up the slab's long corridors.

The core design is complicated by the need to connect the public elevators to the lobby and the service elevators to the housekeeping and other back-of-house areas. This often necessitates two distinct core areas at some distance from each other, although in many hotels they are located together. One common objective is to position the elevator in the middle third of a floor so as to limit walking distances. Rather than integrate the vertical circulation into the body of the tower, the designer may, for planning reasons, add the core to the end of a compact room block or extend it out from the face of the facade.

The actual layout of the core is another determinant of efficiency in the typical plan. In most slab-plan hotels, the vertical cores require space equivalent to two to four structural bays. Usually, the area can be kept to a minimum; certainly fewer guestroom bays are displaced if service areas are located behind the public elevators, rather than beside them or at some distance. Clearly, the efficiency of the plan is improved when the core displaces the fewest number of guestroom units.

Surprisingly, the addition of a distinct elevator lobby is often found in the more efficient layouts. As well as creating an attractive foyer space and isolating the noise and congestion of waiting people from the guestrooms, plans with an elevator lobby tend to have many fewer awkwardly shaped and designed rooms. Thus, efficiency in the

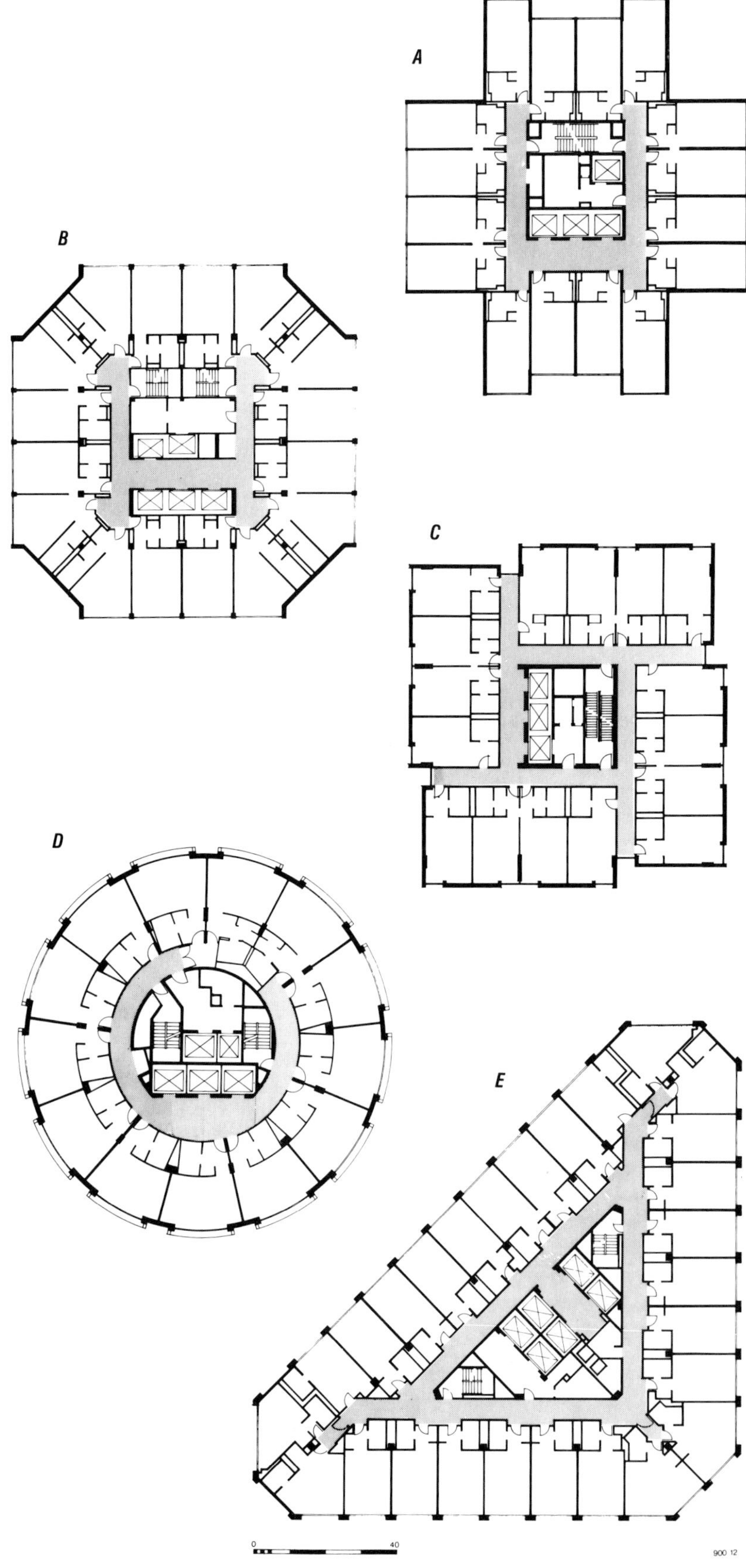

TOWER PLANS

A. PINWHEEL PLAN *(Berkshire Common, Pittsfield, MA): Plan illustrates simple arrangement of 16 rooms in 4 equivalent blocks; the core is extremely efficient with scissor stair, but corridors extended to corners are excessive.*

B. SQUARE PLAN, H CORRIDOR *(Noble Inn, Tampa, FL): Design features extremely economical circulation and core; all bathrooms back to back; unusual yet easily furnished corner rooms.*

C. CROSS-SHAPED PLAN *(Holiday Inn, Ontario, Canada): Layout exemplifies economical corridor plan but increased building perimeter.*

D. CIRCULAR TOWER *(Westin, Seattle, WA): Arrangement shows efficient plan with very compact core and well-laid-out guest bathrooms.*

E. TRIANGULAR TOWER *(New Otani, Los Angeles, CA): Design illustrates well-organized and well-configured core with good access to the ends of the tower.*

core layout comes down to the successful integration of public elevators, service elevators, linen storage, chutes, and vending into a compact vertical core.

The most frequent solutions to the placement of the fire stairs are to locate them at both ends of the corridor, as part of the elevator cores, or within the usual bathroom zone of certain rooms, thereby reducing the guestroom size. These rooms, then, require especially careful planning or are combined with others to form suites. Combining the stairs with one or both of the elevator cores often results in a more efficient overall plan than adding them to the ends of the building.

One limiting factor to the number of rooms on the guestroom floor is the typical building code requirement that there be no more than, say, 200 feet (61 meters) between stair exits. Therefore, one goal in planning the repetitive guestroom floor is to create a layout that does not require a third fire stair. Experienced hotel architects have evolved techniques for lengthening the slab, adding rooms, and manipulating the stairs and corridors to increase the building's overall efficiency.

TOWER PLANS

A second major category of guestroom floor plans are the vertically oriented towers, which are generally organized with a central core surrounded entirely by a corridor and guestrooms (see accompanying plans). The exterior architectural treatment of the tower can vary widely as the geometric shape of the plan changes from square to cross-shaped, circular to triangular. The planning considerations for towers raise similar questions for the designer:

- ☐ **Number of rooms:** How many guestrooms economically fit a particular layout?
- ☐ **Shape:** Which shape is most efficient and permits the desired mix of rooms?
- ☐ **Corridor:** How is hallway access to corner rooms arranged?
- ☐ **Core layout:** How are the elevators, linen storage, and stairs organized?

Unlike the other plan configurations, selection of the tower shape creates specific limitations on the number of rooms per floor. For the most part, towers contain between 16 and 24 rooms, depending on the guestroom dimensions, the number of floors, and the optimum core size. With 16 rooms, the core is barely large enough for two or three elevators, fire stairs, and minimum storage; on the other hand, designs with more than 24 rooms are so large at the perimeter that they contain too much central core area to be efficient.

In most building configurations, efficiency is improved by adding rooms to a floor in which the core and services are only minimally enlarged, if at all, to support them. With the tower configuration, the opposite is true. The analysis of a large sample of actual hotel designs shows that, surprisingly, the *fewer* the number of rooms per floor, the more efficient the layout becomes because the core by necessity must be extremely compact and, as a result, the amount of corridor area is kept to a bare minimum. Inefficient layouts often result from *adding* rooms and by extending single-loaded corridors into each of the building corners.

The shape of the tower has a direct effect on the appearance of the structure and on its perceived scale. The efficiency of the plan, also, is a direct result of the shape because of the critical nature of the corridor access to the corner rooms in the rectangular towers and because of the design of the wedge-shaped guestroom and bathroom in the circular towers. Those plans, which minimize the amount of circulation and, in addition, create unusual corner rooms, exemplify the best in both architectural planning and interior layout.

For the circular towers, the measures of efficiency are judged by the layout of the room as well as the core design. Typically, the perimeter of the wedge-shaped guestrooms is about 16 feet (4.9 meters), whereas the corridor dimension may be less than 8 feet (2.4 meters), thus challenging the designer's skill to plan bathroom, entry vestibule, and closet.

While the design of the core in both rectangular and circular towers is less critical than the arrangement of guestrooms, certain specific issues have to be resolved. Generally, the core is centrally located, and the vertical elements are tightly grouped. The smaller hotels, those with only 16 rooms per floor, generally do not feature an elevator lobby, and the guests in rooms opposite the elevators must tolerate noise from waiting guests. In a few cases, the core is split into two parts, creating roughly an H-shaped circulation zone, effectively providing an elevator lobby. The two fire stairs can be efficiently arranged in a scissors configuration to conserve space.

In the larger tower plans with 24 rooms per floor, inefficiently arranged guestrooms often create excessively large central cores. Simply, the space within the corridor may be larger than is needed for the elevators, stairs, and service areas. Some hotels have "skylobbies" to make this wasted space appear to be a positive feature, or they add conference rooms on every guest floor. Unfortunately, these solutions only show up the problems resulting from poorly conceived and designed guestroom planning. The efficient design of hotel towers requires the simultaneous study of the core layout and of the ring of guestrooms around it, with attempts to compress both as much as possible.

ATRIUM PLANS

A third major category of guestroom floor plans is the atrium design, which was reintroduced by architect John Portman for the Hyatt Regency Atlanta hotel in 1967. The atrium prototype had been used in the past century in both Denver's Brown Palace, still in operation, and San Francisco's Palace, destroyed in the 1906 earthquake and fire. The true atrium configuration has the guestrooms arranged along single-loaded corridors, much like open balconies overlooking the lobby space (see accompanying plans on top of page 166). The following issues must be addressed by the architect:

- ☐ **Shape:** What configuration is to be used for the guestroom structure?
- ☐ **Public elevators:** How are scenic or standard elevators to be arranged?
- ☐ **Service core and stairs:** Where are they to be located?

In addition to the open lobby volume, each atrium hotel is distinguished by the plan of the guestroom floors. While the basic prototype is the square plan with scenic passenger elevators that provide the guest with an ever-changing perspective of the lobby activity as the elevator moves to the upper floors, many of the most recent atrium designs are irregularly shaped to respond to varying site constraints. This sculpting of the building contributes to creating a unique image for the hotel, a primary goal of most developers and architects who select the atrium configuration and who accept the fact that, because of the single-loaded corridors, it is by far the least efficient of the plan types.

Practically all atrium hotels feature scenic or glass elevators, which provide views of the lobby as well as add animation to the space itself. Often these are located on an additional bridge or platform, thereby increasing the amount of circulation on each floor. In some cases, scenic elevators are placed opposite conventional ones, creating the anomaly of two very different experiences.

Service elevators, the housekeeping support functions, and the exit stairs are generally located at both ends of the wings and have relatively little effect on the efficiency of the overall plan. At a practically unfeasible 60 percent usable guestroom space, architects

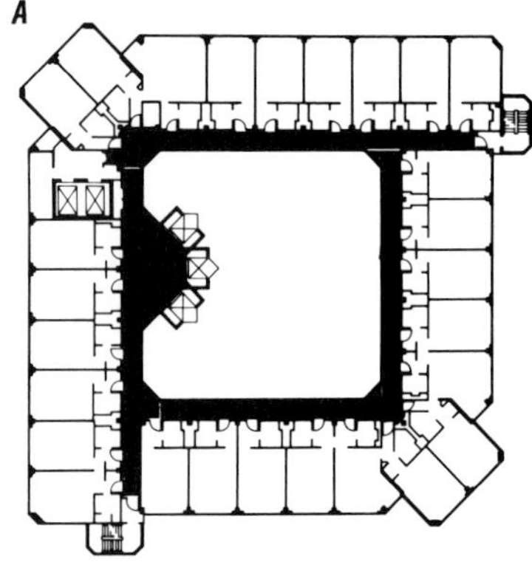

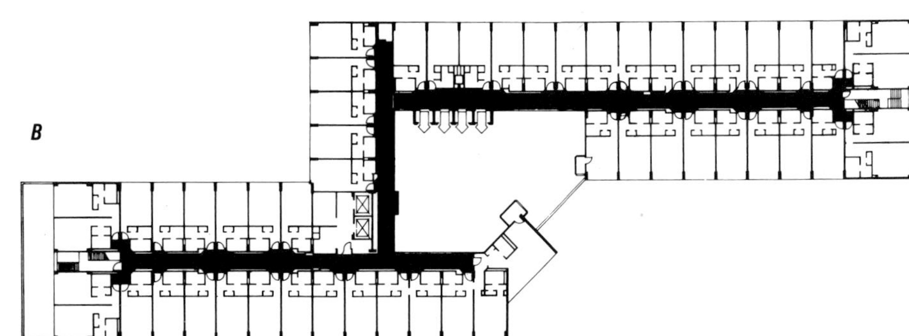

ATRIUM PLANS

A. SQUARE ATRIUM *(Hyatt Regency Louisville, KY): Plan shows variation of classic atrium shape with single-loaded corridors, scenic elevators.*

B. MODIFIED ATRIUM *(Hyatt Regency Cambridge, MA): Design combines small central atrium with two wings of double-loaded rooms to increase efficiency; exposed wall of atrium provides dramatic view of Boston skyline.*

have sought ways to gain the prestige benefits of the atrium while increasing its efficiency. One technique that has been successful in several hotels is to combine an atrium space with double-loaded wings. This effectively and appropriately draws together the architectural excitement of the atrium space—usually on a smaller and more personal scale than in the larger atrium volumes—with the necessary economies of the double-loaded plan.

DEFINING THE GUESTROOM MIX

Following the tentative selection of a plan configuration, the guestroom program requirements must be shaped and modified, if necessary, to fit the architectural concept. The approximate number of rooms in the hotel are identified in the initial market study, in the accompanying financial projections, and in the earliest facilities outline. Typically, these also define the room mix, that is, the number or percentage of guestrooms furnished with a king bed, with two double beds, with a convertible sofa, or whatever. The proposed room mix is intended to reflect the estimated demand of the individual business, group, and leisure market segments. In addition, the preliminary facilities outline developed by the hotel management company specifies precisely the size of the typical room module and the number and type of the proposed suites.

Conceptual plans begin to show how these rooms will be massed in one structure or, in many resorts, in a number of lowrise, scattered buildings. As soon as a tentative building form is conceived, the architect or interior designer should test the plan against the proposed room mix to see what modifications might be necessary in the program or what changes are required in the schematic design. Frequently, critical design modifications are made at this early stage: The width of the guestroom module, the number of bays per floor, or the number of floors are altered to better fit the conceptual design to the program requirements.

One successful approach for studying the room mix is illustrated in the guestroom analysis on the next page, which deals with the following considerations:

- ☐ **Architectural shape:** Identify each room of a different shape or configuration (primarily varying dimensions or bathroom layout).
- ☐ **Bed type:** Label each room by its bed type (twin, queen, king, double-double, king-studio, parlor and handicapped room).
- ☐ **Connecting rooms:** Indicate adjoining guestrooms.
- ☐ **Suite locations:** Position suites, combinations of livingroom and adjoining bedrooms, within the typical room configuration.
- ☐ **Guestroom numbers:** Assign tentative room numbers to the bays to meet the operator's requirements.
- ☐ **Key and bay analysis:** Develop a summary table to tally the number of rentable units ("keys") and room modules for each floor by architectural shape.

The development of such a guestroom analysis early in the preliminary design phase has several important benefits. First, the schematic design is tested against the major element in the space program—the required number of guestrooms—and any necessary changes can be studied.

Second, a format is established so that, as the project proceeds through the later design phases, the designers can continually analyze the guestroom mix and maintain a precise record of the guestroom count.

Third, details of the repetitive guestroom block can be considered at a relatively early phase. For example, the architect can study possible pairing of rooms to increase the number of back-to-back bathrooms and to establish a pattern of wall setbacks at the guestroom doors. The interior designer can begin to analyze the various room layouts and identify any potential problems, such as unusually shaped rooms that might not easily accommodate the necessary furnishings and amenities. Also, the engineering consultants can review the major systems that greatly affect the planning and cost of the rest of the building, such as the elevators, HVAC, and communications.

Frequently, misunderstandings arise over the actual number of rentable guestrooms in a particular project. To avoid this, the following vocabulary should be used consistently.

- ☐ **Key:** A separate, rentable unit
- ☐ **Room:** An individual space, whether separately rentable or not
- ☐ **Bay:** A typical module of the structural bay system

Generally, the hotel management thinks in terms of "keys," which represent the total number of individual guestroom units available to sell. A suite containing a living room and two bedrooms would be considered to contain three keys if the parlor had a full bathroom and convertible sofa, two keys if the living room could not be individually rented. Architects, on the other hand, refer to the individual spaces or rooms and to structural bays, the former being the basis of the contract documents and the latter a chief component of cost estimates for the guestroom structure.

During the development phases, the feasibility consultants are generating estimated revenues, occupancy percentages, and average room rates based on the number of guestroom keys. In addition, both parking requirements and zoning ordinances (used to control project size and density) are usually based on the key count. However, clarification is essential in order to avoid possible misunderstandings and delays. The accompanying example illustrates that the number of bays is larger than the number of rooms, which, in turn, exceeds the number of keys.

Guestroom Analysis. *This case study describes the procedure for analyzing the architectural planning and room layout for a hypothetical 400-room hotel. The two plans illustrate the suite and typical floors, the latter with five different room types—not at all unusual, as the standard room is modified to fit around the elevators, stairs, and support areas. The number of different room types is increased further by special rooms equipped for the disabled and by various suites. The following commentary describes the analysis procedure, resulting in key plans for each floor, labeled with bed type, room number, connecting doors, and so on, and a comprehensive tally of the guestroom mix.*

1. ARCHITECTURAL SHAPE: *Five different room types are identified by the Roman numeral in the top half of the circular code in each room. Room I is the most typical; room II is nearly the same but has a different configuration at the entry vestibule; room III is the corner guestroom with a wider bay and different bathroom; room IV is a two-bay conference suite (the two rooms must be rented together since they have only a single entrance and single bathroom); and room V is a two-bay living room that adjoins two standard guestrooms, although they may have upgraded furnishings.*

2. BED TYPE: *Each room is also designated as a king (K), double-double (DD), parlor (P), conference suite (CS), or VIP suite (VIP). Note that the standard room I is furnished in a variety of different ways.*

3. CONNECTING ROOMS: *Interconnecting rooms are identified by the open circle, for example, the one between rooms 15 and 17. Operating companies seek a specific number of connecting pairs and often designate that, for example, kings connect to double-double rooms.*

4. SUITES: *Two suites are shown: a conference suite in the corner that connects to a standard double-double room, and a VIP suite that connects to two rooms. The VIP suite also counts as a rentable unit, or "key," because it has a full bathroom and a convertible sofa. Often, several large suites are grouped together on the top guestroom floor.*

5. ROOM NUMBERING: *Designating the eventual room numbers at the conceptual design stage is not necessary, except that it aids in communication among the various design professionals and, by doing it early, any confusion caused later by a switch in numbering is avoided. Also, it is a reminder to consider the need for directional and destination graphics.*

6. KEY AND BAY ANALYSIS: *The chart below the plan cross-references the number of room types (I–V) and bed types for each floor. Frequently, a larger chart is developed for the entire hotel showing the stacking of typical and suite floors and providing totals on the number of rooms of each type.*

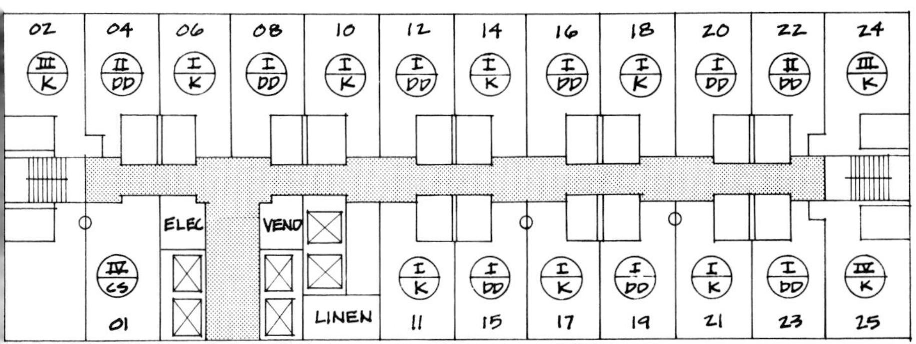

TYPICAL FLOOR

TYPE	BED	NO.	BAYS
I	K	7	7
	DD	6	6
II	DD	3	3
III	K	3	3
IV	CS	1	2
		20	21

CONF. ROOM
CLUB LOUNGE
10 I K
12 VI VIP
16 I DD
18 I DD
20 V VIP
24 III K
ELEC
VEND
LINEN
01 CS
11 I K
15 I P
17 I DD
19 I DD
21 V VIP
25 III K

SUITE FLOOR

TYPE	BED	NO.	BAYS
I	K	2	2
	DD	4	4
	P	1	1
III	K	2	2
IV	CS	1	2
V	VIP	2	4
VI	VIP	1	2
		13	17

16

GUESTROOM DESIGN

"We are going through changes in taste level and demand that is subtle. People are far more discriminating. It requires a lot more attention to design, especially to details."

Guy Ramsey

Design of the individual guestrooms and suites, while clearly more an interior layout than an architectural problem, is still an important part of the architect's responsibility. Along with design of the public spaces, it is also one of the two major duties of the interior designer.

Many hotel operators believe that the guestroom and the guest bathroom make a more lasting impression on the lodging guest than any other single interior space—more than the lobby, the restaurants, or the function space. In part because of the guestrooms' residential character, its irritating deficiencies in layout or equipment—nonworking light switches at the entry, inadequate mirror or counter area in the bathroom, or chair arms that won't fit under the desk—are more obvious to the traveler. These design details call for the coordinated attention of the entire design team: architect, engineer, interior designer, and manager.

The evolution of the hotel guestroom over the past century and a half shows how design and management professionals collaborated to design a better room. Until the Tremont House opened in Boston in 1829, no major hotels with private rooms existed; guests were content to share rooms—even beds—with whatever other travelers were staying in a particular roadhouse. The Tremont's innovative use of private and lockable guestrooms became an overnight success and set the standard for a burgeoning new industry.

Throughout the 19th century, in order to remain competitive, the industry quickly introduced technological advances—gas, then electric lights, voice annunciators, then telephones, and eventually elevators, central heating, and running water. These innovations culminated in the construction of the sumptuous Hotel Statler in Buffalo in 1908 where, for the first time in a major hotel, all the guestrooms included private baths. "A room and a bath for a dollar and a half," the ads proudly proclaimed. Other design innovations of the Statler included bathrooms designed back-to-back for economy, and such features in each room as circulating ice water, full-length mirror, light switch inside the entry door, telephone, built-in radio, and "servidors"—shallow garment-sized compartments constructed in the guestroom door to facilitate pickup and delivery of laundered clothes.

DESIGN CRITERIA

The layout of the hotel guestroom is intertwined with decisions that planners make during the schematic design, when the dimensions of the structural bay, all nontypical room

Hotel guest characteristics

	GUEST CHARACTERISTICS	PURPOSE FOR TRAVEL	GUESTROOM DESIGN FACTORS
Business			
Group	Single or double occupancy; 2–4 night stay; 75% men, 25% women (rising); somewhat price insensitive.	Conventions, conferences; professional associations; sales and training meetings.	King, twin, double–double; bath with dressing area; lounge seating with good work area.
Individual	Single occupancy; 1–2 night stay; 85% men, 15% women; very price insensitive.	Corporate business; sales; conventions, conferences.	King; standard bath with shower; lounge area with exceptional work area.
Pleasure			
Family	Double-plus occupancy (includes children); 1–4 night stay, longer in resort areas; budget or midprice.	Family vacations; sightseeing; sports, family activity.	Double–double, king sofa, or adjoining rooms; lounge area and television; generous, compartmentalized bath; balcony, deck, outside access.
Couples	Double occupancy; 1–7 night stay; midprice to upscale.	Tours, clubs, associations; sightseeing; theater, sports; weekend packages; shopping, vacation.	King; dining, work surface; moderate storage; compartmentalized bath.
Singles	Single occupancy; young professionals; midprice to upscale.	Tours, clubs, associations; culture, arts, theater; shopping.	Queen; dining, work surface; standard bath.

Guestroom design must reflect the needs of the lodger. Commercial hotels, for example, have a high rate of single occupancy and, therefore, need few rooms with two double beds. For the same reasons, they do need better designed and larger work surfaces for the businessperson and full hotel services. The table identifies the principal hotel guest markets, their characteristics, and their influence on the room design.

configurations, and the room mix are determined. These decisions provide the interior designer with the framework to plan the individual spaces creatively and to give the hotel guestrooms a character consistent with the public areas.

Room design entails a series of orderly steps, some of which may have been defined earlier during the architectural planning of the guestroom structure. The designer should establish the following points:

1. Define the lodging guest.
2. Determine the types of guestroom beds.
3. Confirm the guestroom dimensions.
4. Confirm the number and types of suites.
5. Establish the interior design budget.

The best designers recognize the specific needs of the target markets and identify features and amenities that these groups most want and expect. In general terms, the transient business person needs single accommodations, the convention and group markets need double rooms, and the tourist/leisure market rooms to sleep two or more guests. For example, many of the hotel rooms at Walt Disney World in Florida are designed with two double beds and a convertible couch to accommodate a vacationing family of four to six. Also, because each of these market groups uses the room differently, the designer must consider work and meeting functions in one case and family activities in another. The principal market characteristics that influence the layout and furnishing of hotel and resort guestrooms are identified in the above table.

FURNISHINGS

The definition of the market determines not only the most appropriate bed combinations but also all the other furnishings for a particular hotel. Generally, hotels include a mixture of rooms with two beds (generally double beds), one oversized bed (either a queen or king), and suites of various types. The more common alternatives are listed on the top of page 170. While it is uncommon in the United States to have hotel guestrooms furnished with single, twin, or only one double bed, some hotels recently have introduced oversized twin beds in place of two double beds, primarily in convention hotels, in order to provide a more residential atmosphere and to allow more room for other furnishings.

The selection of a proper room mix is important because it influences the hotel's ability to rent 100 percent of its rooms and to generate the maximum revenue. For this reason, rooms with great flexibility, king-size bed plus a convertible sofa, for example, are increasingly popular. Typical room mix percentages for different types of hotel are provided in the figure on the middle of page 170.

The full list of furnishings can be determined by analyzing the guestroom functions—sleeping, relaxing, working, entertaining, dressing—and their space requirements. The typical double–double room has several zones: The bathroom and areas for dressing and clothes storage are grouped next to the corridor entrance; the sleeping area is in the center of the guestroom module; and the seating and work areas are located near the window. New layouts combine the several functions in different ways or find techniques for separating them more fully. For example, suite characteristics are provided in a standard room by adding a screen to separate the sleeping and sitting portions of the space. Or a compartmentalized bathroom is created by isolating the bath and toilet area from the sink and dressing function. Such guestroom zones are illustrated on the bottom of page 170.

With the continuing increase in construction and furnishing costs, it becomes more important to find new solutions to the guestroom layout, that is, designs which combine function and comfort within realistic budgets. One basic approach is to use fewer individual pieces of furniture or to scale them slightly smaller so as to give the perception of a larger or more luxurious room. The designer might include the following:

- ☐ **Queen or 72-inch (1.8-meter) king-size bed:** Beds smaller than the 78-inch (2-meter) king create more open space.

The Remington on Post Oak Park, Houston, Texas. *The 248 guestrooms and suites at the Remington are designed like private residences with carefully constructed details, spacious rooms, and personal amenities to pamper their exclusive clientele. (See also Chapter 9, The Super-Luxury Hotel, and pages 108–109 for more on this hotel.)*

Guestroom bed types

TYPE	SIZE	
Twin	2 twin beds	39 × 80 in. (1 × 2 m)
*Double–double	2 double beds	54 × 80 in. (1.35 × 2 m)
Queen	1 queen bed	60 × 80 in. (1.5 × 2 m)
*King	1 king bed	78 × 80 in. (2 × 2 m)
California king	1 king bed	72 × 80 in. (1.8 × 2 m)
Oversized twin	2 twin beds	45 × 80 in. (1.15 × 2 m)
Queen–queen	2 queen beds	
Double–studio	1 double bed and convertible sofa	
Queen–studio	1 queen bed and convertible sofa	
*King–studio	1 king bed and convertible sofa	
*Parlor	1 convertible sofa	
Wall bed (Sico room)	1 wall bed	

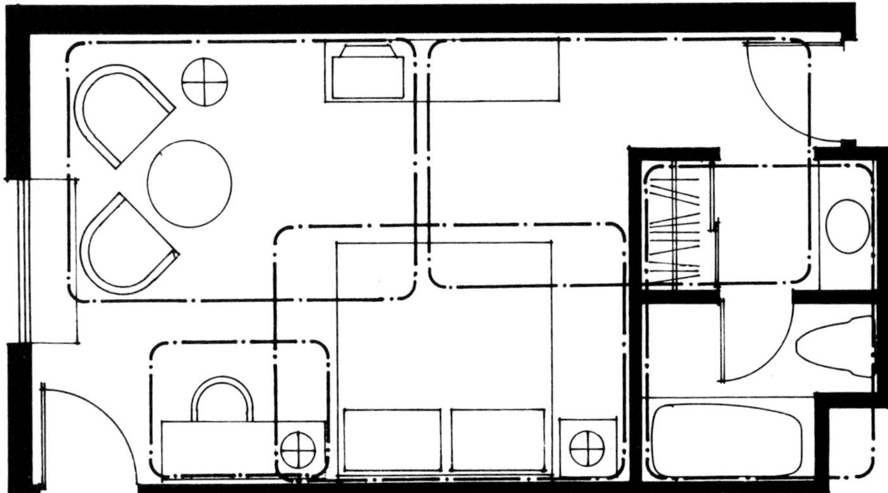

- ☐ **Convertible sofa or wall-bed:** These provide more open space and flexibility, either as the second bed with a double, queen, or king, or as the only bed in a parlor.
- ☐ **Adequate luggage/clothes space:** Sufficient drawers, luggage rack, and closet space reduce the clutter of clothes throughout the room.
- ☐ **Armoire:** Combining drawer space with a television cabinet and possibly a pullout writing ledge in a single unit

ABOVE

Guestroom Bed Types. *Bedrooms come in a great variety of arrangements, generally defined by the type of beds and by the number of room bays. The table provides a comprehensive listing of hotel guestroom types (the more common being identified with an *) and standard bed sizes.*

LEFT

Guestroom Activity Zones. *The hotel guestroom accommodates one to four or more people, sometimes with several activities occurring at one time (for example, bathing and dressing or sleeping and watching TV). The designer needs to be alert to techniques for separating some while combining others, in both cases increasing the flexibility and adaptability of the room to different users. The plan illustrates five guestroom zones.*

BELOW

Guestroom Mix for Different Hotel Types. *Hotel operators have established guidelines for furnishing guestrooms based on the history of the types of guests who stay at a particular type of hotel or resort. This table establishes the room mix objectives for particular types and classes of hotels.*

Guestroom mix for different hotel types

	PERCENT OF TOTAL GUESTROOMS				
TYPE OF HOTEL	DOUBLE-DOUBLE	KING	KING-STUDIO	PARLOR	COMMENTS
Budget inn	100	0	0	0	
Motor inn	60	28	10	2	Trend away from all double-double
Conference center	40	40	15	5	Single occupancy, except needs couples' weekend business
All-suite	10	90	0	100	All rooms connect with a parlor
Super-luxury	20	70	0	10	Double-double replaced with oversize twins
Commercial	20	60	10	10	Limited double occupancy
Resort/family	80	8	10	2	Provide room for cots
Resort/couples	20	70	5	5	
Convention	55	35	5	5	Trend toward replacing double-double with oversize twin
Mega-hotel	55	35	5	5	Double-double provides greatest flexibility for family/group business markets
Casino hotel	40	50	0	10	Depends on strength of tour markets

eliminates the need for two or three separate pieces.

- ☐ **Lounge/desk chairs:** Lounge chairs designed to be used at the work surface eliminate the straight desk chair.
- ☐ **Mirrors:** They enlarge the space visually.
- ☐ **Wall-mounted bedside lamps:** These permit a smaller night table.
- ☐ **Bathroom:** Designs should expand the countertop, mirror, and lighting as much as possible and compartmentalize the tub and/or toilet.

Several details in the room arrangement and furnishing do not have any "best" solution. For example, many operators insist that the telephone should be located next to the beds, whereas others prefer that it be placed at the work area. Similarly, some prefer that the drapes be laminated and combined in a single unit to reduce the number of drapery tracks, whereas others insist on separate sheer, blackout, and overdrape to allow easy cleaning and maintenance. Throughout the room, the designer must balance the conflicting needs of function, safety, maintenance, comfort, and budget and, at the same time, must consider the varying requirements of the several different markets that a single hotel tries to attract.

DIMENSIONS

The guestroom design decision which most influences the rest of the hotel plan is the selection of the room's net width. This establishes the structural module throughout the building, including the public and service areas on the lower floors. The most common dimension is 12 feet (3.7 meters), initially used in the mid 1950s by the Holiday Inn chain as a standard for all their properties. It was designed to accommodate the furniture needed in the roadside motor inn: two double beds against one wall and a desk/luggage rack/TV stand against the opposite wall, with adequate aisle space between. While the room has undergone some minor changes in the last quarter-century, the industry's standard room today is essentially the same one pioneered by founder Kemmon Wilson's Holiday Inns and immediately adopted by Howard Johnson and other companies.

Until then, even the newest and best convention hotels built in the post-World War II period included a variety of room sizes, including a large percentage that were narrower than this 12-foot standard. These hotels, many of them still operating and competing with properties 30 years newer, are greatly limited by the smallness of their guestrooms. In the United States and Canada, no first class or chain-affiliated hotels (except for the budget inns) are built today with rooms less than 12 feet wide, unless, as in the case of renovations of older hotels, the size of a few rooms is limited by unavoidable architectural constraints.

In the past few years guestroom dimensions have become fairly well standardized for different quality levels within the industry (see table below). While a few hotel operators have tried to provide noticeably larger rooms than their direct competitors, guestroom size, quality, and room rate remain closely linked because of the overriding influence of construction and furnishing costs.

The guestroom layouts on pages 172–173 illustrate the standard room design alternatives as well as a number of more innovative solutions. The budget chains have slightly reduced the 12′ × 18′ (3.7 × 5.5 m) motor inn room to lower construction costs, shortening it to between 14 and 16 feet (4.3 to 4.9 meters), which is sufficient to accommodate two double beds. On the other hand, operators who are selling a more luxurious room have experimented with larger guestroom spaces, including more sumptuous bathrooms. Increasing the width of the room module to 13 or 13.5 feet (4 to 4.1 meters) permits one major change in the room layout: two twin beds, or a queen or king-size bed can be positioned against the bathroom wall instead of the side wall, permitting many other arrangements of the furnishings. For example, several designers have placed the bed diagonally instead of against a full wall.

Generally, there is little advantage to increasing the guestroom width beyond 13.5 feet. Even this slightly larger space does not provide improved arrangements, and construction costs are increased dramatically by the increased circulation space and exterior wall area. However, at a room width of 16 feet or more a new set of design alternatives arises: the bed or beds can be positioned against one side wall and the lounge and work area against the opposite wall. Also, the greater width permits unusually luxurious bathroom arrangements, often with four or five fixtures, as well as larger entry vestibules.

The wedge-shaped rooms characteristic of circular towers present their own design problem in the layout of the guest bathroom. The smaller towers have a corridor frontage of only 6 to 8 feet (1.8 to 2.4 meters), the larger plans a more reasonable 10′ feet (3 meters). Although many of these room plans show such positive features as compartmentalized bathrooms (out of necessity), minimum foyer space, a large lounge area, and expansive window wall, today's increasing competition in room size and upscale furnishings has made the smaller cylindrical towers virtually obsolete.

Guestroom dimensions

	LIVING AREA*		BATHROOM		TOTAL GUESTROOM	
	DIMENSIONS, FEET (METERS)	AREA	DIMENSIONS, FEET (METERS)	AREA	DIMENSIONS, FEET (METERS)	AREA
Budget	11′6″ × 15′ (3.5 × 4.5)	172 (16)	5′ × 5′ (1.5 × 1.5)	25† (2.3)	11′6″ × 20′6″ (3.5 × 6.2)	236 (21.9)
Midprice	12′ × 18′ (3.6 × 5.5)	216 (20.1)	5′ × 7′6″ (1.5 × 2.3)	37 (3.4)	12′ × 26′ (3.6 × 6.6)	312 (29)
First class	13′6″ × 19′ (4.1 × 5.8)	256 (23.8)	5′6″ × 8′6″ (1.7 × 2.6)	47 (4.4)	13′6″ × 28′6″ (4.1 × 8.6)	378 (35.2)
Luxury	15′ × 20′ (4.5 × 6.1)	300 (27.9)	7′6″ × 9′ (2.3 × 2.7)	71 (6.6)	15′ × 30′ (4.5 × 9.1)	450 (41.8)

**Living area does not include the bathroom, closet, or entry.*
†Bathroom of budget guestroom includes tub/shower and toilet; sink is part of dressing area.

A
B
C
AC
J
TV
J
SS
F
G
H

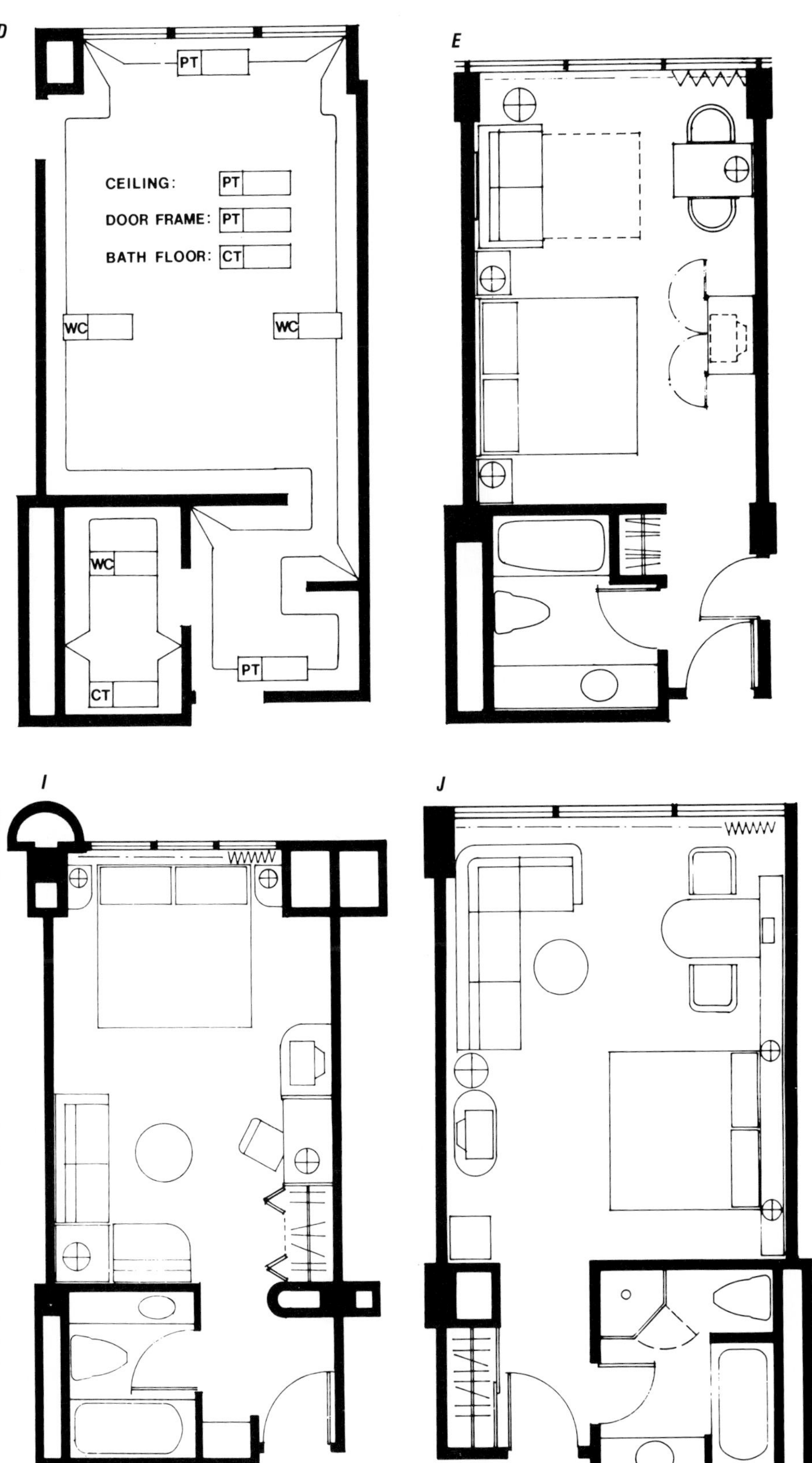

Guestroom Plans. *The room layouts illustrate a variety of solutions to accommodating the family and business markets in hotels, ranging from budget to convention and luxury types. The larger rooms generally provide better lounge and work areas and oversized bathrooms.*

A. *Budget inn double-double (Day's Inn): Small room layout with outside rather than corridor access; limited seating (AC unit used for end table); sink and hanging clothesrod in dressing area.*

B. *Typical double-double: Standard motor inn and hotel room; beds take up 70 percent of living area; limited seating space.*

C. *Typical double-double—electrical/mechanical plan: Identify all electrical outlets, TV, phone, HVAC units; outlets and cable connections should be planned around proposed furnishings.*

D. *Typical double-double—finishes plan: Vinyl wallcovering (VWC), paint (P), carpet (C), ceramic tile (CT) identified and keyed to legend.*

E. *King-studio (Holiday Inn): Standard layout with armoire unit and large lounge area including a convertible sofa.*

F. *Parlor (Holiday Inn): Convertible sofa and small conference area and adjoining typical king and double-double rooms.*

G. *King room—diagonal bed placement (Sheraton Plaza, Palm Springs): Resort layout, larger room size, with bed splayed to reduce institutional look.*

H. *Luxury room (Four Seasons, Montreal, Canada): Room with wider window dimension than depth including luxurious lounge group and oversized four-fixture bath.*

I. *Reversed layout (Sheraton, Washington, D.C.): Unusual room with bed placed in front of window and lounge area near bathroom.*

J. *Luxury king room (Sheraton Grande, Los Angeles): Oversized room with shelf/ledge in place of headboard, large desk surface and lounge area; four-fixture bathroom.*

SUITES

One principal way that a hotel can provide different qualities of accommodations is to include a number of guestroom suites in the room mix. A suite is defined simply as a living room connected to one or more bedrooms. Larger hotels frequently provide a hierarchy of suites, from single-bay living rooms with a sleeping alcove to multiple-bay living rooms with perhaps six adjoining rooms, including dining/conference rooms and several bedrooms. A typical suite breakdown is shown in the table at the right.

Hotel suites, which make up about 10 percent of the total guestrooms, are usually positioned on the upper floors of the tower, but they may be stacked vertically where unusual conditions occur. For example, suites may be used to fill larger structural bays of the typical floor, with mini-suites tucked behind stairs or elevators and others located where the building form provides uniquely shaped rooms.

Over the last 10 years, several new amenities have been added to hotel suites One of these is the inclusion of express checkin and concierge services on the upper floors. In some hotels, these services occur in a single room near the elevator lobby, where the staff serves light hors d'oeuvres, sells beverages, and makes newspapers available. In other hotels, this service has been expanded so that guests on the club floors or towers section bypass the busy lobby registration area and check in at the club floor. The more extensive of these tower club lounges may extend over several bays and contain space for the concierge/registration service, an office, a small seating/television lounge, a conference room, and a large lounge used for continental breakfast, afternoon tea, and cocktails.

Different types of suites

SUITE TYPE	LIVING ROOM	BEDROOMS	KEYS	BAYS	PERCENT
Mini-suite	One bay	Alcove	1	1.5	2*
Conference suite	One bay	1	2	2	3
Junior suite	One bay	2	3	3	4
Executive suite	Two bays	2	3	4	1
Deluxe suite	Three bays	2	2	5	0.5

*Percentage of total rooms, that is, two mini-suites per 100 rooms.

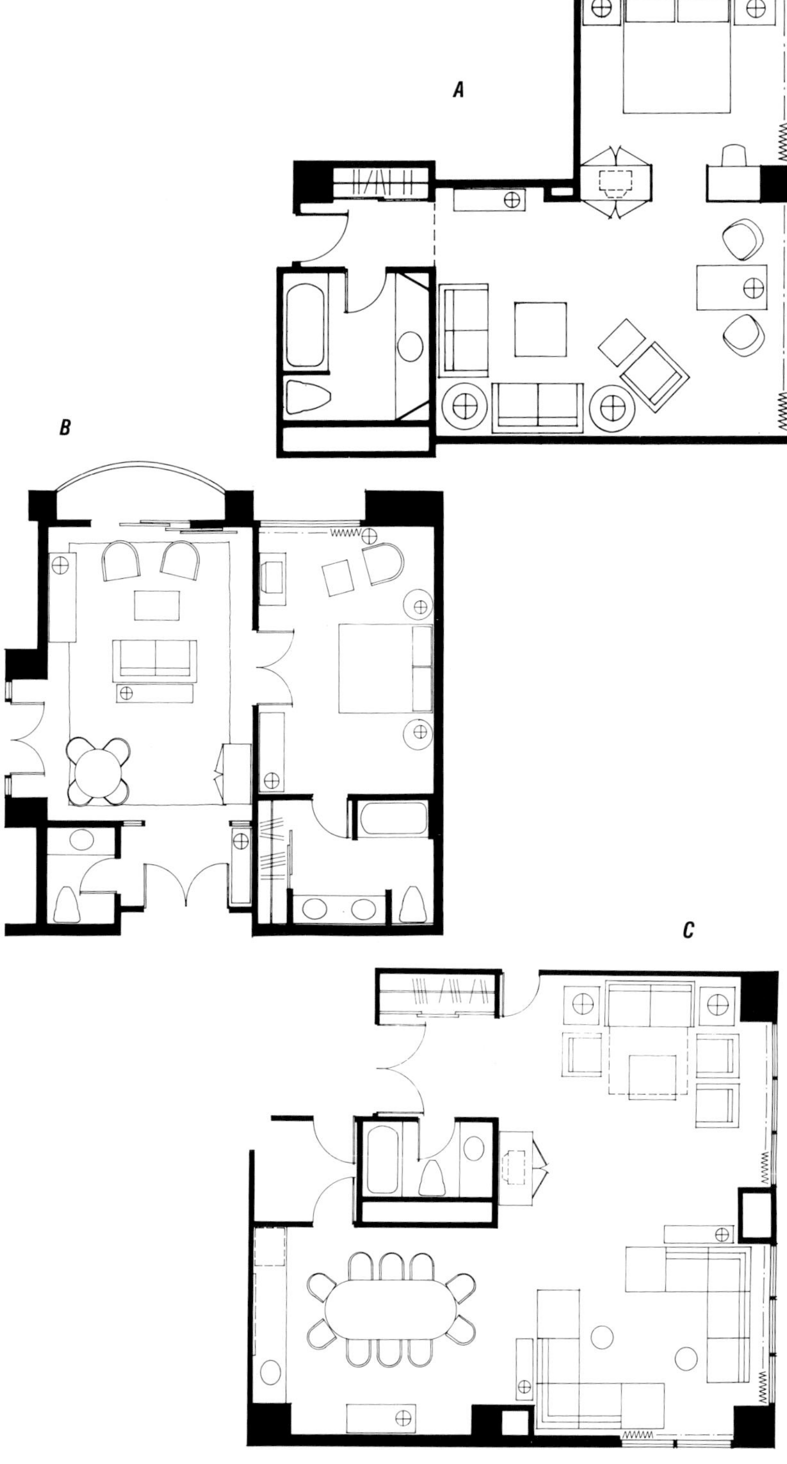

Suite Plans. *Hotel suites combine separate living and sleeping areas and are generally furnished with upgraded fabrics and casepieces. The largest suites may extend for 10 or more structural bays and combine numerous bedrooms and living areas. A range of suites includes: (A) The mini-suite, containing a single bay living room plus a king bed alcove—created by adjacent stairs or elevators. The divider between the two rooms houses the TV and a built-in dressing table.*

(B) The junior suite (Westlake Plaza, Westlake, CA) is equal to the area of two typical rooms. The living area, on an area rug over parquet floors, includes seating and dining areas, while the bedroom features a luxurious compartmentalized bathroom.

(C) Hospitality suites are intended for large groups, such as at conventions where they are the focus of corporate entertaining. The suites show two distinct lounge areas in addition to the conference/dining area with its own pantry; one or more bedrooms generally interconnect.

INTERIOR DECOR AND EQUIPMENT

While guestroom layouts are a major factor in guest satisfaction, the interior design details are equally important. Guestrooms are no less an integral part of the total design concept than the lobby and public areas. Interior design of the guestrooms must show a continuity of design and somehow recall the style and ambience of the public space. Thus, the designers should seek basic design patterns and motifs that can be adapted to both the large-scale public areas and the more residential guestrooms.

Because of the sheer number of guestrooms, the designer has to be particularly conscious of budget economies in their layout. Because of their importance in influencing the guests' perception of the hotel as well as these cost factors, developers usually build a full-scale mockup or model room to test the design before purchasing the furnishings. This provides the perfect setting for final coordination of many furnishing, room finish, and mechanical decisions that affect the final guestroom design.

Some furniture alternatives have already been discussed and illustrated in the various room layouts. The following table lists additional elements that the design team must integrate into guestroom design:

A

Elements needed for complete guestroom design

FURNISHINGS	
☐ **Casepieces**	Desk, dresser, tables, chairs, nightstands, headboard, and TV stand.
☐ **Soft goods**	Bedspreads, drapes, and upholstery fabrics; carpet sometimes included.
☐ **Lighting**	Lamps at the bedside, desk, and lounge seating areas.
☐ **Accessories**	Mirrors, art, planters, other amenities. (Items such as wastebaskets, ashtrays, and luggage racks are part of the operators' equipment.)
GUESTROOM FINISHES	
☐ **Floor**	Generally carpet over padding although resorts might have tile (warm climates) and suites may have wood parquet with area rugs.
☐ **Wall**	Vinyl wall covering preferred or paint.
☐ **Ceiling**	Acoustical treatment.
☐ **Doors**	Wood, prefinished, or painted—all solid core.
☐ **Door frames**	Painted to match doors, walls, or accent color.
BATHROOM FINISHES	
☐ **Floor**	Ceramic or other tile—not carpeted.
☐ **Walls**	Ceramic or marble tile around tub; vinyl wallcovering or paint elsewhere.
☐ **Ceiling**	Paint.
ACOUSTICS	Guestroom walls should be designed for STC ratings of 48.
ELECTRICAL/ MECHANICAL	
☐ **Outlets**	Minimum of 5 duplex outlets: 2 at the beds, one each at desk, dresser, lounge area arranged for the planned layout.
☐ **Cable**	Television, telephone, fire alarm, room status, or other communications system.
☐ **Mechanical**	HVAC integrated with room layout; bathroom exhaust.
☐ **Fire protection**	Minimum of one heat or smoke detector and one sprinkler in each guestroom; some areas require additional sprinklers in closet and bathroom. All interior furnishings should be carefully checked for fire retardant and nontoxic qualities.

ABOVE AND PAGES 176–177

Guestrooms. *Hotel guestroom decor shows a strong move toward subtly patterned and colored residential designs in contrast with the bold motel schemes of 10 years ago. Downtown hotel designs are patterned after that of the public spaces: (A) Sheraton in Washington, D.C., features highly polished chrome and glass surfaces much like its lobby; (B) Adolphus in Dallas takes its direction from the traditional and luxurious finishes elsewhere in the hotel; (C) Melrose in Dallas recreates the elegant moldings and French windows of the 1924 original.*

Suburban and small town hotels such as (D) Hyatt Regency in Princeton, New Jersey, and resorts life; (E) Sheraton Plaza, Palm Springs, California, illustrate striking contemporary designs with atypical layouts and details. Resort rooms require more space to accommodate a longer stay and double occupancy.

Luxury and suite hotels feature many of the extra amenities found in the better resorts. Hotels such as (F) The Mansion on Turtle Creek in Dallas and (G) La Reserve in White Plains, New York, show the designers' attention to every detail, including the many residential accessories so uncommon in commercial hotels. (See also other guestrooms on pages 172–173.)

B

D

C

E

F

G

1

PUBLIC SPACE DESIGN

"All lobbies should establish contact with the shops, bar, and restaurants, and enable a guest to feel like he's in the heart of the hotel."

Vladamir Sanda

While the hotel guestrooms take up the majority of the floor area in virtually all hotels, it is the public space that defines the differences among the various types. Because the lobby, restaurants and lounges, meeting and banquet space, and recreation facilities vary so greatly (from only 6 percent in a budget inn to 20 percent in a conference center), understanding the distinctions among the different hotel types is crucial to programming and designing a successful project.

In the table opposite, the key differences in public space for the different hotel types are identified. Convention hotels and conference centers, for example, have immense meeting and banquet space; resorts and, more recently, conference centers include major recreational components; downtown and luxury hotels, among others, have fewer but generally high-quality food operations.

In addition to providing the appropriate mix of facilities for each type of hotel, the architect must create an organization that meets the functional requirements of the developer and the hotel management company. The budget and midprice companies insist on tight and economical layouts, which give special attention to such operational areas as the back-of-house and the front office. The first class and deluxe operators, while they too strive for efficiency, are equally concerned with the visual qualities of the building and frequently will accept a less economical plan in order to accommodate more appealing architectural and interior design features.

An overall objective of the planning and design requirements for hotel public areas is that they be clustered around the lobby (see accompanying diagram). This arrangement assures that the hotel guests can find the various facilities with a minimum of difficulty and provides the opportunity for overlap of function, especially true with atrium lobbies or with such hotels focused around a central lobby/recreation core as Holiday Inns' "Holidome."

EXTERIOR APPROACH AND ENTRANCES

The architectural aspects of the building are, of course, best observed on the approach to the front entrance, and the details of the site and exterior design—the landscaping, the night illumination, the entry drive and canopy—all contribute to the guests' anticipation of their hotel stay. Larger hotels may develop a number of different entrances to help separate overnight guests and visitors, to reduce the amount of unnecessary traffic through the building, to establish a distinct identity for a restaurant or other facility, or to provide increased security. The designers should as-

Public space matrix*

TYPE	LOBBY	FOOD AND BEVERAGE AREAS	FUNCTION SPACES	RECREATION	PARKING†
Downtown	Moderate	Small	Varies	Small	Small
Suburban	Moderate	Moderate	Moderate	Moderate	Large
Airport	Small	Moderate	Large	Small	Moderate
Roadside	Small	Moderate	Small	Small	Moderate
Resort, beach golf, tennis	Moderate	Large	Moderate	Large	Large
Resort, condo	Small	Moderate	Small	Large	Moderate
Vacation village	Small	Small	Small	Large	Moderate
Convention	Large	Large	Large	Moderate	Moderate
Conference center	Moderate	Moderate	Large	Large	Large
Condominium	Small	Small	Small	Moderate	Moderate
Suite	Small	Moderate	Moderate	Moderate	Moderate
Super-luxury	Small	Moderate	Small	Small	Moderate
Renovation	Varies	Varies	Varies	Small	Moderate
Mega-hotel	Large	Large	Large	Large	Moderate
Mixed-use	Large	Large	Large	Moderate	Moderate
Casino	Large	Large	Large	Large (casino)	Moderate

**Key:* "Small" means lobby < 6 sq ft/room; food and beverage areas < 1 seat/room; function spaces < 2 seats/room; recreation area = pool plus limited other facilities; parking < 1 car/room.

"Moderate" stands for lobby 6–10 sq ft/room; food and beverage areas 1–1.5 seats/room; function spaces 2–4 seats/room; recreation area = pool and health club plus limited other facilities; parking for 1–1.3 cars/room.

"Large" indicates lobby > 10 sq ft/room; food and beverage areas > 1.5 seats/room; function areas > 4 seats/room; recreation areas = extensive facilities; parking > 1.3 cars/room.

†Parking: Some types of hotels require additional parking for buses.

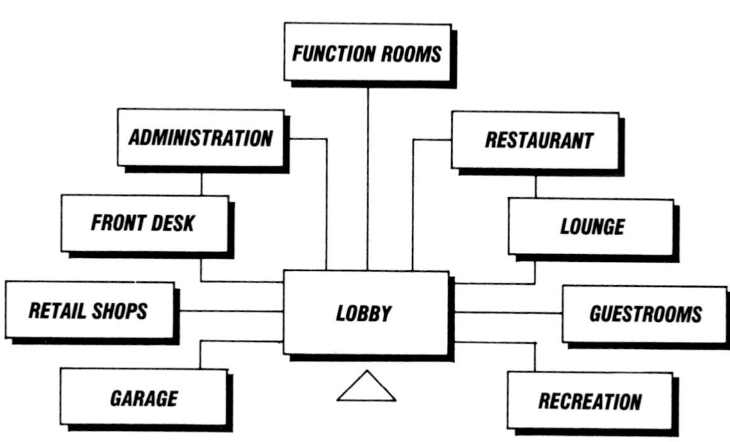

sess the relative need for the following entrances:

- ☐ Main hotel entrance
- ☐ Ballroom/banquet entrance
- ☐ Restaurant/bar/nightclub/casino entrance
- ☐ Tour bus/airport bus entrance
- ☐ Suite or apartment entrance

Each entrance needs to be clearly marked according to its function with a canopy, signage, special illumination, or other architectural treatment. Some entrances require space for waiting taxis or buses, others require temporary luggage storage, and the apartment entrance requires special security. The design requirements for the hotel entrances can be summarized briefly:

- ☐ **Canopy;** Provide a porte cochere or covered dropoff at the main entrance and principal secondary entrances (ballroom) to protect guests from inclement weather; include lighting, signage, heat, if necessary; ensure sufficient height for buses.
- ☐ **Driveways:** Predict the amount of traffic congestion and provide space for

ABOVE

Public Space Adjacency Diagram. *The schematic diagram illustrates the principal requirement that as many public facilities as possible—front desk, guest elevators, restaurants and bars, meeting and banquet rooms, and recreational facilities—be located close to, and visible from, the main lobby. Many problems in hotel planning can be resolved if guests can find their way easily around the building.*

OPPOSITE PAGE

Seoul Hilton International, Seoul, Korea. *The Henry Moore sculpture in the lobby of the Seoul Hilton creates an exciting and memorable experience for hotel guests and visitors alike and emphasizes the great opportunities for exhibiting artwork throughout hotels.*

waiting taxis, loading and unloading of passengers and bags, and short-term standing including valet-delivered cars and tour or airport buses.

- ☐ **Parking:** Make garage entrances convenient to and from the main entrance; if there is valet parking, establish a location for the attendant's booth near the main entrance.
- ☐ **Sidewalks:** Design pedestrian areas sufficiently wide for handling baggage, storing baggage carts, and providing doorman or bellman station; at bus locations provide space for groups.
- ☐ **Doors and Vestibules:** Develop weather vestibule with revolving or automatic doors to limit temperature differences; include access into luggage storage room from curb; provide ramps if necessary for both disabled guests and luggage.

Examples of successful hotel entry areas such as The Bostonian, The Remington, Stanford Court, and the Four Seasons Olympic, are illustrated in Part 1 of this book.

LOBBY

Among the many public areas of the hotel, the lobby makes the single greatest impact on the guest. Its design—whether intimate or expansive, formal or casual—sets the tone of the hotel or resort. Therefore, the planning of the major lobby elements and the design of the details are crucial to making a positive and lasting impression on the guest. The most successful designs carefully balance two key factors: visual impact and function.

For several decades, until the Hyatt Regency Atlanta opened in 1967, most hotel lobbies were relatively small, designed along the same economical principles as the rest of the hotel. However, in the 70s emphasis shifted toward larger lobbies, not only in convention hotels and mixed-used complexes, but also in smaller hotels built in suburban areas and at airports. The current decade, with its increase in hotel specialization, shows evidence of a return to more intimate interior spaces, especially in the super-luxury, all-suite, and conference center categories. Thus, an initial decision facing the developer and architect that is central to the concept is what should the scale, atmosphere, and image of the lobby be.

Planning objectives

The planning requirements of most hotel lobbies are similar regardless of the type of hotel (see lobby design checklist). In addition to establishing the image of the hotel, the lobby serves as the main circulation space, directing guests to the front desk, elevators, food and beverage outlets, meeting and banquet facilities, recreation complex, and other public areas; as guests linger, it serves as an informal gathering space. It also functions as a control point, with the staff visually supervising access to the building. The several planning objectives for the lobby can be summarized as follows:

- ☐ **Entrances:** Consider additional exterior entrances for main lobby, banquet facilities, restaurants, health club, or other high traffic areas.
- ☐ **Front desk location:** Locate the desk so that it is immediately visible to the entering hotel guest; in addition, have the front desk staff visually oversee access to the passenger elevators.
- ☐ **Office access:** Provide entrances to the front office, safe deposit area, executive offices, and sales and catering offices.
- ☐ **Guest elevators:** Locate elevators close to the desk and the main entrance with sufficient elevator lobby space for guests and their luggage.
- ☐ **Seating area:** Provide a seating area near the desk and entrance; the area may also be contiguous with the lobby bar.
- ☐ **Circulation:** Establish clear paths to the front desk, elevators, restaurants and bars, meeting and banquet areas; where possible, separate hotel guest traffic from purely convention traffic.
- ☐ **Retail areas:** Provide lease space convenient to the guest circulation areas.
- ☐ **Bellman/luggage:** Position bellman station near front desk, elevators, and front entrance, with separate rooms for baggage, carts, and locked storage.
- ☐ **Support functions:** Locate such accessory functions as toilets, coats, house phones, public phones, directory, and assistant manager's desk conveniently in relation to other areas.

The space program for the lobby must recognize the type of hotel and the amount of circulation within the public areas. Larger hotels, such as convention properties and those located within mixed-use projects, require tremendous amounts of space to accommodate the number of guests and visitors drawn to the variety of facilities. Smaller hotels and those that cater to few outsiders other than hotel guests require very little floor area. Most hotels provide per guestroom between 6 and 10 square feet (.6 and .9 square meters) of floor area in the lobby, not including circulation to remote functions (see Chapter 14, Facilities Programming).

Locating bars, restaurants, and retail kiosks within the lobby is one way to increase the apparent size of the space without adding additional gross area. Architect John Portman refers to this concept as "shared space," in which the many lobby functions are planned to create variety not only in scale but in relative level of activity, with fluctuations throughout the day. In order to accomplish this diversity successfully, the best plans provide a clear definition of the several functions that occur within the lobby and make their organization obvious to the guest.

Lobby design checklist

FRONT DESK AREA
- ☐ Registration station, number
- ☐ Cashier station, number
- ☐ Mail/information stations, number
- ☐ Total desk length
- ☐ Assistant manager's desk
- ☐ Bellman station
- ☐ Bellman cart storage
- ☐ Luggage storage
- ☐ House phone
- ☐ Pay phone
- ☐ Meeting directory

SEATING AREA
- ☐ Seating, number of seats
- ☐ Food or beverage service
- ☐ Fountain or other focus

CIRCULATION
- ☐ Passenger elevators
- ☐ Access to restaurants and lounges
- ☐ Access to meeting and banquet rooms
- ☐ Access to recreation facilities
- ☐ Access to retail shops and other public areas
- ☐ Access to parking garage

RETAIL AREA
- ☐ Newsstand
- ☐ Drugstore
- ☐ Giftshop
- ☐ Travel agent/tours
- ☐ Airline counters
- ☐ Car rental
- ☐ Barber/beauty shop
- ☐ Jeweller
- ☐ Florist
- ☐ Bank
- ☐ Men's wear
- ☐ Women's wear
- ☐ Toys
- ☐ Specialty shops (leather, linens, glass)
- ☐ Bookstore

Lobby Design Checklist. *Successful lobby planning requires the designer to carefully consider the relative layout of several major functional elements (front desk, guest elevators) and uncountable minor ones (house phones, meeting directory). Some relate to the lobby space itself, others to the perimeter, and others to movement through the area. The checklist identifies the essential elements of good lobby planning.*

Design objectives

The written design objectives for the lobby provide a detailed description of the front desk, seating area, circulation, and secondary functions. To a large extent, the architect and interior designer must first study these areas individually, designing the registration and cashier area, the traffic flow areas, and so forth. Planning the front desk, for example, requires independent decisions about the following features:

- ☐ **Size of desk:** Provide 6 feet (1.8 meters) long stations for registration and cashier based on the number of guestrooms; assume two stations for first 150 rooms, one more for each additional 100 rooms; also provide one mail/information station for each 600 rooms or fraction.
- ☐ **Queuing space:** Provide sufficient space in front of the desk for guests to stand at the counter; for convention hotels at least 20 feet (6.1 meters) clear of circulation.
- ☐ **Assistant manager's desk:** If required, provide a desk, three chairs, and storage near the front desk for a concierge or assistant manager; the desk may be a major decorative feature within the lobby.
- ☐ **Bellman station:** Provide a bellman station near the front desk and main entrance; provide public phone, house phone, paging, and electrical outlet.
- ☐ **Baggage storage:** Provide a lockable storage area adjoining the bellman station with shelving for checked luggage; provide direct access to the curb.
- ☐ **Telephones:** Include house phones close to the front desk and public phones convenient to the lobby; a minimum of 1 to 100 rooms.
- ☐ **Directory/signage:** Locate a directory with listings of all special functions and meetings near the front entrance; provide clear signage to all hotel areas.
- ☐ **Furniture and fixtures:** Establish ambience of lobby area by providing special millwork detailing and finishes, front desk, bellman station, assistant manager's desk, and furnishings (lounge seating, decorative lighting, artwork) to establish the image of the hotel.

The design of the other areas of the lobby deals with fewer functional elements but requires more manipulation of the space. The definition of circulation, seating, and retail areas is usually advanced by such standard design techniques as level changes, floor materials, varying ceiling heights, special lighting, signage programs, articulation of decorative details, and custom millwork. Many of these are evident in the illustrations of lobbies throughout Part 1.

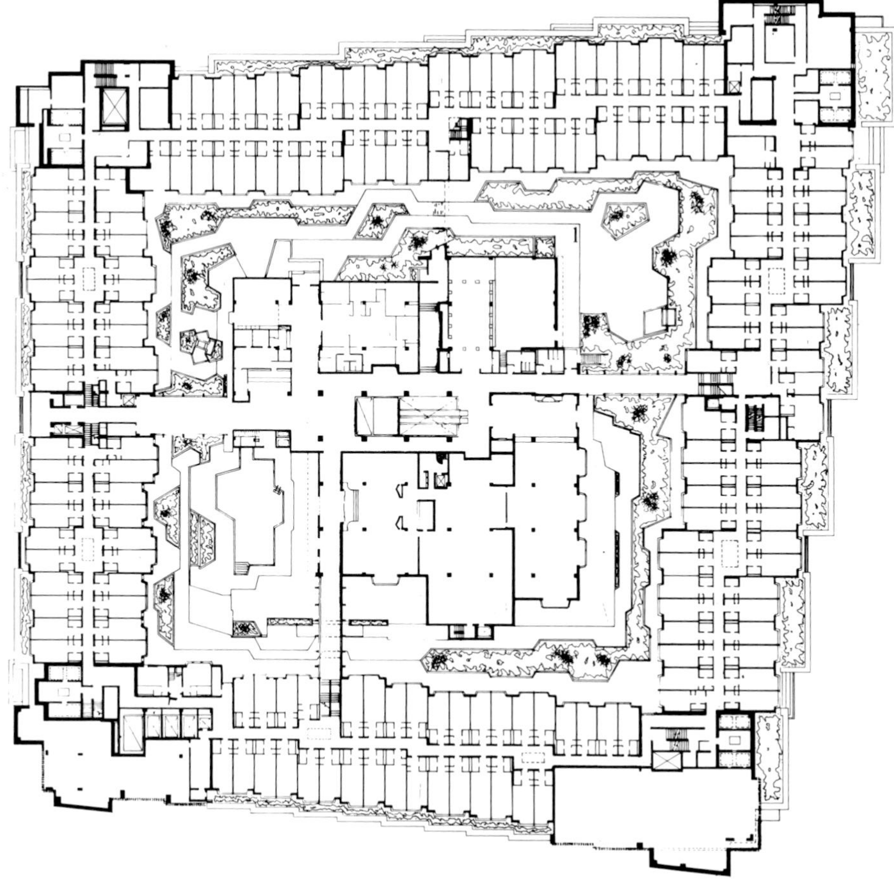

Lobby Planning. *The arrangement of the public areas in The Bonaventure Hilton International in Montreal, Canada, shows the clustering of restaurants, cocktail lounges, and shops around the main lobby with the access to the function space from the central stair and escalators. The lobby and restaurant look out on the pool and carefully landscaped roof gardens.*

FOOD AND BEVERAGE OUTLETS

Generally, one or more restaurants and cocktail lounges are clustered conveniently around the hotel lobby. These and other more specialized types of food and beverage outlets—specialty, rooftop, and theme restaurants, deli and snack bars, lobby, bar, and entertainment lounges—form a second more complex category of public spaces. However, these vary so widely in quality and character that the program and design of each outlet must be developed individually based on a survey of the total market and existing competition.

Hotel food service has gone through frequent cycles of popularity with the public. Until a decade ago, the great majority of American hotel restaurants had a reputation for poor food and uninspired design. Their mediocrity may have been due to the fact that often hotel restaurants were only profitable at breakfast, when the overnight guests could be depended on to fill the dining rooms; guests scarcely used them at lunch and hardly more at dinner. Only in the mid 1970s, in a climate of increased competition, did the hotel industry recognize the marketing opportunities of improved restaurant and lounge operations. They found that well-conceived food and beverage outlets increased the demand for guestrooms and meetings, attracted the general public, especially at the low volume lunch and dinner periods, and generated additional profits.

Designing successful restaurant and bar operations must be based on a recognition of the public's changing attitudes. For example, more people now eat outside conventional meal times, foregoing breakfast but taking a larger morning coffee break or putting off dinner for a late-evening meal or snack. Travelers appreciate restaurants that provide self-service elements—buffet lines or salad bars—from which they can choose among various displayed foods and have better control of their time or choose outlets that wel-

Food concept checklist

GENERAL
- ☐ Name of outlet
- ☐ Location
- ☐ Capacity
- ☐ Operating hours
- ☐ Market description
- ☐ Financial projection
- ☐ Staffing

FOOD CONCEPT
- ☐ Menu
- ☐ Style of service
- ☐ Food/wine display
- ☐ Exhibition cooking
- ☐ Atmosphere
- ☐ Entertainment

DESIGN/LAYOUT
- ☐ Entry sequence
- ☐ Host/maitre d'
- ☐ Cashier
- ☐ Seating mix
- ☐ Self-service/buffet
- ☐ Service station
- ☐ Food/wine display
- ☐ Exhibition cooking
- ☐ Level change
- ☐ Entertainment area
- ☐ Kitchen entry
- ☐ Service bar

DESIGN/DECOR
- ☐ Atmosphere
- ☐ Finish
- ☐ Tables/chairs
- ☐ Feature elements
- ☐ Window treatment
- ☐ Lighting
- ☐ Color scheme
- ☐ Tabletop
- ☐ Artwork
- ☐ Plants

UNIFORMS
- ☐ Uniform design

SPECIAL EQUIPMENT
- ☐ Exhibition cooking equipment
- ☐ Tableside carts
- ☐ Point-of-sale computers
- ☐ Order writing system
- ☐ Sound system

come informal dress. These considerations should be part of the market analysis, which defines both the hotel guest and the local customer, so that the hotel's food and beverage facilities can enjoy the largest possible audience.

Developing food and beverage concepts

The high visibility of hotel restaurants suggests that designers should think through their detailed operations early in the development phase. However, often in smaller hotels, restaurant menus are not developed until a few months before the hotel opens. As a result, the restaurant may not be designed until well after the building shell is complete, when changes to the lobby entrances and kitchen access or the addition of level changes, display features, or special ceiling treatments are impossible. The result is an unexceptional restaurant.

Experienced hotel management companies evolve food and beverage concepts in two ways. Some, like Marriott, define the operations early in the development process and establish the type of food and service, the hours of operation, the theme and general atmosphere including even the name and logo. The architect and interior designer are then expected to develop a schematic building design that accommodates these themes. The components of restaurant and lounge design should be based on food and beverage concept checklists shown above.

The other procedure is to establish only rough space requirements at the program phase and, after the architect has conceived the organization of the hotel, to develop the food and beverage concepts in light of the actual location and type of space provided. For example, at the Hyatt Regency Buffalo, a converted office building, the theme and design for the entertainment lounge was developed only after it was located within the 50-year-old restored Genesee Building; it contrasts markedly with the other beverge outlet (the contemporary lobby lounge), which is located within the exposed trusses of the new atrium space. (Also, see the discussion of the Hyatt Regency Buffalo, Chapter 10.)

A recent approach to hotel food service has been to develop a single restaurant with several distinct moods that are appropriate to the different meals and levels of informality. At the 400-room Berkshire Place in New York, Dunfey Hotels operates such a restaurant, Rendezvous, which includes an area overlooking the street that is furnished like a sidewalk cafe, intermediate zones that are modeled after a French bistro, and a rear section, that is lavishly decorated as a more formal dining room. The distinct atmospheres of the Rendezvous are created by such techniques as changing the floor materials and levels, table accessories, and lighting.

Larger hotels and resorts have several restaurants requiring individual and distinctive themes. If a property includes only two outlets, they usually are a coffee shop—or "cafe"—and a specialty restaurant. A third outlet might be a small gourmet dining room and a fourth a deli or a pastry shop. Each restaurant has its own image, and while attracting hotel guests, it also attempts to compete for different groups of outside diners.

Many food and beverage concepts include conscious attempts to merchandise the food in novel ways such as through display and

Beverage concept checklist

GENERAL
- ☐ Name of outlet
- ☐ Location
- ☐ Capacity
- ☐ Operating hours
- ☐ Market description
- ☐ Financial projections
- ☐ Staffing

BEVERAGE CONCEPT
- ☐ Bar/lounge emphasis
- ☐ Entertainment
- ☐ Atmosphere

DESIGN/LAYOUT
- ☐ Entry sequence
- ☐ Host
- ☐ Bar
- ☐ Pickup station
- ☐ Drink rail
- ☐ Bar storage
- ☐ Food/snack counter
- ☐ Seating mix
- ☐ Stage
- ☐ Dance floor
- ☐ Disco booth
- ☐ Special entertainment
- ☐ Level changes

DESIGN/DECOR
- ☐ Atmosphere
- ☐ Bar/other fixtures
- ☐ Finishes
- ☐ Tables/seating
- ☐ Window treatment
- ☐ Lighting
- ☐ Color scheme
- ☐ Decorative elements

UNIFORMS
- ☐ Uniform design

SPECIAL EQUIPMENT
- ☐ Remote liquor/beer
- ☐ Performer lighting
- ☐ Sound system
- ☐ Point-of-sale computers

open food preparation areas. Increasing th visibility of the food choices and developin unusual food combinations can greatly in crease revenues. Some of the many oppor tunities for better food merchandising ar listed on the next page.

Bar operations are similarly varied. Whil most motor inns include a small cockta lounge, larger hotels offer a lobby bar, a entertainment facility, and, occasionally, rooftop lounge where the view warrants it Additional small outlets for food and beverag may complement and support a hotel's recre ation facilities, such as the pool bar, marin bar, or the bar and restaurant at the golf c tennis resort's clubhouse.

Before considering the detailed plannin and design issues of hotel restaurants an lounges, designers should become familia with such operational aspects of food servic as marketing, menu planning, service, an food preparation techniques. This enable them to communicate better with the managers who establish the following basic restaurant and lounge criteria:

- ☐ Market characteristics
- ☐ Type of menu
- ☐ Style of service
- ☐ Hours of operation
- ☐ Number of covers
- ☐ Average guest check
- ☐ Turnover
- ☐ Demand fluctuations (day, week, season)
- ☐ Average party size
- ☐ Food preparation techniques
- ☐ Bar operations
- ☐ Service station requirements
- ☐ Host and cashier functions
- ☐ Food/beverage merchandising
- ☐ Staffing
- ☐ Financial projections

Planning objectives

The planning requirements for restaurants and lounges are as critical as for the other public areas, but, to a large extent, each outlet is independent of the others. Nevertheless, the following points are essential to an effective organization:

- ☐ All food outlets need direct, close access to the kitchen except outlets with minor food service that may be served from pantries.
- ☐ All beverage outlets need service backup, either to the kitchen or to bar storage areas.
- ☐ All outlets should be easily located from public flow areas; the cafe should be visible from the lobby.
- ☐ Most food outlets should have a bar adjacent or should include a small holding lounge.
- ☐ Larger restaurants and bars should be planned so that sections can be closed during slow periods.
- ☐ Restaurants and bars should have exterior frontage and direct outside access.

The optimal number of restaurant and bar seats varies with the size, type, and location of the hotel and with the relative emphasis that the operator gives to that part of the operation. A good starting rule of thumb is to provide restaurant seats equal to .75 times the number of guestrooms and lounge seats equal to .5 times the number of guestrooms. This initial program objective can be increased or decreased according to the consultants' market study and the hotel operator's further financial analysis.

Convention hotels, at which the breakfast meal creates the largest peak demand, usually have larger coffee shops and more active room service. Remote destination resorts, where all the guests must be served three meals, plan flexible use of outdoor areas—breakfast terraces and pool snack bars, for instance—or introduce two sittings to accommodate peak numbers. At certain suite hotels, where the average length of stay is often several weeks or longer and where the guests may prepare their own breakfast and dine out in the evening, only minimal food and bar service is needed. But today's new transient suite hotels often serve free breakfast as well as provide generous cafes and lounges.

Experienced hotel operators approach the food and beverage program with an instinct about the relative size of the several outlets. Thus, a 400-room hotel might feature, instead of a 300-seat restaurant (.75 times the number of guestrooms), a moderate-price food outlet for 175 to 200 people and a more expensive restaurant with 100 to 125 seats. The table on page 184 gives guidelines on restaurant and bar capacities for different size hotels before the necessary modifications for site and market conditions.

Downtown hotels, especially in shopping and tourist areas, provide special opportunities for independent-appearing restaurants. For example, Cafe de l'Auberge in Toronto, Fourneau's Ovens in San Francisco, and LaRecolte in New York, while all part of deluxe hotels, are recognized as high caliber, free-standing restaurants. These operations can be added to the recommended program of restaurant seats because hotel guest use is relatively small.

Opportunities for better food merchandising

Multiple themes	Several small restaurants with distinct ethnic or other themes operate from a single commissary; the O'Hare Hilton in Chicago has a cluster of English pub, French bistro, Balkan grill, and Swiss specialty restaurants, ranging in size from 30 to 80 seats.
Exhibition cooking	Food is prepared in the restaurant or at an area visible from the seating areas and is used as the source for many menu items; examples include grill, bakery, pasta making, rotisserie, and Chinese wok.
Food display	A display area either at the entrance or located near the center of the outlet serves either as a source for food or as decoration; examples include appetizers, carved roasts, desserts, wines, special coffees, ice carvings, and "horns of plenty."
Buffet	Display area is used for guest self-service.
Tableside service	Service carts are rolled to each table with the presentation or preparation of individual entrees; or specialty appetizers, Ceasar's salad, desserts, and liqueurs.
Takeout	In downtown hotels, especially in shopping and tourist areas, fast service and informal outlets with takeout counters may be installed with such items as ice cream, pastries, sandwiches, and specialty foods.
Lobby breakfast	Temporary cart service is provided in the lobby to sell coffee, juices, and pastries during peak breakfast hours.
Atrium restaurant	Exposed and visible food outlet, such as a sidewalk cafe in the lobby, increases awareness of the restaurant and encourages guest use, whatever the theme.

Restaurant design objectives

Design objectives follow directly from a clear and well-researched operational and marketing concept. Based on the menu and such operational aspects as the type of service, method of beverage service, check handling, and use of entertainment, designers create the desired mood, function, layout, finishes, lighting, and furnishings.

Each restaurant outlet, depending on its type and quality level, must have very different design treatment. For example, the hotel's main three-meal restaurant needs a theme that will permit the mood to vary from light and casual at breakfast to more formal at dinner. This may be accomplished by providing variable lighting, changing from placemats to table linen, closing the counter seating, presenting a food display, and extending room dividers to make smaller and more intimate dining areas. The design of a hotel coffee shop should include the following considerations:

- ☐ **Cashier/hostess station:** Provide a combined station to control access to all sections of the room, handle guest checks, and supervise coat check area.
- ☐ **Separate sections:** Divide restaurant into two or more areas so that portions can be closed during periods of low occupancy.
- ☐ **Flexible arrangement of tables:** Provide paired deuces, flip-top fours (table leaves to convert a square table into a larger circular one) to provide for large parties.

- ☐ **Counter seating:** Provide about 10 percent of total seats at counter for singles.
- ☐ **Buffet/display areas:** Provide an area for self-service buffet or food display.
- ☐ **Service stations:** Provide service stations for every 100± seats to supply water, coffee, linen, tableware, and soiled dish areas.
- ☐ **Adaptable lighting:** Provide dimmers so that the mood can be changed from breakfast to dinner.
- ☐ **Background music:** Consider including soft music.
- ☐ **Uniforms and graphics:** Design to complement the coffee shop or hotel theme.

Similarly, design objectives can be established for a hypothetical higher-priced restaurant. The specialty or signature restaurant may be open daily only for dinner, although lunch service is profitable in urban locations and Sunday buffet brunch in the suburbs. Its mood and decor reflect a theme developed, primarily, around the menu and the style of service. Decorative touches in materials, detailing furnishings, planting, artifacts, artwork, and tabletop design further reinforce the theme. The design objectives, modified and refined by analyzing the market and developing a unique food concept, include the following:

- ☐ **Entry sequence:** Establish a foyer space to set the mood for the restaurant.
- ☐ **Maitre d':** Provide a host station at the entrance to the restaurant.
- ☐ **Focal point:** Organize all seats to take advantage of some focal point, either inside (food display, fountain) or outside the dining room.
- ☐ **Seating areas:** Arrange dividers, level changes to create intimate, semiprivate groups of tables.
- ☐ **Table seating:** Provide clear definition to the seating areas, separating them from the aisles, service, buffet, and host areas. Each table should have some privacy from other tables.
- ☐ **Food display:** Arrange a food display either near the entrance or central to the seating.
- ☐ **Exhibition cooking:** Based on the food concept, consider providing an area for food preparation such as a grill, bakery, or Japanese Teppanyaki feature.
- ☐ **Entertainment:** Provide a small stage and dance floor or consider how the plan might be modified to accommodate entertainment in the future; ta-

Restaurant and bar capabilities for different size hotels

	NUMBER OF GUESTROOMS					
	200	**300**	**400**	**500**	**750**	**1000**
Coffee shop	150*	225	200	200	250	275
Specialty restaurant			100	125	175	175
Theme restaurant					125	125
Deli/pastry shop				50	50	75
Cocktail lounge/oyster bar	100	115	125	150	100	150
Lobby bar		35	50	75	75	100
Restaurant holding bar			25	25	25	25
Entertainment lounge					175	225

*Food and beverage capacities in number of seats.

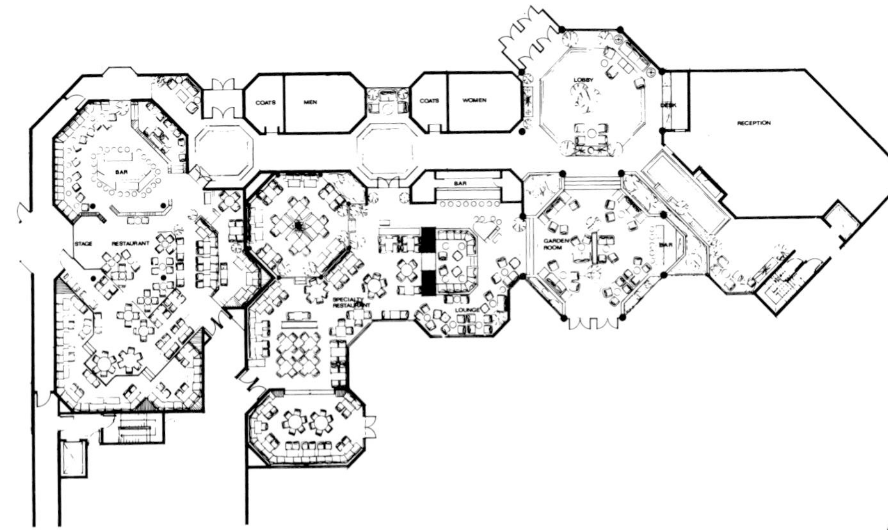

A

B

C

bles should be organized with views toward this focal point.

- ☐ **Service stations:** Develop inconspicuous service stations, without compromising staff efficiency.
- ☐ **Bar or holding bar:** Provide beverage service from an adjacent cocktail lounge or a separate holding bar designated for the specialty restaurant, or from a kitchen service bar.
- ☐ **Intimate lighting:** Design the variable lighting to create a more formal mood at dinner, yet allow for brighter levels at lunch and for maintenance; fluorescent lights should not be used in any area.
- ☐ **Uniforms, tabletop, graphics:** Select all design accessories to complement and reinforce the specialty theme of the room.

Most other restaurant outlets feature aspects of these two dining types. Theme restaurants may combine the counter seating and cashier functions—creating some of the informality of the coffee shop—with a very specific food display or exhibition cooking element from the specialty restaurant. A deli operation, for example, which might be open 24-hours in an urban hotel, would feature imaginatively designed display cases and sandwich preparation areas, counter seating plus a small number of booths, high lighting levels, and easily maintainable finishes.

Lounge and bar design objectives

Similiar to restaurants, the hotel operating company establishes bar and lounge concepts, the architect prepares preliminary plans that accommodate these requirements, and the interior designer develops these concepts more fully, including their furnishings and fixtures.

Even more than the restaurants, the lounge areas vary much more extensively be-

Food and Beverage Outlets. *The restaurants and lounges at Stouffer's Bedford Glen Hotel in Massachusetts (opposite page middle) are grouped together near the front entrance and overlook an interior courtyard. Each of the rooms is broken into intimate seating areas with a variety of decorative treatment and layout, some focusing on a stage, or the bar, or the landscaped grounds. The garden room functions as a visual focus for the lobby and an adjunct to the specialty restaurant and its bar.*

A. *Sheppard's (opposite page bottom, Sheraton on Harbor Island, San Diego, CA) was created in existing space to give the character of an exclusive yacht club, with views to the adjacent marina from three distinct seating areas.*

B. *The crisp art deco Garden Court (above, The Melrose, Dallas) is appropriate for casual meals as well as elegant dinners and includes a secluded private dining room for small parties.*

C. *The lobby bar (left, Meridien, Houston) provides a brightly daylit focus to the more formal hotel lobby.*

tween different types of hotels. In a downtown property, the primary beverage outlet may be a quiet and luxuriously furnished lobby bar, whereas in a convention, casino, or resort property, it may be an action-oriented entertainment lounge and a major nighttime focus for the hotel. Variation among entertainment lounges is usually based on the opportunities of the local market and on the expected hotel clientele. Therefore, it is especially important that the designer be given a clear set of design objectives for the facility.

The lobby bar was developed in the 70s as a method of creating activity and excitement, first, in the open atrium spaces and after its success as a revenue generator was proven, even in conventional locations. Open to the lobby space, separated only by planters, water features, or a level change, it functions as additional lobby seating as well as a bar. The designer should attempt to include the following features in the lobby bar:

- ☐ **Visibility:** Provide an open area that is obvious to hotel guests and visitors.
- ☐ **Seating:** Furnish the bar primarily with lounge seating—sofas, lounge chairs, end tables—or with a combination of lounge and bar seating; provide a few seats at a service bar.
- ☐ **Service bar:** include a small bar for beverage service with nearby storage or backup from the kitchen.
- ☐ **Entertainment:** Specify a location for a piano or other limited entertainment.
- ☐ **Food service:** Consider access for limited food service, especially continental breakfast, hors d'oeurves, and snack service.

The second beverage outlet is a cocktail lounge, often with careful provision for entertainment and dancing. Quite different from the quiet lobby lounge, the entertainment lounge is completely enclosed to reduce high noise levels and features lower light levels and more closely spaced seating. Some management companies, recognizing the variable nature of the business from midweek to weekend, provide a "flexible entertainment facility" with features to accommodate both recorded and live entertainment and for different size groups. The designer, in developing the layout and design of entertainment lounges, should consider the following:

- ☐ **Entry sequence:** Develop an enclosed entrance to maintain acoustic and visual separation between the lounge and the hotel circulation areas.
- ☐ **Separate sections:** Establish distinct zones for the bar, the entertainment/dancing area, and quieter lounge area.
- ☐ **Bar (about 10 to 25 percent of the lounge area):** Provide a large bar that is visible from the entrance and is situated so that guests can view the performers; provide pick-up stations for the staff; provide bar storage adjoining the lounge.
- ☐ **Entertainment area (50 to 65 percent):** Develop an integrated section with stage, dance floor, and seating so that at least half of the guests are involved with the entertainment; add platforms to provide better views of the performers.
- ☐ **Lounge area (20 to 30 percent):** Design a separate lounge area where guests can sit quietly without being disturbed by the entertainment; consider soft lounge seating.
- ☐ **Lighting:** Install flexible lighting, controlled at the bar, including stage lighting and dance floor lighting.
- ☐ **Sound system:** Provide a complete sound system for the performers with speakers focused on the dance floor area.

Developing the restaurant and lounge concepts and establishing design goals are only part of the process. Often, the constraints of the building's schematic design greatly influence, for better or worse, the success of the food and beverage areas. The designer needs to combine the programmatic requirements with the operational standards to create a workable scheme.

Hotel restaurants and bars, because they face such severe outside competition, create the greatest of all interior design challenges. While guestrooms and meeting spaces include various pragmatic requirements, the dining experience, combining food, service, and design, requires more imaginative skills.

FUNCTION SPACE

The third principal category of public space includes the meeting, banquet, reception, and exhibit spaces, which form a major core in many medium and large hotels and in conference centers. Variously referred to as "function space," "meeting and banquet area," or "convention complex," the cluster of individual spaces generally includes a large ballroom, intermediate-size banquet rooms, and smaller breakout rooms. In fact, the principal distinctions among types of hotels often focus on the size and mix of the function space.

Introduced a century ago to accommodate important civic and social gatherings, hotel function space has been developed more recently to meet the needs of corporations and of professional associations. The two create very different demands. The corporate group market mainly requires a variety of relatively small but high-quality spaces for sales and management meetings, launching new products, and continuing-education programs for executives. The association market primarily needs facilities for large group meetings, smaller rooms for seminars and workshops, and extensive exhibition space. In addition, local organizations use hotel meeting space for a variety of meetings, banquets, and reception functions. The table at right lists the primary types of hotel function space and their essential characteristics.

Generally, the hotel feasibility study recommends a mix of function space that is based on an analysis of the demand for different types of business and social uses. Motor inns, for example, generally offer a single multipurpose ballroom, which is simply decorated and intended to accommodate a full range of small meetings, civic lunches, wedding receptions, and local product displays. It is not often intended to attract business to fill the hotel guestrooms.

On the other hand, convention hotels and conference centers provide a wide range of facilities—large and small, simple and elegant, with and without high-tech audiovisual equipment—as the principal attraction to the hotel. Meeting planners select the hotel, to a large extent, for its ability to provide complete meeting facilities, which, in turn, sells large blocks of guestrooms.

In resort hotels, where seasonal demand for recreational facilities creates a low for several months of the year, the hotels have begun to add conference wings to increase the demand for guestrooms throughout the shoulder- and off-season periods. In superluxury hotels, which have relatively fewer rooms and which place an important emphasis on intimacy and exclusivity, only small meeting facilities are encouraged; the function rooms more often are used for receptions and banquets and to cater to the surrounding community rather than to the hotel guests. In all but the smallest properties, function space is an essential ingredient of the successful hotel.

Planning objectives

The design of the function space is a cooperative effort among the architect, interior designer, consulting engineers, and operator. The success of meeting and banquet sales depends on a number of planning considerations, interior decor, proper lighting, acous-

Function room characteristics

SPACE	USES*	TYPE OF HOTEL*	SEATING CAPACITY*	PRINCIPAL FEATURES
Ballroom	Meetings, banquets, receptions, exhibits	Motor inn, Resort, transient, Convention	1.5–2 × GR .5–1.5 × GR 2–2.5 × GR	Divisibility, high ceiling, direct food access, no columns
Ballroom foyer	Reception, meeting registration, flow	Motor inn, transient, Resort, Convention	.2 × BR, .25 × BR, .25–.3 × BR	Access to all ballroom sections, toilets, phones
Meeting rooms	Meetings, banquets	Transient, resort, Convention	— .2–.4 × BR .4–.6 × BR	Built-in A/V, food access desirable
Banquet rooms	Banquets, meetings, receptions	Transient, resort, Convention	— .2–.4 × BR .4–.6 × BR	Divisibility, direct food access
Boardroom	Meeting, banquet	Transient, convention	— .05–.1 × GR	Superior finishes, separate from other meeting rooms
Exhibit hall	Exhibition	Convention	— 1–2 × BR	Display access, high ceiling, high lighting level
Theater	Lectures, A/V presentation	Convention	— .2–.4 × GR	Stepped levels, built-in A/V

**Key: GR, number of guestrooms; BR, capacity of ballroom.*

tical and mechanical engineering, and other technical requirements. The adjacency requirements are illustrated on the top of page 188; these are reflected in the following schematic planning requirements:

☐ Group all function areas together, although in major convention hotels some separation may be desirable.

☐ Provide a separate function entrance from the street or parking area.

☐ Locate the function space close to and easily accessible from the hotel lobby.

☐ Locate additional function areas such as exhibit hall or audiovisual theater close by but not adjacent to the ballroom foyer.

☐ Include adjacent public support areas: toilets, coatrooms, telephones, convention services office.

☐ Provide direct food service access to the ballroom and all banquet rooms; any banquet pantry must be on the ballroom level.

☐ Include essential meeting and banquet storage adjacent to the ballroom.

☐ Design the ballroom and other larger rooms to be independent of the guestroom tower so as to simplify the building structure.

These planning objectives are further refined by analysis of the exact size of the various function spaces and by their proposed use. One consideration is the relative clustering of the function areas. Convention hotels tend to attract one major group or no more than four or five smaller groups at one time. For the occasions when a single major convention is in the hotel, it is convenient to have the ballroom, junior ballroom, and several meeting rooms immediately adjacent to each other, perhaps sharing a foyer or prefunction area. This is the usual and preferred arrangement in smaller hotels of 250 to 400 guestrooms.

When multiple functions are to be accommodated, it is preferable to separate the principal meeting and banquet areas so that several groups can assemble simultaneously without interference or distraction. At the 1400-room, convention-oriented Sheraton Centre in Toronto, for example, the ballroom and exhibition hall are on a basement floor, whereas two junior ballrooms are in separate areas on a mezzanine level; each of three groups can easily meet without interference or direct contact with the others. For the same reason, small conference centers frequently arrange the meeting rooms and breakout areas in several clusters so that each group is assured privacy.

Design criteria

The coordination among the design team is epecially important in the evolution of the details for the function space. The architectural aspects (proportions, divisibility, access), the interior design considerations (finishes, furnishings, lighting), and the engineering requirements (mechanical, sound system, fire protection) are clearly related and heavily influence each other.

Function Room Characteristics. *Most hotels include a variety of meeting and banquet spaces ranging from an expansive ballroom to intimate boardrooms. Each type of function space is used for particular activities that affect their size and design criteria as listed here.*

Connecting these facts are several overall issues. One is the relative specificity of the various function areas, that is, the degree to which each is designed as a multipurpose room or, instead, is intended particularly for board meetings or film presentations. The principal considerations include size, divisibility, complexity of services, and quality of finishes. The better defined the use of a particular room, the more specific the interior design can be. Larger hotels, and those with a clear market orientation such as luxury properties and conference centers, can afford to provide very specific meeting and banquet rooms and further assure their use by groups with individual needs. The motor inn must use its single ballroom for so many varied functions that, unfortunately, none is particularly well served.

A second consideration is planning the divisibility of ballroom and larger function rooms. Practically all hotel ballrooms are divided into several sections so that a smaller group is in a more appropriately sized space, two or more groups can use the room simultaneously, or one group can use part for a meeting and the adjoining section for meals. Two approaches for subdividing the ballroom are illustrated below.

A third aspect is how the proposed use affects the probable arrangement of the function rooms as well as their capacity. The ap-

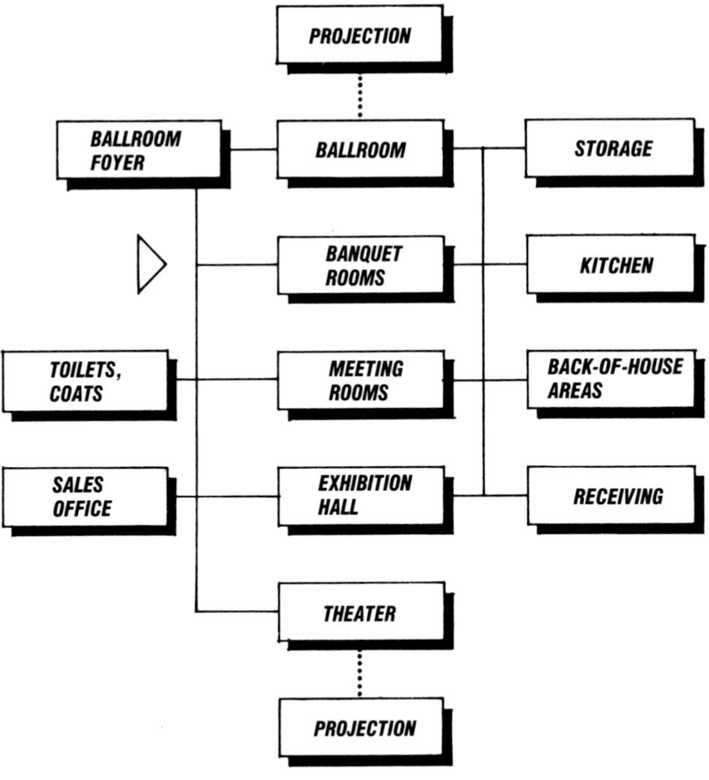

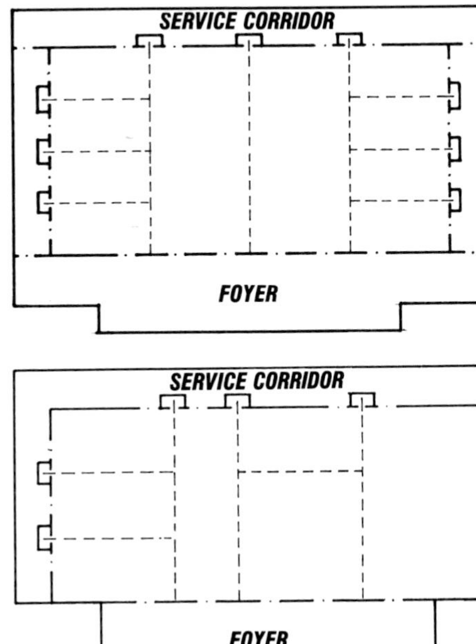

ABOVE LEFT

Schematic Diagram. *The diagram illustrates the recommended arrangement of meeting and banquet facilities and their connections to public and back-of-house areas in the hotel. Generally, the function space should be separated from the other public facilities and developed, in addition, with some differentiation among the ballroom, meeting, and banquet spaces. Support services should be provided nearby.*

ABOVE

Ballroom Divisibility. *The principal method for providing flexibility in the function areas is by using a subdivisible ballroom. In motor inns and smaller hotels the room is often divided in half or thirds. Two common arrangements for larger hotels are illustrated, the top one favored by Marriott and the bottom one by Hyatt. The first has more potential rooms but fewer possible sizes; the second has relatively few divisions, but they can be combined into rooms with a variety of capacities. The strategy for using the main ballroom is important for a hotel's ability to compete for major meetings.*

OPPOSITE PAGE

Function Area Plan. *The floor plan from the Prince Hotel in Toronto, Canada, illustrates many of the best planning features of function areas: divisible ballroom and meeting rooms, separate foyer areas, direct access from parking, separation from other hotel public areas, direct food access to the ballroom and several banquet rooms (2, 3, 5), meeting rooms with windows (rooms 4, 6, 7, 8), toilets, coats, and telephones within area, pantry adjacent to ballroom, adequate storage.*

Design criteria for meeting space

ARCHITECTURAL	
Divisibility	Number of subdivisions and proportions of each, storage of dividing walls, acoustic rating of dividing walls.
Proportions	Location of and views to head table or stage.
Structure	Full span, no columns.
Ceiling height	Projection booth, use for exhibitions, chandeliers, cost of divisible walls, implications for second floor.
Floor load	Use for displays and exhibits.
Access/egress	Public and service access to each subsection, storage, display access, emergency exits.
Windows	Desirability, blackout requirement.
INTERIOR DESIGN	
Floor	Carpeting, patterned to assist furniture placement, portable dance floor.
Walls	Various finishes, chair rail, folding wall finish to match perimeter, doors to cover wall storage compartments.
Ceiling	Various, needs downlights, chandeliers, track lighting, emergency lighting, HVAC diffusers and air return, sprinklers, smoke detectors, sound system, wall tracks in integrated pattern.
Windows	Full blackout capability.
Lighting	Combination of functional, decorative, display, and accent lighting.
Ferniture	Round banquet and rectangular meeting tables, stacking chairs, risers, lectern, A/V equipment for function rooms; seating in foyer areas.
MECHANICAL/ELECTRICAL	
All	Fully separate controls in each room and subdivisions of larger rooms.
Lighting	Fully dimmable, control at podium, flexible track lighting where required.
Electrical	208 volts available in ballroom and exhibition areas.
Sound	Television, telephone, microphone jacks in each area, control from sound and light booth.
Mechanical	Full air conditioning, fire protection.
Plumbing	Wet utilities available near ballroom and exhibition areas.

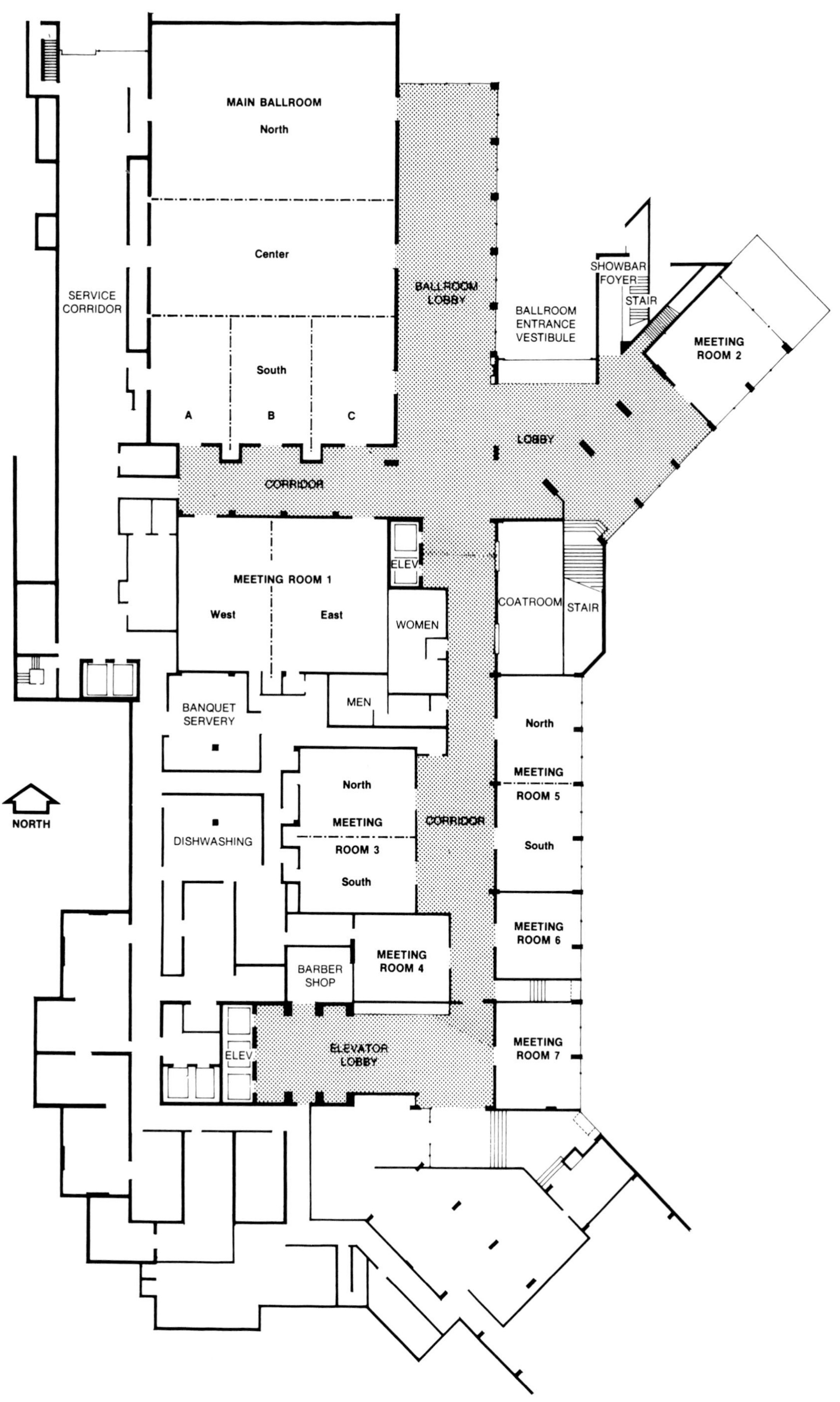
MAIN BALLROOM
North
Center
South
A
B
C
SERVICE CORRIDOR
BALLROOM LOBBY
BALLROOM ENTRANCE VESTIBULE
SHOWBAR FOYER
STAIR
MEETING ROOM 2
LOBBY
CORRIDOR
ELEV
MEETING ROOM 1
West
East
WOMEN
COATROOM
STAIR
BANQUET SERVERY
MEN
North
MEETING ROOM 5
South
North
MEETING ROOM 3
South
CORRIDOR
NORTH
DISHWASHING
MEETING ROOM 6
BARBER SHOP
MEETING ROOM 4
ELEV
ELEVATOR LOBBY
MEETING ROOM 7

Area requirements for function rooms

SPACE		RECEPTION*	AUDITORIUM*	BANQUET*	CLASSROOM*	BOARD-TABLE*
Ballroom	[>10,000 sq ft (929 sq m)]	7	8	10	—	—
Ballroom	[>3,000 sq ft (278.7 sq m)]	8	8	11	12	—
Banquet room	[<3,000 sq ft (278.7 sq m)]	9	10	12	14	—
Meeting room		9	10	12	14	16–20
Boardroom		12	—	15	—	20–25
Theater		—	8–12	—	12–15	—

**The approximate area requirement is given in square feet.*

proximate area requirements for different types of seating in different size function rooms is given in the following table. Typical table layouts for each type are illustrated in the accompanying plan.

Many designers and hotel operators have found that the single most critical element in the meeting and banquet rooms is the design of the ballroom ceiling. When a hotel ballroom is set up for a banquet or meeting, most of the floor and the lower part of the walls are obscured. The ceiling, though, is totally visible and contains downlights, chandeliers, and track lighting, as well as mechanical diffusers and return grills, sprinklers, speakers, smoke detectors, and movable wall tracks. All must be integrated into a single, cohesive, organized, and attractive pattern.

Another design aspect that too often is ignored during design development is provision of sufficient electrical and communication services to the ballroom, meeting rooms, and, especially, the exhibit hall. Not only electrical outlets, but telephone, television, and microphone jacks, controls for the projector, projection screen, and lights, and, in some cases, a wet utility panel must be provided (see accompanying table above). Exhibit halls, for example, should contain electrical outlets every 10 feet (3 meters) in the floor, ceiling mounted spotlight tracks 30 feet (9 meters) on centers, and convenient water and drain connections for exhibitors.

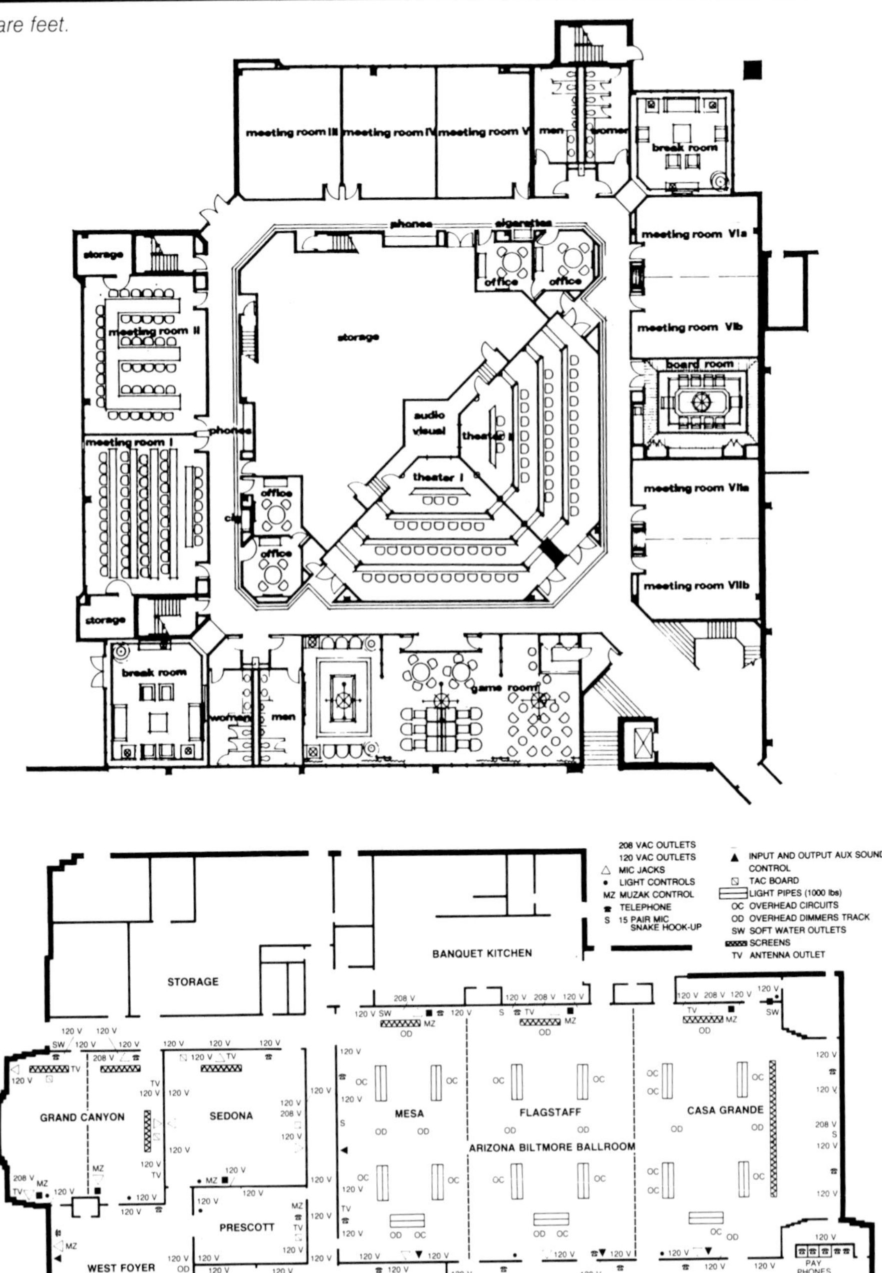

ABOVE

Meeting Room Layout Alternatives. *The lower-level plan of the 400-room Dallas/Fort Worth Hilton Hotel and Conference Center at the airport shows the variety of meeting rooms essential for a successful hotel. On this level alone, in addition to the tiered theaters, there are nine meeting rooms, two breakout rooms, four offices for conferees, and a boardroom pictured with a number of different seating arrangements. Immediately above are a larger auditorium, additional meeting rooms, sales offices, and an informal restaurant for the attendees.*

RIGHT

Mechanical/Electrical Requirements. *Ballroom and other function spaces require electrical and mechanical services to properly handle major meetings and exhibitions. Operators must describe these for the meeting planner, as in this example from the Arizona Biltmore.*

A

Function Area Design. *Hotel meeting rooms exhibit a tremendous diversity in design since they are oriented toward different markets. (A) Traditional hotels such as the Hotel Inter-Continental New York show fine detailing as shown in the carefully hidden presentation cabinets behind the far panels. (B) New high-tech conference centers like Arrowwood (also see pages 94–95) include tiered audio visual amphitheaters. (C) International convention hotels such as the Doha Sheraton (also see page 93) incorporate major conference facilities with luxurious appointments and full translation services.*

C

B

RECREATION FACILITIES

Increasingly, motels and hotels provide recreational facilities, ranging from an outdoor pool at a small family-operated motel, to major health clubs in downtown hotels, to extensive golf, tennis, or ski complexes in destination resorts. While surveys of the use of swimming pools and other sports facilities at hotels show that relatively few guests actually use them, nonetheless many guests expect them and providing recreational amenities is essential.

To counter low use, some hotels expand rather than minimize their recreational features and profitably promote them to the community as well as the hotel guest. In a highly competitive market, this is one more area in which a hotel can gain an edge over other properties. Downtown hotels, for example, are including full-size health clubs to complement their other business-oriented facilities; suburban and small town motor inns are enclosing their pool complexes to provide a swim club for the community; and conference centers are adding extensive outdoor jogging, tennis, and golf facilities to attract the high-level executive retreats. The accompanying checklist shows the principal types of recreational facilities that might be provided.

In the midprice range especially, recreational facilities have been developed as the focus for the hotel's public space. Holiday Inns' Holidome Recreation Center combines informal restaurants and bars, meeting assembly, seating, and walkways with a full recreational complex. The latter includes the swimming pool, wading pool, whirlpool/hot tub, table tennis, shuffleboard, children's play area, and coin-operated games. In addition, the main lobby and front desk connect to the center and as many guestrooms as possible look into the Holidome space.

The hotels discussed in Part 1 illustrate the kinds of recreational facilities that are commonly found at different types of properties. Generally, the smaller, budget, and midpriced motels and hotels, those which attract a large number of price-conscious family travelers, include little more than an outdoor swimming pool and a gameroom. Larger hotels and especially those with a business market frequently add health clubs, including exercise rooms, saunas, and perhaps racquetball. Resorts and other lodging types, catering to longer-staying guests, and hotels in outlying areas, where land costs are less, feature additional outdoor facilities. The following table identifies in broad terms the typical program for recreational facilities by hotel type (see also the accompanying recreation and fitness facilities checklists).

Fitness facilities checklist

ACTIVITY	MINIMUM OVERALL SIZE SQ FT	(SQ M)
Swimming pool	800	(75)
Total including deck area	2400	(225)
Exercise room	600	(56)
Nautilus circuit	400	(37)
Exercycles	50/unit	(4.7)
Rowing machines	50/unit	(4.7)
Weight machines	50/unit	(4.7)
Aerobic classroom	800	(75)
Gym	2400	(225)
Health club		
Whirlpool/hot tub (single)	50/person	(4.7)
Whirlpool/hot tub (group)	20/person	(1.9)
Sauna	20/person	(1.9)
Steam bath	20/person	(1.9)
Plunge (hot/cold)	20/person	(1.9)
Swiss shower	30/person	
Loofah bath	100/person	
Herbal Wrap	100/person	(9.3)
Massage	100/person	(9.3)
Facial	100/person	(9.3)
Barber/hairdresser	70/person	(6.5)
Manicure/pedicure	70/person	(6.5)
Suntan	70/person	(6.5)
Inhalator	20/person	(1.9)
Rest area	100/person	(9.3)
Medical/stress test	150/person	(14)

Swimming pool

Nearly all hotel management companies require that a swimming pool be included in the hotel's design, although minimum sizes vary. The pool area should be separated from other public spaces so that guests dressed in bathing suits need not pass through the hotel lobby. Other planning considerations include the following:

- ☐ **Location:** Place the pool so that guests can reach it from guestroom elevators without passing through the lobby; provide some guestrooms with views of the pool; screen any exterior views toward the pool.
- ☐ **Orientation:** Position the pool so that it receives unobstructed sunlight from midmorning to late afternoon.
- ☐ **Size:** Plan the pool to accommodate the swimming and sunbathing needs of the guests but no less than about 20′ × 40′ (6 × 12 m) with at least 10 feet (3 meters) of deck space on all sides.
- ☐ **Support functions:** Provide toilets, lockers where required, towel issue area, snack bar or vending, equipment room, and furniture storage.
- ☐ **Safety:** Do *not* provide a diving board; include slip-free deck surface, depth markings, underwater lighting, safety or "pool rules" signage.
- ☐ **Wading pool, whirlpool:** Include additional pools within view of the swimming pool but slightly separated.
- ☐ **Indoor pool:** Design either operable roof or glass walls to provide direct sunlight and ventilation.

Health club

A second major component of hotel recreational facilities is the health club, a feature that has developed only in the past decade. Its main focus is a combination of exercise equipment such as Nautilus or Universal and

Recreational facilities by hotel type

Downtown	Pool, health club, jogging track (roof)	**Conference center**	Pool, health club, racquet sports, golf
Motel, roadside	Pool, gameroom	**All-suite**	Pool, health club
Suburban, airport	Pool, gameroom, health club	**Super-luxury**	Pool, health club
Resort	Varies depending on location (beach, mountain, desert)	**Condominium**	Pool, health club
		Mixed-use	Varies
Convention hotel	Pool, gameroom, health club, racquet sports	**Mega-hotel**	Pool, gameroom, health club, racquet sports, golf, water facilities
Casino	Pool, health club		

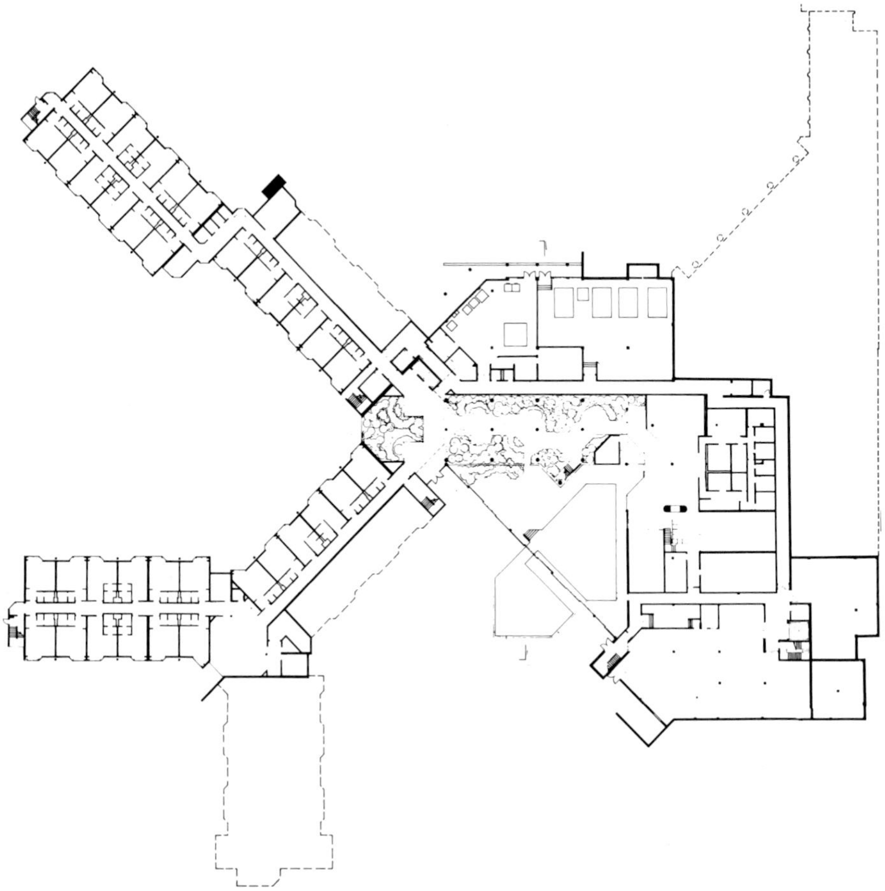

Health Club. *Hotel health clubs combine exercise, racquet sports, swimming, and sauna/whirlpool facilities in a single controlled complex. At Arrowwood, the club is located between the conference facilities and the residential wing with views over the landscaped grounds.*

health facilities such as steamrooms, whirlpool baths, and saunas. Larger complexes add racquetball or squash courts, and a multipurpose room for aerobic exercise. Frequently, especially in business-oriented markets, the health club may dominate all other recreation facilities, including the swimming pool. The following items should be considered during the planning phase:

- ☐ **Location:** Plan the club so that guests can reach it directly from the guestroom elevators and members from the street or parking area without passing through the hotel lobby.

Recreational facilities

INDOOR FACILITIES

- ☐ Swimming pool
- ☐ Whirlpool, jacuzzi
- ☐ Wading pool
- ☐ Exercise room
- ☐ Locker rooms, sauna
- ☐ Game room
- ☐ Pingpong, billiards
- ☐ Racquetball, squash
- ☐ Tennis
- ☐ Jogging track
- ☐ Mini-gym
- ☐ Multi-use sports court (includes volleyball, badminton)
- ☐ Aerobic exercise classroom

OUTDOOR FACILITIES

- ☐ Swimming pool
- ☐ Whirlpool, jacuzzi
- ☐ Wading pool
- ☐ Tennis
- ☐ Platform tennis
- ☐ Volleyball, badminton
- ☐ Shuffleboard*
- ☐ Basketball*
- ☐ Handball*
- ☐ Jogging, par track
- ☐ Miniature golf*
- ☐ Putting green*
- ☐ Golf course (includes driving range)
- ☐ Pitch and Put golf
- ☐ Beach swimming
- ☐ Sailboating
- ☐ Motor boating, marina
- ☐ Windsurfing, surfboard
- ☐ Waterskiing, parasailing
- ☐ Scuba diving, snorkel trails
- ☐ Fishing
- ☐ Sightseeing tour boats and glass-bottomed boats
- ☐ Snow skiing
- ☐ Riding stable
- ☐ Ice-skating rink
- ☐ Marina

**Occasionally provided indoors.* Note: *see Fitness Facilities Checklist for saunas, exercise room. For required dimensions and areas of sports courts, see International Athletic Standards. Add approximately 10% to above areas for landscaping, drainage, and circulation.*

☐ **Program:** Include the following depending on the market:
- Toilets, showers, lockers
- Sauna
- Steam room
- Whirlpool
- Plunge bath
- Massage rooms
- Exercise room
- Control, attendant
- Lounge, waiting
- Equipment sales
- Juice counter, vending

☐ **Adjacencies:** Plan the complex with the control area and lounge most visible and with the private functions either shared (exercise room) or back-to-back (saunas) (see accompanying plan).

☐ **Shared space:** Consider whether certain elements, especially the swimming pool or lounge, can be combined with other hotel functions, such as the lobby or coffee shop.

PARKING

The provision for sufficient parking can be a crucial element, in both the budgeting and conceptual planning for a hotel or motel. Motor inn developers know they must provide 1 space per room plus additional spaces for employees and for any public areas—restaurants, bars, meeting space, or recreational facilities—that attract guests from the community. Land cost is an increasing problem in suburban and rural locations, making it necessary for developers to program their parking requirements more carefully.

However, the more critical concern is at downtown hotels and at those other types where extremely high land costs preclude extensive amounts of parking space. Often, the developer and architect attempt to appeal zoning regulations, if justified, following an analysis by traffic experts. One technique is to project hourly parking requirements, recognizing that the hotel guest, conferee, and employees create peak demands on parking at different periods of the day (see accompanying table).

However, one caution is necessary: An otherwise successful hotel can be seriously affected—especially its local banquet business—by insufficient or inconvenient parking. The key objective should be to provide optimum but not excessive amounts of parking. Unless unusual conditions (sports complex, large banquet facility, retail center) exist, the parking provision for different types of lodging properties falls within the ranges shown in the table on the right.

Parking analysis

The following steps describe an approach to calculating parking requirements based on the changing needs of the guestrooms and other hotel facilities throughout the day. The maximum parking demand in most properties is created not by the rooms but by the meeting and banquet space. The provision of parking must recognize the sum of the various components and the interrelationship of the peaks and valleys over a 24-hour period.

PART I:
Determine the components of the parking requirement: overnight guests, restaurant and bar patrons, meeting attendees, and other visitors (see part III).

PART II:
Calculate the maximum number of cars that might be reasonably anticipated, planning to accommodate full demand on 80–85 percent of all days, but not peak demand for *each* component. The overnight guest calculation is illustrated by the following example:

Number of rooms	400
Percent occupancy	85
People per room	1.4
Percent arriving by car	40
People per car	1.5

The equation for calculating the guests' parking requirement is as follows:

$$\frac{(\text{Rooms}) \times (\%\ \text{occupancy}) \times (\text{people/room}) \times (\%\ \text{by car})}{(\text{People/car})}$$

$$\text{Example: } \frac{400 \times .85 \times 1.4 \times .40}{1.5} = 127 \text{ cars}$$

The calculation for the other components includes similar factors as appropriate, such as food and beverage covers, percentage of diners arriving by car, and number of employees by shift.

PART III:
Develop a table showing hourly parking use factors (example shows 4-hour periods). For example, the parking facility needs to accommodate all (100 percent or 1) overnight guest cars from midnight to 4:00 A.M. but, because of checkouts, only 60 percent (.6) during the midday periods.

	MORNING			AFTERNOON		
AREA	**MIDNIGHT TO 4:00**	**4:00 TO 8:00**	**8:00 TO NOON**	**NOON TO 4:00**	**4:00 TO 8:00**	**8:00 TO MIDNIGHT**
Hotel guests	1	.95	.6	.6	.9	.95
Restaurant and bar patrons	.05	.1	.1	.1	.2	.25
Meeting/banquet attendees	.05	—	.1	.1	.4	.4
Health club members	—	.2	.1	.2	.2	.05
Visitors	—	.1	.2	.1	.2	.4
Employees	.25	.25	.4	.4	.35	.35

PART IV:
Combine the parking requirements for each component (part II) with the use table (part III) to calculate the total amount of parking necessary during each time period. In this example, hotel guests would require 127 parking spaces (1 × 127) at midnight but only 76 spaces (.6 × 127) at noon. Recognize that high evening demand, for example, might be partially met by available parking nearby.

Parking needed for different types of hotels according to spaces per room

Downtown	0.4–0.8	Assumes limited function space
Suburban	1.2–1.4	Heavy local meeting/banquet use
Airport	0.6–1.0	Moderate rental car use
Highway	1.0–1.2	Some local banquet/F&B use
Resort	0.2–1.4	Varies by location and proximity to urban centers
Convention	0.8–1.4	Regional convention hotels need higher provision
Conference Center	1.0–1.3	If full house, minimum local use
Residential	1.2–2.0	May need two spaces/condominium
All-suite	0.8–1.2	Limited public functions
Super-luxury	1.0–1.2	Limited public functions
Mega-hotel	1.0–1.2	Limited local business; high rental car use
Mixed-use	0.6–1.2	Highly variable depending on other activities
Casino	0.8–2.0	Varies by location; for example, Atlantic City requires extensive bus parking

SIGNAGE AND GRAPHICS

Much of the visual impression of a hotel, in addition to its architectural and interior design, is created by the signage and other graphic features. These need to be carried out consistently, from the exterior building signage to the most minor printed items throughout the hotel. A coordinated signage and graphics system provides visitors with information and directions, while at the same time creating the desired atmosphere and reinforcing the hotel's marketing efforts. The graphics program should include the following:

Exterior signage
- ☐ Building identification
- ☐ Vehicular directional signs
- ☐ Pedestrian directional signs

Interior signage
- ☐ Meeting directory
- ☐ Directional signs
- ☐ Room identification
- ☐ Room image (restaurant logo)

Printed graphics
- ☐ Stationery, forms, matchbooks
- ☐ Restaurant menus

Uniforms

As with many other components of hotel design, the graphics program requires the collaboration of a number of professionals. The architect and interior designer are joined by graphics, print, and lighting consultants, as well as a uniform designer. All details refined by these several consultants should relate visually to reinforce the desired image.

Exterior signage establishes the hotel's identity not only within the community but to the new guest. In highway and suburban hotels especially, signage is critical to the property's visibility. Some firms, more often in the restaurant field, such as Howard Johnson's and McDonald's, use the combination of signage and building design—the orange roof and the golden arches—to create a highly successful marketing image. (To a lesser extent, the Howard Johnson's Motor Lodge gatehouses do the same thing.)

Although cities such as Washington, D.C., and San Francisco have taken great strides in eliminating rooftop signs, identification of the hotel is no less essential. Limited in size and number by local ordinances, hotel signage

Information

Hotel

Information

Hotel Information

Lost and Found

Hotel Reservation

Meeting Point

Bedrooms

Room Key Return

Check-in Registration

Bellman Bellwoman

Cashier

Baggage Claim

Baggage Check-in

Ticket Purchase

Baggage Lockers

Safe Deposit Boxes

Keys

Graphics Program. *Original graphics programs are important to establish a unified image for a hotel. At the Sheraton Grande in Los Angeles, the bird of paradise flower, both in abundant bouquets and as a printed logo, is consistently used. For the Hotel Europa, the designers developed a stylized tulip—representing the owner's Dutch heritage—and used it as an imprint on glassware and other hotel items. Shown here are some international symbols used to designate services in hotels.*

must be carefully thought through and integrated with the architectural design to obtain maximum impact. Often, corporate or individual property logos are applied to the building exterior in place of less attractive rooftop signs.

For the convenience of hotel guests and visitors, ground level directional signage is required to identify not only the main lobby but restaurant and ballroom entrances as well. Secondary signs provide directions within the parking areas, identify wheelchair routes, and locate taxi or other special areas.

Interior signage, including directional and room identification types, must be equally well integrated into the overall design. Directional signage occurs throughout the hotel, pointing the way to the front desk, meeting room areas, recreational facilities, and other public functions. Room identification signage begins at the registration desk, where it is defined along with the cashier and mail stations. It continues at each guestroom, meeting or banquet room, administration offices, toilets, telephones, and other guest support areas. The use of international symbols has recently become more popular in hotels as the number of foreign visitors has increased. The American Hotel and Motel Association, for example, has approved over 100 symbols to identify both principal public areas and such secondary functions as housephones, guestroom key return, and safe deposit boxes.

Instead of standard symbols or signage, the hotel's major public areas frequently have specially designed graphic images to complement the restaurant or lounge theme, identify the major ballroom, or add elegance to the deluxe suites. These often are fabricated out of special materials, requiring the review of samples and full-size mock-ups for approval.

In addition to signage, a graphic consultant will often be called upon to design advertising and promotional material for use during the preopening months and later within the hotel. Hundreds of items are specially imprinted with the property's name and logo including guestroom amenities, guest bathroom supplies, menus and wine lists, restaurant and bar accessories, and accounting and front office forms.

Uniforms for the front-of-house employees are frequently specified by the hotel company or may be custom designed for a particular hotel. Often, costumes for the dining room and lounge employees may be specially developed to reflect the theme of the interior design, while those for the front office, bellman, and housekeeping staffs are more traditional. Throughout the hotel, signage, printed graphics, and uniforms play important roles in integrating design with the operational elements of the property.

18
ADMINISTRATION OFFICES

"The front office is the nerve center, the contact point between guest and hotel."

Jerry Lattin

The design of the front desk and administration offices is critical to the guests' positive reaction to the hotel. While all guests have contact with the front desk, many visitors each day meet with the sales and catering staff or with assistant managers. Therefore, the proper planning, design, and equiping of the hotel's office space deserves no less attention than that given to the guestrooms and public areas. The planning and interior design of the workplace and the provision of the correct equipment are essential not only to the morale and productivity of the staff but also to the public's perception of the quality and value of the hotel.

The offices, as the administrative plan shows, are generally divided into four clusters (the personnel office usually is located near the employee entrance):

- ☐ Front desk and front office
- ☐ Accounting
- ☐ Executive
- ☐ Sales and catering

While there are substantial advantages—shared reception and support areas, closer communication among the staff, and better visibility to the guest—in having offices located together, most hotels of over a few hundred rooms separate the groups into two or three clusters. The sole advantage is that the sales offices can be located near the function space. More than anything else, though, such arrangements are the result of unclear programming and hastily conceived schematic designs. Often, space initially allocated to offices near the desk must be replanned for other support functions that had not been sufficiently recognized in the program and early design phases.

FRONT DESK AND FRONT OFFICE

The front office is the largest of the four clusters and the one with which the casual guest is most familiar. It includes the following areas (also shown schematically in the figure on top of page 198):

- ☐ Front desk
- ☐ Reception
- ☐ Assistant manager
- ☐ Director of rooms
- ☐ Reservations area
- ☐ Reservations manager
- ☐ Telephone operators
- ☐ Fire control room
- ☐ Safe deposit area
- ☐ Counting room
- ☐ Work area/mail
- ☐ Other: toilets, storage, copying

In planning the front desk, collaboration among the design team is necessary: The architect establishes the general location, the

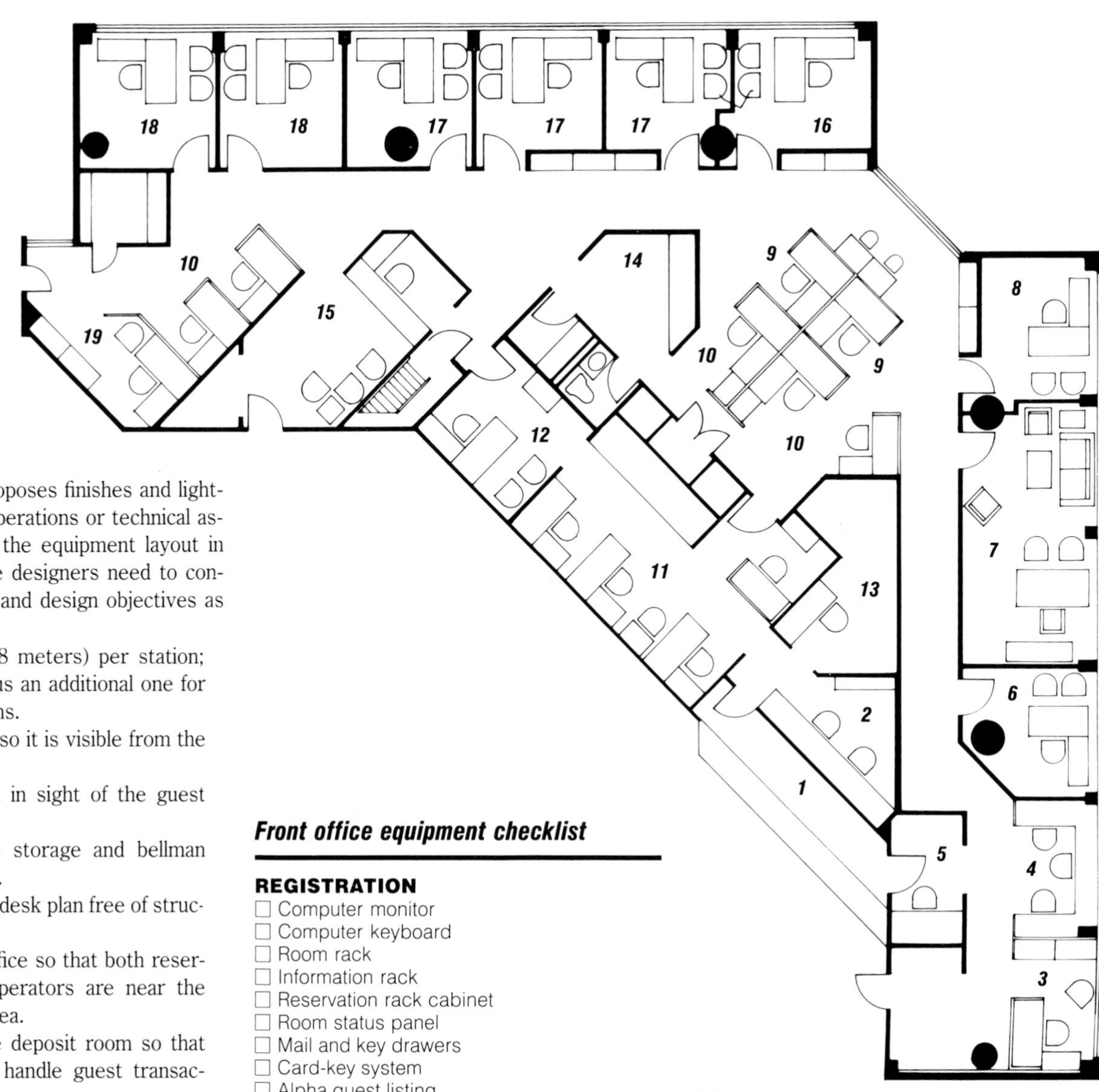

interior designer proposes finishes and lighting, and the hotel operations or technical assistance staff plans the equipment layout in the workspace. The designers need to consider such planning and design objectives as the following:

- ☐ Allow 6 feet (1.8 meters) per station; one station plus an additional one for each 150 rooms.
- ☐ Locate the desk so it is visible from the entrance.
- ☐ Locate the desk in sight of the guest elevators.
- ☐ Position luggage storage and bellman near the desk.
- ☐ Establish a front desk plan free of structural columns.
- ☐ Plan the front office so that both reservations and operators are near the registration area.
- ☐ Lay out the safe deposit room so that a cashier can handle guest transactions.
- ☐ Plan the front desk so that the cashier and registration functions can be staffed flexibly.
- ☐ Screen guests' views into office work areas.
- ☐ Recognize requirements for support functions: house phones, brochure display, concierge or assistant manager, and bell station close to front desk.
- ☐ Provide decorative focus at the desk: counter material, lighting, treatment of backwall, and signage.

The checklist at right of front office equipment identifies basic front desk systems.

The front office provides support to the registration and cashier functions. Its area requirement varies from between about 3 to 5 square feet (.3 to .5 square meters) per guestroom. The key elements in terms of layout are the reception and work areas, around which most of the other offices are clustered. In smaller hotels, where employees may be required to perform a variety of duties, such functions as telephone and reservations need to be convenient to the front desk. This is especially true at night when only one person may be on duty.

Front office equipment checklist

REGISTRATION

- ☐ Computer monitor
- ☐ Computer keyboard
- ☐ Room rack
- ☐ Information rack
- ☐ Reservation rack cabinet
- ☐ Room status panel
- ☐ Mail and key drawers
- ☐ Card-key system
- ☐ Alpha guest listing
- ☐ Message waiting panel
- ☐ Reserve key drawer
- ☐ Credit card imprinters
- ☐ Automatic wake-up system

CASHIER

- ☐ Cash registers
- ☐ Invoice trays
- ☐ Telephone meter system
- ☐ Folio printer
- ☐ Computer monitor
- ☐ Computer keyboard
- ☐ In-room movie recorder

OTHER

- ☐ Safe deposit boxes
- ☐ Telex
- ☐ Fire control system
- ☐ Employee paging

ABOVE

Administration Office Layout. *The office layout of the Doubletree Hotel in Overland Park, Kansas, illustrates the principle of clustering private offices around the central secretarial or work areas. One entrance leads to credit manager, front office manager, and safe deposit boxes; the other leads to a reception area near which both the executive and sales groups are conveniently located.*

(1) Front desk, (2) telephone, (3) front office manager, (4) reservations, (5) fire control center, (6) rooms manager, (7) general manager, (8) food and beverage manager, (9) restaurant manager, (10) secretary, (11) accounting, (12) controller, (13) computer area, (14) copy/mail, (15) reception, (16) marketing director, (17) sales, (18) catering, (19) convention coordinator.

LEFT

Front Office Equipment Checklist. *Hotel operating companies provide technical assistance in the planning and equipping of such areas as the front desk and back-of-house spaces. The items in the checklist need to be provided at or in close proximity to the front desk.*

PRECEDING PAGE

Hilton at Walt Disney World, Lake Buena Vista, Florida. *A row of computer consoles hidden behind the marble counter at the Hilton's front desk tie together all aspects of the rooms department in a hotel noted for its state-of-the-art technology.*

FRONT OFFICE

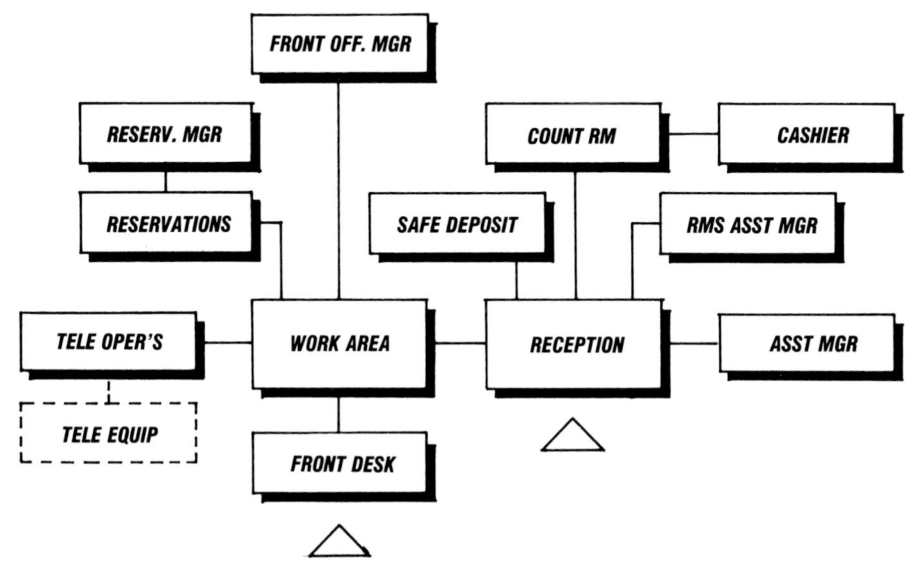

Front Office Diagram. *Organization of the hotel front office, adjacent to the registration/cashier desk, is clustered around the reception and work areas. The most important connection is to the accounting offices where possible.*

ACCOUNTING

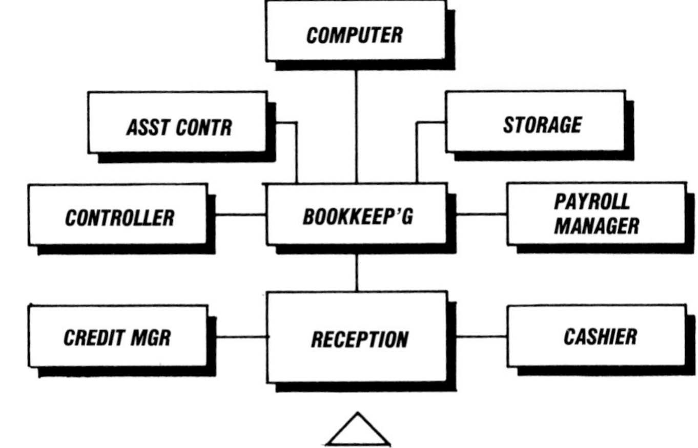

Accounting Office Diagram. *The accounting functions are simply arranged around a central bookkeeping work area. If the counting room is part of the front office, then a drop box into the cashier area must be provided.*

ACCOUNTING OFFICE

The accounting office, while best located as part of the main complex near the front desk, can operate satisfactorily at some distance. Their main connection to the front office is the need to have a counting room, where managers of such outlets as restaurants, bars, and retail shops can count and deposit their daily receipts. Even when the general cashier is located within the accounting area, a counting room must be included within the front office area.

The accounting cluster includes the following positions:

- ☐ Reception
- ☐ Controller
- ☐ Assistant controller/auditor
- ☐ Cashier
- ☐ Payroll manager
- ☐ Accounting work area
- ☐ Computer room
- ☐ Secretary
- ☐ Other: storage, copying

The layout of the accounting area is not complicated by special operating requirements or technical equipment except that with increased computerization the offices need to be flexible enough to accommodate new desktop systems as they are developed. These emerging special systems are briefly discussed in Chapter 20. The architect should allocate approximately 3 square feet (.3 square meters) per room for the accounting offices.

EXECUTIVE OFFICE

The executive office complex is the smallest of the four clusters. In smaller hotels, it is generally combined with the front office, the general manager assuming the duties of rooms department manager. In larger hotels, the executive office, diagrammed in the accompanying figure includes the following:

- ☐ Reception area
- ☐ General manager
- ☐ Executive assistant manager
- ☐ Food and beverage manager
- ☐ Secretary
- ☐ Conference room
- ☐ Other: toilets, storage, copying

The general manager is often highly visible, greeting dignitaries and hosting special visitors. Thus, his office and conference area may begin to resemble public reception and lounge areas. Where this is the case, the offices need to be larger and should be located where guests can readily find them and where security can be assured. Some senior managers prefer their office to be located near the receptionist, whereas others insist on its being at the very back, away from the distractions of the office routine.

Executive assistant managers, who share in policy decisions, are usually clustered with the general manager rather than with their respective departments.

SALES AND CATERING OFFICES

The fourth group, the sales and catering offices, is responsible for attracting group business and servicing the meetings and banquets once they are in the hotel. The cluster includes the following:

- ☐ Reception
- ☐ Director of sales
- ☐ Sales representatives
- ☐ Director of public relations
- ☐ Catering manager
- ☐ Banquet manager
- ☐ Banquet representatives
- ☐ Convention services manager
- ☐ Function book room
- ☐ Secretaries
- ☐ Other: toilets, storage, copying

Since the sales staff frequently shows prospective guests the available meeting and banquet facilities, the office suite is frequently located near the function area in the hotel rather than in the lobby. As with the other areas, the most common arrangement is to group the private offices around a secretarial work area (as shown above). This allows all the sales and banquet representatives to be close to the single function book, the master record of all functions scheduled in the hotel, which is often kept 3 or more years in advance.

The sales and catering offices get increasingly large in convention and other properties that cater extensively to group rather than individual guests. The space programming, which varies depending on the type of hotel, usually falls between 2 and 4 square feet (.2 and 4 square meters) per guestroom.

Executive and Sales Offices Diagram. *The executive offices are often paired with the sales and catering complex because the high incidence of visitors requires that they both be easily accessible, as well as contain highly finished reception and conference spaces. Alternately, the sales and catering group could be placed adjacent to the ballroom or meeting complex.*

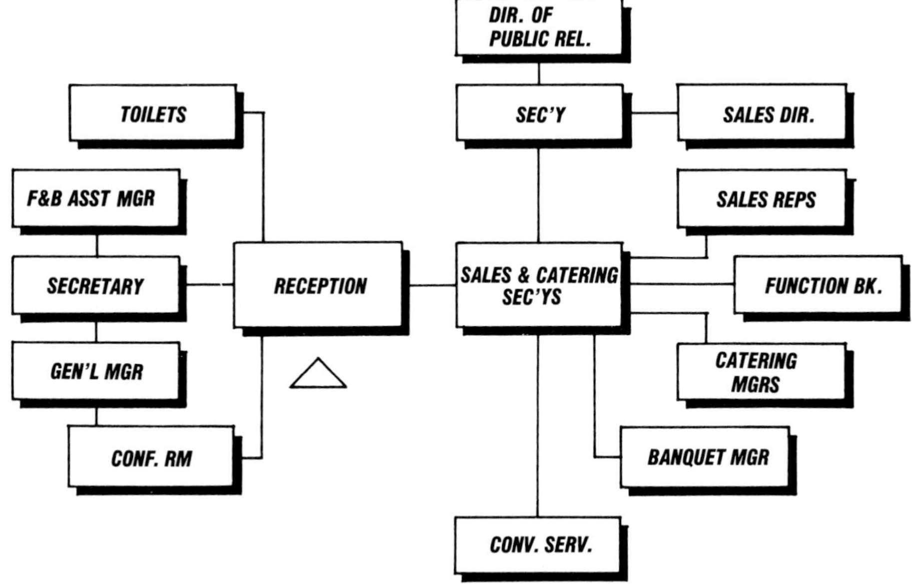

19
SERVICE (BACK-OF-HOUSE) AREAS

"The success or failure of a hotel depends on how efficiently the guests can be serviced."

Morris Lapidus

The planning and design of the back-of-house or service areas of the hotel, which the hotel guest rarely sees, are critical to the eventual success of the hotel. Comprising between 10 and 15 percent of the total floor area in all lodging types except motels and budget inns, the service areas influence the staff's ability to provide efficient housekeeping, repair, engineering and food and beverage services to the hotel.

The functional areas include the following:

- ☐ Food preparation and storage
- ☐ Receiving, trash, and general storage
- ☐ Employee areas
- ☐ Laundry and housekeeping
- ☐ Engineering and mechanical areas

These spaces vary considerably from hotel to hotel, depending on the type of property and on its size and location. Resorts, for example, may need to provide their own engineering services, including electricity, fresh water, as well as employee housing. In contrast, those motels that have neither restaurants nor a laundry need to provide only minimal storage for guestroom linen and for outdoor maintenance equipment.

Larger hotels require that these back-of-house areas function economically and efficiently so that staff can reach all areas of the hotel without passing through the lobby and other public spaces. Consequently, the service functions must be clustered around the receiving area and the employee entrance or near a major service corridor, and the food outlets need to be grouped around the kitchen and its satellite pantries (see diagram on page 202). The operational characteristics and planning and design criteria for each area will be discussed in detail.

FOOD PREPARATION AND STORAGE AREAS

Of all the service areas in a hotel, the kitchens and related food preparation areas require the most design attention, in part because the mechanical, electrical, and plumbing systems must be integrated with the layout of the kitchen equipment. In addition, the design of the kitchen, usually the largest single back-of-house area, critically influences labor costs for the life of the building. Distances should be as short as possible, related activities should be located close together, and layouts should be flexible. Therefore, the planning and design aspects of the kitchens require the coordinated attention of a variety of specialized kitchen and engineering consultants.

Planning objectives

Among the many planning requirements that the architect should address during the conceptual design, the most-important goal is to locate the receiving area, food storage, kitchen, and all outlets (restaurants and banquet areas) on a single floor. When this goal is not possible, which is almost always the case in downtown hotels and properties over 400 rooms, the designer must assess the relative merits of alternate groupings of service and public functions. The following checklist identifies the critical adjacencies:

Essential

- ☐ Food storage to main kitchen
- ☐ Main kitchen to restaurants
- ☐ Room service area to service elevators
- ☐ Banquet pantry to ballroom

Desirable

- ☐ Receiving to food storage
- ☐ Main kitchen to banquet pantry
- ☐ Banquet pantry to smaller banquet rooms
- ☐ Banquet pantry to prefunction area
- ☐ Coffee shop pantry to room service area
- ☐ Kitchen to cocktail lounges
- ☐ Kitchen to garbage/trash holding
- ☐ Kitchen to employee dining

These adjacency requirements are illustrated schematically in the accompanying figure below.

The amount of floor space required in the kitchen and food and beverage storage areas depends on the number of meals served, the complexity of the menu, and the delivery schedule. One goal, because of the high cost of equipment, energy, and labor, should be to design the smallest kitchen that meets the operational objectives. For example, many downtown hotels, where space is at a premium because of high land costs and where most foods are readily available, operate with a minimum food storage area. Yet, while some small kitchens function well because of

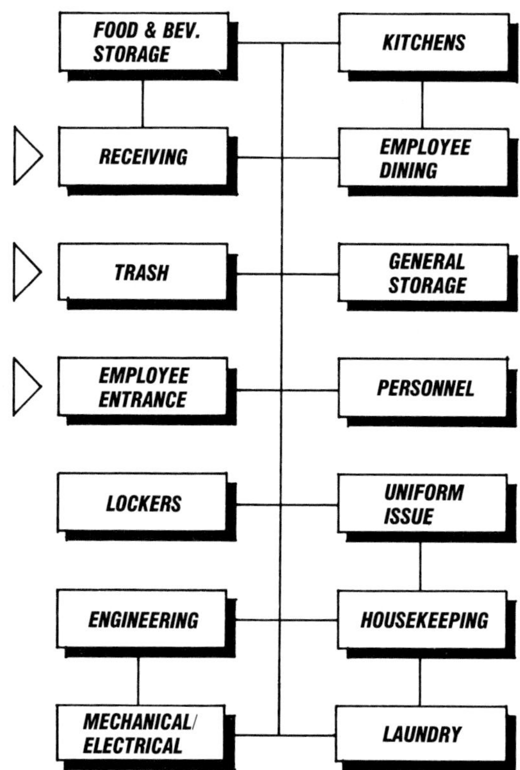

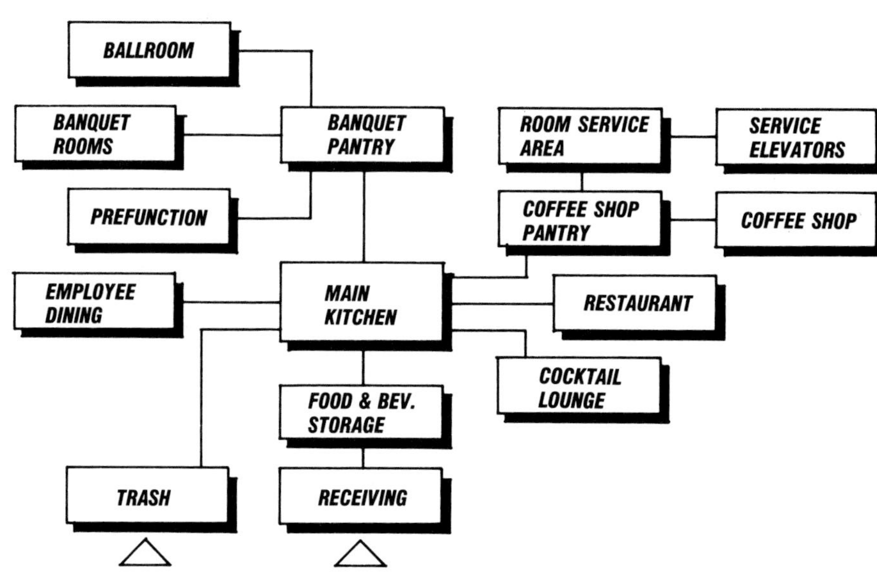

ABOVE

Back-of-House Adjacency Diagram. *The most efficient hotel support areas combine all the food service and other back-of-house functions on one floor. The diagram illustrates one arrangement where the following pairs of spaces are adjacent: receiving to food storage, food storage to kitchen, kitchen to employee dining, employee entrance to personnel, laundry to housekeeping, housekeeping to uniform issue, and uniform issue to lockers.*

RIGHT

Food Service Adjacency Diagram. *Among all the service areas, the location of the food preparation areas—the main kitchen and satellite pantries—is the most critical in terms of efficient operations and guest satisfaction. The essential connections include storage to kitchen, kitchen to restaurants, room service to elevators, and banquet pantry to ballroom.*

PRECEDING PAGE

Commercial Kitchen. *Hotel service areas require careful planning to improve staff productivity and guest satisfaction. The kitchen shows the difficulty of integrating such design goals as lighting, equipment, ventilation in an acoustically successful design.*

Checklist of Kitchen Areas. *Food service design focuses on organizing the movement of food through the kitchen and laying out the individual component areas identified in the checklist. Each area can, to some extent, be sized and designed independently and then combined to create a compact and efficient total layout. The kitchen must be closely related to the receiving and trash areas as well.*

the close proximity of these elements, the layout of larger hotels must compensate for separation of storage, preparation, cooking, serving, and washing areas.

Rules-of-thumb for space allocation vary depending upon the quality level of the hotel. However, an average starting point is to base kitchen size on the number of restaurant and banquet seats and hotel guestrooms and to refine it as the food and beverage concepts are better defined. The following formula establishes the initial space requirements for hotel kitchens:

Main kitchen (total of the following)

- ☐ 6 sq ft (.6 sq m)/restaurant seat
- ☐ 2 sq ft (.2 sq m)/ballroom and banquet seat
- ☐ 1 sq ft (.1 sq m)/cocktail lounge seat
- ☐ 1 sq ft (.1 sq m)/hotel guestroom

Food and beverage storage

- ☐ .3–.5 × main kitchen area

The accuracy of these rules-of-thumb is affected by the size of the hotel; the smaller hotels (fewer than 200 rooms) and satellite restaurants require a larger allocation per seat in order to equip even a minimum kitchen. Food preparation areas for representative types of hotels are included in the sample space programs illustrated in Chapter 14.

Designing the main kitchen

After the food preparation area space has been allocated during the early design phases, the food service consultant proposes a preliminary design. If major planning criteria are met, such as providing a single main kitchen close to the restaurants and function outlets, the overall design can be greatly simplified and the duplication of equipment eliminated. While the food facilities consultant prepares the kitchen plan, the architect needs to understand the flow of food and personnel throughout the kitchen areas. The accompanying checklist identifies the individual kitchen areas that must be integrated into a workable layout.

The kitchen planner usually approaches the design in two opposing ways: to locate departments (such as the bake shop or dishwashing station) within the larger kitchen space and to develop each work station by combining the equipment (range, fryer, broiler) to meet the following overall objectives:

- ☐ Provide straight-line flow of food from storage to serving.
- ☐ Eliminate cross-traffic and back-tracking.
- ☐ Minimize distance between kitchen serving area and restaurant seating.
- ☐ Arrange compact work centers.
- ☐ Locate secondary storage near each station, as required.
- ☐ Place shared facilities centrally.
- ☐ Consider sanitation and employee safety.
- ☐ Provide the minimum of heat-generating equipment.
- ☐ Plan for the efficient use of all utilities.

The kitchen planner incorporates complete design details, coordinating them with the architect so that the kitchen space can accommodate the intended equipment layout. In addition to standards for lighting and finishes, the detailed plan for the food service areas must include the following features:

- ☐ Provide automatic fire protection systems throughout, especially over cooking equipment.
- ☐ Depress floor slabs for refrigerated storage so that the finish floor is even with the kitchen floor.
- ☐ Group all walk-in refrigerators and freezers together to share common walls and compressors.
- ☐ Provide service vestibules between the kitchen and all outlets, banquet pantry, and ballroom; baffles between service corridors and banquet rooms.
- ☐ Locate soiled dish dropoff immediately inside doors from each restaurant, feeding a single dish-washing area.
- ☐ Provide for security at the kitchen service bar.
- ☐ Plan aisles at a minimum of 42 inches (1.1 meters).
- ☐ Set equipment on concrete curbs.
- ☐ Provide space for dining room cashier near waiter circulation.

Kitchen area checklist

RECEIVING

STORAGE
- ☐ Dry food storage
- ☐ Refrigerated food storage
- ☐ Liquor storage
- ☐ Refrigerated beverage storage
- ☐ Nonfood storage (china, silver)

PREPARATION AREAS
- ☐ Butcher shop
- ☐ Bake shop
- ☐ Vegetable preparation area
- ☐ Meat preparation area
- ☐ Salad and dessert preparation area

COOKING AREAS
- ☐ Main cooking
- ☐ Short order cooking

SANITATION
- ☐ Dishwashing
- ☐ Pot washing
- ☐ Garbage/trash removal

SERVING
- ☐ Restaurant(s) pickup
- ☐ Banquet pickup
- ☐ Room service area

OTHER
- ☐ Chef's office
- ☐ Service bar
- ☐ Staff toilets

Designing the food and beverage storage areas

The food and beverage storage areas in most cases are located adjacent either to the receiving area or to the kitchen, with the latter arrangement preferable. The storage and control requirements for hotels require that supervision and security be available at all times. The approximate area breakdowns of storage spaces are as follows:

STORAGE AREA	PERCENT
Dry food storage	30
Refrigerated food storage	25
Frozen food storage	10
Beverage storage	15
Refrigerated beverage storage	5
Nonfood storage (china, silver, paper)	15

A key feature in planning kitchen storage areas is to cluster all the refrigerated storage. Walk-in refrigerators and freezers require a depressed floor slab (to accommodate floor insulation) and share common insulated walls and compressor system, which is best located away from the storage. The closely grouped storage areas are clearly designated on the accompanying kitchen plan on the top of page 204.

RECEIVING, TRASH, AND GENERAL STORAGE AREAS

The hotel's receiving and trash areas, while located at the loading dock, require clear separation. Only in smaller hotels and motels are the two functions combined in a single area. The individual spaces are identified in the space program checklist in Chapter 14 and in the schematic diagram on the bottom of page 204.

The receiving and trash areas must be adjacent to the hotel's back-of-house areas. In addition to the major connection to the kitchens for incoming food and liquor and for outgoing garbage, sufficient area must be available to move goods to the laundry, house-

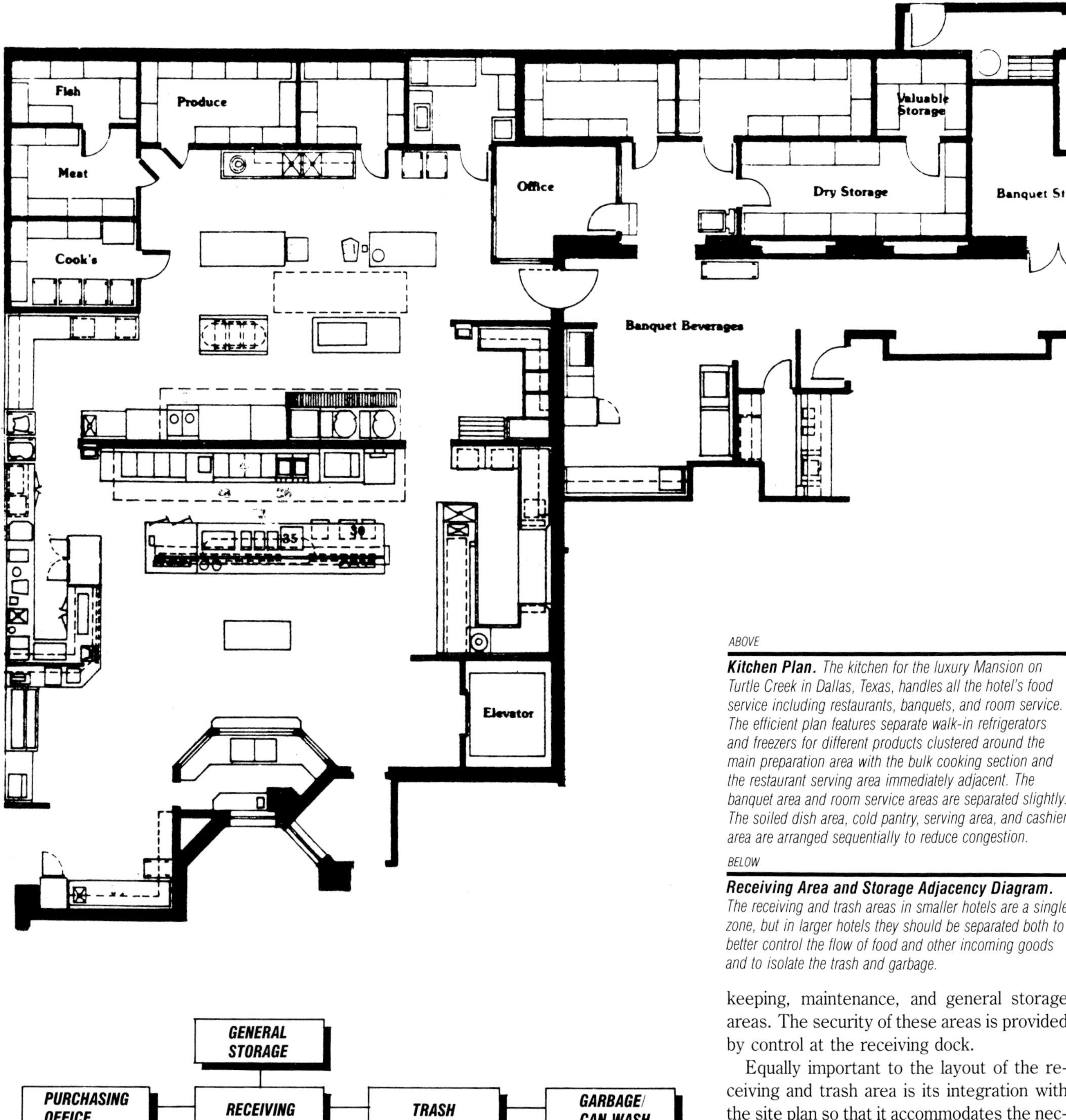

ABOVE

Kitchen Plan. *The kitchen for the luxury Mansion on Turtle Creek in Dallas, Texas, handles all the hotel's food service including restaurants, banquets, and room service. The efficient plan features separate walk-in refrigerators and freezers for different products clustered around the main preparation area with the bulk cooking section and the restaurant serving area immediately adjacent. The banquet area and room service areas are separated slightly. The soiled dish area, cold pantry, serving area, and cashier area are arranged sequentially to reduce congestion.*

BELOW

Receiving Area and Storage Adjacency Diagram. *The receiving and trash areas in smaller hotels are a single zone, but in larger hotels they should be separated both to better control the flow of food and other incoming goods and to isolate the trash and garbage.*

keeping, maintenance, and general storage areas. The security of these areas is provided by control at the receiving dock.

Equally important to the layout of the receiving and trash area is its integration with the site plan so that it accommodates the necessary movement of trucks without disrupting guest parking, yet is hidden from the hotel guestrooms and such public areas as restaurants, lounges, and recreational areas. An otherwise well-designed hotel can be severely downgraded by the poor location of its receiving and trash areas.

The overall planning requirements include the following:

Receiving

- ☐ Provide a raised dock area large enough to accommodate two trucks at one time;

three trucks if over 600 rooms.

☐ Enclose the receiving area so that it is secure, weather protected, and sounds and odors are contained.

☐ Include windows between the receiving office and both the dock and receiving area.

☐ Arrange access to the area to avoid cross-traffic between incoming goods and garbage.

Trash/garbage

☐ Separate the trash/garbage holding area from the receiving dock.

☐ Provide refrigerated area for garbage and area for washing cans.

☐ Enclose compactor area, yet allow accessibility at all times.

☐ Provide a small compactor at the outlet of the trash chute to reduce the bulk of paper waste.

The receiving and trash areas require between 2 and 3 square feet (.2 and .3 square meters) per guestroom, but the size of the area is determined only in part by the number of guestrooms. More important is the relative amount of restaurant, lounge, and function space—reflecting the volume of food and beverage operations—and the quality level of the hotel.

Hotels require considerable amounts of storage area. Most of this space is associated with specific activities: food storage near the kitchen, function room storage near the ballroom and banquet rooms, linen storage on each floor and with housekeeping, and records storage at the administration offices. However, in addition, two categories of storage are often located near the receiving area: outdoor equipment and general storage. The first, generally requiring a few hundred square feet (except in resorts), is for building and grounds maintenance equipment and outdoor furniture. The second, often occupying an area as large as the entire receiving and trash area, is for extra furnishings and equipment, record storage, printed material, and unassigned items.

While they must be near receiving, these storage areas have different requirements. Often omitted from the program, space for outdoor equipment such as for lawn care and snow removal should be located at grade level. The general storage area needs to be secure, perhaps comprised of two or three caged areas, so that different operating departments control separate sections of the room. Although the general storage area is necessary for a variety of miscellaneous items, it does not replace the need for adequate storage at each of the back-of-house functions previously discussed.

EMPLOYEE AREA	SQUARE FEET	SQUARE METERS
Personnel	1.5–2.5*	.14–.23*
Timekeeper/security	0.3–0.5	.03–.05
Men's lockers/toilets	1.5–2	.14–.19
Women's lockers/toilets	1.5–2.5	.14–.23
Employee dining	1.8–2	.17–.19
Employee housing	Varies	Varies

*Area requirements per guestroom.

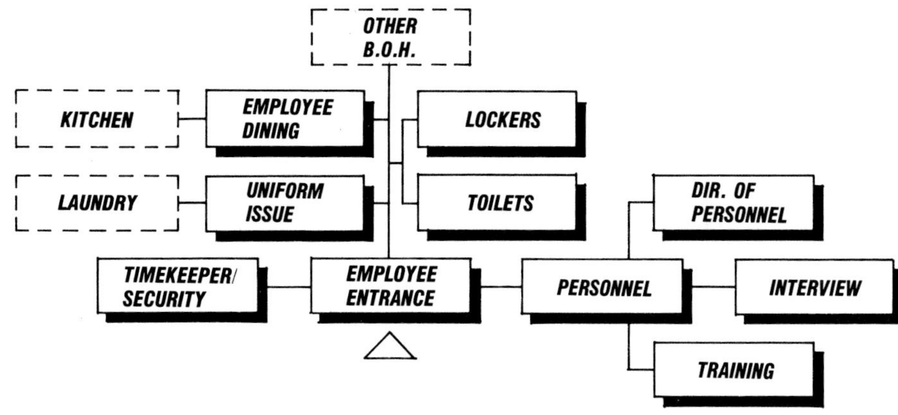

Employee Areas Adjacency Diagram. *The employee areas should be organized so that the timekeeper and personnel areas are immediately adjacent to the entrance. Also, the food service, housekeeping, maintenance, and other employees should be able to reach the locker areas, uniform issue, and employee dining room without interfering with the receiving function.*

EMPLOYEE AREAS

The staff areas form a third major part of the hotel's back-of-house areas. While in smaller and lower-quality properties these areas may be limited, adequate space for the hotel staff is essential to a full-service operation in any hotel. (In a few cases, primarily resorts and overseas hotels, the developer may even include large-scale staff housing.)

The usual components—personnel offices, lockers, and employee dining—are somewhat independent from each other and relate to other back-of-house areas as much as or more than to each other. For example, the personnel function is related closely to the employee entrance, the lockers to the uniform issue area and to the timekeeper, and the employee cafeteria to the main kitchen. The adjacency requirements are described schematically in the above figure.

The area requirements, totaling between 6 and 10 square feet (.55 and .9 square meters) per room include the following units:

Security, circulation, and equipment requirements for the employee areas are less rigid than for other back-of-house functions, allowing greater flexibility in their location within the service block. The architect, nevertheless, must incorporate the following operational features into the planning and design:

Personnel and timekeeper offices

☐ Locate timekeeper and security office immediately inside the employee entrance.

☐ Provide visual control of the entrance and main service corridor.

☐ Include small, private offices for interviewing and counseling employees.

☐ Provide a training room for staff meetings and education.

Lockers and toilets

☐ Provide separate facilities sized according to the staff program and shift schedules.

☐ Consider separate lockers for banquet staff.

☐ Plan separate access to toilets without passing through lockers.

Employee dining

☐ Plan cafeteria near kitchen or, if on different floor, near employee locker rooms.

☐ Design cafeteria to contain service line, seating, and soiled-dish-holding area.

☐ Include vending machines.

☐ Provide sufficient capacity for peak periods (consider numbers at shift change).

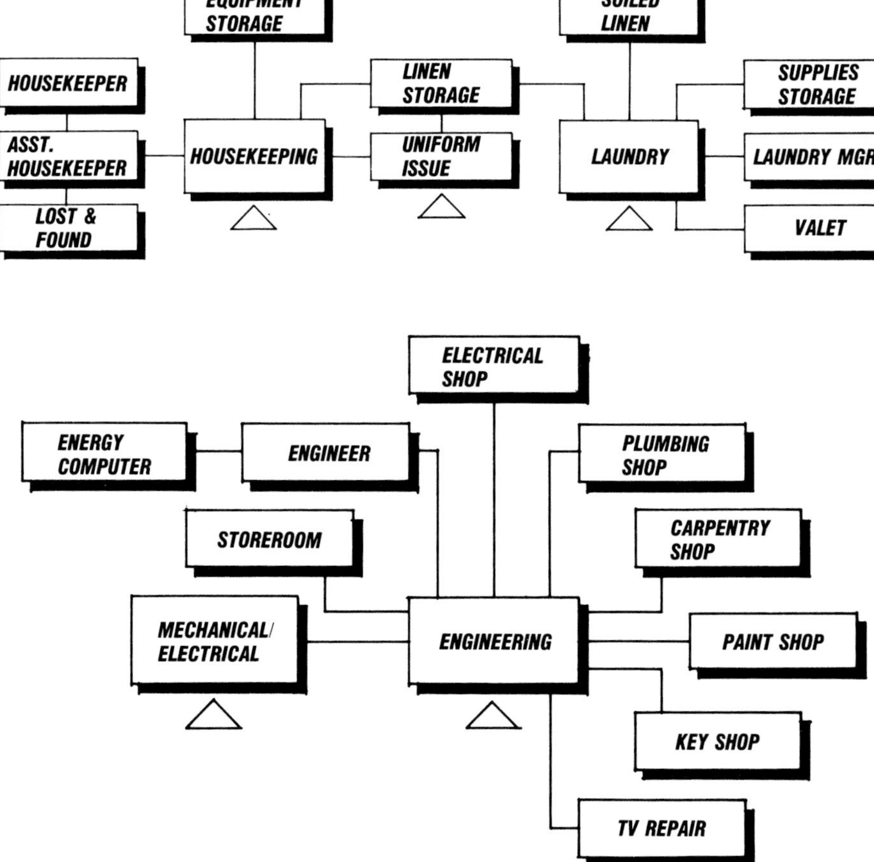

TOP

Laundry and Housekeeping Areas Adjacency Diagram. *The laundry and housekeeping functions, although separate for better control and supervision, must adjacent so that clean linen and guest laundry can be moved easily from the laundry to the housekeeping and uniform issue areas. Each area has its own storage and offices as required.*

ABOVE

Engineering Areas Adjacency Diagram. *The engineering area combines a number of different repair and maintenance shops with a small office area, the latter getting more important with the addition of energy management computers and frequent refurbishing or renovation projects. The mechanical and electrical areas should adjoin the engineering area although various equipment rooms may be somewhat removed.*

Employee housing

- ☐ Provide manager's apartment as part of guestroom program.
- ☐ Where necessary, include two-bedroom apartments for senior management and one-bedroom apartments for junior staff; plan dormitory units for other employees.
- ☐ Provide appropriate commons areas such as recreation room, self-service laundry, pool, and lounges.

Most major hotel chains now require that their general manager live in the hotel in an apartment. Often, this unit is the equivalent of a five-bay suite, including a two-bay living room, one-bay dining room and kitchen, and two bedrooms.

In both destination and highly seasonal resorts, where no community is close enough to provide housing for the full staff, hotel developers must include adequate staff housing. The same is the case in many developing regions, where trained employees in addition to managers must be accommodated. For example, in much of the Middle East, where virtually all hotel employees are imported, a major housing complex—effectively a second hotel—must be built. While entailing substantial capital cost, such housing complexes can be justified in terms of lower payroll costs and such operating advantages as reduced absenteeism, lower turnover, and greater employee productivity and promptness.

LAUNDRY AND HOUSEKEEPING

The laundry and housekeeping areas create the fourth key element of the service facilities of a major hotel. Even the smallest motel provides some space for storage and control of guestroom linen; in larger hotels this space is extensive and includes major laundry facilities.

Among the key issues for back-of-house areas in properties with fewer than 150 rooms is whether or not to include a laundry. In small inns, when construction and equipment costs are added to the operating expenses, the developer or operator may find it more economical to rent linen or to send it out to a commercial laundry than to handle it in-house. On the other hand, virtually all mid-price and better hotels operate their own laundries in order to control quality and availability of linens.

The laundry and housekeeping areas are closely related and should be adjacent, even though they are separately managed. But even where laundries are omitted, extensive areas are required for collecting, loading, receiving, and storing linen. The main function, of course, is to clean and distribute guestroom (bed and bath) and table linen, uniforms, kitchen laundry, and guest clothing. Resort hotels may have additional laundry demands, such as swimming pool towels.

The laundry and housekeeping areas have key adjacency requirements, related to servicing the guestrooms and providing staff uniform and other linen.

Essential

- ☐ Linen chute to soiled linen area
- ☐ Soiled linen area to laundry
- ☐ Receiving to housekeeping (if no hotel laundry)

Desirable

- ☐ Laundry to housekeeping (linen storage)
- ☐ Housekeeping to uniform issue
- ☐ Uniform issue to employee lockers
- ☐ Valet to housekeeping
- ☐ Housekeeping to service elevators

The area requirements are fairly standard—from 10 to 14 square feet (.9 to 1.3 square meters) per room—because the great majority of laundry demand is generated by the guestrooms. Two types of hotels, motor inns and commercial hotels of over 600 rooms, are at the low end of the range. On the other hand, resort hotels, properties with extensive food and beverage and function facilities, and first-class and luxury propertie reach toward the high extreme. The necessary space is about equally divided betwee the laundry and housekeeping areas, including their respective support spaces (see th hotel program checklist in Chapter 14).

The laundry layout is often designed by th technical services staff of the hotel management company or by laundry design consultants, representing the major equipmen manufacturers. Laundries should be locate preferably at the hotel's lowest floor to avoi noise and vibrations from interfering wit any guest area. In hotels with over 80 guestrooms tunnel laundries have proved t

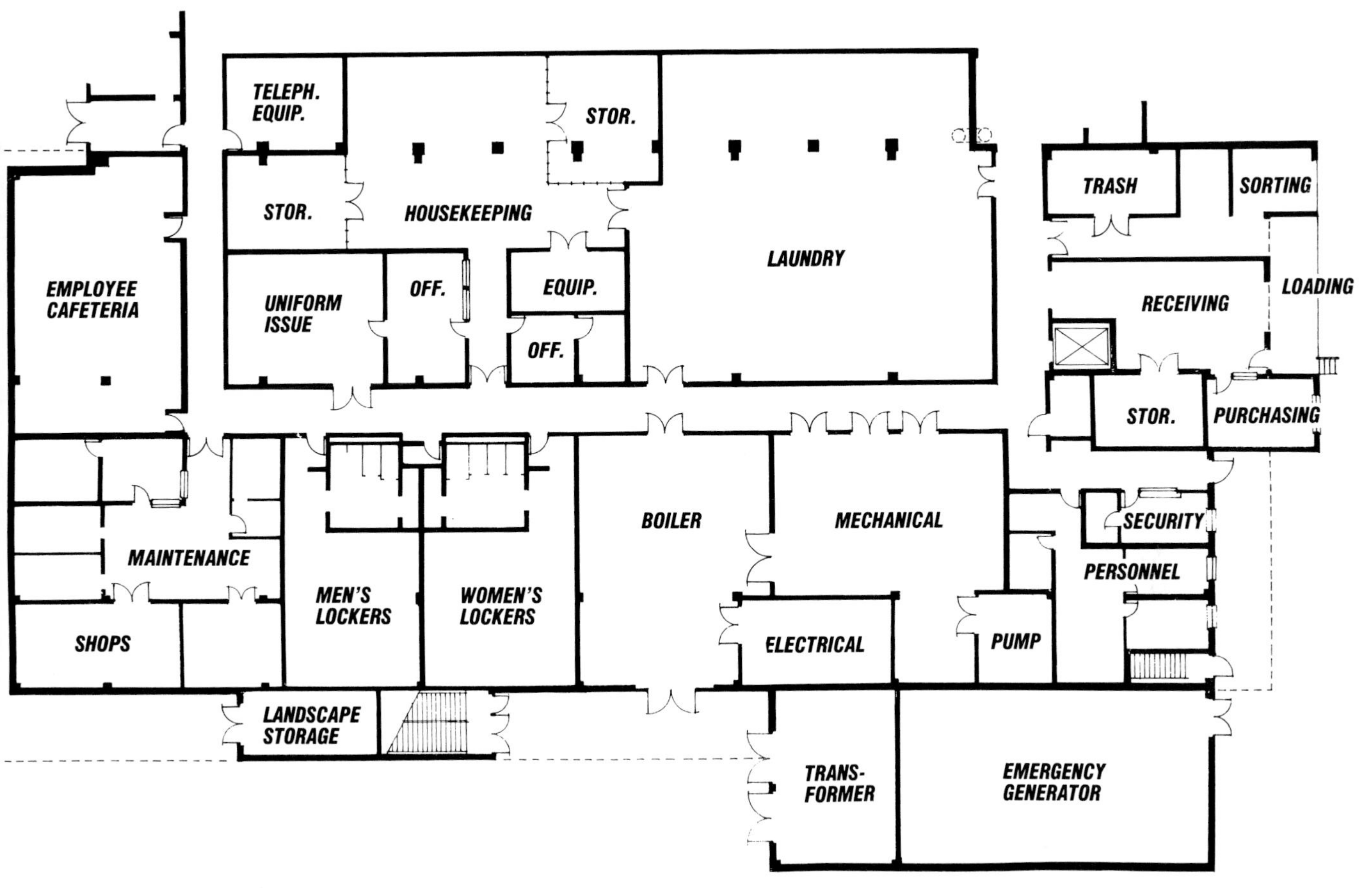

ack-of-House Areas Plan. *The service areas for the yatt Regency Austin in Texas are located on a single level xcept for the main kitchen, which is immediately above he receiving area. The layout illustrates the successful rouping of related functions: laundry, housekeeping, and niform issue are a single block; uniform issue and mployee lockers are together; receiving and trash are eparated; personnel is at the employee entrance; mainte-ance and engineering areas are clustered; the cafeteria is ear the lockers, although distant from the kitchen.*

e most efficient and should be installed. Among the operational requirements and de-ign objectives for the two areas are the fol-owing:

- ☐ Provide a linen chute including provisions for smoke control, venting, and locked access.
- ☐ Locate offices so that they visually control the laundry and housekeeping areas.
- ☐ Establish separate locked linen storage for particular departments, such as food and beverage or pool.
- ☐ Create separate accessible areas for night staff (cleaning equipment and supplies).
- ☐ Consider energy conservation approaches such as heat recovery for all equipment.
- ☐ Plan continuous flow of linen and uniforms through the laundry cycle.

Engineering and Mechanical Areas

The final back-of-house area contains three related functions supervised by the hotel's chief engineer: engineering offices, repair and maintenance shops, and mechanical and electrical areas. Too often these activities are given insufficient space with architects and engineering consultants planning the mechanical areas but only allocating leftover space to the offices and shops.

The mechanical equipment areas do not need to be immediately adjacent to the other service areas, although they should be close to the laundry, kitchen, and other high energy use areas for most effective operation. In fact, the equipment rooms can be organized along a separate service corridor for better control and supervision. However, the engineering function operates 24 hours a day and thus must be directly connected to back-of-house areas and to the service elevators. The organization within the offices and shops, illustrated in the bottom figure on page 206, shows the various repair and maintenance areas clustered around the offices.

The offices and shops require between 3 and 5 square feet (.3 and .5 square meters) per room; the area requirements for the mechanical and electrical areas vary considerably, depending on such factors as climate, size of hotel, type of construction, orientation, and operational objectives. Plans for the engineering spaces should include the following considerations:

Engineering offices

- ☐ Locate the secretarial area to control all access to the shops and mechanical areas.
- ☐ Group engineer, assistants' offices, and record and drawing storage around control area.
- ☐ Provide energy management computer room as required.

Maintenance shops

- ☐ Position the carpentry, upholstery, and paint shops adjacent to each other.
- ☐ Provide exhaust system from paint shop (fumes) and carpentry shop (airborne sawdust).
- ☐ Provide additional electrical service to all shops.
- ☐ Connect TV antenna system to television repair shop.

Mechanical/electrical areas

- ☐ Locate mechanical areas so that noise and vibration do not affect guests.
- ☐ Locate so that large equipment can be replaced reasonably easily.

20

CONSTRUCTION

"We look at every design decision in terms of life-cycle-costing. It becomes cost effective in the long run to invest in good design."

Isadore Sharp

Just as the planning issues in hotel development are critical to the success of a particular project, so too the construction methods and materials are essential to maintaining the overall concept, schedule, and budget. For the most part, the structure and mechanical systems as well as construction techniques are similar to those of other building types. Yet the nuances of hotel design and operation greatly influence such choices as structural materials, bay spacing, and HVAC systems. The following elements, even the most subtle of which influence construction alternatives, affect hotel projects:

- ☐ Small, repetitive guestrooms and large public and service areas, suggesting a combination of short- and long-span structural systems.
- ☐ Residential and assembly spaces, with different building code requirements.
- ☐ Frequent requests to accelerate the construction schedule so that parts of the building may be occupied before substantial completion.
- ☐ Differing objectives of the owner, developer, and hotel operator.
- ☐ Requirement, in some cases, to adapt prototype designs to different climates, availability of materials, and site constraints.
- ☐ Frequent need to evaluate lower initial capital cost versus reduced life-cycle costs.

These elements combine to make hotel projects, whether they are small budget inns, medium-size conference or suite projects, or large convention or mega-hotels, a unique building type. Further, because of the 24-hour-per-day operation, hotels receive constant physical wear, must be easily maintained, and cannot afford to be closed for repair. The checklist of construction alternatives on the top of page 209 outlines some principal design options available to the hotel architect, ranging from massing and structural questions to materials and building systems.

A variety of external factors also influence the design and construction of hotels. In addition to the availability of utilities, favorable soil conditions, and zoning, among the most crucial factors are the building and life safety codes. These establish strict requirements for maximum occupancy, number and size of exits, fire resistance of materials, compartmentation, and the provision of fire protection systems. The design of a fire-safe building requires the integration of proper design—the passive element in protection—with adequate detection, alarm, and sprinkler systems—the active portions of a complete fire protection program.

Satisfying guests also depends on the mechanical and electrical systems of the building. These total about 35 percent of the cost of construction and, as a result, are major elements in budget control. Newer designs have generated improved solutions, not only for heating and cooling but for such specialized hotel requirements as ventilation and smoke evacuation from open atrium spaces and heat recovery for kitchen and laundry areas. Solar energy systems—used for some years to provide hot water in restaurants—are only beginning to be applied in the hotel field.

CONSTRUCTION SYSTEMS

A particular hotel site and its environs suggest the form for the building, especially the guestroom structure. The rooms tend to be grouped into relatively compact highrise slabs and towers or lowrise horizontal wings. They can be built of any of several materials and systems. Lowrise resort cottages differ very little from wood-frame residential buildings, mediumrise motor inns might be built of load-bearing masonry walls, and highrise hotels are likely to incorporate either a flat-plate reinforced concrete system or a steel or reinforced concrete frame. A few hotels in the United States, most notably the Hilton Palacio del Rio in San Antonio, Texas, and the Contemporary Hotel at Florida's Walt Disney World, have been built by stacking individual prefabricated guestroom modules, and, internationally, many others have used precast concrete panel systems.

A second structural decision concerns the typical bay or column spacing. Some systems are more efficient if the structure is spaced every two guestrooms, or about 25 to 28 feet (7.6 to 8.5 meters) apart; others are more economical when the columns are placed at every guestroom wall. In general, steel frame buildings have the wider column spacing while reinforced concrete structures are based on the narrower module. The wider spacing allows considerably more flexibility in the planning of the lower public and service floors.

One design decision that marries the construction and esthetic concerns is the choice of the exterior materials. The amount and type of glass and the selection of the brick, concrete, or other cladding material affects not only the guests' reaction to the hotel but the cost of construction, including mechanical systems, and of operating the heating and air conditioning systems.

Construction alternatives checklist

MASSING
- ☐ Highrise
- ☐ Mediumrise
- ☐ Lowrise
- ☐ Scattered

GUESTROOM CONFIGURATION
- ☐ Slab (rooms arranged along a single- or double-loaded corridor)
- ☐ Tower (rooms cluster around a central elevator core)
- ☐ Atrium (rooms located around or overlooking a multistory space)
- ☐ Combination of configurations
- ☐ Individual cottages

TYPE OF STRUCTURE
- ☐ Reinforced concrete frame or flat plate
- ☐ Steel frame
- ☐ Masonry bearing wall
- ☐ Panel (precast floor and wall units)
- ☐ Modular (prefabricated guestroom modules)
- ☐ Wood frame (residential quality)
- ☐ Indigenous methods and materials

COLUMN SPACING
- ☐ Single bay (columns at each guestroom partition)
- ☐ Double bay (columns at every other partition)
- ☐ At thirds (usually four columns across the width of a guestroom wing, the two interior ones being approximately at the one-third and two-third positions)
- ☐ No interior columns (staggered truss)

BUILDING MATERIALS
- ☐ Exterior (glass-to-wall ratio; performance characteristics of all materials)
- ☐ Interior architectural finishes
- ☐ Interior decorative finishes

MECHANICAL/ELECTRICAL SYSTEMS
- ☐ Central versus individual "package" units
- ☐ Fan-coil versus heat pump system
- ☐ Horizontal versus vertical distribution
- ☐ Two pipe versus four pipe hot and chilled water distribution
- ☐ Location of mechanical areas
- ☐ Relative first cost versus life-cycle cost
- ☐ Heat recovery alternatives
- ☐ Submetering of individual areas
- ☐ Cogeneration

The architect and other design professionals must make hundreds of choices between approximately equal options. Often, these don't influence esthetics but do affect the relative efficiency of the building plan or of the construction system. Many alternatives further reflect on future costs such as energy consumption or replacement cost.

LEFT AND TOP PAGE 210

Contemporary Hotel, Walt Disney World, Orlando, Florida. *The 1970 prefabricated hotel pioneered the use of lightweight guestroom modules held within the steel A-frame structure. The rooms were constructed off-site, trucked to the theme park, and lifted into position by crane. The room interiors were completed and entirely furnished at the factory.*

PRECEDING PAGE

Hyatt Regency Grand Cypress, Orlando, Florida. *The 750-room mega-hotel surrounded by lush gardens was constructed in relatively short time, in part because of the separation of the guestroom structure from the lowrise public space and extensive recreation facilities. (See Chapter 11, The Mega Hotel, and bottom of page 130 for more on this hotel.)*

Frame structures

The nature of hotel spaces — long-span ballrooms, and lobbies combined with small, repetitive guestrooms—has created a group of structural solutions typical for high-rise hotels. Where possible, the conceptual structural analysis for a hotel should:

- ☐ Separate guestroom and public/service portions of the hotel because of the different structural and mechanical requirements.
- ☐ Investigate the use of flat plate, post-tensioned, or other thin slab struc-

ture for the guestroom portions of the building.

- ☐ Consider lightweight steel for the public and service areas of the hotel.
- ☐ Weigh the impact of wind loading on highrise structures before determining the guestroom tower configuration.
- ☐ Analyze the construction timetable versus benefits of earlier opening.
- ☐ Consider the influence of structural systems on future adaptability of hotel functions.

Unlike office and commercial buildings, which require suspended ceilings, the guestroom portion of the hotel is more easily built with a flat-plate concrete structure or with precast floor slabs. With no need for HVAC ducts or recessed lighting, the underside of the floor construction can easily be given an appropriate ceiling finish. The extra beam depth and necessary fireproofing of the typical steel frame is much less appropriate for hotel guestrooms. Only in extremely tall buildings or where concrete is considerably more expensive is steel preferable.

Other approaches have been tried for highrise hotels. Ellerbe Associates has designed a group of hotels using a staggered truss structure for the upper floors. They substitute a series of skeletal walls across the width of the guestroom floor, supported by the exterior columns, speeding construction and eliminating interior columns on all floors. This solution creates medium-span spaces [about 60 feet (18.6 meters) wide] on the public levels.

Bearing wall structures

A second approach to hotels is to eliminate the structural frame entirely and, since the guestrooms contain parallel walls roughly 13 feet (4 meters) apart, to use these as load-bearing partitions. Not a new concept (most of the early skyscrapers a century ago used bearing walls that were several feet thick at the base), the innovation is in maintaining only an 8-inch (.2-meters) thick concrete block partition for 12 or more floors. Architects Hendrick and Mock have designed a number of bearing wall hotels and cite the quality control, speed, and economy of construction, the acoustic benefits, and the integral fireproofing. One 200-room, 8-story project in San Diego, California, took less than

LEFT

Hyatt Regency Flint, Flint, Michigan. *The centerpiece of downtown renewal efforts, the 375-room Hyatt Regency was designed with a staggered truss system to speed construction and provide column-free space. The system was developed in the 1960s as an economical framing system—U.S. Steel claims a 40 percent reduction in structural steel—for tall, narrow buildings.*

five months to complete and open.

Though it is logical for use in the guestroom structure, the bearing wall limits the planning flexibility of the ground floor. It is necessary, even more than with frame structures, to separate the lowrise public areas from the bearing wall structure; otherwise the ground floor layout is controlled by the location of columns or the partial wall structure supporting the upper floors.

Other architects have taken advantage of the wide availability of precast concrete to design hotel wings using precast and prestressed wall and floor slabs. The Forest City Dillon (FCD) process, for example, includes structural components (precast concrete walls, stairs, and spandrel panels, prestressed floor and facade slabs), preassembled service cores (back-to-back bathrooms), elevator shaft components, and non-load-bearing interior partitions and curtain walls. FCD maintains that partial prefabrication methods, like theirs, can reduce the construction period by 50 percent because of the speed of erection and the reduced need for interior finishing. They have refined the process to the point where they can erect two floors per week, while, on the lower levels, contractors connect the finished service cores, add electrical wiring, and finish the interiors.

Modular construction

A third construction approach that has found some support in hotels is modular construction, highlighted by the factory manufacturer of guestroom-size modules, complete with walls and ceiling, plumbing, finishes, and furnishings. The pioneer hotel was the Hilton Palacio del Rio, built in San Antonio, Texas, in 1967 to meet the deadline of a regional trade fair. Five hundred concrete modules were built off-site, transported by truck, and lifted into position by crane. Assisted by a helicopter rotor mounted on each box to control sway, the 30,000-pound (13,620-kilogram) modules were literally piloted into position.

The Hilton was matched for innovation by the later Contemporary Hotel at Florida's Walt Disney World, where 1500 rooms were prefabricated of light-weight steel studs and gypsum board—much like a mobile home—in part because of the poor subsoil conditions at the Orlando site. The excitement created by these two projects produced several variations: one concrete system offered choices of brick and barn-board textures cast in both the exterior and corridor facades. Other manufacturers hurried to begin producing factory-built motel rooms for the budget and lower ends of the hotel market. These continue to be popular, primarily in the southern areas of the United States.

International Systems (ISI) has built concrete modules for several overseas hotels in both the Middle East and the Pacific. These projects require inverting the usual construction sequence. Interior designs for the guestrooms must be completed first, while the construction documents for the rest of the hotel are incomplete. The modules are cast, interiors finished, and shipped while the foundations and public areas are built conventionally. For the 335-room Hyatt Regency Hotel in Macau, Houston architects CRS/SIRRINE shipped over 400 modules to Hong King, from where they were barged to Macau and the guestrooms erected in little more than 1 month.

BUILDING AND LIFE SAFETY CODES

All buildings are subject to a variety of regulations from health codes to sign ordinances. Once the proposed hotel meets the zoning requirements regulating use, height, site coverage, and density, the detailed design must comply with the building and fire codes. Their intent is to protect the public against faulty design or construction; therefore, they principally address structure (including materials, live and dead loads) and fire conditions. The goal is to build a structure that will resist fire or other emergencies and protect the occupants until they can exit from the building. Plumbing and electrical codes further regulate those technical disciplines.

While the codes in most countries are highly specific and have been continually updated as a result of fires or building failures, significant variations remain within the United States as well as internationally. For example, in building renovations, owners may not be required to bring the full facility up to the standard of the code; however, this policy is changing so that even minor remodelings bring with them substantial price tags for safety modifications. Typical building and life safety codes address the following:

- ☐ **Fire resistance:** Codes define for different construction elements the number of hours they should withstand fire, ranging from 45 minutes to 4 hours.
- ☐ **Compartmentation:** Codes outline the required fire separation between different uses (for example, assembly and parking).
- ☐ **Flame spread:** Codes rate interior finishes according to their ability to limit fire growth as measured by "flame spread rating," ranging from 0 (asbestos board) to 100 (red oak) to over 500.
- ☐ **Fire resistance of furnishings:** Codes describe furnishings in terms of both fire and and smoke propagation, especially to reduce toxicity.
- ☐ **Fire detection, fire alarm, and fire suppression systems:** Codes now require fire detectors and alarm systems and, for highrise hotels, assume full sprinkler protection.
- ☐ **Limited building height and single floor area:** In special cases where hotels are not built of fire-resistive materials, codes limit the height and maximum area per floor.
- ☐ **Occupant load:** Codes establish maximum room occupancies based on floor area and define the number and size of the exits for a particular type and size space.
- ☐ **Exit requirements:** Codes require at least two independent routes of escape and establish requirements for their width and protection from flame and smoke.

Even the codes that are most up to date are subject to varying interpretations, especially by so-called experts. Therefore, the tables on page 213 do not attempt to state legal standards that vary significantly among different cities and states but rather provide relevant requirements as established by international hotel chains. (However, these are standards are generally adaptations of several American and international codes.) These standards are not meant to take the place of codes; in fact, it is essential that the architect and engineers study the codes and standards for a particular location and comply fully with all the requirements.

Requirements for finishes and furniture

The interior finishes and hotel furnishings create the single largest potential fire hazard. Statistics show that furnishings, primarily bedding, are the source of over 40 percent of hotel fires and nearly 60 percent of motel fires. Although stringent standards exist for making interiors fire resistant, recent hotel fires have been fueled by the improper application of combustible interior finishes.

The most flame-resistant materials must be used without exception. These are rated according to the materials' ability to limit the spread of fire and minimize the danger from smoke, as noted in the table on the right on page 213. Even though the National Bureau of Standards has developed mathematical models to predict how different furnishings

Fire resistance and compartmentation

FIRE RESISTANCE OF CONSTRUCTION ELEMENTS

3-Hour rating
- ☐ Structural frame
- ☐ Load-bearing and fire walls
- ☐ Doors in 3-hour walls

2-Hour rating
- ☐ Floor construction
- ☐ Roofs
- ☐ Walls enclosing vertical shafts (stairs, elevators, chutes)
- ☐ Most non-load-bearing exterior walls

1.5-Hour rating
- ☐ Doors in 2-hour walls
- ☐ Windows in 2-hour walls

1-Hour rating
- ☐ Interior partitions

.75-Hour rating
- ☐ Doors in 1-hour partitions
- ☐ Openings in most exterior walls

SEPARATION OF HOTEL USES

3-Hour separation
- ☐ Theaters and nightclubs

2-Hour separation
- ☐ Ballroom, meeting and banquet rooms, exhibit halls
- ☐ Enclosed restaurants and lounges
- ☐ Offices and computer rooms
- ☐ Laundries and dry cleaning areas
- ☐ Projection booths
- ☐ Maintenance shops (carpentry, painting, furniture refinishing)
- ☐ Boiler, transformer, switchgear, and emergency generator rooms
- ☐ Parking garage
- ☐ Storage area

1-Hour separation
- ☐ Guestrooms
- ☐ Mechanical areas
- ☐ Kitchens

Codes rate construction elements in general and further define various use groups (such as assembly and storage) and their required separation in hours of resistance to the spread of fire. Ratings of between 45 minutes and 4 hours are established for the structural frame and for such major elements as floors, walls, and doors. Ratings for separation between uses fall between 1 and 3 hours. Where mixed uses occur close together, for example, storage areas adjacent to a hotel ballroom or restaurants next to a kitchen, the higher rating prevails.

will behave during a fire and various laboratories have tested actual samples, many materials react differently in a unique application or situation. For example, flame spread ratings vary depending on fabric dyes, cleaning solvents, wear, and varying installation techniques. Custom-built products, which are so common in hotel guestrooms and public areas, usually are not tested or the results are averaged.

To counteract these problems, architects and designers need to document fully the selection and specification of finishes and furniture. They might assign responsibilities at each stage to the manufacturer, fabricator, installer, or owner as appropriate. It is essential that the specifier record any substitutions, retain product and material samples, and verify that the product guarantees actually cover the type of installation envisioned.

A second aspect of interior finishes and furnishings also deserves mention. Because of the highly decorative nature of many hotels, the interior designer assumes major responsibility for the selection of the materials, and the relationship between the designer and architect is more crucial than that for most other building types. There are numerous areas in which they must share in the decision making, and these often result in unclear responsibility for specification, purchasing, and budgeting. As a result, many hotel companies have adopted checklists that define the responsibilities among the design professionals and assign the items to an appropriate budget category. (The latter are detailed in Chapter 24, Professional Practice.)

The single component that leads to the largest number of problems is the "fixed decoration." This includes decoration applied walls and ceilings in restaurants, lounges, and boardrooms; such millwork as the front desk, bar, host or bellman stands; built-in planters and railings, especially at minor level changes in the several public areas; and special lighting. Actually, it makes little difference how these are controlled, so long as architect and designer fully coordinate their efforts.

ACOUSTICS

Hotel designers must recognize the importance of noise control in hotels, especially in the guestrooms and meeting rooms that are among the more sensitive areas. But in practically every part of the hotel including the public areas (lobbies, meeting room foyers, entertainment lounges, bars), recreation facilities, service areas (kitchens, laundries, mechanical, receiving, and trash areas), and guestrooms (because of television and hospitality uses) there is the potential of unwanted noise. In addition, proximity to highways and airports, while important in attracting guests, creates additional noise problems.

Standards have been established to identify the required acoustic separation needed between areas to reduce noise levels. For example, meeting room dividing partitions are rated at 44 to 48 STC (sound transmission class), which reflects the average reduction in decibels attained by a particular construction. Guestroom partitions should be rated at 50 or higher, while others may vary between 35 and 50. The more severe acoustic separation problems that must be addressed by the architect and consultants occur between:

- ☐ Adjoining guestrooms (including guest bathrooms)
- ☐ Adjoining meeting rooms
- ☐ Exterior areas and meeting rooms or guestrooms
- ☐ Elevator lobby and guestrooms
- ☐ Entertainment rooms and guestrooms
- ☐ Kitchen and restaurants
- ☐ Service pantries and banquet rooms
- ☐ Mechanical areas and public rooms or guestrooms
- ☐ Rooftop cooling towers and penthouse suites
- ☐ Laundries and adjoining public areas

ENGINEERING SYSTEMS

The highly variable use of the hotel, determined by seasonal and daily occupancy fluctuations, creates the need to design and install extremely adaptable mechanical, electrical, and plumbing systems. The increase in fuel prices over the past decade has provided further impetus to finding innovative systems that run both efficiently and cost effectively. Energy costs alone now average over $1000 per room each year in major hotels and approach $1400 in many resorts.

The separation in hotel facilities between the guestrooms and the public and support areas has implications for building's mechanical systems as well as for the architectural and structural design. The need for separation is clear in the relative difference in cost in the systems needed in each area (as percentages of the total construction cost), as shown on the table on page 214.

This table indicates, for example, how the mechanical, plumbing, and electrical capital costs vary substantially depending on the function of the space; savings should be sought primarily in the more costly areas. Also, the architect should consider such alternatives as providing greater building mass for

Flame-resistant guestroom

MATERIALS
- ☐ Glass fiber wall coverings
- ☐ Spandel* drapes, sheers, and blackout liners
- ☐ Spandel bedspread fabrics, mattress ticking, and pillow coverings
- ☐ Fire-retardant foam cushions, fire-resistant liners and upholstery fabrics
- ☐ Flame-resistant nylon carpeting
- ☐ Wood furniture in place of plastic laminates
- ☐ Nonflammable materials (mirror, glass, tile, metal furnishings)

EQUIPMENT
- ☐ Built-in cabinets with fire blankets and fire extinguishers
- ☐ Television used as fire enunciator
- ☐ Smoke detectors that activate exhaust fans to create negative pressure
- ☐ Halon gas extinguishers in rehabilitation projects where permitted

SPACE DESIGN
- ☐ Hard floor entry foyer as a firebreak
- ☐ Fire-rated door with drop seal as smoke barrier
- ☐ Second door between room foyer and guestroom to isolate room from corridor
- ☐ Furniture with minimum of folds, buttons, pillows to limit the opportunity for cigarettes to ignite upholstery

**Spandel is a woven fiberglass chemically coated to increase wear and feel.*

Occupant load and exit requirements

MAXIMUM CAPACITY (based on floor area per person)

	SQUARE FEET	SQUARE METERS
☐ Guestrooms	200	18.6
☐ Offices	100	9.3
☐ Retail at grade	30	2.8
☐ Retail on upper floors	60	5.6
☐ Assembly spaces	7	.7
☐ Theaters (fixed seating)	Actual number of seats	
☐ Parking garage	Number of parking spaces	

NUMBER OF EXITS (based on the room capacity)

	EXITS
☐ 1000 people or more	4
☐ 601–999	3
☐ 50–600	2

CAPACITY OF EXITS (based on the number of people per exit unit)

	PEOPLE PER 22 INCHES (.55 METERS) WIDTH
☐ Guestroom and assembly area stairs	113
☐ Guestroom and assembly area doors	150
☐ Office and retail stairs	90
☐ Office and retail doors	150

MAXIMUM TRAVEL DISTANCE TO PROTECTED EXIT (for sprinklered hotels)

	FEET	METERS
☐ Guestroom areas	150	46
☐ Assembly areas	200	60
☐ Through atrium space	100	30
☐ Deadend corridor	20	6

SAMPLE CALCULATION (based on 10,000 sq. ft. ballroom)

• Capacity:	1428	(10,000 ÷ 7)
• Number of exits:	4	(capacity > 1000)
• Total width of doors:	220″	(1428 ÷ 150 = 10 × 22)
• Total width of stairs:	286″	(1428 ÷ 113 = 13 × 22)

Flame spread and smoke development

FLAME SPREAD RATINGS

	RATING
Interior finishes	
Guestrooms	200
Ballrooms, meeting and banquet rooms	200
Restaurants and lounges	200
Offices	200
Ballroom foyer, hotel lobby	75
Stairs, exit corridors	75
Carpeting	
Floors, all areas	75
Wallcovering	25
Fabrics	
Furniture upholstery	75
Curtains, drapes, wallcoverings	25

SMOKE DEVELOPMENT RATING

Hotel companies do not permit the use of any interior finish materials, fabrics, or other furnishings that have a tested smoke development rating of over 300.

ABOVE LEFT

Flame-Resistant Guestroom. *A recent project by Owens-Corning Fiberglas Corporation's Life Safety Laboratory developed six prototype flame-resistant guestrooms for budget, commercial, and luxury resort hotels. Designed by GKR, Inc., The Walker Group, and Hirsch/Bedner and Associates, the layouts were designed to address the over 10,000 hotel fires each year. They focus on the use of fire-resistant materials, especially glass fiber fabrics and fire-resistant liners for foam cushions, protective equipment, and space design concepts.*

ABOVE

Flame Spread and Smoke Development. *Building finish materials and furnishings are rated according to their relative ability to resist combustion and the further development of toxic smoke. For example, the assigned "flame spread" rating and "smoke development" rating for asbestos board is 0 and for red oak 100, and those for other materials range as high as 500. Decorative finish materials and fabrics must be selected carefully to assure compliance, and highly flammable materials such as polyurethane foam should be avoided. The standards shown here assume complete sprinkler protection throughout the hotel.*

LEFT

Occupant Load and Exit Requirements. *Exit requirements including the number and size of doors, width of corridors and stairs, and travel distance are based on the assumed maximum capacity of a space, usually determined by dividing the floor area by an appropriate area per person. Code officials generally calculate a conservative occupant load. They may require that any assembly space be rated at 7 square feet (.7 square meters) per person even if, for example, the restaurant is furnished to accommodate one-half to one-third that number.*

The necessary exit calculations can be extremely involved. Consider the simplified analysis for a hotel ballroom of 10,000 square feet (929 square meters), based on the tables above. In addition, each meeting room, foyer space, and so on must be added and exit routes from the building determined.

Need for separation of guestrooms and public/service areas

COST CATEGORY	GUESTROOMS, PERCENT	PUBLIC/ SERVICE, PERCENT
Architectural and structural	60–65	60–65
Heating, ventilation, and air conditioning (HVAC)	10–12	16–18
Plumbing	8–9	4–5
Sprinklers	3–4	3–4
Electrical	11–13	8–10
General conditions (site overhead)	4–5	4–5

passive heating and cooling, solar shading, and reduced glass area, modifying the building orientation and even its color, and installing highly efficient mechanical systems to reduce the capital and operating costs by significant margins.

Energy conservation goals should be part of the architect's original plan. Since most critical design decisions are made early in the planning phases, architectural and systems decisions need to be integrated from the beginning. For example, at the new Hilton Hotel at Walt Disney World, the architectural massing evolved in part to meet the energy performance requirements of the developer. The highrise guestroom structure was positioned to the south of the main public facilities, shielding them so that their exposed glass areas receive a minimum of direct sun. Most of the hotel windows were deeply recessed, further reducing heat gain and, consequently, the capacity of the building's environmental systems. Public areas such as the lobbies and restaurants were located to receive considerable indirect daylight, lowering their lighting costs. Other areas, meeting rooms, offices, and back-of-house facilities, which receive intermittent use, were equipped with occupancy sensors that automatically turn off lighting when the rooms are vacant. The hotel expects to see a 50 percent reduction in electrical consumption from these sensors.

Atrium engineering systems

Over the past two decades the open atrium design has been one of the most visible new building forms. In office and retail uses, as well as hotels, atrium lobbies or gallerias have become increasingly popular because of such factors as an exciting public image, increased daylight and visibility, and, with proper design, reduced operating costs.

In office buildings especially, where lighting consumes nearly two-thirds of the energy, atrium or courtyard designs that provide more natural light have flourished. In these cases, the atrium roof in effect replaces large areas of the perimeter window wall, substantially decreasing the energy required for space heating and cooling and offering the opportunity of designing a passive solar system. Current practice is to heat or cool only the lower and upper 10 feet (3 meters) of the atrium and consider the remainder to be dead air space if the atrium is surrounded by building on four sides.

In hotels, the open corridor design of most atriums leads to other engineering solutions. Because the corridors are emergency exit routes, the system must be designed to quickly and effectively control the spread of smoke within the atrium space. Generally, the system is designed to draw smoke from the fire area into the atrium and exhaust it at the roof. Stairwells and corridors not open to the atrium are kept under positive pressure to keep smoke from entering. These designs must be connected to the building's emergency power to assure operation at critical times.

Many fire protection experts believe atrium hotels are safer than conventional designs because they assure a thoroughly developed fire safety system, noncombustible construction, full sprinklers, and a complete smoke evacuation plan. In addition, the conditions of the fire can be observed better and, therefore, actions can be taken more quickly. In contrast traditional hotels, with their long corridors, may fill quickly with smoke even from small fires that may go undetected for some time. Happily, conventional hotels are now installing the same safeguards the atrium hotels were forced to do a decade ago.

The smoke evacuation system for atrium hotels, more complicated than for other corridor designs, should include the following features:

- ☐ Fire zone kept at negative pressure (air supply ducts are closed).
- ☐ Non fire floors kept at positive pressure (fresh air is supplied at corridor ends remote from the atrium; return air fans shut off; dampers closed).
- ☐ Stairwells kept at positive pressure (fresh air is supplied, often by dedicated HVAC systems; all doors well sealed against smoke infiltration).
- ☐ Atrium kept at negative pressure (induction jet at center of atrium floor directing smoke upward; entry doors automatically open; exhaust smoke at roof).
- ☐ Computer-controlled smoke dampers in supply and return ducts; all air-handling components not part of smoke control system shut down; manual back-up system at the fire control room.

Cogeneration systems

With continual inflation in energy prices, hotel developers and operators are seeking ways to reduce energy costs without detracting from the guests' satisfaction. One concept gaining advocates is cogeneration, which combines on-site electrical generation with the use of the waste heat for heating, air conditioning, and domestic hot water. It is most appropriate in areas with high electric rates (such as New York City, San Diego, and the Caribbean Islands) and with demand charges and for those hotels that have emergency generators.

The typical system includes a reciprocating engine/generator set, fueled with either natural gas or diesel fuel. It is sized to accommodate the electrical baseload required (lighting of public areas, including guestroom corridors; pumps and fans; and refrigeration compressors) and whatever additional load might be economically feasible. Where utilities charge additional rates for peak demand use or have "time-of-day" billing, it may be cost effective, for example, to generate close to 100 percent of a hotel's electrical requirements.

Generating electricity is itself only part of the cogeneration system. Equally important is the ability to harness the waste heat from the cooling exhaust and systems and use it to meet the thermal requirements for the hotel. Systems can be designed to provide:

- ☐ Domestic hot water
- ☐ Steam for kitchen and laundry
- ☐ Space heating
- ☐ Air conditioning (with an absorption chiller)
- ☐ Swimming pool heating

Cogeneration systems are feasible where both the electricity and the waste heat can be profitably used in the operation, where it is compatible with local codes, and where energy costs are likely to rise. There are installations in hotels as small as 80 rooms and as large as 680. For example, the Hotel del Coronado in San Diego, California, installed a major $2.2 million system in 1982. Their staff reports that it provides 30 percent of the resort's electrical requirements and nearly all its thermal needs, including steam and space heating. In 1981, the Ramada Inn at the Philadelphia airport installed a relatively small system that provides much of the electricity, hot water, space heating, and public area air conditioning.

Solar energy

Solar energy, with its great untapped potential, is only in its early years of becoming cost effective for hotels. However, one substantial installation has been made in the temperate, often cold, north: The Radisson Plaza Hotel in St. Paul, Minnesota, incorporates two different solar systems in an experimental government-supported demonstration program. The hydronic system consists of 4400 square feet (410 square meters) of traditional flat-plate solar collectors on the sloping atrium roof. The southern exposure generates a projected 35 percent of the 250-room hotel's hot water requirements. A complementary air-to-air system is built into the southwest facade of one of the stairtowers, drawing outside air through glass collectors, heating it, and eventually distributing it throughout the 14 guestroom floors. In the summer, this heated air supplements the first system in producing hot water.

Lighting

The electrical systems are a major part of any building project and no less important in a hotel. However, the designer should consider hotel lighting more a design element than a building science. The success of the lobbies, atriums, restaurants, entertainment areas, meeting and banquet rooms, and guestrooms depend as much on comfortable and creative lighting than on any other single design element. The requirements are often based on common sense. Guestroom lighting needs to be adequate for reading in bed, working at the desk or table, and shaving or applying makeup. If any of these is poor, the guest registers at least subconscious irritation. Meeting room lighting must also be highly adaptable. It should combine incandescent lighting for ambience with fluorescent fixtures for meeting use and track lighting for displays or accents. Special decorative restaurant lighting is essential to create the desired mood in food outlets.

Developers may hire a specialized lighting designer—or assign the lighting design to the interior designer—for the primary public spaces while relying on the architect's and engineer's judgment for offices and back-of-house areas. However, many locations have special restrictions for overall energy. Massachusetts, for example, requires that hotels not have over 1 watt per square foot of lighting.

Radisson Plaza, St. Paul, Minnesota. *The solar panels covering the atrium roof supply one-third of the hot water requirement for the 250-room downtown hotel, supporting the promise of solar energy even in northern climates.*

Exterior areas also require proper application of illumination effects. The architect must consider exterior lighting of the building, parking, grounds, and exterior recreational areas for identification and security. The night illumination of a hotel can help create a memorable image and must be considered as part of the lighting program.

21
SPECIAL SYSTEMS

"Traditionally, every communication and control system required separate wiring. Now, microelectronics permits a few wires or fiber optic cables to accomplish everything."

United Technologies ad

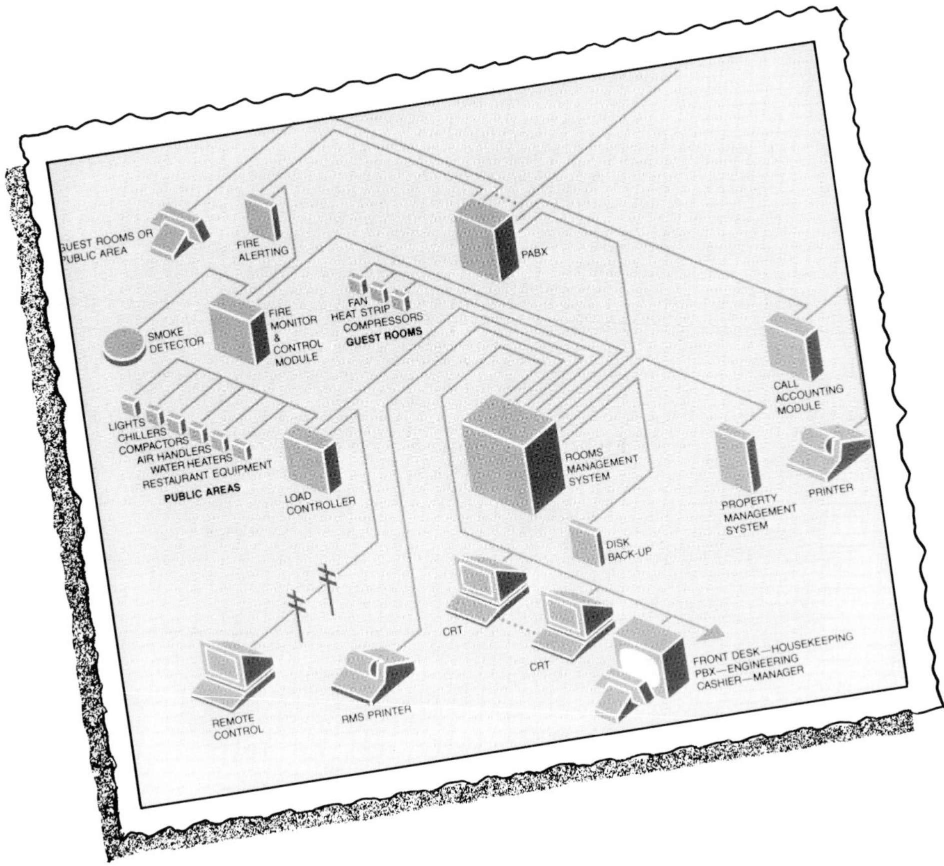

Technology has evolved at such a fast pace since 1980 that advances in the various types of systems have dramatically changed the methods of operation in the hotel industry. From computerized check-in to automatic wake-up call systems, electronic locks to closed circuit televisions, fire and security protection systems to teleconferencing, no buildings have ever been more systemized than today's hotel and resort. These specialized systems fall into six broad categories that are being continuously refined by manufacturers and that have become the focus of thorough study by the major hotel companies as well as by the American Hotel and Motel Association (AH&MA):*

- ☐ Information processing
- ☐ Telecommunications
- ☐ Energy control
- ☐ Life safety systems
- ☐ Security systems
- ☐ Audio/video systems

The rapid advances and changes aren't limited to one or two categories; they cross all lines, reflecting the influence of the miniature microchips on computers and various types of specialized control systems. Also, as the AH&MA study points out, most of the specialized hotel systems now on the market—including sophisticated energy management controls, "card-key" locking systems, and telephone call-accounting systems—were not even available, much less cost effective, until just a few years ago.

The various integrated systems that tie several operational requirements together include a reservations system which checks the availability of rooms for individuals or for groups, assigns room types, tracks deposits, and prints management reports. As a front desk system, it handles registration and check-out, automatically posts guest accounts, provides telephone operators with a room directory, updates accounts receivables, and tracks housekeeping staff. As an accounting system, it handles guest accounting, night audit, and all back-office accounting functions. With available options, the same system supports energy management, monitors life safety systems, and controls telecommunications equipment.

Today more than 600 vendors supply over 3000 models of equipment to the hotel industry. The challenge for operators and developers is to use the technology to improve guest service as well as the financial operation of the hotel.

Imagine, for example, an automated front

*American Hotel and Motel Association, *The State of Technology in the Lodging Industry,* New York: 1983.

desk at which computer terminals, much like automatic bank tellers, register guests, record credit card information or accept cash, assign rooms, and issue magnetic card-keys that are good only until the designated check-out. The card-key provides access to the guestroom, turns on the heating and air conditioning, permits use of in-room vending (snacks, soft drinks, and liquors) and electronic services (business computers, local information, movies, and entertainment) available through the television, with the appropriate charges automatically recorded at the front desk. These automated operations are routine, for example, at the business class Shinjuku Washington Hotel in Tokyo.

To these operations, American systems being developed add a print-out of guest messages at the check-in counter, additional room sensors for security and fire protection, and push-button phones that also control lighting, television, room temperature, and drapes; check-out is handled at a computer terminal in the guestroom or in the lobby, where the itemized bill is displayed on a monitor and approved by a signature with a light pen. The cost of these features, if separately wired, would be prohibitive. But they are possible through integrated building systems that allow new options to be added as available.

Information Processing

One area in which technology has already advanced rapidly is in information processing, including the use of companywide reservations networks and, at individual hotels, room-management systems, point-of-sale charging, accounting, word processing, and personal computing. Not surprisingly, the industry has moved dramatically away from such nonelectronic equipment as cash registers and accounting machines, replacing these with computerized and electronic equipment that integrate conventional data-processing applications with such other hotel systems as energy control and communications systems.

Computerized reservations systems were first centralized by Sheraton in 1956, further developed by Holiday Inns in the early 1960s and, since then, have gone through generations of refinement. Practically every major hotel chain has its own computerized reservation service or one based on readily available software. For example, a package originally developed for Westin Hotels is now used by Ramada and is the basis for modified or expanded programs by Days Inns, Holiday Inns, Hyatt, and Marriott. A specialized reservations program is being developed for the unique requirements of condominium hotels.

A second major area of information processing is the broad category of property management systems. Over the past decade, according to the AH&MA survey, as the technology has matured, the number of systems that perform a host of management tasks at the property level has grown 20 times. They ably and reliably perform not only reservation functions but also room management, front- and back-office accounting, and operational reporting including:

- ☐ Guest reservations
- ☐ Guest registration and folio accounting (the record of guest charges for room, food and beverage, and telephone)
- ☐ Accounting, including night audit, city ledger, accounts payable, and general ledger
- ☐ Travel agency accounting (record of commissions to be paid)
- ☐ Guest history and other marketing reports
- ☐ Daily and monthly operating reports
- ☐ Payroll and related reports
- ☐ Inventory

The many vendors now competing to satisfy the individual requirements of a particular hotel or resort can be expected not only to supply the computer equipment and the software but to modify them to accommodate the specific needs of the property. In addition, vendors will integrate their systems with other automated and nonautomated parts of the hotel. For example, the more sophisticated systems are able to interconnect with other equipment that monitors telephone calls, energy consumption, restaurant and bar purchases, and fire and security conditions.

Point-of-sale systems have become commonplace in many food outlets, restaurants, and clubs, as well as hotels. A system allows the waiter to place an order at a console located in the dining room, which then prints out in the kitchen where the production staff begins to prepare the food. In addition to saving steps, the restaurant systems reduce errors in calculating and totaling the final check, immediately post the charge to the guest's room account, and provide a variety of analyses including daily accounting and food inventory reports.

More revolutionary than property management systems has been the sudden growth just since 1983 in the use of desk-top personal computers in hotels. Marriott has a personal computer in each hotel for shared use by different departments, while Ramada has used them to replace their reservation terminals. The desk-top models are limited to relatively specialized and individualized applications, including financial analyses (budget projections and capital projects reports), operations monitoring (staff scheduling, equipment records, function room bookings), word processing, guest histories, and numerous accounting functions. Middle management is only beginning to understand how computers can assist them. Several larger hotels have purchased small computers and assigned them to different departments where the staff can experiment with various analytical programs and use them for such specialties as menu costing or energy consumption.

Telecommunications

The second technological area that has had a major influence in the hotel industry recently is telecommunications, including electronic telephone systems, call accounting systems, and video conferencing. With the continued deregulation of the communications industry, competition among the private companies should reduce the cost and add increasing numbers of features to hotel telephone service. In addition, the 1981 ruling by the U.S. Federal Communications Commission that allowed the resale of telephone service provides hotels with the opportunity to add a surcharge to telephone calls and thereby turn a deficit operation into a profit-making department. The larger hotel chains are considering establishing their own telecommunications networks—even booking travel reservations and other services—to capitalize on the capabilities of their equipment.

Electronic systems offer hotels the same advantages they do to residential customers: quicker dialing, data transmission (increasingly important as guests carry portable computers on business), and expanded features. For example, in Canada, the VuPhone provides a visual display similar to that of a memory typewriter for the hearing impaired; the phone "rings" with a flashing light. A number of companies already have developed sophisticated telephone systems that:

- ☐ Contact typical hotel services by dialing a single number (front desk, housekeeping, room service, bell captain, restaurants, and wake-up).
- ☐ Reach outside services with a code number (travel reservations, car rental, and ticket agencies).
- ☐ Place a call on hold, receive a second

Diagram of Central Building Nervous System. *Much like the human body, the hotel's special systems are becoming more fully integrated into one "central building nervous system," illustrated by this diagram of Honeywell's System 80. (With permission, System 80, Honeywell, Commercial Division.)*

call, and transfer a call to the hotel's message center.

- ☐ Record incoming messages so that a guest hears the caller's voice rather than a written message, or divert all incoming calls to the message center yet make outgoing calls.
- ☐ Control room amenities (television on/off, channel, and volume); adjust room temperature within a pre-set range; open or close drapes.
- ☐ Provide fire safety information by serving as a loudspeaker for emergency messages.
- ☐ Transmit alarms to front desk from smoke detector or motion or other security sensors.
- ☐ Function as a room status system to track cleaning of occupied rooms and preparation of unoccupied rooms.

The new telephone call-accounting systems are profitable because they permit the automatic identification of long-distance calls so that the hotel guest can be charged accurately without operator assistance. Among other savings, this service permits calls to be made at the cheaper station-to-station rates or through private interconnect companies. Studies have shown that even smaller hotels at which guests make as little as $1000 worth of long-distance calls per month can benefit from installing call-accounting equipment. In addition to overall reliability, ease of maintenance, and technical issues, the AH&MA study cautions that in selecting a system the operator should consider the following points:

- ☐ Accuracy of charge calculations.
- ☐ Ability of the system to interconnect with different phone equipment, hotel computer systems, and private transmission companies.
- ☐ Capacity of the call-record storage.
- ☐ Ability to merge calls on to the guest bill and to surcharge guest calls but not administrative calls.
- ☐ Format of reports and speed of output.

Communications systems will grow enormously in the future, and the hotel operator should consider ease of expansion in making equipment decisions. For example, the increased use of guest computers will require the installation of additional trunk lines to accommodate longer connection times to offices and data banks.

An equally large advance in the telecommunications field has been the recent increase in video conferencing. Since it erected its first receiving "dish" in 1980, Holiday Inns has installed several hundred earth stations at its hotels to provide both conference capability and in-room entertainment. Other companies, instead of providing their own systems, make use of newly established satellite service companies. Some video-conferencing experts expect that the number of video-conference meetings will increase 20 times over by the mid-1980s alone. Obviously, this new meeting service affects the design of the hotel's function areas, which must now be planned to accommodate the rapidly changing technology of teleconferencing (see Chapter 17 for a discussion of how to plan meeting space).

ENERGY CONTROL

Energy management features have become increasingly popular since the first drastic rise in energy prices created by the 1973 oil embargo. Technological advances that were formerly cost prohibitive have become common as a result of rising prices, increased efficiencies of the systems, and reductions in capital equipment costs. The greatest savings are in the design and operation of the heating, ventilation, and air conditioning (HVAC) systems, lighting, and water heating with the relative benefit depending on climate, orientation, type of hotel, size, and construction materials.

The AH&MA study surveyed the use of 13 possible energy control technologies. The more common ones, those used by at least 10 percent of the hotels polled, include:

- ☐ **Water flow restrictors:** Limit water flow in guestroom showers and sinks, reducing the use of hot water.
- ☐ **Automatic time clocks:** Turn lighting and equipment on and off according to a preestablished schedule.
- ☐ **Automatic lighting controls:** Provide programmed control of lights by cycling or dimming particular areas.
- ☐ **Load cyclers/programmable controllers:** Provide programmed control of motors and other equipment according to schedule.
- ☐ **Peak demand controllers:** Limit the total energy consumed at any one time by turning off equipment.
- ☐ **Heat recovery systems:** Reuse waste heat from the kitchen, laundry, and mechanical areas.
- ☐ **Turndown of guestroom HVAC systems at checkout:** Allows front desk staff to turn down guestroom heat and air conditioning.

While others, such as central building automation, cogeneration, solar, or guestroom motion sensors (to control HVAC) have found much less favor to date, they will become more practical and cost efficient in the future. Overall, energy control technologies vary from the extremely simple to the complex. Plastic or metal disc water flow restrictors, which reduce the diameter of the opening in a faucet, cost only pennies and can be installed in minutes. At the other end of the scale are central building systems that combine the sophisticated controllers from the above list with numerous options and that include the ability to integrate security, fire alarm, telephone, and data processing components. They include computers that continuously monitor building functions, turning on equipment only when it is needed.

Energy management technology is rapidly increasing to meet the rising expectations of the industry. Unfortunately, hotel operators often don't comprehend the value of energy conservation techniques as easily as they see the virtues of accounting or security systems. One general manager expressed this disconcerting opinion: "My engineer and I have never heard of some of the types of energy control technology listed on the questionnaire. I'm busy greeting guests and paying the electric company. My engineer can't keep up with the lightbulb changes and clogged sinks. How the hell can we tell what technology we should have?"*

LIFE SAFETY SYSTEMS

Because of increased public concern over fire disasters, such as that at the MGM Grand Hotel in Las Vegas, Nevada, protection systems in hotels have been substantially upgraded since the late 1970s. Testing and research on the causes of hotel fires have improved design methods and standards and new technology has advanced the quality of detection, alarm, and fire extinguishing systems. Hotels lacking state-of-the-art fire protection systems are no longer safe.

One issue that affects the provision of life safety systems is the mandate of building codes. The electrical fire at the Westin Hotel in Boston early in 1984 caused the city to modify its standards for the protection of emergency generators. Other hotels then under construction upgraded their plans even though they had complied with previous codes. A serious fire at a Fort Worth, Texas, hotel in 1984 was the impetus for requiring sprinklers even in lowrise guestroom wings. An earlier fire at the Hyatt Regency O'Hare near Chicago in the mid-1970s resulted in code changes that required increased exhaust systems to draw smoke away from atrium guestroom corridors.

As a result of these and several other fires, the National Fire Protection Association

*AH&MA 1983 Survey, p. 63.

(NFPA) and the AH&MA have urged developers to incorporate new technology even where codes don't require it. The ultimate goal, of course, is to install fail-safe protection in all hotels worldwide. Life safety technology includes the following:

- ☐ Manual fire alarm system
- ☐ Heat and smoke detectors
- ☐ Automatic sprinklers, standpipe system, and portable extinguishers
- ☐ Central annunciator panels
- ☐ Guest evacuation sound systems
- ☐ Firefighters' voice communication system
- ☐ Fire and smoke dampers
- ☐ Smokeproof and pressurized exit stairs
- ☐ Exit signage and emergency lighting
- ☐ Emergency electrical generator

Also, building codes specify numerous construction details to further protect the building occupants as well as the property. The United States has several building codes in addition to the NFPA life safety code on which most individual city or state codes are based. England, France, Germany, and other nations also have precise building regulations. Although similar, the detailed requirements vary somewhat from code to code—the number of sprinklers required in a hotel guestroom, for example, varies from one to four depending on the code in force—so that hotel standards must be designed to meet the most stringent requirements of all codes. (Building codes are discussed in more detail in the previous chapter.)

Because of the high priority given to fire safety by the hotel industry, large national and international hotel companies have established their own fire safety standards that exceed most local codes, thereby reducing the problem of satisfying varying regulations in different localities. Up-to-date, consistent company standards that go beyond codes are also becoming the key to "legal safety" as well. Today, owners who fail to apply the latest safety or security measures throughout a hotel or chain may risk liability. For example, after a hotel in Washington, D.C., installed electronic locks in its new addition, it was held liable for a theft in the older building because its locks were less secure. Attempts have been made to apply this legal principal also to life safety issues; therefore, operators and designers must carefully consider safety standards and consistently implement them in all hotels under the same ownership or management.

It is essential in all projects—expansion and renovation as well as new construction—that the architect, engineers, and interior designers, in collaboration with life safety consultants, if necessary, carefully consider the latest fire protection design methods and systems and consistently apply them early in the planning phases to assure the development of a fire-safe hotel.

Smoke or heat detectors are now required by most codes in hotel guestrooms as well as public areas. The AH&MA study found a 4-fold increase in guestroom smoke detectors in the three years before the 1983 survey. The detectors are usually located above the guestroom bed and at regular intervals along the guest corridors. Heat detectors are usually provided in such service areas as kitchens, laundries, and mechanical areas but are set to recognize the usual high temperature. While also sounding a local alarm, an integrated system ties these detectors to the telephone switchboard room and to a control panel near the front desk, which is easily accessible to firefighters. It also automatically notifies the local fire department.

Because of the excellent record of life safety protection in hotels with sprinklers, it is surprising that any hotels resist installing complete sprinkler and smoke detection systems. Even the strict Las Vegas, Nevada, code requires only that all guestrooms above the sixth floor be equipped with sprinklers. One New York City hotel installed sprinklers just six months after it opened, even though they were not required, at 3 times what they would have cost if originally included, because the owner recognized the increased safety and reduced insurance costs for both fire and liability.

With the increased use of heat and smoke detectors, hotel company standards require that these be hard-wired, rather than battery operated, to a central annunciator panel where the alarm is identified by its zone location in the building. This panel must be close to an entrance where firefighters can readily reach it as well as in the telephone switchboard room—the main point from which directions can be quickly communicated to hotel guests. The AH&MA found that the number of hotels with central annunciator panels had doubled in the 1980–1983 period, a trend that clearly should continue.

A major issue in hotel fires is the approach taken to notify guests of the emergency. Some hotels have attempted to put out a local fire without evacuating the building. Often, in emergencies, guests have been uninformed about whether they should try to leave their room or remain there until the emergency is over. Various approaches to establishing sound systems connected to hotel guestrooms have been implemented, including speakers in the corridors loud enough to be heard in the guestrooms. Some regulations insist that a guest evacuation sound system be carried over the telephone system, master television antenna (MATV), or independent low-voltage systems.

Often as part of the same network with the central annunciator and guest evacuation sound system, hotels provide firefighters with voice communications to areas within the building. These usually include jacks in the elevators and in each stairway at the floor landing. By connecting their handsets to the system, the firefighters can report to the fire control room and receive instructions.

Recognition that much of the danger from fires comes from smoke rather than the fire itself has created an increased awareness of the importance of controlling the spread of smoke. This goal is accomplished horizontally by closers on guestroom and other doors and by installation of fire doors at elevator lobbies that are held open magnetically and, when detectors sense a fire, close automatically. The problem is more severe vertically because of elevators, stairs, mechanical ducts and shafts, and numerous small penetrations through the floor slabs. All vertical openings must be protected with fire-rated automatic dampers to isolate smoke and fire between adjoining floors. These dampers, adding substantially to the capital costs of a project, can be designed to also help control energy use.

Vertical stairtowers present a similar smoke problem. Two common solutions are to pressurize the stairs so that when any door is opened the higher air pressure keeps the stair clear of toxic smoke or to provide for smoke evacuation in stair vestibules. Elevator shafts require similar specialized systems. In Germany codes require pressurization of elevator shafts, while in France all elevator openings are further protected by automatic fire shutters.

SECURITY SYSTEMS

While improved life safety systems protect the public against fire or such other emergencies as earthquakes, new security systems protect guests, employees, and the physical property from crime. The systems and the procedures set up by management may be developed, at least in part, to meet the requirements established by the hotel's legal and insurance advisors and to help ward off lawsuits.

To protect against theft, physical assault, vandalism, arson, and terrorism, the hotel security system has three principal components: locking systems, television surveillance cameras, and various types of alarms. These are outlined on the accom-

Hotel keying schedule

MASTER KEY	SUBMASTER KEY	PRIVACY KEY
Administration	Executive offices Sales and catering offices Accounting offices Personnel	Cashier's office (safe) Accounting files Safety deposit area
Rooms division	Front office Entrances Guestrooms (by floor)	Retail shops
Food and beverage	Kitchens Food outlets Beverage outlets Food and beverage storage Food and beverage offices, purchasing Receiving area	Wine and liquor storage Refrigerators and freezers China and silver storage Entertainers' dressing rooms
Function areas	Function rooms Function storage	Audiovisual equipment storage
Housekeeping	Guestrooms (by floor or other maid unit) Linen/housekeeping Lockers and employee dining	Lost and found
Laundry	Laundry Linen storage	
Engineering	Engineering offices Engineering shops Mechanical areas Electrical areas	Electrical transformer room
Recreation	Health club and pool Remote facilities (tennis club, golf club, pool)	

The master key schedule should be based on the need to separate functional areas so that employees have access only to discrete zones of the hotel. For example, the engineering department has a master key that provides access to all engineering areas, submaster keys for offices, shops, mechanical and electrical areas except the transformer room, individual keys for each space, and a privacy key for the transformer room. In small hotels several master keys from the following list may be combined (administration and rooms, food and beverage and function areas, housekeeping and laundry, for example).

Security checklist

SURVEILLANCE CAMERA LOCATIONS

Grounds
- ☐ Exterior grounds, as required
- ☐ Remote recreation areas (pool, golf club)

Entrances
- ☐ Main entrance
- ☐ Ballroom entrance
- ☐ Loading dock
- ☐ Employee entrance

Interior locations
- ☐ Front desk (cashier)
- ☐ Escalators (for safety)
- ☐ Food storage areas
- ☐ Wine and liquor storage
- ☐ China and silver storage
- ☐ Service elevators

Casino areas
- ☐ Entrances to gaming areas
- ☐ "Eye in the sky"
- ☐ Cashier's cage
- ☐ Counting rooms
- ☐ "Money path" to armored cars

ALARM LOCATIONS

Manual alarm
- ☐ Front desk (each station)
- ☐ Cashier's office
- ☐ Safe room
- ☐ Security office
- ☐ Casino cashier areas

Door alarm
- ☐ All entrances (except main entrance)
- ☐ Food storage areas
- ☐ Wine and liquor storage
- ☐ China and silver storage
- ☐ Casino cashier areas

Most hotel security systems include both closed circuit camera systems and alarms. Surveillance cameras are most useful for monitoring public areas, entry-exit points such as the receiving area, and storage and other employee areas. Alarm systems are generally supplied for locations where cash and valuables are handled and storage areas that have limited activity.

panying keying schedule and hotel security checklists.

The keying system is the largest element in hotel security and has undergone the most change over the past few years. Traditional mortise locksets have been improved with the addition of separate deadbolt latches, while mechanical card-access systems have been used to upgrade existing hotels and electronic card systems have been installed in many first class hotels and resorts. These report a marked drop in thefts as well as high approval ratings by guests.

The major concern, in addition to the guest's safety, is the cost of rekeying a hotel with a traditional system. Urban hotels report the loss of an average of one key per guestroom per week. The result is that most locks are not rekeyed, which presents a serious security problem. Card-access systems provide for the quick reassignment of codes to a particular room or floor and assure much better security. Nonelectronic card systems that must be rekeyed at each door are primarily suitable for renovation projects; electronic card systems, on the other hand, which are controlled at the front desk, can be recoded at will and can generate reports of unauthorized attempts to enter a particular room.

Most hotel key systems include the following levels that must be accommodated by whatever system is selected:

- ☐ **Grand master key:** Opens all doors.
- ☐ **Master key:** Opens all doors within a major functional area such as resort recreational facilities or convention hotel function spaces.
- ☐ **Submaster key:** Opens all doors within a specific area such as kitchens or accounting offices; in guestrooms might be called a "floor master."
- ☐ **Maid key:** Opens designated guestrooms and housekeeping service areas.
- ☐ **Guest key:** Opens only a single guestroom door.
- ☐ **Emergency key:** Overrides deadbolt lock on guestrooms and opens all hotel doors except the following.
- ☐ **Privacy key:** Opens specific doors requiring additional security such as wine and liquor storage, silver storage, freezers and refrigerators, accounting records storage, and safe rooms.
- ☐ **Special keys:** Opens other doors such as on linen and trash chutes, desks, and file cabinets.

A second major part of the hotel's security systems is closed circuit television (CCTV). The television surveillance system is controlled and monitored in larger hotels at a security office and in smaller properties at the receiving office or other control point. Cameras can be used to scan outdoor areas and specific indoor locations where theft or unauthorized access is a problem. They may be programmed to run only when an alarm is sounded or when a particular door is opened. In other cases, especially in casinos, the CCTV systems monitor areas continuously. The hotel areas most often protected by closed circuit television include the several hotel entrances, storage rooms, and areas where large amounts of cash are handled. These are listed in the security checklist.

The third element in a security plan, in addition to employee training, is the installation of intrusion alarms at critical points. These incorporate various types of electrical circuits, light beams, and motion detectors, including such modern technology as photoelectric beams, seismic detectors, infrared beams, microwaves, and radio-frequency fields. Obviously, these depend on standby or emergency power systems to protect the hotel completely. Intrusion detectors can be used for all areas of the hotel: grounds, doors and windows, unoccupied rooms including guestrooms and storage areas, and selected locations such as the safe and safety deposit boxes. Connecting these alarms to a security console permits the operator to notify authorities of the exact location of the alarm before he or she takes action.

All these security systems increase the safety of the guests and employees and help reduce the hotel operator's insurance premiums. As with other specialized systems, the security components are generally available as part of an overall, integrated package including life safety and energy management.

AUDIO AND VIDEO SYSTEMS

The last area of new technology that applies to hotels and resorts is audiovisual systems. These include a variety of guestroom and meeting room entertainment and business options that are becoming more and more common as the costs become lower and the systems more reliable. Typical audiovisual systems (excluding video conferencing, discussed as part of telecommunications) include the following:

- ☐ Employee paging
- ☐ Meeting room sound reinforcement
- ☐ Closed circuit television
- ☐ Large screen television entertainment
- ☐ Guestroom terminals
- ☐ Master antenna systems including entertainment, information, and integrated life safety, security, and energy management

For the most part, these systems have been available for many years and, although they have been refined as low-voltage networks have been established throughout new hotels, they exhibit limited technological innovation. One area, though—the use of guestroom computer terminals for entertainment, business, and information purposes—is seeing exploding growth. Videotel, a supplier of in-room electronic services, recently surveyed hotel guests in Boston and found that more than 20 percent were willing to pay additional charges for special services. These included cable TV, video games, on-line airline schedules, local information (about restaurants, films, shopping, and so on), wire service news, and daily stock prices and other financial news. Very few guests cited any interest in word processing or access to outside computer services. The company indicated that it was developing automated room service ordering and in-room check-out that would also be connected through the master antenna system.

The industry surveys, such as the technology overview conducted by the AH&MA, show growth and innovation in other areas, although it is moderated by high capital investment and limited programming. Some experts expect, for example, that the standard television will be replaced by flat, large screen wall units that can project multiple-screen images. As more components are added to the basic low-voltage network the cost of each system will be significantly reduced to the point where it becomes both cost effective and competitively essential.

Part 3
SPECIAL CONCERNS

Successful hotel development requires familiarity with more than the vital planning techniques and design criteria outlined in Parts 1 and 2. Equally essential is an understanding of the many financial, operational, and organizational procedures and processes that must be taken into consideration when designing a hotel so that it prospers as a business enterprise.

The chapters in Part 3 trace the hotel development scenario beginning with the feasibility study. The hotel's operations and management are analyzed and practical technical design and construction applications are examined—for example, how life safety or energy management techniques should be integrated into its design. The responsibilities of various design professionals, from the engineer who surveys the site to the landscaper who eventually plants it, are also discussed in detail.

Finally, dynamic projections for the future of hotels, including the effects of global socioeconomic trends as well as space explorations, conclude the book.

22

FEASIBILITY STUDIES

"No lending officer of a bank or insurance company will loan money without a feasibility study. They are his hedge insurance in case the facility fails."

Donald Lundberg

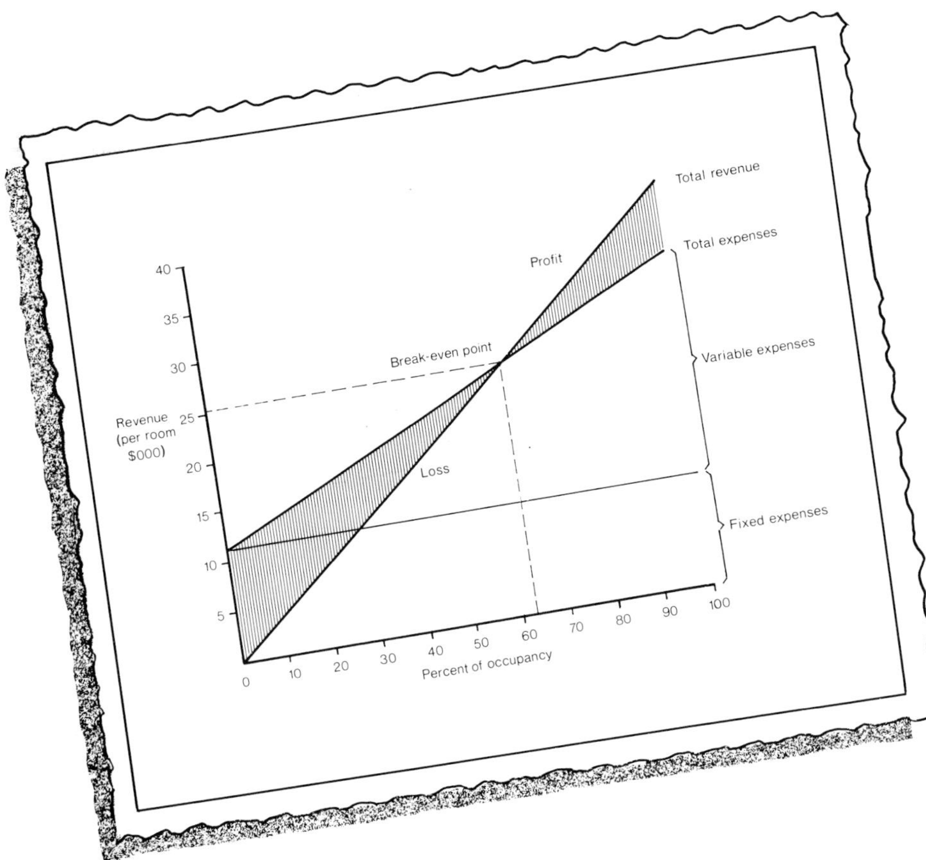

Among the first steps that the developer of a new hotel must take is the preparation of a feasibility study. The study, usually assembled by a consulting firm and further refined by the hotel's senior operations staff if it is to be operated by a management company, has two key aspects. First, it assesses present and future demand for lodging and such other hotel services as meeting areas, restaurants and bars, and recreational facilities. Second, it estimates operating income and expenses for several years after the opening.

There is no single formula for success. Projects with optimistic feasibility studies may do poorly, while occasionally those built despite a negative report do surprisingly well. However, the more successful projects do combine several ingredients: good location, continuing strong demand, the proper mix of facilities, and professional management. To some extent, the prototypical feasibility studies common to the hotel industry critically assess all these factors.

Feasibility studies often have differing objectives. Most are used to increase the confidence of others in a project's success and to obtain permanent financing. Thus, it is often a basic component of the developer's package to prospective lenders. Other feasibility studies may be used to obtain a franchise or management contract or to attract equity participation. Similar reports but with different emphases may be used in negotiations with city boards to support a developer's request for a zoning variance or to reinforce his or her contention that the project will increase sales and real estate taxes and add new jobs. Occasionally in recent years, feasibility studies have been commissioned by a municipality or a public agency in an attempt to attract new private development.

Only infrequently do these studies actually assess the feasibility of a project. This is because any calculation of relative success depends on much more than the objective analysis of the lodging market. Not only does it depend on accurate projections of future conditions, but it must also take into account such confidential factors as the developer's investment strategies and tax status.

Assuming the study doesn't go beyond projecting cash flow available after fixed charges (such as real estate taxes, property insurance, and management fee), the typical outline includes:

Local area evaluation

- ☐ Analyze the economic vitality of the city or region.
- ☐ Describe the suitability of the project site for a hotel.

Lodging market analysis

☐ Assess the present demand for lodging (and other revenue generators) and future growth rates for each of several market segments.

☐ Identify the existing supply of competitive properties and their probable growth.

Proposed facilities

☐ Propose a balance of guestroom and public facilities including restaurants, bars, meeting and banquet rooms, retail shops, recreation facilities, and parking.

☐ Assess the competetive position of the subject property.

Financial analysis

☐ Estimate income and expenses for the hotel over a five-year period to show its potential cash flow.

However, these sections are not treated in equal detail in the typical study. The parts that have the most direct relationship to the architectural solution—the site analysis and the facilities list—are perhaps the least highly refined. The supply-and-demand analyses and the financial projections, on the other hand, are usually the most specific, understandably since the study is prepared by market and economic consultants. The following discussion and the accompanying tables adapted from an actual report will highlight the principal aspects of a feasibility study.

ANALYZING THE LOCAL AREA

As a prelude to the market analysis, most feasibility studies present data illustrating the economic climate in the area—from the entire city or region to the particulars of the specific project site. Many critics consider them no more than boiler plate, yet they are helpful in providing necessary background to lenders from outside the local community and in establishing a relative sense of the lodging markets. In broad terms the local analysis includes:

☐ Growth trends in population, employment, income, tax receipts, new construction, and so on.

☐ Major public and private facilities including those for education, health, government, transportation, religion, tourism, and so forth.

☐ Travel analysis, including volume and percentage of traffic by car, air, train, bus, and ship as appropriate.

The emphases of the study should reflect the probable type of hotel project. For example, a resort hotel would be only marginally concerned with industrial and commercial influences, perhaps only as secondary markets for off-season periods. Instead, it should focus on natural attractions and other recreational opportunities in the area and on airline and highway networks from the principal market areas. For the same reason, area analyses for hotels sited near a university or a major medical complex should deal with trends in these institutions rather than with those of the larger industrial and commercial sector.

The area evaluation should also include a detailed site analysis. In addition to the obvious site description—size, boundaries, topography, and so forth—the analysis should emphasize visibility, accessibility, and suitability to hotel use. The first two are most critical for motel and motor inn properties that attract predominantly highway business, much of it without reservations. The suitability discussion may emphasize such site advantages or potential constraints as views, natural features, proximity to local attractions or businesses, adjacent uses, room for expansion, zoning, or utility availability.

ANALYZING THE LODGING MARKET

The largest part of the feasibility study is the analysis of the demand for guestrooms and other hotel services and the enumeration of existing competitive hotel rooms. The study must acknowledge future shifts in demand, as individual market segments expand or contract and as neighborhoods undergo change. Making assumptions about these future changes, as well as about growth rates, improves the sophistication of the analysis but adds considerably to the risk. Therefore, the developer must be prepared to analyze and review the consultant's assumptions.

The demand for lodging can be calculated in two complementary ways. In one approach, estimates of the need for guestrooms are assembled from interviews and meetings with local businesspeople representing the various generators of lodging demand: industries, government and commercial offices, university and medical centers, amusement parks, and so forth. For the most part, the demand is separated into three major market segements: convention and other group business, commercial business, and tourists. Occasionally, the report identifies airport traffic or other specific markets as well. It analyzes each of these thoroughly in terms of its weekday/weekend characteristics, seasonality, price sensitivity, amount of double occupancy, and, most important, its anticipated growth over the succeeding several years. It assesses group meeting business, restaurant demand, and other hotel services at the same time.

The second and quicker way to estimate total demand is to know the current year's occupancy rates at the competitive hotels. A simple calculation for each hotel (number of rooms times average occupancy percentage times 365 days) results in a figure that represents the total areawide annual demand for guestrooms. Unfortunately, the use of the average occupancy rates fails to take into account daily or seasonal fluctuations in demand and, importantly, fails to identify the "fill days" when the local hotels are at 100 percent occupancy and must turn away potential guests.

Estimates of future demand for each segment are obtained by extrapolating the current demand figures on the basis of various growth assumptions. These inflation factors—so critical to the conclusions of the market study are based on identifiable trends, economic projections, and the consultants' judgment and experience. A market segment analysis, including the application of the growth factors, appears on top of page 226.

The supply calculation is much simpler. Usually, the competitive hotels of a quality level similar to the proposed property are simply listed with their physical characteristics (number of guestrooms, size of restaurants, bars, meeting and banquet areas, recreation facilities, and parking) and fundamental operating statistics (occupancy percentage, "rack" or listed rates, average rate—resulting from discounting—and double occupancy) as demonstrated in the accompanying figure. In smaller communities, where there are few or no competitors in the subject property's class, less competitive properties may be added to the analysis. The supply analysis includes adjustments for future years to reflect the construction of new hotels, the expansion of existing properties, the renovation to competitive status of lower-quality hotels, as well as anticipated deletions from the market.

DEFINING THE PROPOSED FACILITIES

Feasibility consultants include in the body of the report a general description of the proposed facilities. As illustrated here, this description includes the following elements, outlined in only the broadest terms:

☐ Number and mix of guestrooms.

☐ Restaurants and bars with their capacities.

☐ Meeting and banquet facilities with their capacities or floor area.

Breakeven Analysis. *Feasibility consultants project future revenue and expenses in order to forecast a hotel's economic vitality. The breakeven analysis compares the total of fixed and variable expenses at different occupancy levels with anticipated revenues to determine the exact point of profitability for a 600-room hotel.*

Projected guestroom demand by market segment

MARKET DEMAND SEGMENT	GROWTH FACTOR	CURRENT DEMAND	YEAR 1985	1986	1987	1988	1989
Commercial	3	92,000	94,750	97,600	100,500	103,500	106,400
Convention/group	5	35,000	36,750	38,500	40,500	42,500	44,600
Tourist/vacation	3	59,000	60,700	62,600	64,500	66,400	68,400
Local	3	20,000	20,600	21,200	21,800	22,500	23,200
Estimated total demand		**206,000**	**212,800**	**219,900**	**227,300**	**234,900**	**242,600**
Competitive supply		250,000	250,000	359,500*	359,500	359,500	359,000
Estimated occupancy (area-wide, annual)		82.4	84.8	61.2	63.1	65.3	67.4

Existing guestroom demand by hotel

PROPERTY	ROOMS	OCCUPANCY (%)	COMMERCIAL DEMAND	CONFERENCE/ GROUP DEMAND	TOURIST/ VACATION DEMAND	LOCAL DEMAND	TOTAL DEMAND
Hotel A	200	85	34,500	9,500	12,000	6,050	62,050
Hotel B	200	82	29,300	8,200	14,160	8,200	59,860
Hotel C	165	74	22,000	4,500	13,500	4,560	44,560
Hotel D	135	80	6,200	12,800	19,340	1,190	39,530
Total	**700**	**80.6**	**92,000**	**35,000**	**59,000**	**20,000**	**206,000**

- ☐ Recreational facilities.
- ☐ Parking.
- ☐ Additional amenities, including retail shops, car rental, theaters, and special services.

The facilities description, substantially based on the supply and demand analysis, is the one section of the report that most directly influences the predesign and planning phases of the hotel development project. It establishes the number of guestrooms and a list of the major public facilities that provides the necessary order-of-magnitude framework for the preliminary space program. Although the report describes the public areas briefly, it neglects entirely the back-of-house service areas and administrative offices.

Some developers feel the typical definition of the public areas isn't detailed enough. They request that the consultants identify specific operational and design features that will help assure the hotel's success and discuss how these influence the positioning of the hotel. Many studies, though, do little more than suggest that the property "will be developed as a first class hotel and be expertly managed and promoted."

The competitive standing of the hotel can be projected once its size, facilities, rate, and level of quality are determined. This part of the analysis focuses on guestroom occupancy percentage and average room rate. The "fair-share" concept, which assumes that a new hotel will attract at least its proportionate share of the aggregate market demand, is at the center of the competitive evaluation. On occasion, the consultants may propose that a particular hotel will capture more than its fair share of a specific market segment because of its location, facilities, chain affiliation, or, perhaps, nothing more than its newness. The following table, which refers to the earlier example, shows how the competitive standing is arrived at.

Facilities list

Guestrooms	**Units**	**Bays**
Double-double	180	180
King	98	98
Sico room (sleeping–meeting room)	10	10
Parlor (one-bay)	10	10
Suite (two-bay; connects to typical rooms)	2	4
Manager's apartment	0	4
Total	**300**	**306**
Food and beverage outlets	**Seats**	
Multipurpose restaurant	140	
Specialty restaurant	100	
Cocktail lounge	110	
Lobby bar	40	
Total	**390**	
Function rooms	**Seats**	
Ballroom	700	
Meeting rooms, total	400	
Boardroom	30	
Total	**1130**	
Other public facilities		
Indoor swimming pool		
Health club, sauna, exercise room		
Retail shops	2,000 sq ft (185 sq m)	
Parking	450 cars	

Market penetration

PROPERTY	ROOMS	OCCUPANCY (%)	COMMERCIAL DEMAND	CONVENTION/ GROUP DEMAND	TOURIST/ VACATION DEMAND	LOCAL DEMAND	TOTAL DEMAND
Estimated total demand			92,000	35,000	59,000	20,000	206,000
Proposed hotel (fair share)			27,600	10,500	17,700	6,000	61,800
Market share			.8	1.2	1.0	.8	—
Proposed hotel	300	52	22,080	12,600	17,700	4,800	57,180
Hotel A	200	62	26,210	6,080	8,400	4,600	45,290
Hotel B	200	60	22,270	5,250	9,910	6,230	43,660
Hotel C	165	54	16,720	2,880	9,450	3,460	32,510
Hotel D	135	56	4,720	8,190	13,540	910	27,360

This refinement of the aggregate demand figures will allow one to begin to assign occupied guestrooms to area hotels in proportion to their current standing as modified by the introduction of the new property in the marketplace. Commonly, occupancy during the first two or three years is several percentage points below a stabilized or target operating year because the hotel needs this time to develop its full sales potential. The third year is frequently used as the standard to represent the probable operating results in a stable year.

In addition to guestroom occupancy, the feasibility report projects estimated average room rates for the new hotel based on existing rates at similar quality hotels inflated to "future dollars." The average rate is expanded to represent room sales for each year, and this figure, based on numerous assumptions and estimates, provides the basis for many of the financial projections, which often fill one-fourth of a typical feasibility report.

It is common for the hotel management company, the future chain operator, to review the feasibility recommendations critically and to modify them to reflect their own operating strategies as well as perceptions about the local market. Though depending on the feasibility report for background material and for the objective judgment of experienced hospitality consultants, experienced and sophisticated developers may alter significant portions of the facilities outline or the occupancy and rate assumptions to better support their own image of the project.

PREPARING THE FINANCIAL ANALYSIS

The typical feasibility report has two clearly different sections. The main body of the study analyzes the local area, identifies supply-and-demand characteristics, and proposes a project of a specific size. The second part, the financial projections, contains 10 or more pages of financial tables estimating the income and expenses of the subject property for several years—usually five or more—following its opening. These are simplified below and illustrated with a full example of projected cash flow.

The financial analysis is based on averages of hotel operations established by two major consulting/auditing firms—Pannell Kerr Forster and Laventhol & Horwath—both of which publish annual statistics comparing hotels by size, region, type, age, and, for smaller properties, those with and without restaurants. The developer of a new property should be familiar with the basic organization of and approximate values reflected in these financial reports.

In selecting the feasibility consultant, the developer should seek a firm with experience and high industry credibility. The consultant must be neutral and objective if he or she is to prepare an independent report that will be accepted by lenders. In addition, the developer must insist on complete documentation of sources and explanations of assumptions. People and companies interviewed for the study may purposely exaggerate or simply be too optimistic; similarly, such assumptions as growth rates, inflation, and market penetration, if even slightly in error, can substantially alter the reliability of the study.

A well-prepared study can establish the basis, in terms of both financial and facilities goals, for a profitable and sharply conceived hotel. The narrower the focus, the more precise will be the market analysis, the selection of truly competitive hotels, the definition of rate and occupancy, and the outlining of a facilities list. The developer must be able to critique the drafts of the study and insist on a clear and logical presentation of the competitive environment.

Projected cash flow

REVENUE	
Rooms	$5,000,000
Food and beverage	2,500,000
Beverage	2,000,000
Telephone	250,000
Other	100,000
Total	**$9,850,000**
DEPARTMENTAL EXPENSES	
Rooms	$1,300,000
Food and beverage	3,500,000
Telephone	300,000
Other	20,000
Total	**$5,120,000**
GROSS OPERATING INCOME	**$4,730,000**
UNDISTRIBUTED OPERATING EXPENSES	
Administrative/general	$ 550,000
Marketing	250,000
Energy	400,000
Property operation/ maintenance	230,000
Total	**$1,430,000**
GROSS OPERATING PROFIT	**$3,300,000**
FIXED CHARGES	
Real estate taxes	$ 400,000
Property insurance	50,000
Reserve for replacement	300,000
Management fee	750,000
Total	**$1,500,000**
CASH FLOW AVAILABLE FOR DEBT SERVICE AND TAXES ON INCOME	**$1,800,000**

23 Hotel Operations

"If the bed was hard, and if the eggs were cold in the morning, how nice the building was makes very little difference."

Houston architect

Hotel design affects two major groups: the guests of the hotel and the people who operate it. The best designs not only anticipate the guests' needs and expectations, but also consider the functional requirements of the management and staff. Therefore, it is important that those involved in developing and designing hotels understand hotel operations and management.

A standard hotel organization plan does not exist. The size of the staff and their specific duties are determined by such factors as the type, size, and location of the hotel, its chain affiliation, the abilities of the management team, and the type of ownership. In small hotels, many functions may be combined and performed by one person. In larger hotels, the staff will be larger and more specialized in order to service the guests properly.

Because hotels vary not only in size but in type of clientele and in activities offered, priorities differ from one hotel to the next. Security, for example, may be a separate department in a downtown property, but be part of the engineering department in a suburban hotel. Similarly, in a convention hotel where the meeting and banquet facilities produce a substantial share of the total income, the banquet manager may be removed from the control of the food and beverage manager and established in an executive position. The management in each hotel must determine the necessary departments and decide upon the required number of employees.

The organization chart on top page 229 illustrates the chain of command in a medium-size hotel and identifies the major department heads who report directly to the resident and executive assistant managers. The organization chart should be altered to suit a particular hotel's operating policies. For example, in many larger hotels, such department head positions as director of security, executive chef, and front office manager may be added.

The accompanying figure illustrates the sources of hotel income and the categories of expenses that control management's ability to operate profitably. For several decades, revenue from guestrooms as a percentage of total income has been approximately 60 percent in American hotels, while little more than 50 percent in international properties where food, beverage, and minor operating departments contribute a larger share. However, despite the great difference internationally in hotel operations, especially in staffing and salary levels, payroll and other operating expenses are similar in North America and overseas.

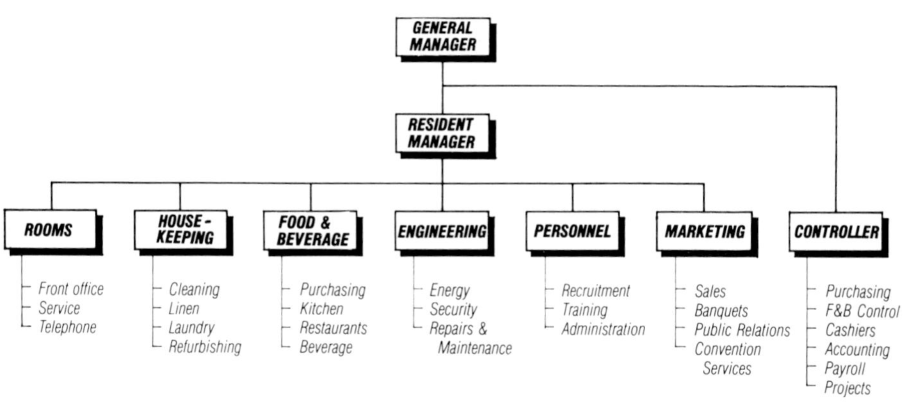

INCOME

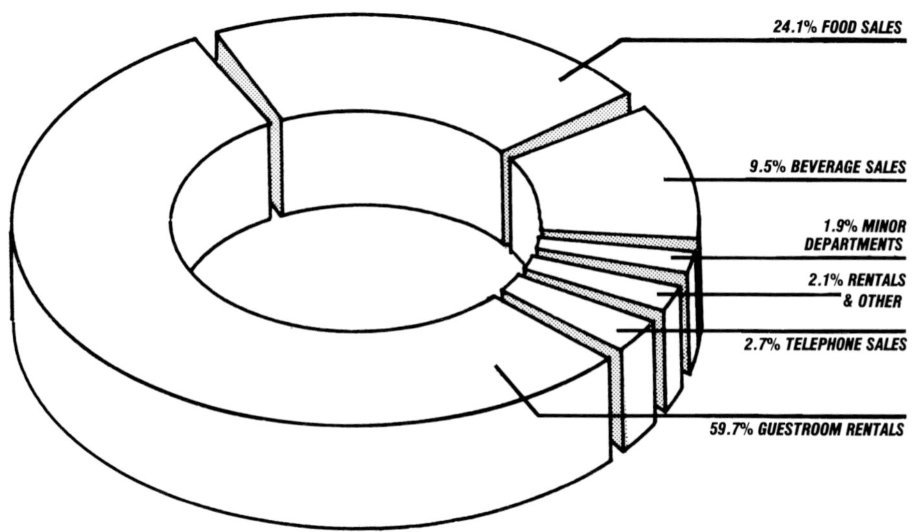

EXPENSE

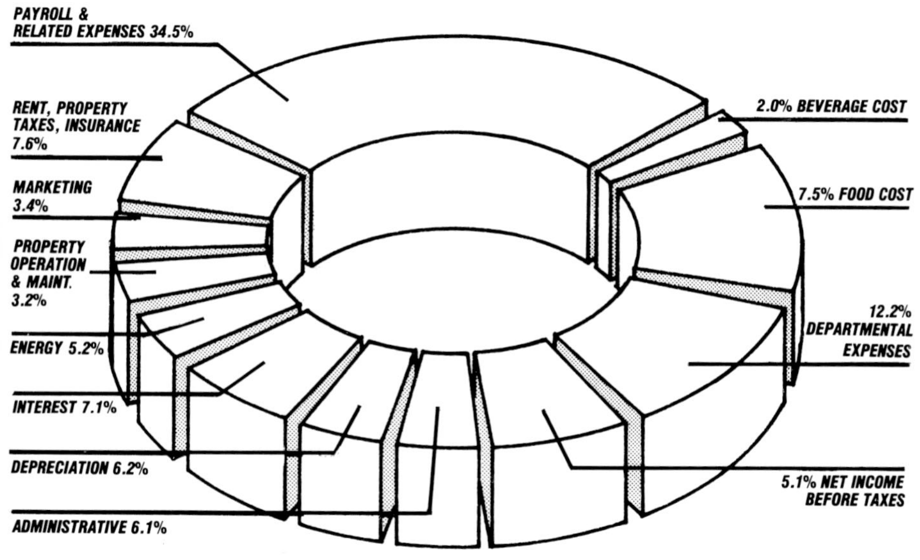

SOURCE: Laventhol and Horwath, **U.S. Lodging Industry**, 1983.

ROOMS DEPARTMENT

A hotel is often characterized by the number and quality of its guestrooms and suites. The rooms department, responsible for the comfortable lodging of guests during their stay at the hotel, performs the following functions:

Front office
- ☐ Reservations
- ☐ Registration
- ☐ Mail, messages
- ☐ Information
- ☐ Cashier
- ☐ Concierge

Service
- ☐ Doorman
- ☐ Bellman

Telephone

Clearly, the most critical policy decision within the rooms department is establishing the room rates and guidelines for discounting to the corporate, convention, and tour group markets and for weekends and off-season periods. The full price overnight charge, or "rack rate," initially positions the hotel among a group of competitive properties. Setting the rate too high may discourage business and even permit rival hotels to inch their rates up profitably without losing occupancy. Setting it too low, on the other hand, may contribute to increasing occupancy percentages but make it difficult to meet fixed costs. Operations

ABOVE

Hotel Organization Chart. *The chart represents the organization of a medium-size hotel (300 ± rooms) with a resident manager supervising most of the day-to-day operations. Larger hotels would need more department heads, for example, in the front office, elevating the front office manager and reservations manager to the Executive Committee. Most of the department heads submit reports to their corporate counterpart in addition to the hotel's management. That is, the chief engineer or building superintendent would forward energy-use data to the corporate director of energy for analysis.*

LEFT

The American Lodging Dollar: Income and Expense. *The division of hotel revenue and expenses is shown in typical categories. Hotel consulting firms annually publish statistics on the national and international lodging industry that are useful for comparing any existing or proposed project to industry averages. Generally, the data are broken down into such categories as size and type of hotel, regional location, age of buildings, and occupancy percentage. International hotels differ from those in North America in that food and beverage and minor departments generate nearly half of their income; operating expenses, on the other hand, nearly parallel each other (adapted from Laventhol and Horwath,* U.S. Lodging Industry, *1983).*

PRECEDING PAGE

Sheraton Washington, Washington, D.C. *The hotel guest's first impressions—of the building and of the quality of service—are created at the hotel entrance and at the front desk. Illustrated here is the reconstructed registration area at the Sheraton Washington.*

continually struggle to find the proper balance between rate and occupancy that results in the greatest profit.

Like the airlines, the hotel's product is highly perishable. The revenue from an unoccupied guestroom can never be recovered. Therefore, the rooms department attempts to accurately forecast demand for each night months in advance, fine tuning the rate for short periods and even overbooking where no-shows are projected. Thus, while taking reservations, checkin and checkout of guests, and other visible functions are routine, behind the scenes management continually adjusts the price and availability of the rooms in a highly competitive market.

To serve guests better and to assure return business, hotel management regularly implements new procedures and services. These include express checkin and checkout (the guest indicates he or she is leaving by depositing a card at the front desk, is billed later, and avoids the wait in line at the cashier), club floor services (registration and checkout at an upper floor concierge desk), and electronic systems that handle wake-up, messages, and mail. These are usually established as corporate operating policies or are proposed by the front office or rooms department manager and adopted by the hotel's management.

HOUSEKEEPING

The hotel housekeeping function, while important to the guest's perception of quality and service, tends to be fairly routine. The department includes an executive housekeeper, assistant housekeepers or "inspectors," and a cadre of maids and housemen, responsible for cleaning all areas in the hotel. The principal housekeeping activities include:

Cleaning
- ☐ Guest rooms
- ☐ Public areas
- ☐ Back-of-house areas

Linen supply
- ☐ Linen storeroom
- ☐ Uniform issue

Decorative refurbishing
- ☐ Drapes, upholstery, carpeting
- ☐ Scheduled painting

Some operating companies still recommend that guest room floors be planned on a multiple of 14 rooms (that is, 28 or 42 rooms per floor), the standard day's work for one maid. This policy may be beneficial to scheduling the housekeeping staff and assigning rooms; however, in general, the many other architectural and functional considerations do not permit such planning.

There is some flexibility in the operating details of guest room housekeeping. For example, there are alternate procedures for stocking linen carts or guestroom floor storerooms each afternoon or in the morning shift, depending upon such planning aspects as number of service elevators, size of guest floor linen rooms, and use of linen and trash chutes.

The management and coordination of small-scale repair and refurbishing is often directed by the executive housekeeper; larger renovation and major redecoration projects may be handled by the housekeeping or by any of a number of other staff: the engineer, an assistant manager, or a director of rehabilitation (a new position in larger hotels). Nevertheless, the housekeeper should know precisely the furnishings for each room and keep records of such scheduled cleaning duties as rugs, drapes, upholstery, touch-up painting, and so on.

FOOD AND BEVERAGE DEPARTMENT

Despite the fact that rooms usually provide the largest source of income for a hotel, a quality food and beverage operation can be a hotel's best advertisement. The food and beverage department is one of the few departments that differs greatly from one type of hotel to another. For a downtown or suburban property, the restaurant may be the single most identifiable feature and be used as a marketing tool to measure demand for other facilities. Even the smaller property may benefit from a restaurant operation. Lodging statistics show that motels with restaurants operate at a higher average occupancy than those without.

While about half of the total revenue in the industry comes from food and beverage sales, due to the complexity of departmental operations, little more than 15 percent of the overall operating profit comes from the food and beverage department. The limited food and beverage profitability is the result of such factors as fluctuating food costs, high staffing levels, and lack of inventory controls.

The food and beverage department is responsible for the following functions:

Purchasing and storage
- ☐ Ordering
- ☐ Receiving
- ☐ Issuing
- ☐ Storage

Kitchen
- ☐ Food preparation
- ☐ Cooking
- ☐ Baking
- ☐ Dishwashing, potwashing
- ☐ Trash, garbage

Restaurant service
- ☐ Host/maitre d'
- ☐ Wait staff
- ☐ Bus staff
- ☐ Cashier

Beverage service
- ☐ Bartenders
- ☐ Porters

In addition to food and beverage service to restaurants and lounges, catering is an important function at many hotels—it is generally the largest profit maker in the food and beverage area. The catering department books and coordinates all banquets, receptions, and any other type of meeting that takes place in hotel function rooms. The catering manager, therefore, works closely with the food and beverage department to plan food preparation and service.

In high-quality or large operations, room service is critical to the reputation and success of the hotel. In some properties, food service personnel are permanently assigned to room service, a reflection of its increased importance. In a handful of super-luxury hotels, there is a pantry on each guestroom floor for simple food and beverage preparation or where final tray assembling occurs. The pantry includes toasters and coffee machines, as well as storage space for flatware, glassware, and linen. Though the pantry system is extremely labor intensive, it permits more consistent and high-quality service to the guest.

Many commercial and convention properties have added concierge or "executive" floors that combine guest checkin and an open lounge where continental breakfast, coffee, tea, cocktails, snacks, and magazines are provided. A butler may be employed who is responsible for seeing to every guest need from serving light meals to valet service.

ENGINEERING DEPARTMENT

In recent years, the energy crisis and the general desire to contain cost has focused more management attention on the engineering department because of its impact on the overall profitability of a hotel operation. The following activities are performed in engineering:

Repairs and maintenance

Energy management
- ☐ Monitor equipment
- ☐ Analysis
- ☐ Conservation measures

Security
- ☐ Guest protection

HOW TO MANAGE A HOTEL*

An Allegory for Tired Innkeepers

Introduction

In the past several years I have often been approached by some person or other who has told me he just bought a hotel and would like to read a book on how to run it.

Unfortunately, such a book has not been available. It is such an easy matter that I can't really see why someone hasn't written one.

I find that I now have a few spare hours so I plan to write that book. I know all hotelmen will find it helpful to be able to give it to friends who have just bought a hotel.

Chapter I: The Back of the House

The use of the expression, "back of the house," strikes terror into the hearts of the uninitiated. This is an unfounded fear.

The back of the house is merely that area of the building which faces the back parking lot. You will notice it immediately as you drive into the lot. However, as simple as it might appear, don't dismiss it. The good operator sees to it that it is kept well painted, that broken windows are repaired, and the garbage is hidden from public view.

So much for the mysterious back of the house.

If one enters the hotel from this area, he will usually find himself in the kitchen. This is a warm, wonderful place, full of the good smells of cooking food. The kitchen is an area to be avoided during busy periods as your presence could make the chef and other employees nervous.

The chef can be easily recognized as the man in the T-shirt, with a cigarette hanging out of his mouth, talking to his bookie. At this time, it is customary to greet the chef, ask him how things are going, taste his soup, and then be on your way.

Other areas of the kitchen such as dishwashing, potwashing, and pantry pretty much run themselves. In the event anything goes wrong, you know that the chef is there to take care of things.

Chapter II: The Front of the House

The front of the house is the same as the back of the house, only, of course, on the opposite side. This area should also be kept well painted and broken windows repaired.

If one enters the hotel from this direction, he will usually find himself in the lobby. The lobby is pretty much a fun area with a lot of sofas and potted plants, pictures on the walls, and a guide to church services in the area. The latter is most important because the majority of the people checking into your hotel are good, God-fearing people, and are anxious to go to services on Sunday mornings.

Somewhere, in about the center of the lobby, is the front desk. You have probably already decided by this time that hotel people are a little strange about identifying things by where they sit physically on the property (back of the house, front of the house, front desk). It might be because of all the drinking they do, and they want to know just where they are supposed to be going.

The front desk is usually occupied by no one. The person in the room just behind the desk, smoking a cigarette, drinking a cup of coffee and talking to his girl friend on the phone, is the desk clerk.

A good operator will go into the back room and ask the clerk three questions:

"How's the coffee?"

"How's the girl friend?"

"How's the house?"

The answer to all three will be, "Fine."

Chapter III: The Side of the House

For some reason unknown to me, this expression is not used in hotels. This suggests, of course, that the sides of the house are not important. It would be unwise on your part to draw the conclusion that the sides of the house need not be kept well painted, nor is it necessary to replace broken windows.

Chapter IV: Food and Beverage Control

This is the key to the good operation, and, perhaps, the most important chapter in the book.

The hotel business offers many temptations. There is always a ready availability of vast amounts of food and liquor at the disposal of the operator. It is critically important that the operator control the amount of food and beverage that he consumes.

Remember—no one likes a fat, drunken hotel manager.

Chapter V: Other Departments

There are other departments in the hotel that the new operator may be interested in.

The first is the maintenance department, which is usually located somewhere in the basement of the hotel. This department is of little consequence, and can be virtually ignored because nothing ever goes wrong during the maintenance man's normal duty hours. If one cares to see him, the maintenance man can usually be found sleeping at his desk.

Next is the housekeeping department which is also usually found in the basement of the hotel. The task of housekeeping is to keep the hotel relatively clean with as little effort as possible. This area often has in it a lot of dirty linen and other unpleasant things. It's a good place to avoid.

Then we come to the dining room, which doesn't deserve a full chapter because it is basically a very simple operation. The guest sits down, the waitress takes the order, goes to the kitchen (see Chapter I) for the food, gives it to the guest who eats it, gets up, pays and leaves. The process is repetitious and has a tendency to get boring. However, it doesn't hurt, while standing at the bar, to look in once in a while and see how things are going.

Chapter VI: You, the Operator

There is an old saying that "no system operates well without a good head." (A Navy expression, I believe.) The implication is, of course, that the operator has to have complete control and a constant good mental attitude. As is obvious from the preceding chapters, the job is time-consuming and creates a great deal of mental strain.

The operator must have his sanctuary, a place to retreat to gather his thoughts, and to do his personal work in private. This brings us to the manager's office. Ideally, the office should be located in another building, across the street, or, perhaps, down the block. But this is not always practical. You may be forced to have your office on the property.

High traffic areas, such as off the lobby or near the banquet rooms, should not be considered. This type of location encourages department heads and other troublesome people to drop in and bother you with their problems. These people never seem to understand that you have your own problems and that they must really learn to take care of themselves.

The decision on the location must be yours, but remember, the fewer people who know where you are will insure you that you will get the peace and quiet to do your job and do it well.

Conclusion

This book may also be used by someone who has just gone into the restaurant business. Everything applies—just forget about the guest-rooms.

By Thomas C. Chevoor; Reprinted with permission from the Cornell Hotel and Restaurant Administration Quarterly, *August 1976.*

☐ Property protection
☐ Fire safety

Over the last decade, hoteliers have recognized the need to continually renovate public and guestroom areas. In very large properties, a projects manager, who reports directly to the general manager, is responsible for rehabilitation; however, in most hotels, the function normally occurs within the engineering or housekeeping department.

In the early years in the life of a hotel property, engineering work consists of minor repairs and maintenance. As the hotel ages, scheduling of major renovation and redecoration projects becomes important in order to minimize the downtime of a guestroom, guestroom floor, restaurant, or other public area. Consequently, the work is often done in off-peak days or seasons.

Energy control and management have become an important function of the engineering department. In recent years, energy costs have escalated rapidly and currently range between 4 and 6 percent of gross revenues. Because of the magnitude of this expense, energy conservation strategies are vital, demanding staff training as well as systems decisions. Even the choice of light fixtures in public spaces, though seemingly a minor concern, can have a major impact on a hotel's annual utility bill. Present technology allows a hotel property, with the aid of a microcomputer, to analyze its energy costs and set up conservation procedures. This is the essence of energy management.

Security recently has become a consideration of guests when selecting a hotel. To better coordinate anticrime and life safety measures, large downtown and convention hotels have created a separate security department. Sometimes, however, such services are performed by engineering department personnel. In step with the advances in technology, many hotels have recently spent large sums of money on such sophisticated electronic devices as keyless locks, closed circuit television, and intrusion detectors. It is important to note that simple installation of state-of-the-art security systems does not ensure the safety of guests and property. Training programs must be estimated so that each employee if fully aware of hotel security policies.

PERSONNEL DEPARTMENT

The personnel department in a hotel is a modern phenomenon. The days are gone in which the owner or general manager hired department heads who in turn hired their own staffs. Historically, human resources management policies were loosely applied and rarely documented, a modus operandi that is ineffective in today's complex hospitality setting. Absentee and chain management, labor laws and regulations, comprehensive benefits packages, inflation, automation, and endless paper work have all contributed to the growth of the personnel department.

The following activities occur in the personnel department:

Recruitment
Training
Administration

☐ Staff planning
☐ Benefits
☐ Scheduling
☐ Safety

More frequently today than ever before, the hotel industry is making a real effort to train employees systematically. Larger hotels establish training departments to structure and control this process better, not only for lower-level employees, but also for managers. Many hotel companies require that people entering managerial positions first participate in a corporate training program. Others have implemented successful mid-management programs, such as that conducted at Hilton International's Career Development Institute.

While the personnel department has growing authority, many personnel decisions are made at the corporate level. These include the initial staffing of a hotel, uniform wage and salary guidelines, benefits packages, and allowable personnel changes due to increases or decreases in business volume.

ACCOUNTING DEPARTMENT

The accounting function has not changed much in the past 10 years, except that there is now more pressure on the department to forecast accurately. Generally, a controller joins the preopening team 6 to 12 months before the hotel opens to coordinate the preparation of the preopening budget. The budget is based on management reports from the general manager and department heads, including sales data on tenative and guaranteed bookings; occupancy projections; food and beverage forecasts; furniture, fixtures, and equipment figures from purchasing; and staffing requirements for the departments. The accounting areas, therefore, must be designed to accommodate few people but increasing numbers of sophisticated equipment.

Computerization has allowed hotels to reduce the number of people on the bookkeeping staff. The controller must be familiar with computers and accounting software. This knowledge is especially important when opening a new hotel because the decision about what computer software will best serve its needs is usually made at the property level.

MARKETING DEPARTMENT

The marketing department in a hotel is traditionally staffed by sales personnel. However, increasing competition has changed its orientation so that now the hotel develops a marketing strategy based upon the consumer rather than on the product to be sold. By identifying potential customers and understanding their needs and wants, the sales personnel can be more effective in the field. There is a new realization that hotels are selling a service, not a product, and that marketing a service must differ from marketing a product.

The following activities occur in the marketing department:

☐ Sales
☐ Banquets
☐ Convention services
☐ Public relations

A major function of the marketing department is booking group business. Group bookings are made at discounts from the rack rates. Groups consist of business and tour groups and even such parties as airlines or the government that need to reserve blocks of rooms on a regular basis. Discounting is also a strategy to attract individual guests. The emergence of weekend packages and discount coupons are marketing efforts to bring in new guests during seasonal or weekend occupancy lulls.

Each year over 25,000 conventions are held in the United States with a total attendance of 12 million people. Convention and conference services are a large function of many hotels and allow hotels to know far in advance that rooms and public space will be fully used. Smaller properties such as conference centers have joined the move to accommodate group business. Convention business has also proven beneficial to resort hotels; in response to rising operating costs, resorts book conventions before and after peak seasons to boost occupancy percentages.

The marketing department also services meetings and banquets. Convention and conference hotels have elaborate brochures for meeting planners that provide floor plans of the function facilities, square footage, occupant capacities, and a list of all the support equipment the hotel will provide. Hotel marketing will continue to grow and to become increasingly important in the profitable operation of all types of hotels.

24 PROFESSIONAL PRACTICE

"When describing the restaurants and hotels of their creation, designers without hesitation speak in fervent tones about aesthetics and form; yet there is always, lurking beneath the surface, the practical matter of fee."

Mark Kristal

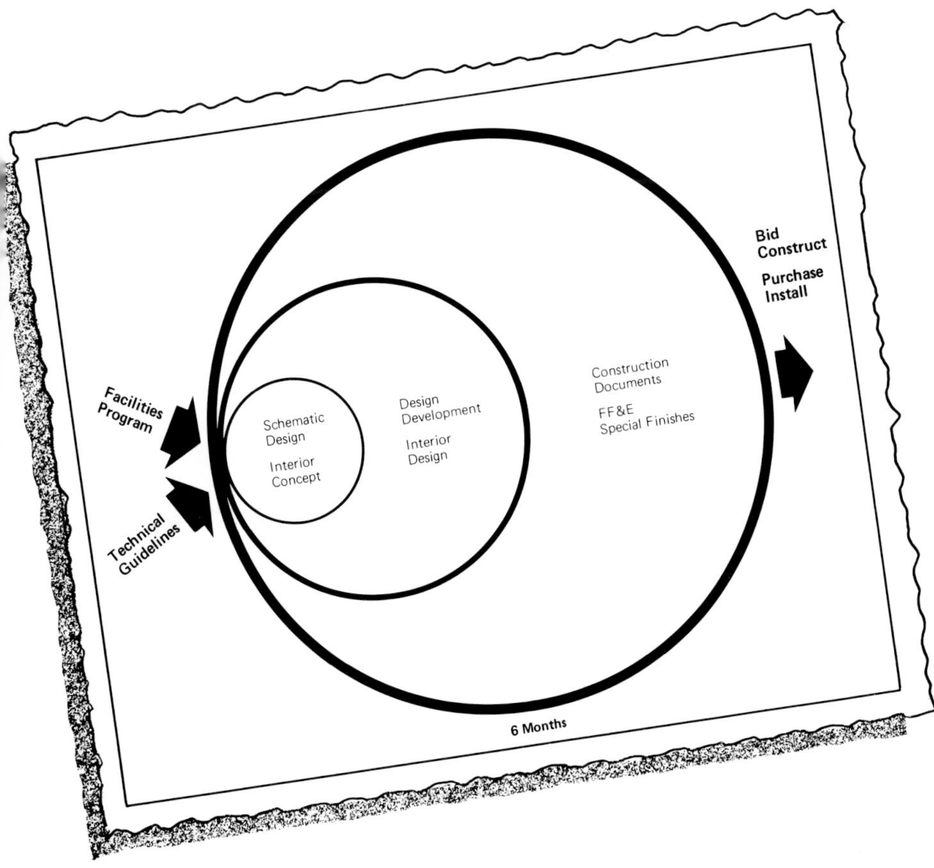

In the hotel boom following World War II, the expanding chains searched for architects with hotel experience. Having built few hotels during the previous 15 years, some turned to the experienced firm of Holabird and Root, responsible for several of the last hotels including Chicago's Stevens Hotel and the Washington Statler, to develop new designs and technology. Two young designers working in collaboration with the firm, William B. Tabler and Richard E. Smith, fresh from service in the Pacific, developed the first major post-war hotels, including the Statler in Los Angeles.

As experts on hotels, Tabler then became exclusive consultant to Statler-Hilton for a time, while Smith joined Inter-Continental Hotels, establishing the specialized fields of hotel architecture and corporate technical services. Tabler's firm went on to design over 300 hotels, while Smith continued supervising consulting architects worldwide for over 25 years. Other leaders in the field include Joseph Rosenthal, design director for Hilton for many years, and such worldwide construction advisors as William Rizzo of Sheraton.

The success of many hotel companies, and America's prominence in the hotel field, is in no small measure due to the experienced in-house technical departments developed by each hotel company. From the facilities programming of hotels to developing design standards and guiding the many talented consulting architects and interior designers, a relative handful of corporate architects and specialists has upgraded the quality and efficiency of hotel design and construction worldwide.

This unique form of professionalism, fostering creative interaction among teams of architects, interior designers, and in-house operational specialists, developers, and other expert team members, has led to a golden age in hotel planning and design.

The techniques developed to effectively deal with the design and construction of hotels require special coordination procedures among the owner, developers, operators, architects, and consultants including the following team members shown in the table on the next page.

Extensive guidance is provided by the operator (under management and technical services agreements) and/or the franchisor (under a franchise agreement) during the design process to assure that the structure complies with standards required by the operator or franchisor. To this end, the hotel company makes its technical assistance available to

Diagram of Hotel Design Phases. *The hotel design phases diagrammed here—from initial programming and technical standards to final bid and purchase documents—are essential to coordinate the progress of the project team.*

Typical design team members

TEAM MEMBER	DESCRIPTION
Owner	The owning company, which may also be the developer, an equity investor, operator, government, or a combined joint venture of any of the above.
Developer	The entity initiating and actively managing the overall development process.
Operator	The hotel company that holds a management agreement and, normally, a technical services agreement with the owner; the operator may also be an owner, or joint-venture partner or developer.
Franchisor	The hotel company that holds a hotel franchise agreement with the owner (or franchisee).
Lender	Institution providing primary debt financing; may also be an owner or joint-venture partner.
Construction lender	Institution providing temporary financing until construction is complete.
Feasibility consultant	Independent accounting or similar professional firm recognized in the field of hotel development and finance. (See Chapter 22, Feasibility Studies.)
Design consultants	(See table on types of consultants and contractors below)
Lender's inspecting architect	Architect independently reviewing design and construction for the lender.
Contractors	(See table below)
Construction manager	Consultant employed by the owner to manage the construction and equiping of the hotel if not managed directly by the owner or operator.

help select the design consultants, supply specialized hotel information, review and approve drawings, and, in some cases, perform portions of the design itself, such as provide preliminary concept drawings, back-of-house planning, or interior or kitchen designs by its in-house professionals.

Since the hotel company continually improves and refines its operational methods, its latest input is needed by consultants as a basis for their designs. Advice from operating company technicians is provided in such areas as food and beverage services and computerized hotel systems as well as architecural, engineering, and interior design. Since the operator has a large stake in the hotel's success, it needs to participate fully in the design and approval process.

Developers from other fields are often unprepared for the additional responsibilities inherent in hotel development. "It's like building an apartment house, shopping mall and offices all under one roof, including all their tenant furnishings, as well as a training school for employees before it opens," said one.

The required consultants and a synopsis of the special provisions of their agreements as they specifically relate to hotels are outlined in this chapter. One of the main objectives on each hotel project is to tie all written agreements together to ensure that (1) all necessary services are provided; (2) duplication or overlapping of responsibilities is eliminated; and (3) the primary cost responsibility for each budget item is assigned *contractually* (that is, to the architect, interior designer, construction manager, purchasing agent, and so on). If the budget estimate is exceeded in any design phase, the team member responsible can be made to redesign, respecify, reestimate, or rebid as necessary to maintain the initial agreed upon project cost (see section on Estimating and Budget Control later in this chapter).

TYPES OF CONSULTANTS AND CONTRACTORS*

In addition to architects and interior designers, the following types of consultants and contractors are usually required on hotel projects.

Responsible to the owner; selected by the owner and operator

- ☐ Architect
- ☐ Interior designer
- ☐ Food service equipment consultant
- ☐ Laundry equipment consultant
- ☐ Graphic consultant (print graphics, menus, and so on)
- ☐ Geotechnical engineer
- ☐ Site surveyor
- ☐ Environmental impact consultants (see the environmental planning checklist in the Appendix)
- ☐ Construction manager (as required)

*Although all fees and contract agreements described below have been written in quasi-legal terms, the material should not be excerpted for use without consultation with attorneys.

Responsible to the architect; selected by the architect and subject to approval by the owner and operator

- ☐ Structural engineer
- ☐ Mechanical, electrical, and elevator engineers
- ☐ Civil engineer
- ☐ Fire protection consultant
- ☐ Audiovisual consultant
- ☐ Acoustical consultant
- ☐ Traffic and parking consultants
- ☐ Landscape architect
- ☐ Estimator

Responsible to the interior designer; selected by the designer, subject to approval by the owner and operator

- ☐ Lighting consultant
- ☐ Graphics consultant (for interior signage)

Responsible to the owner; bid and awarded by the owner, subject to approval by the operator

- ☐ General contractor for construction
- ☐ Separate construction subcontractors (if construction management system used)
- ☐ Separate contractor for interior finishes and millwork
- ☐ Purchasing agent and installer of furniture, fixtures, and equipment
- ☐ Suppliers of special artwork and artifacts
- ☐ Sign contractor
- ☐ Menus and printing supplier
- ☐ Uniform supplier
- ☐ Suppliers of miscellaneous expendables, consumables, and inventories

CORPORATE TECHNICAL SERVICES FEES AND CONTRACTS

Technical services agreements should require all design information and guidance needed from the operator including: facilities and area programs [that is, number, size and type of guestrooms, guestroom bays, suites, seating capacities of food, beverage, banquet and meeting areas, recreation, retail, parking, and other special requirements); technical guidelines; circulation flow diagrams; special systems layouts (for example, for telephones, business, and communications equipment and computers; service areas, laundries, front desk), operating and design themes for food and beverage areas; general staffing requirements (such as lockers and offices); requirements for office layouts and equipment, signage, room numbering, and all other detailed hotel requirements affecting the design and budget].

The coordination, review, and approval of consultants and all phases of design from initial program orientation and concept to final design documentation, field inspection, and acceptance should be included to ensure that the operator's needs are fully met.

The diagram on page 233 indicates the stages at which facilities program information, design guidelines, and other hotel technical data are incorporated into the architectural and interior design documents as well as the review and approval phases by the owner and operator.

Technical services fees based on the above scope range about $300 to $400 per room, with a minimum total of $150,000. A full-time project representative is also generally required at a cost of approximately $60,000 per year plus about 10 percent for reimbursables (note the capital cost outline). But technical services costs vary between different operators based on the extent of their participation, including detailed document reviews and additional scope of services.

ARCHITECTURAL FEES AND CONTRACTS

The architect's agreement should contain the following special provisions:

General

The architect shall perform the following professional services pertaining to the hotel and be responsible to the owner. The hotel operator's approval shall be obtained on all matters required by the management agreement.

Architect's services

Basic Services: These shall consist of the following six phases including normal structural, mechanical, electrical, fire protection, elevators, civil engineering, landscaping, sitework, parking, acoustical, audiovisual, lighting, security, estimating, and coordination of all required consultants as approved by owner. The architect shall provide value architecture and engineering services consisting of evaluation of all reasonable design components, systems, and methods for efficiency, economy, life safety, and adaptability to the site. The architect warrants that documents shall be in full compliance with all applicable codes and regulations. All construction estimates shall be prepared by a qualified estimator in adequate detail to evaluate the architect's work at each phase, according to the following schedule, not to be exceeded, except for reasonable cause, by either architect or owner (insert agreed completion dates for each phase here). The owner shall have the right to require modifications to achieve its desired goals with respect to overall design and operation of the hotel.

Schematic Design: Based on the hotel facilities list and design program, hotel design guide, construction budget, and other data furnished by the owner, the architect shall prepare single-line plans and variations of buildable schemes, indicating all relationships of hotel components. The architect shall further refine the concept selected by the owner, presenting all floor plans, exterior elevations, building sections, exterior color perspectives, and cost estimates.

Design Development: Based on approved schematic design documents, the architect shall prepare more detailed drawings and outline specifications describing all aspects of the hotel's size and character, including architectural, structural, mechanical, electrical, and fire protection systems, materials, and an updated cost estimate. In compliance with energy conservation codes and standards, the architect shall prepare a comparative analysis of capital costs and operating expenses of alternate mechanical, electrical, and energy-saving systems so that the owner can select among them.

Construction Documents Phase I (50 percent complete documents): Based on approved design development documents, the architect shall prepare final detailed drawings and specifications of all construction requirements for the hotel, coordinating in the documents all data provided by the owner and its consultants on guestroom layouts, kitchen, bar, and laundry equipment and layouts, exterior signs, and other standard details. The architect shall provide the interior designer with drawings of fixed interior elements of hotel, but not including movable furnishings or other work provided by the owner's consultants. The architect shall refine engineering subsystems and advise the owner of any adjustments to the cost estimate.

Construction Documents Phase II (90 percent complete documents): The owner and its consultants shall give the architect material and color selections and data on any additional systems or equipment to be incorporated on final documents including front desk, computers, and telephones. The architect shall submit updated drawings and specifications, advise of any adjustments to the cost estimate, and assist the owner in preparing necessary bidding documents.

Construction Documents Phase III (100 percent complete documents and bidding): The architect shall finalize drawings and specifications and file them on behalf of the owner with appropriate regulatory agencies for issuance of the building permit, with the owner paying all associated fees. The architect will submit updated cost estimate and assist the owner in clarifying documents during bidding. Where considered necessary to ensure that the budget is met, the architect will organize specified portions of the design as bid alternates.

Construction Phase: The architect shall promptly review and take appropriate action on the contractor's submittals to make sure they conform with the design concept and construction documents and forward them to the owner. The architect shall visit the site as appropriate, but not less than once each month, to make recommendations to the owner about progress of the work, evaluate the contractor's applications for payment, issue certificates of payment, endeavor to guard against defects in the work, but not to guarantee performance by the contractor or supervise construction means, methods, or safety precautions. The architect shall interpret all documents and provide certificates of substantial and final completion of the work.

Construction Costs

The architect agress that the construction budget is a maximum of (*insert amount here*) and its best efforts shall be made to delineate the design bidable within this sum, but if exceeded by lowest bona fide bids, the owner shall: (1) approve increase: (2) authorize rebidding; or (3) cooperate in revising the scope, materials, or details to reduce the cost. In such case, the architect without additional charge shall modify final documents to bring the cost within the construction budget.

Compensation to Architect

The owner's payments shall be made on approved invoices at the completion of each of the following phases:

PHASE (based on designer's services listed above)	PERCENT FEE PAID
Schematic design	10
Design development	35
Construction documents phase I	55
Construction documents Phase II	70
Construction documents phase III	80
Construction (final phase payable monthly in accordance with construction's progress)	100

Renegotiation of Compensation

If the scope of the hotel is changed substantially after approval of the schematic design phase or the architect's services, through no fault of the architect, have not been completed within six months after the originally scheduled completion date, the architect's compensation for the then uncompleted portion shall be subject to renegotiation.

Ownership of Documents: All documents shall be the property of owner.

Insurance

The architect shall maintain during service, and for a minimum of five years after their completion, professional liability insurance specifically covering errors and omissions, as well as during workman's compensation, employer's liability, and comprehensive general liability insurance services (specify amounts here). The architect shall submit certificates of insurance naming the owner and operator as additional insureds to the extent permitted by the carrier. Such insurance shall not limit the architect's liability. The architect shall hold the owner and operator harmless from liability, loss, or property damage resulting from the architect's acts or omissions.

Fees

The Architect's fees for the scope of services defined in the above agreement are normally a lump sum amount ranging from 3 to 4 percent of the agreed estimate of the construction cost of the work designed by the architect and related consultants. The exact fee depends on the size and complexity of the hotel. If full technical services are not provided by the hotel company, the architect's fees may be increased by up to 1 percent.

Fees may vary from the above averages due to unique conditions. But more than any other factor, a hotel company's information, decisions, and approvals, saves time and work for the consultants, enabling them to reduce their fees accordingly.

INTERIOR DESIGN FEES AND CONTRACTS

The interior designer's agreement should contain the following special provisions.

General

The designer shall perform professional services pertaining to the hotel and be responsible to the owner. The operator's approval shall be obtained on all matters required by the management agreement. The designer's services shall include the following spaces: public areas including lobbies, corridors, elevator lobbies, elevator cab interiors, restaurants, cafe, coffee shop, snack bar, cafeteria, pool bar, bars, cocktail lounges, entertainment facilities, night clubs, discos, meeting rooms, conference rooms, function rooms, seminar rooms, boardrooms, ballroom, junior ballroom, exhibit areas, prefunction areas, preassembly areas, outdoor dining areas, pool terraces, front desk area, executive offices, sales offices, catering office, accounting office, personnel office, administrative office, front offices, recreation rooms, health clubs, employees dining room, public restrooms, upper-floor lounges and registration area; and guestroom areas including typical guestrooms, special guestrooms, typical suites, deluxe and special suites, hospitality suites, office suites, guest bathrooms, vending areas, guest self-laundry, corridors, guest and service elevator lobbies, and guestroom balconies.

Designers Services

Basic Services: These shall consist of the following six phases including normal interior design services for furniture, fixtures, and accessories (F&F), special finishes, graphics, uniforms, and table top items and coordination of consultants approved by the owner. The designer shall coordinate with the architect and other consultants. The designer warrants that documents shall be in full compliance with all applicable codes and regulations. All interiors estimates shall be prepared by a qualified estimator in adequate detail to evaluate the designer's work at each phase, according to the following schedule, not to be exceeded, except for reasonable cause, by either the designer or the owner (insert agreed completion dates for each phase). The owner shall have the right to require modifications to achieve its desired goals with respect to overall design and operation of the hotel.

Concept Phase: Based on hotel facilities list and design program, hotel design guide, room mix, suggested operating and design themes for food and beverage areas, budget for F&F and special finishes, available architectural plans, and other data furnished by the owner, the designer shall prepare preliminary floor plans and variations indicating proposed furniture layouts for public areas and guestrooms, sketch perspectives of overall design concepts including colors and samples of proposed materials, catalogs, and photos of furnishings, alternate selections, and cost estimates.

Preliminary Design Phase: Based on approved concept documents, the designer shall prepare preliminary room layouts for all public areas, guestrooms, and suites including furniture, ceiling and lighting designs, and electrical outlet locations, with color perspective renderings and presentation boards containing color, fabric, and material samples of floor, wall, and ceiling finishes, window treatments, furniture and furnishings fabrics and materials including drawings and photos of standard and custom-fabricated furniture, fixtures, and accessories for presentation to the owner. The designer shall present a preliminary design direction for graphics, uniforms, and artwork to the owner and submit a preliminary line item estimate of F&F and special finishes.

Documentation phase I (working drawings of furniture and special finishes and mock-up room specifications and review): The designer shall prepare complete working drawings including floor plans of all furniture and furnishings identified by type, size, and total number of each item, coded on the drawings and crossreferenced to all other specification data. Drawings shall include elevations, sections, and ceiling plans identifying wall and window treatments, location of special finishes and materials, variations in ceiling heights and floor levels, location of lighting and outlets for electricity and TV. The designer shall prepare specifications for a mock-up of a typical guestroom and assist in installation and adjustments to meet the owner's approval and also present all seating for food and beverage areas for the owner's approval at that time.

Documentation phase II (millwork and special finishes drawings, complete specifications, and confirmation of budget): The designer shall prepare final working drawings and bid specifications for all millwork and special finishes including floor and ceiling plans, sections, elevations, and details of all fixed furniture, furnishings, fixtures, and finishes including floor, wall, and ceiling decorative elements and level changes and coordination of all engineering outlets. Each decorative item shall be detailed and identified by manufacturer. The designer shall provide a finish schedule and specification books of swatches illustrating all materials, fabrics, colors, details, or catalog cuts of F&F, crossreferenced to drawings and specifications; carpet and fabric designs including color tufts or samples; itemized schedules and bid specification sheets including alternate sources of supply; design and procurement coordination for artwork and special accessories; and a final estimate breakdown conforming with the budget for F&F and special finishes for approval of the owner, operator, and their designated purchasing agent.

Documentation phase III (graphics,

uniforms, and table tops): The designer shall provide a graphics program throughout the hotel including specialty signage for each food and beverage area and required drawings, specifications, and color samples for all interior signs for the owner's approval. Estimates shall be included in the budget for F&F. The designer shall assist the owner in reviewing uniform designs and selections of table top items including glassware, china, linen, and related service pieces, menus, and accessories designed by others.

Construction and Installation Phase: The designer shall verify that construction and installation of interior spaces conform to documents; review and approve color and material samples, shop drawings, and manufacturers' detail submittals of furniture, fixtures, and millwork; provide on-site coordination with the installation contractor to approve furniture arrangements; locate decorative materials, artwork, and accessories; and prepare a final punch list of detective items.

Cost of F&F and special finishes

The designer agrees that the budget for F&F and special finishes is a maximum of (insert amount here), and best efforts shall be made to delineate designs bidable within this sum, but if exceeded by lowest bona fide bids, the owner shall: (1) approve increase; (2) authorize rebidding; or (3) cooperate in revising scope, materials, or details to reduce cost. In such case, the designer, without additional charge, shall modify final documents to bring costs within the F&F and special finishes budget.

Compensation to Designer

Owner's payments shall be made on approved invoices at completion of each of following phases:

PHASE (based on designer's services listed above)	PERCENT FEE PAID
Concept design	25
Preliminary design	40
Documentation phase I	50
Documentation phase II	70
Documentation phase III and bidding	80
Construction and installation (final phase payable monthly in accordance with progress of services)	100

Provisions for renegotiation of compensation, ownership of documents, and insurance should be similar to those discussed under the architect's agreement above.

The interior designer's fees for the scope of services defined in the above agreement are normally a lump sum amount ranging from 6 to 9 percent of the agreed cost estimate of the work designed and specified by the interior designer and his or her consultants. The exact fee depends on the size and complexity of the hotel (for example, the number of restaurants or special suites). But, for extensive renovation services, fees range up to 12 percent.

FOOD SERVICE EQUIPMENT CONSULTANT'S FEES AND CONTRACTS

The foodservice equipment consultant's agreement should contain the following special provisions:

General

The consultant shall perform professional services pertaining to the hotel and be responsible to the owner. The operator's approval shall be obtained on all matters required by the management agreement. The designer's services shall include the following areas: main kitchen, room service, cafe and restaurant pantries, service stations, cafeteria, display cooking, service bars, banquet service pantries, food and beverage storerooms, refrigeration rooms, lobby bar, entertainment lounge bar, pool snack bar, pastry shop, employees' cafeteria, receiving area, garbage refrigeration room, can washing room, guestroom floor vending, ice-machine areas, and guestroom pantries, kitchens, or bars.

Consultant's services

Basic Services: These consist of the following four phases including normal design services for all food service equipment (FSE), layouts, and coordination with the architect, interior designer, and other consultants. The consultant warrants that documents shall be in full compliance with all applicable codes and regulations. All equipment estimates shall be in adequate detail to evaluate the consultant's work at each phase according to the following schedule not to be exceeded, except for reasonable cause (insert agreed completion dates for each phase).

Preliminary Design Phase: Based on hotel facilities list and design program, hotel design guide, suggested operating and design themes for food and beverage areas, budget for FSE, available architectural plans and other data furnished by the owner, the consultant shall prepare preliminary layout plans indicating all equipment, counters, shelving, and hoods; a schedule describing types and quantities of equipment; and a cost estimate with equipment in place ready for final utilities connections.

Documentation Phase: Based on approved preliminary designs, the consultant shall prepare final plans with dimensions and locations of all equipment, shelving, counters, and hoods; dimensions, sizes, and capacities of all required plumbing, electrical, gas, and steam services and exhaust hoods; schedule and specifications of all equipment by their manufacturers, models, and utilities requirements as well as specially fabricated items by their sizes, shapes, materials, and finishes. Documents shall be in adequate detail for bidding and contracting supply and setting in place of all required FSE. The consultant shall submit an updated cost estimate for approval.

Bidding Phase: The consultant shall recommend at least three qualified bidders; review any clarifications or proposed alternatives to documents with bidders; assist the owner in analyzing bids and making acceptable revisions, if required, to negotiate a contract within the approved estimate.

Construction Phase: The consultant shall review and approve shop drawings, manufacturers' equipment cuts, and samples; coordinate with the architect and other consultants as required; inspect installation, prepare a corrective punch list, verify compliance, and recommend final acceptance of all equipment.

Cost of FSE

The consultant agrees that the budget for the FSE is a maximum of (insert amount here), and best efforts shall be made to delineate designs bidable within the sum, but if exceeded by lowest bona fide bids, the owner shall: (1) approve increase; (2) authorize rebidding; or (3) cooperate in revising scope, materials, or details to reduce cost. In such case, the consultant, without additional charge, shall modify the final documents to bring costs within the FSE budget.

Compensation to consultant

The owner's payments shall be made on approved invoices at completion of each of the following phases:

PHASE	PERCENT FEE PAID
Preliminary design	35
Documentation	80
Bidding	90
Construction	100

Provisions for renegotiation of compensation, ownership of documents, and insurance should be similar to those described under the architect's agreement above.

The food service equipment consultant's fees for the scope of services defined in the above agreement are a lump sum amount ranging from 3.5 to 4.5 percent of the agreed cost estimate of the FSE designed or specified.

PURCHASING AGENT FEES AND CONTRACTS

The purchasing agent's agreement should include coordination, scheduling, estimating, procurement, ordering, expediting, and installing all furniture, fixtures, equipment, accessories, supplies, and inventories for the hotel including:

1. Coordination with the owner, operator, interior designer, architect, and other consultants and contractors; monitoring design; and recommending materials, methods, vendors, and alternates for the owner's consideration wherever required to maintain the budget.
2. Issuing schedules and reports on procurement and shipping status including advice on any items affecting completion.
3. Providing itemized estimates with comparisons of line item to budget for the owner's approval.
4. Bidding, negotiating, and awarding purchase orders for approved budget items, with copies to the owner, and invoicing the owner accordingly, including any discounts.
5. Expediting manufacture, routing, and shipping to ensure the lowest costs consistent with the agreed delivery, installation, and completion schedule, and supervising receiving procedures including processing claims for damaged and missing materials.
6. Supervising and installing all work in accordance with approved completion schedule and providing applicable warrantees, guaranties, and operating manuals.

The purchasing agent's fees usually range from 4 to 5 percent of the cost of the work procured.

CONSTRUCTION MANAGER'S FEES AND CONTRACTS

Construction management (CM) is often provided directly by the owner, developer, or operator through their construction staff or by a professional CM firm. Agreements with construction managers should be on a fixed fee basis, averaging about 2 percent of construction costs, depending on the project's size. Their responsibilities and reimbursable expenses should be clearly defined, using the American Institute of Architects Document

Capital cost outline for typical 500-room hotel

ITEM	PREDESIGN ESTIMATE BASIS*		AMOUNT ($)
Land	Purchase		**2,000,000**
General construction			**23,000,000**
Sitework		$1,000,000	
Utilities	Allowance	200,000	
Surface parking, roads	600 cars × 1,000	600,000	
Structured parking	None		
Landscaping	Allowance	200,000	
Basic building	500 bays × 600 sq ft (55.7 sq m) = 300,000 sq ft (27,870 sq m) 300,000 sq ft × 70	21,000,000	
Interior finishes	500 bays × 2,000	1,000,000	
Furniture, fixtures, and equipment	500 bays × 14,000		**7,000,000**
Furniture and fixtures	55% × 7,000,000	3,850,000	
Kitchen, laundry, back-of-house equipment	25% × 7,000,000	1,750,000	
Inventories (linen, china, glassware, utensils, uniforms, supplies, printing)	15% × 7,000,000	1,050,000	
Purchasing fee	5% × 7,000,000	350,000	
Special systems			**550,000**
Telephone	500 bays × 900	450,000	
Computer (leased)	Allowance for conduit	50,000	
Special audiovisual equipment	Allowance	50,000	
Technical expenses			**2,450,000**
Architect-engineers (total)	3.5% × 22,000,000	770,000	
Architect (balance)	54% × 770,000	415,800	
Structural	12% × 770,000	92,400	
Mechanical, electrical, elevators, and civil engineering	28% × 770,000	215,600	
Audiovisual, acoustical, life safety, and landscape	6% × 770,000	462,000	
Interior designer (including lighting, signage graphics)	6.5% × 4,800,000†	312,000	
Menu graphics consultant	Allowance	20,000	
Food service equipment consultant	3.5% × 800,000	280,000	
Laundry equipment consultant	2% × 400,000	80,000	
Site survey	Allowance	5,000	
Environmental consultant	Allowance	20,000	
Geotechnical consultant	Allowance	5,000	
Soils testing	Allowance	7,000	
Construction manager	2% × 25,000,000	500,000	
Hotel operator's technical services	500 bays × 300	150,000	
Project field administration	1.5 years × 120,000	300,000	
Mock-up of typical guestroom	Allowance	25,000	
Lender's inspecting architect	Allowance	50,000	

ITEM	PREDESIGN ESTIMATE BASIS*		AMOUNT ($)
Reimbursables	Allowance	150,000	
Construction testing	Allowance	150,000	
Permits	.2% × 25,000,000	50,000	
Feasibility study	Allowance	25,000	
Legal, financial, administrative			**650,000**
Financing fees	Debt: 70% × 40,000,000 = 28,000,000	320,000	
Loan commitment fees	1% × 28,000,000	280,000	
Brokerages	.5% × 28,000,000	140,000	
Owner's legal fees	Allowance	45,000	
Lender's legal fees	Allowance	55,000	
Developer's fee	None		
Appraisal	Allowance	10,000	
Investment tax credit study	Allowance	50,000	
Real estate taxes	Allowance	50,000	
Title insurance	Allowance	60,000	
Builder's risk insurance	Allowance	45,000	
Liability insurance	Allowance	40,000	
Liquor license	Allowance	10,000	
Preopening expense	500 bays × 2,000		**1,000,000**
Working capital	500 bays × 500		**250,000**
Employee housing	None		
Interest during construction	Debt: 70% × 38,400,000 13% × 18 months × .55 (average cash flow balance)		**2,900,000***
Contingency	5% × 30,000,000		**1,500,000**
Total			**41,300,000**
Total cost per bay	**$41,300,000 ÷ 480 keys**		**86,400**

The predesign estimate includes major headings only and requires detailed breakdown of construction, interior finishes, FF&E, and preopening expense items as soon as schematic design is complete. It should be updated and modified as required at each design phase in accordance with the budget. The figures represent a moderate quality hotel.

†Cost of furniture, fixtures, accessories, and interior finishes designed and detailed by the interior designer.

B801a as a basis. Fees and reimbursables should be divided into separate guaranteed maximum amounts for the preconstruction and construction phases and should require quantity survey cost estimates at each phase of the architect's and interior designer's services. But if estimates or bids exceed the construction budget, the construction manager must advise on cost reductions to meet the budget without an additional fee.

ESTIMATING AND BUDGET CONTROL

While the complexity of hotel developments demands that several separate cost headings with thousands of individual line items be estimated and monitored, the following budget control steps and capital cost outline should help ensure that all major items are included and budget overruns avoided.

BUDGET CONTROL STEPS

Design Phases

1. Detailed estimates must be made by appropriate experts for all items to be capitalized and such estimates rechecked and updated at each design phase.
2. In addition to the estimates required by the architect and other consultants, a second estimate should be obtained, normally by a quantity estimating firm or the construction manager, with any differences in the estimates resolved by mutual agreement.
3. Design consultants must be held contractually responsible for redesigning and respecifying to meet the initial agreed-upon budget without an additional fee.
4. Due to the almost direct link between cost and area, budget control is often to a large extent a matter of space control. Designs must therefore be continually checked to ensure that unnecessary areas, as well as equipment or finishes, are not added beyond that required by the facilities program. Any increases must be justified by the owner based on their additional revenue-producing potential.

Construction Phase

1. All bidding must be competitive.
2. Design consultants must be contractually required to make reductions if budget estimates or bids are exceeded.
3. No construction commitments should be made until virtually all major items are under guaranteed maximum contract or at least reasonably firm allowances have been established and required design reductions have been already implemented wherever necessary to meet the budget.

Value design, as required under the section on Architectural Fees and Contracts above, provides the single most important tool for controlling costs. It eliminates waste space not contributing to guest appeal or hotel revenue and carefully evaluates those building shapes most appropriate to the land and to the required internal layouts for the particular type of hotel. Value design is the main reason why the Embassy Suites prototype became more cost efficient than that of other suite hotels (see Chapter 8) and why the Crowne Plaza Hotel in New Orleans, Louisiana, could be built for well under $50,000 per room (see Chapter 2). While the more attractive finish on a door knob costs pennies, a smarter, more effective building configuration can save hundreds of thousands of dollars. This is the least understood and best kept secret of successful cost control and the factor that separates the professionals from the novices in the field.

Rough cost estimates for hotels that are based on average unit costs per square foot on per room can only be considered as preliminary at best because there are so many variable factors. Accurate estimates based on specific hotel design are essential as soon as the drawings permit, and they must be reevaluated at every stage of the design. A summary of items to be budgeted for a typical hotel is indicated in the table.

25 THE NEXT STAGE

"Hotel people, architects, and designers must recognize that a great deal more profit could be made if a hotel had a really distinctive personality, if it were a place where people really wanted to be."

Warren Platner

While hotel development is primarily driven by room demand, it is also highly stimulated by competition among different chains, operators, and developers as well as by the creative ideas of architects and designers. Barring any physical and economic constraints such as the lack of adequate sites, sources of financing, sufficient room rates, or reasonable construction, energy, or staffing costs, hotels will continue to be built wherever rooms are scarce (see the market survey in Chapter 22).

Obviously, this assumes a peaceful and cooperative political climate, since progress in hotels, like other types of economic development, is quickly reversed and set back for years by unfortunate political turmoil such as occurred in Lebanon and Iran. Political stability is essential for freedom of travel and hotel growth. In many countries governments have vigorously promoted hotel and tourist development, while in other regions, restrictive controls have continued to inhibit tourism and hotel development. The difference is now clearly visable in China, for example, in its dramatic turnabout from a former state of restricted growth to a new era of vast tourist and hotel expansion.

It is also true that the need for hotel rooms can trigger uncalled-for overbuilding in a given area, as too many developers rush in to fill a void. Once started, the momentum is not easily slowed, resulting in serious hotel operating shortfalls instead of reasonable profits. In such cases, it may take several years for new room demand to catch up with the oversupply and for the original pro-forma financial projections to be finally achieved. For example, in 1983, occupancy rates in Dallas and Houston, Texas, fell below 45 percent compared with the minimum 65 percent needed to stay out of the red. Too many new hotels had opened within a narrow timeframe, causing a sudden bulge in supply in a normally healthy and steadily growing region. The situation was such that one Dallas hotel invited guests to fill in their own room rates, while a new Houston hotel offered free airline travel to attract its first few thousand weeklong occupants!

But in Houston, even where 8500 hotel rooms were added precipitously over a three-year period, its occupancy slump eventually bottomed out and began rebounding in 1984. However, in Boston, approximately 5000 new hotel rooms entered the market in 1983–84 in anticipation of an expanded new convention center previously announced by the city. But after considerable hotel construction was committed, the convention facility was delayed until 1988, with serious losses of profit expected by the hotels for the intervening period. While growth in hotel room demand correlates on a national basis with normal economic indicators, forecasting such demand locally for a specific project is risky, particularly for the short term. At best, hotels are a cyclical business, subject to shifts in local supply, although rising steadily in the long run. For this reason, hotel investment is considered most appropriate for those with deep pockets who can weather temporary gaps in supply and demand in the marketplace.

The problem of cyclical oversupply could easily be alleviated if a greater contingency factor were allowed in the hotel's pro-forma revenue projections based on unforeseen (that is, previously unannounced) competition entering the market. However, what may seem to be excessive expansion in one local area may often make sense to a large chain or developer on an overall basis. Due to economies of scale, growth is often necessary to stay competitive. Greater size reduces the hotel company's costs per room for advertising, reservations, purchasing, administration, and other systems costs and increases its ability to market its other hotels. With a large network of hotels it becomes easier to hold customers who feel more comfortable dealing with the same chain particularly for multiple bookings on extensive trips. Prestige is often linked to size and may also help attract higher quality staff interested in career-growth opportunities.

Whether practiced by independent entrepreneurs or chains, competitive factors are primarily responsible for quality improvements, with each operator attempting to best please the guest through its own individual style and methods. Since management policies vary and such differences make companies more successful than others, designers must know their client's current philosophy, marketing objectives, and operating methods. Comprehensive design manuals and technical staffs provide such guidance, but direct contact with the chief executive is required where such information is lacking. If we compare some overseas chains with cars, for example, over the years Hilton International seems to be trying to be the Cadillac with many frills, Sheraton the Lincoln Continental with impressively large areas, Hyatt the Corvette displaying its high-tech contemporary flavor, and Inter-Continental the Mercedes with its emphasis on operations and more comfortably crafted spaces.

In addition to personality, operation, and service quality, competition is also matched between varying systems of ownership and management: (1) chain-brand owned and managed, (2) independent or joint-venture owned and chain-brand managed, (3) independently owned and managed under a chain-brand franchise, and (4) independently owned and managed. Creative new methods of financing have also become competitive factors in fueling needed expansion (for example, syndications, underwritings, limited partnerships, timesharing and condominiumization, joint-venture mixed-use complexes, and obtaining government subsidies through grants, low-interest loans, favorable ground leases, tax abatement, landmark write-offs). With the various options available, financial expertise is required, as well as a detached view in the board room, resisting risky projects wherever capital cost budgets cannot be reasonably guaranteed or pro-forma revenue forecasts have been developed by overly optimistic staffs.

PRECEDING PAGE AND ABOVE

Model Photo of Space Colony. *Space colonies, or "spacetels," as pictured in this NASA model, are anticipated not long after the turn of the century.*

But like other public corporations that need to protect themselves against potential takeovers, hotel companies must maintain their stock prices at high levels. Since high-growth rates are required to maintain investor interest, chains are under continuous pressure to expand or perish, which often leads to overbuilding in certain areas.

The effect of overexpansion has been mitigated by the growth rate of population age groups that use hotels most (see the Preface). Not only are new types of destination resorts and tourist attractions rapidly multiplying, but convention attendance, extended business stays with families, and more frequent patronage of downtown and suburban hotel amenities have all become more widely accepted customs. Competition causes more luxurious features to be introduced into popular-priced hotels—from granite-topped vanities to Maxim's restaurants—and continues to present hotels as showplaces of modern technology. But, as with other luxury products, hotels must be *sold,* and it is the *imaginative design and marketing of hotels* that has created new demands.

That the upscale hotels are enjoying the highest of all occupancies indicates the guest's growing taste and ability to pay for comfort. That hotels are becoming more specialized shows greater consumer sophistication. That the small downtown hotel and the country inn are making a comeback augers well for the individual entrepreneur at a time when the major expansion in other hotel sectors is being dominated by chains. This shows there is still room for growth for the independent operator, particularly in hotels with fewer than 200 rooms that still claim the largest sector of the market. That hotels have rapidly expanded their sports and fitness facilities points up their ability to quickly adapt to new lifestyle trends.

That budget motels are expanding again indicates the industry's cost effectiveness and ability to better serve a new body of price-conscious consumers. That the modern hotel is now far safer and provides more automated fire protection, security, and communications systems than any other type of building exemplifies the hotel field's rapid technical response to serious concerns.

That restoration and adaptive reuse are more prevalent in hotels than in any other building type demonstrates the industry's willingness to convert its long-standing renovation experience into leadership in preservation. That the super-luxury hotel is expanding at the fastest rate in its history shows that dedication to the old-fashioned art of personalized service can still flourish in an age of mechanization. That hotels are rapidly becoming prime catalysts in mixed-use and planned community development has earned them a pivotal role in the continual renewal and reshaping of cities.

The next several years will not only see a surge of worldwide expansion in the above areas, but the continued widespread extension of hotel management into residential and business life through such avenues as time-sharing, condominium resorts, downtown, and suburban condo hotels, and residential communities with hotel-type amenities, as well as office suites, business service centers, and executive conference centers. Hotel-like facilities will increasingly serve society, and potential outerspace settlements will be patterned on hotel structures.

Design professionals and students, as well as investors and managers, can best prepare for such vital future roles by working together in improving today's hotels.

Environmental planning checklist

DATA	DESCRIPTION	SOURCE
Location map	Indicating limits of project site in relation to the surrounding area	Planner
Topographic map	Scale: 100 ft = 1 in.	Surveyor
Land use analysis	Compatibility with surrounding uses, plans, and policies Appropriate mix of uses and phases in which market would absorb them	Planner
Traffic analysis	Calculate average daily trips generate, distributed to road systems Identify roadway capacity problems Evaluate traffic count data Evaluate road safety data Analyze intersection capacities Provide data for air quality and noise analysis Mass transit, monorails Pedestrian walks and bridges	Traffic consultant
Air quality analysis	Compliance with standards: Project generated Traffic generated	Environmental engineer
Noise analysis	Compliance with standards: Project generated Traffic generated	Environmental engineer
Urban design analysis	Preservation of scenic qualities of and from site Effect on views Sun angles, effect on shadows Compatibility with adjacent land uses and existing built environment Building orientation to minimize adverse energy impacts Parking locations to minimize coverage Landscaping design character	Planner
Growth inducement	Visitor-serving uses Attraction of population to area	Planner
Employment opportunities	Availability of employees to fill positions From local sources From outside locations	Economist
Public services	Police, security Fire, emergency, rescue Proximity to health facilities Recreation, parks, waterfront activities, boat slips, jogging trails, bicycle paths, nature walks, and potential development Wildlife protection	Planner
Archaeological resources	Survey, testing of known sites: Excavation test pits Radiometric dating to determine significance Excavation if justified by presence of artifacts	Archaeologist
Grading plan	Indicating finished grade elevations, overlaid on existing topography including: Area to be graded (acres) Volume to cut (cubic yards) Volume of fill (cubic yards) Source of fill or destination of spoil if earthwork is not balanced on site Description of any proposed retaining walls (height, length, location)	Civil engineer
Site utilities design	Location and configuration of: Water mains Sewer mains Drainage system, including quantity, direction, and velocity of projected surface runoff flows Filtration ponds Electric, telephone, natural gas Offsite improvements	Civil and mechanical engineer

Environmental planning checklist (continued)

DATA	DESCRIPTION	SOURCE
Site plan and building elevations	Showing location and size of uses proposed on site: Building locations Description of uses Area (sq ft/sq m) Access points Road and walkway circulation Parking spaces (number and location) Building materials and colors	Architect
Landscape concept	General description of types of landscaping proposed: Species list Lakes, water features, fountains, lagoons Outdoor recreation Preservation of existing vegetation	Landscape architect
Geotechnical report	Description of existing geologic conditions including: Stratigraphy of bedrock and surficial units Geologic structure and map Identification of any geologic hazards or constraints including: Faults Landslides Adverse soil conditions Significant mineral resources Assessment of potential effects on project due to geologic hazards and constraints including: Grading (soil ripability) Slope stability (artificial, natural) Seismic ground shaking, rupture, and effect on foundation soils, structures (soil liquification, differential settlement) Adverse soil conditions (expansive, erodible soils) Specific engineering recommendations to reduce or avoid adverse impacts Existing surface water drainage, groundwater levels, fresh water ponds, saltwater tidal ditches; if any adverse effects on project (for example, through flooding, hurricane type floods), identification of mitigating measures	Soils engineer

Differentiation checklist*

To avoid duplications or omissions in developing capital cost budgets, the members of the design and construction team should be assigned the following specific responsibilities for cost estimation, design preparation of contract documents, purchasing, and installation of all the specialized building elements, equipment, and furniture.

Areas of Responsibility	BUDGET CAT'GRY	EST. BY	DESIGN BY	CONTR. DOC'S	PURCH. BY	INST'LD BY
1. General construction	C	CE	A/ST/ AC/F	A/ST	GC	GC
2. Furniture (seating, casepieces, etc.)						
a. Movable	FFE	I	I	I	PA	PA/IN
b. Fixed/Millwork	FD	I	I	I	GC/MC	GC/MC
3. Artwork and artifacts	FFE	I	I	I	PA	PA/IN
4. Flooring						
a. Carpeting and pad	FFE	I	I	I	PA	PA/IN
b. Marble, decorative tile, wood	FD	I	I	I	GC	GC
c. Concrete, resilient tile, ceramic tile bathrooms, quarry tile kitchens and pantries	C	CE	I/A	A	GC	GC
5. Wall covering						
a. Vinyl						
(1) Guestrooms	C	CE	I	A	GC	GC
(2) Public areas	FD	I	I	I	PA	GC
b. Paneling, marble,	FD	I	I	I	GC/MC	GC/MC

Differentiation checklist* (continued)

Areas of Responsibility	BUDGET CAT'GRY	EST. BY	DESIGN BY	CONTR. DOC'S	PURCH. BY	INST'LD BY
other decorative finish						
c. Masonry and plaster or drywall, paint and ceramic tile bathrooms, kitchens and pantries	C	CE	I	A/I	GC	GC
6. Ceiling finishing						
a. Spray on or paint	C	CE	I/A	A	GC	GC
b. Lay-in acoustic tile	C	CE	I/A	A	GC	GC
c. Coffered or other decorative treatments	FD	I	I/A	I/A	GC/MC	GC/MC
7. Doors (finishes, hardware, door frames, seal-stripping, view holes and rate notice frames)	C	CE	I/A	A	GC	GC
8. Movable partitions (ballrooms, meeting rooms)	C	CE	I/A	A	GC	GC
9. Lighting						
a. Decorative fixtures						
(1) Plug-in	FFE	I	I	I	PA	PA/IN
(2) Fixed	FFE	I	I/LT	I/A/EE	PA	PA/IN
b. General lighting	C	CE	I/A/EE	A/EE	GC	GC
c. Conduit, wiring and dimming systems	C	CE	A/EE	A/EE	GC	GC
10. Mechanical, electrical, life safety and security systems (sprinklers, standpipes, fire hoses, smoke detectors, alarms and fire extinguishers)	C	CE	A/ME/EE/F	A/ME/EE	GC	GC
11. Elevators and escalators						
a. Equipment	C	CE	A/EV	A/EV/EE	GC	GC
b. Cab interiors, doors and frames	C	CE	I/A	A	GC	GC
12. TV System						
a. Conduit	C	CE	A/EE/S	A/EE	GC	GC
b. Equipment and wiring	SS	S	S/V	S/V	O*	V
13. TV surveillance system						
a. Conduit	C	CE	A/EE/S	A/EE	GC	GC
b. Equipment and wiring	SS	S	S/V	S/V	O*	V
14. Telephones						
a. Conduit	C	CE	A/EE	A/EE	GC	GC
b. Equipment and wiring	SS	S	S	S	O*	V
c. Public phones	SS	O	O/V/I	V/I/A	O*	V
15. Computer and reservation systems						
a. Uninterrupted power supply (UPS) for computers and conduit	C	CE	A/EE/S	A/EE	GC	GC
b. Equipment and wiring	SS	S	S/V	S/V	O*	V
16. Audiovisual systems						
a. Fixed equipment and wiring	SS	S	A/S/AV	A/AV	GC	GC
b. Movable equipment	SS	S	S/AV	S	O*	O/V
c. Conduit	C	CE	A/S/EE	A/EE	GC	GC
d. Built-in projection screens	C	CE	A/AV	A	GC	GC
17. Foodservice equipment						
a. Kitchen, bar and pantry equipment (set in place) including walk-in coolers and freezers, refrigeration, hoods, and stainless	FFE	K	K	K	PA	GC

LEGEND

BUDGET CATEGORIES

- **C** Basic Construction
- **FD** Fixed Decor (Millwork and Special Finishes)
- **FFE** Furniture, Fixtures, and Equipment
- **OP** Operating Supplies, Inventories, and Consumables
- **SS** Special Hotel Systems

TEAM MEMBERS

- **A** Architect
- **AC** Acoustical Consultant
- **AV** Audiovisual Consultant
- **CE** Construction Estimator (construction manager or professional estimator)
- **CIV** Civil Engineer
- **EV** Elevator Consultant
- **EE** Electrical Engineer
- **F** Fire Protection Consultant
- **G** Graphics Designer
- **GC** General Contractor
- **I** Interior Designer
- **IN** Installation Contractor for FFE Items
- **K** Kitchen, Bar, and Foodservice Consultant
- **L** Laundry Consultant
- **LS** Landscape Consultant
- **LT** Lighting Consultant
- **MC** Millwork Contractor
- **ME** Mechanical Engineer
- **O** Operator/Purchasing Department†‡
- **PA** Purchasing Agent for FFE Items‡
- **S** Systems Consultant
- **ST** Structural Engineer
- **V** Vendor
- † Denotes items subject to lease or purchase in the checklist
- ‡ Subsidiary corporations are often formed by hotel companies to handle all FFE purchasing

*Adapted from checklist prepared for Ramada Inns by W.A. Rutes.

Differentiation checklist* (continued)

Areas of Responsibility	BUDGET CAT'GRY	EST. BY	DESIGN BY	CONTR. DOC'S	PURCH. BY	INST'LD BY
steelwork						
b. Ice machines	FFE	K	K	K	O	GC
c. Vending machines	FFE	K	K	K	O*	V
d. Disposal equipment	FFE	K	K	K	O*	V
e. Mechanical and electrical rough-in and final connections	C	CE	K/A/ ME/EE	K/A/ ME/EE	GC	GC
f. Foodservice carts	FFE	K	K	K	O	O
18. Laundry and dry-cleaning						
a. Equipment (set in place)	FFE	L	L/A/ ME/EE	L/A/ ME/EE	PA	GC
b. Mechanical and electrical rough-in, final connections, and ventilation	C	CE	L/A ME/EE	L/A ME/EE	GC	GC
c. Linen chute	C	CE	A	A	GC	GC
19. Housekeeping and maintenance equipment (vacuum cleaners, maid's carts, floor polishers, mops, tools, and maintenance shop equipment)	OP	O	O	O	O	O/V
20. Storage shelving						
a. Fixed wood	C	CE	A	A	GC/MC	GC/MC
b. Metal movable	FFE	O	A/O	A/O	O	IN
21. Office and front desk equipment						
a. Office furniture, files, vaults, business machines, copiers, etc.	FFE	O	O	O	O	O
b. Safe deposit boxes	FFE	O	O	O	O	GC
c. Baggage carts	OP	O	O	O	O	O
22. Meeting room equipment (movable stages, dance floors, lecterns, easels, etc.)	FFE	O	I/O	I/O	PA	PA/IN
23. Recreation facilities						
a. Pools, courts, etc.	C	CE	A	A	GC	GC
b. Equipment	FFE	O	O/A	O/A	O	O
24. Window coverings						
a. Draperies, tracks, blinds	FFE	I	I	I	PA	PA/IN
b. Valances	FD	I	I	I	GC/MC	GC/MC
25. Shower curtains	FFE	I	I	I	O	IN
26. Shower rods or door assemblies	C	CE	I/A	A	GC	GC
27. Vanities	C	CE	I/A	A	GC	GC
28. Mirrors						
a. Public areas and guestrooms	FD	I	I	I	GC/MC	GC/MC
b. Bathrooms	C	CE	I	A/I	GC	GC
29. Accessories						
a. Towel bars and shelves, tissue dispensers, paper holders, robe hooks, grab bars, ceramic soap dishes, retractable clotheslines	C	CE	I/A	A	GC	GC
b. Ash urns						
(1) Fixed	FD	I	I/A	I	GC	GC
(2) Movable	FFE	I	I	I	PA	PA/IN

Areas of Responsibility	BUDGET CAT'GRY	EST. BY	DESIGN BY	CONTR. DOC'S	PURCH. BY	INST'LD BY
c. Closet shelving and rods	C	CE	I/A	A	GC	GC
d. Clothes hangers	OP	O	O	O	O	O
e. Luggage racks	FFE	I	I/O	I	PA	PA/IN
30. Bedspreads	FFE	I	I	I	PA	PA/IN
31. Mattresses and boxsprings	FFE	O	O	O	O	IN
32. Linens, bedding, and terry materials	OP	O	I/O	I	O	O
33. Uniforms	OP	O	I/O/V	O	O	O
34. Tableware (china, glassware, flatware, holloware, tablecloths, napkins, place mats)	OP	O	I/O	I	O	O
35. Kitchen and bar utensils and smallwares	OP	O	O	O	O	O
36. Food and beverage consumables	OP	O	O	O	O	O
37. Working inventories						
a. Office supplies; cleaning, laundry, and maintenance supplies; guestroom (wastebaskets, ashtrays, etc.) and bathroom supplies (soaps, tissues, etc.)	OP	O	O	O	O	O
b. Menus and printed forms	OP	O	G	O/G	O	O
38. Interior signage						
a. Directional signs and room numbers	FFE	I	I/G	I	GC	GC
b. Restaurant and lounge identification	FFE	I	I/G	I	GC	GC
39. Exterior signage						
a. Building identification signs	SS	O	O/A	O/A/V	O	V
b. Directional, traffic, and parking signs and striping	C	CE	A/G	A	GC	GC
40. Interior landscaping						
a. Fixed planters	C	CE	I/A/LS	A	GC	GC
b. Movable planters	FFE	I	I/LS	I	PA	PA/IN
c. Planting	FD	I	I	I	O*	V
d. Fountains	FD	I	I/A/ME	I/A/ME	GC	GC
41. Exterior landscaping						
a. Planters	C	CE	A/LS	A	GC	GC
b. Irrigation and drainage	C	CE	A/CIV/ LS	A/CIV	GC	GC
c. Planting, water features, and hardscape	C	CE	A/LS	A/LS	GC	GC
42. Roadways, parking, and walks	C	CE	A/CIV/ LS	A/CIV	GC	GC
43. Vehicles (vans, golf carts, grounds maintenance trucks)	OP	O	O	O	O*	O

SELECTED BIBLIOGRAPHY

HOTEL AND RESORT PLANNING

Aloi, Giampiero. *Hotel Motel.* Milano: Hoepli, 1970.

Architect's Journal, ed. *Principles of Hotel Design.* London: The Architectural Press, 1970.

Davern, Jeanne, ed. *Places for People.* New York: McGraw-Hill, 1976.

End, Henry. *Interiors 2nd Book of Hotels.* New York: Whitney Library of Design, 1978.

Gee, Chuck Y. *Resort Development and Management.* East Lansing. MI: Educational Institute of the American Hotel and Motel Association, 1981.

Hoyt, Charles K., ed. *More Places for People.* New York: McGraw-Hill, 1982.

Lawson, Fred. *Hotels, Motels and Condominiums.* Boston: Cahners, 1976.

———, and Manuel Baud-Bovy. *Tourism and Recreation Development.* London: The Architectural Press, 1977.

Penner, Richard H. *Hotel Design and Development.* Council of Planning Librarians Exchange Monticello, IL: Bibliography No. 1399, 1977.

Portman, John, and Johnathan Barnett. *The Architect as Developer.* New York: McGraw-Hill, 1976.

Weisskamp, Herbert. *Hotels: An International Survey.* New York: F.A. Praeger, 1968.

FOODSERVICE AND RESTAURANT PLANNING

Kazarian, Edward A. *Foodservice Facilities Planning,* 2d ed. Westport, CT: AVI Publishing Co., 1983.

Kotschevar, Lendal H., and Margaret E. Terrell. *Foodservice Planning: Layout and Equipment.* New York: Wiley, 1977.

Lawson, Fred. *Restaurant Planning and Design.* New York: Van Nostrand Reinhold, 1973.

———. *Designing Commercial Foodservice Facilities.* New York: Watson-Guptill, 1973.

Wilkinson, Jule, ed. *The Anatomy of Foodservice Design 1.* Boston: CBI (Cahners), 1975.

———. *The Anatomy of Foodservice Design 2.* Boston: CBI (Cahners), 1978.

HISTORY

Kramer, J.J. *The Last of the Grand Hotels.* New York: Van Nostrand Reinhold, 1978.

Limerick, Jeffrey, Nancy Ferguson, and Richard Oliver. *America's Grand Resort Hotels.* New York: Pantheon, 1979.

McGinty, Brian. *The Palace Inns: A Connoisseur's Guide to Historic American Hotels.* New York: Stackpole, 1978.

Pevsner, Nikolaus. *A History of Building Types.* Princeton, NJ: Princeton University Press, 1976. Chapter 11, pp. 169–192.

Williamson, Jefferson. *The American Hotel: An Anecdotal History.* New York: Alfred A. Knopf, 1930.

OTHER

Technology

American Hotel and Motel Association. *The State of Technology in the Lodging Industry.* New York: AHMA, 1983.

National Fire Protection Association. *Hotel Fires: Behind the Headlines.* Quincy, MA: NFPA, 1982.

Saxon, Richard. *Atrium Buildings, Development and Design.* New York: Van Nostrand Reinhold, 1983.

Operating Statistics

Laventhol & Horwath. *U.S. Lodging Industry.* Philadelphia, PA. Annual editions.

Pannell Kerr Forster. *Trends in the Hotel Industry.* Houston, TX. Annual editions.

Hotel Directories

Official Meeting Facilities Guide. New York: Ziff-Davis. Semi-annual editions.

Hotel and Motel Red Book. New York: American Hotel & Motel Association. Annual editions.

PERIODICALS

Architectural Record. New York: McGraw-Hill.

Cornell Hotel and Restaurant Administration Quarterly. Ithaca, NY: School of Hotel Administration, Cornell University.

Hotels and Restaurants International. Boston: Cahners.

Interior Design. New York: Whitney Communications.

Interiors. New York: Billboard Publications.

Lodging. New York: American Hotel & Motel Association.

Lodging Hospitality. Cleveland: Penton/IPC.

Restaurant Business. New York: Bill Communications.

Restaurant and Hotel Design. New York: Bill Communications.

List of Hotels and Credits

The following list includes the credits for the architects (A), interior designers (ID), photographers (P), and other consultants whose projects are illustrated in this book. The authors express our deep appreciation to them for making the material available to us. Additional noteworthy hotels and resorts that we believe are worth a visit are also listed.

THE DOWNTOWN HOTEL

The Akasaka Prince, Tokyo, Japan
A and ID: Kenzo Tange
P: Courtesy Cole and Weber
Alameda Plaza, Kansas City, MO
A: Kivett and Myer
Bangkok Peninsula, Bangkok, Thailand
A: Wimberly Whisenand Allison Tong & Goo
ID: P49, Rifenberg/Rirkrit
Boston Marriott/Long Wharf, Boston, MA
A and ID: Cossutta & Associates
ID: Marriott Hotels
The Bostonian, Boston, MA
A: Mintz Associates
ID: Graham Solano
P: Sam Sweezy
Four Seasons Hotel Philadelphia, Philadelphia, PA
A: Kohn Pederson Fox Associates
ID: Frank Nicholson Associates, John S. North
P: © Jock Pottle/ESTO, Lawrence Williams
Holiday Inn Crowne Plaza (Post Oak), Houston, TX
A: Golemon & Rolfe Associates
ID: Holiday Inns
P: Barry Whitehead
Holiday Inn Crowne Plaza, New Orleans, LA
A: DMJM/Curtis and Davis, concept design by Wally Rutes and Nadine Papon (HII)
ID: Holiday Inns
P: Alan Karchmer
Holiday Inn Crowne Plaza, White Plains, NY
A: Fuller & D'Angelo
ID: Holiday Inns
Hotel Inter-Continental, New Orleans, LA
A: Perez Associates
ID: Donghia Associates
Hyatt on Capitol Square, Columbus, OH
A: Pringle and Patrick
ID: Hirsch/Bedner and Associates
Hyatt Regency Atlanta, Atlanta, GA
A and ID: John Portman and Associates
Hyatt Regency Macau, Macau
A and ID: CRS/SIRRINE
ID: Dale Keller & Associates
Inter-Continental Hotel, Jeddah, Saudi Arabia
A: William B. Tabler
ID: Grusczak Associates
P: Louis Checkman
Model built by George Awad
La Mansione del Rio, San Antonio, TX
A: WZMH Group
ID: Barry Design
P: Zintgraff
The Madison, Seattle, WA
A: The Callison Partnership
ID: Robinson Mills & Williams
Meridien, Houston, TX
A: Lloyd Jones Brewer Associates
ID: Guillon, Smith, Marquart & Associates
P: Rick Gardner
New Otani Hotel and Garden, Los Angeles, CA
A: William B. Tabler, Kajima Associates
ID: Kajima Associates
Parker Meridien, New York, NY
A: Philip Birnbaum
ID: Tom Lee
Pavillion Inter-Continental, Singapore
A and ID: John Portman and Associates
ID: Hirsch/Bedner and Associates
P: Courtesy John Portman and Associates
Radisson Plaza, St. Paul, MN
A: Bergstedt Wahlberg Bergquist Rohkohl
ID: CSA
P: Courtesy BWBR
Ramses Hilton, Cairo, Egypt
A and ID: Warner Burns Toan & Lunde
Semiramis Inter-Continental Hotel, Cairo, Egypt
A: Benjamin Thompson & Associates, Sabour Associates
ID: Dale Keller and Associates
P: Nick Wheeler
Seoul Hilton, Seoul, Korea
A: Jong Soung Kimm, Edward Killingsworth (consulting architect)
ID: Graham Solano
P: George Mitchell
Sheraton Grande, Los Angeles, CA
A: Maxwell Starkman
ID: Merchant Associates
Sheraton Halifax, Halifax, Nova Scotia
A: Lydon Lynch
ID: Graham Solano
Vista International (Hilton International), Washington, DC
A: Holle & Graff, Smith/Williams Group
ID: Graham Solano
Warwick Post Oak, Houston, TX
A: I. M. Pei & Partners
ID: Tom Lee
P: Richard Payne
The Westin Hotel, Tabor Center, Denver, CO
A: Urban Design Group
ID: Hirsch/Bedner and Associates
White Swan, Canton, Peoples Republic of China
A: P. D. Mok, Sheh Chun Han
ID: Hirsch/Bedner and Associates
Williams Plaza (Westin), Tulsa, OK
A: Neuhaus-Taylor
ID: Design International, Hirsch/Bedner and Associates

THE SUBURBAN HOTEL

Boston Marriott Burlington, Burlington, MA
A: WZMH Group
ID: Graham Solano
P: Edward Jacoby
Doubletree, Aurora, CO
A: Architectural Development
ID: Victor Huff & Associates
Doubletree, Overland Park, KS
A and ID: Thompson, Ventulett and Stainbeck
Fragrant Hill, Beijing, People's Republic of China
A: I. M. Pei & Partners
ID: Dale Keller and Associates
P: L. C. Pei
Holiday Inn Crowne Plaza Park 10, Houston, TX
A: Golemon & Rolfe Associates
ID: Holiday Inns
Hyatt Regency Princeton, Princeton, NJ
A: Skidmore Owings & Merrill
ID: Hirsch/Bedner and Associates
P: Steve Rosenthal
Loews Glenpointe, Teaneck, NJ
A: Barrett A. Ginsberg
ID: Tom Lee
Noble Inn, Tampa, FL
A: Mastin Associates
Raleigh Marriott, Raleigh, NC
A: Clark Tribble Harris and Li Architects
ID: Marriott Hotels
Sheraton Meadowlands, Hackensack, NJ
A: The Hillier Group
ID: Trisha Wilson and Associates
P: Leigh Photographic Group
Stouffer's Bedford Glen, Bedford, MA
A: Sasaki Associates
ID: Jutrus & Nobili Associates
Westlake Plaza, Westlake, CA
A: Thompson Architectural Group
ID: Lee-Rovtar Associates
Wyndham Hotel at Greenspoint, Houston, TX
A: Morris*Aubry
ID: Trisha Wilson & Associates
P: Courtesy of Morris*Aubry

THE AIRPORT HOTEL

Holiday Inn Crowne Plaza, Los Angeles Airport, CA
A: Maxwell Starkman
ID: Holiday Inns
Rendering by Tom Tomonaga
Holiday Inn Orlando Airport, Orlando, FL
A: Russell, Martinez, Holt
ID: Holiday Inns
P: Courtesy of Russell, Martinez, Holt
Hyatt Regency O'Hare, Chicago, IL
A and ID: John Portman and Associates
P: Courtesy of John Portman and Associates
Miami Airport Hilton, Miami, FL
A: The Nichols Partnership
ID: Kenneth E. Hurd & Associates
P: Steven Brooke Studios
Ramada Renaissance, Atlanta, GA
A: Rabun Hatch Portman McWhorter Hatch & Rauh
ID: Trisha Wilson & Associates
P: Rion Rizzo, Eric N. Richards
Sheraton Plaza La Reina, Los Angeles, CA
A: Welton Becket Associates
ID: Hirsch/Bedner and Associates
P: Courtesy of Welton Becket Associates

THE ROADSIDE AND SMALL TOWN HOTEL/MOTEL

Columbus Hilton, Columbus, GA
A: Pound Flowers & Dedwylder
ID: Design Continuum
Corning Hilton, Corning, NY
A: Sasaki Dawson & DeMay
ID: Jutras & Nicholson
Courtyard by Marriott, Atlanta area, GA
A and ID: Marriott Hotels
P: Courtesy of Marriott Hotels
Hampton Inn, Memphis, TN
A: Archion
ID: Holiday Inns
Hotel Europa, Chapel Hill, NC
A: O'Brien/Atkins Associates
ID: Omnia Design
La Quinta, San Antonio, AZ
A: La Quinta Motor Inns
ID: La Quinta Motor Inns
P: Zintgraff

THE COUNTRY INN

The American Club, Resort and Conference Center, Kohler, WI
A: William Weeks (remodeling)
ID: Peabody International
P: Courtesy The American Club
New Harmony Inn, New Harmony, IN
A and ID: Woollen Associates
P: Balthazar Korab
Systematics Guest House, Little Rock, AK
A: Cromwell Truemper Levy Parker & Woodsmall
ID: Cromwell Interior Design
P: Gary Stone
Woodstock Inn (Rockresorts), Woodstock, VT
A: William B. Tabler
ID: dePolo Associates

THE BEACH, GOLF, AND TENNIS RESORT

Arizona Biltmore (Westin), Phoenix, AZ
A: Albert McArthur, Frank Lloyd Wright Foundation
ID: Frank Lloyd Wright Foundation
Boca Raton Hotel and Club, Boca Raton, FL
A: Killingsworth, Stricker, Lindgren, Wilson & Associates
ID: Erickson Associates
P: Julius Shulman
The Boulders (Rockresorts), Carefree, AZ
A: Robert Bacon
ID: Warner Interiors
Camino Real (Westin), Cancun, Mexico
A: Ricardo Legoretta
ID: Design International
P: Courtesy Westin Hotels
The Greenbrier, White Sulphur Springs, WV
A: Small, Smith and Reeb
ID: Dorothy Draper
P: Courtesy The Greenbrier
The Halekulani, Honolulu, HI
A: Killingsworth, Stricker, Lindgren, Wilson & Associates
ID: Terry & Egan
Hotel del Coronado, San Diego, CA
A: James and Merritt Reid
P: Courtesy Hotel del Coronado
Hyatt Regency Maui, Maui, HI
A: Lawton & Umemura, Wimberly, Whisenand, Allison, Tong & Goo
ID: Hirsch/Bedner and Associates

LIST OF HOTELS AND CREDITS

P: David Franzen
Inter-Continental Hilton Head, Hilton Head, SC
A: Rabun Hatch Portman McWhorter Hatch & Rauh
ID: Trisha Wilson & Associates
P: David Guggenheim
Kahala Hilton, Honolulu, HI
A: Killingsworth, Stricker, Lindgren, Wilson & Associates
ID: Terry & Egan
Kapalua Bay, Maui, HI
A: Killingsworth, Stricker, Lindgren, Wilson & Associates
ID: Merchant Associates
La Salinas Sheraton, Lanzarote, Canary Islands
A: Fernando Huigueras
P: Courtesy Sheraton Hotels
Loews Paradise Valley Resort, Paradise Valley, AZ
A: Frizzell Hill Moorhouse Beaubois
ID: Hirsch/Bedner and Associates
P: Courtesy of Loews Hotels
Loews Ventana Canyon Resort, Tucson, AZ
A: Frizzell Hill Moorhouse Beaubois
ID: Hirsch/Bedner and Associates
P: Courtesy Loews Hotels, FHMB
Mauna Kea Beach Hotel (Westin), Kamuela, HI
A and ID: Skidmore Owings & Merrill
P: R. Wenkham
Mauna Lani Bay, Big Island, HI
A: Killingsworth, Stricker, Lindgren, Wilson & Associates
ID: Richard Crowell & Associates
P: Julius Shulman
Royal Hawaiian (Sheraton), Honolulu, HI
A: Warren and Westmore
P: Courtesy Royal Hawaiian
Sheraton El Conquistador Golf and Tennis Resort, Tucson, AZ
A: Gary Nelson Associates
ID: George Gobel
Sheraton Plaza, Palm Springs, CA
A: Thompson Group
ID: Integrated Design Associates
P: Paul Bielenberg
Sheraton Princeville, Kauai, HI
A: Boone & Associates
ID: Adams Design
Rendering by Larry Segedin

THE HEALTH SPA

Bonaventure Inter-Continental Hotel & Spa, Fort Lauderdale, FL
A: Charles Giller Associates, Michael A. Schiff and Associates
ID: Jeffrey Howard & Associates
P: Courtesy Bonaventure Inter-Continental
The Golden Door, Escondito, CA
A: Mosher Drew and Watson
ID: Deborah Szekely, Robert Mosher
The Houstonian, Houston, TX
A: Kendall Heaton Associates
ID: Mary Ann Bryan
Safety Harbor Spa Resort, Safety Harbor, FL
ID: Richard Bostain
The World of Palm-Aire, Pompano Beach, FL
A: Thor Amlie, Charles Giller Associates
ID: Wells Squier
P: Gary Kufner

THE VACATION VILLAGE

Club Mediterranee, Cherating, Malaysia
A: Daniel Paterne
ID: Daniel Paterne
P: Courtesy Club Mediterranee
Club Mediterranee, Mauritius
A: Daniel Paterne
ID: Daniel Paterne
Club Mediterranee, Pompadour, France
A: Noelle Janet
ID: Christian Demonchy
P: Courtesy Club Mediterranee
Mediterranean Village, Williams Island, FL
A: The Alan Lapidus Group
ID: Jeffrey Howard & Associates
Tanjong Jara Beach Hotel and Rantan Abang Visitors Center, Kuala Terengganu, Malaysia
A: Wimberly Whisenand Allison Tong & Goo, Akitek Bersekutu Malaysia

THE TIMESHARING AND CONDOMINIUM RESORT

Playa Linda Beach Club, Aruba, Netherlands Antilles
A: Associated Architects, N.V.
ID: Kappy King Cole
P: Harold Zipkowitz, Tom Hurley
San Luis, Galveston, TX
A: Morris*Aubry
ID: Richard Pedroza Associates
The Sandestin Beach Hilton, Destin, FL
A: Collins & Kronstadt
ID: Designers II
The Towers of Quayside, Miami, FL
A: Arc-tech Associates, Sandy and Babcock
Restaurant consultant: Joseph Baum

THE MARINA HOTEL

Abu Dhabi Inter-Continental, Abu Dhabi, U.A.E.
A and ID: Benjamin Thompson & Associates
P: Gregory Murphey
Bahia Mar Hotel and Yachting Center, Fort Lauderdale, FL
A: David Jacobson Associates
ID: Ellen L. McCluskey and Associates
Biscayne Bay Marriott Hotel and Marina, Miami, FL
A: Toombs Amisano & Wells
ID: Marriott Hotels
Inter-Continental San Diego, San Diego, CA
A: Hope Consulting Group
ID: Hirsch/Bedner and Associates
P: Mike Muckley
Mariners Boathouse and Beach Resort, Ft. Myers Beach, FL
A: Architectural Resources
ID: Robb and Stucky
Pier 66, Fort Lauderdale, FL
A: Py-Vavra
ID: Integrated Design Associates

THE SKI LODGE

Avoriaz Ski Resort, Avoriaz, France
A: Atelier d'Architecture
Deer Valley Resort, Park City, UT
A: Esherick Homsey Dodge and Davis
ID: Andrew Delfino
Flaine Ski Resort, Haute Savoie, France
A: Marcel Breuer Associates
P: Courtesy Gatje Papachristou & Smith
Poste Montane, Beaver Creek, CO
A: Bull Volkmann Stockwell
ID: Erickson & Associates
P: David Lokey
Snowbird, Alta, UT
A: Brixen & Christopher
ID: Robert Richins
Westin Vail, Vail, CO
A: ROMA
ID: Design International
P: Russell Abraham

THE TOURIST/SIGHT-SEEING RESORT

Al Ain Inter-Continental, Al Ain, U.A.E.
A and ID: Benjamin Thompson & Associates
P: Gregory Murphey
Cidade de Goa, Goa
A and ID: Charles Correa
Contemporary Hotel, Orlando, FL
A: Welton Becket Associates
ID: Scollard Maas
P: Balthazar Korab
Hilton at Walt Disney World Village, Orlando, FL
A: Alan Lapidus
ID: Kovacs-McElrath
P: Herbert Boelter, Courtesy Hilton Hotels
Oberoi Mèna House Giza, Giza, Egypt
ID: Dale Keller and Associates (consultant)
Petra Forum, Wadi Mousa, Jordan
A and ID: Architects Collaborative
P: Vince Nauseda
Royal Orleans, New Orleans, LA
A: DMJM/Curtis and Davis
ID: Henry End Associates, Jutras + Nobili Associates
P: Frank Lotz Miller
Salt Lick Lodge (Hilton International), Kenya
A and ID: Allen Williams

THE MULTIRESORT COMPLEX

Babin Kuk, Dubrovnik, Yugoslavia
A and ID: Edward Durrell Stone Associates; **A:** CENTAR 51; Edward D. Stone Jr. & Associates (master plan)
Bernardin Resort Complex, Piran, Yugoslavia
A and ID: Architects Collaborative
Cancun, Mexico
P: Courtesy FONATUR
El Morro Tourist Complex, Barcelona, Venezuela
A: Edward D. Stone Jr. & Associates (master plan)
Ixtapa, Mexico
P: Warren Shuman
Kanapali Beach, Maui, HI
P: Courtesy of Kaanapali Beach Operators Association
Porto Carras Resort, Sithonia, Greece
A: The Architects Collaborative
ID: Dale Keller and Associates
P: Serge Crijanovic

CONVENTION HOTELS

Atlanta Marriott Marquis, Atlanta, GA
A and ID: John Portman and Associates
ID: Marriott Hotels
P: Clyde May
Doha Sheraton Hotel and Conference Center, Doha, Qatar
A: William L. Periera Associates
ID: Dale Keller and Associates
P: John Lawrence
Holiday Inn Crowne Plaza, Memphis, TN
A: Taylor and Crump, Lindy Associates
ID: Holiday Inns
Hyatt Regency Austin, Austin, TX
A: Py-Vavra
ID: Hirsch/Bedner and Associates
Hyatt Regency Cambridge, Cambridge, MA
A: Graham Gund Associates
ID: Jutras and Nicholson Associates
Hyatt Regency Flint, Flint, MI
A: Ellerbe Associates
ID: Hirsch/Bedner and Associates
P: Courtesy Ellerbe Associates
Hyatt Regency Long Beach, Long Beach, CA
A: Archisystems International
ID: Singer and Christiansen
P: Wes Thompson
Hyatt Regency Louisville, Louisville, KY
A: Welton Becket Associates
ID: Hirsch/Bedner and Associates
Hyatt Regency Memphis, Memphis, TN
A: Walk Jones & Francis Mah
ID: ISD
J. Willard Marriott, Washington, DC
A: Mitchell Giurgola
ID: Hirsch/Bedner and Associates
New York Marriott Marquis, New York, NY
A and ID: John Portman and Associates
ID: Marriott Hotels
The Registry Hotel Dallas, Dallas, TX
A: William B. Tabler
ID: Joyce K. Wynn
P: Jim Zerschlin
Sheraton Premiere, North Hollywood, CA
A: William L. Pereira Associates
ID: Graham Solano
P: Ronald Moore
Sheraton Seattle, Seattle, WA
A and ID: John Graham
Sheraton Washington, Washington, DC
A: Hellmuth, Obata & Kassabaum
ID: Dale Keller and Associates
P: Tom Crane, Ankers Capitol Photographers
The Waverly (Stouffer), Atlanta, GA
A: FABRAP
ID: Cannell & Chaffin
Westin Crown Plaza, Kansas City, MO
A: Harry Weese and Associates
ID: PBNL Architects, Design International
Wyndham Franklin Plaza, Phila delphia, PA
A: Geddes Brecher Qualls Cunningham
ID: Semanko & Brobrowicz
P: George Cserna

THE CONFERENCE CENTER

Arrowwood of Westchester, Rye Brook, NY
A and ID: The Hillier Group
P: Jim D'Addio
Breckenridge Hotel and Conference Center, St. Louis, MO
A: Henmi & Associates
ID: HRP Hotel/Restaurant Planners
Chaminade Whitney at Santa Cruz, Santa Cruz, CA
A and ID: Whitney Design Group;
A: Neal Lindstrom

Hilton Hotel and Conference Center, Dallas/Fort Worth, TX
A: Larry Lacy
ID: Richard Pedroza Associates
Minaki Lodge (Radisson), Minaki, Ontario, Canada
A: CSA
ID: CSA
P: Courtesy Radisson Hotels
Scanticon-Princeton, Princeton, NJ
A and ID: Warner Burns Toan & Lunde; **A:** Friis & Moltke
P: Courtesy Scanticon-Princeton

RESIDENTIAL AND CONDOMINIUM HOTELS

Four Seasons Hotel Boston, Boston, MA
A: WZMH Group
ID: Frank Nicholson
P: Courtesy Four Seasons
Moscow World Trade Center, Moscow, U.S.S.R.
A: Welton Becket Associates
ID: Scollard Maas
P: Courtesy Welton Becket Associates
The Ritz-Carlton, Boston, MA
A: Skidmore Owings & Merrill (addition)
ID: Graham Solano
U.N. Plaza Hotel and Tower (Hyatt International), New York, NY
A and ID: Kevin Roche John Dinkeloo and Associates
P: Brian Rose

THE SUITE HOTEL

Brock Residence Inns, Denver, CO
P: Kevin Saehlenow
Embassy Suites, Crystal City, Arlington, VA
A: Stinson-Cappelli
ID: Gary Edwards
Embassy Suites, Philadelphia, PA
A: Jung/Brannen
ID: Trisha Wilson and Associates
Embassy Suites, Overland Park, KS
A: DMJM
ID: Richard Pedroza Associates, Holiday Inns
P: Paul Kevitt
Guest Quarters, Charlotte, NC
A: Clark Tribble Harris and Li Architects
ID: Guest Quarters
Guest Quarters, Tampa, FL
A: Morris*Aubry
ID: Guest Quarters
La Reserve, White Plains, NY
A: Matthew Warshauer
ID: RTKL Associates
Windsor Court, New Orleans, LA
A: Morris*Aubry
ID: Frank Nicholson

THE SUPER-LUXURY HOTEL

Campton Place, San Francisco, CA
A: Sagar McCarthy & Kampf
ID: Hirsch/Bedner and Associates
P: Jaime Ardiles-Arce
Grand Bay Hotel, Coconut Grove, FL
A: The Nichols Partnership
ID: Jeffrey Howard & Associates
P: Dan Forer
La Reserve, Geneva, Switzerland
A and ID: Design International
L'Hotel, Paris, France
A and ID: Robin Westbrook
The Mansion on Turtle Creek (Rosewood), Dallas, TX
A: Shepherd + Boyd USA
ID: Hirsch/Bedner and Associates
P: Jaime Ardilles-Arce; Kitchen: Thomas Ricca Associates
No. 1022, New York, NY
A: Michael Wolfman
ID: Georgina Fairholme
Regent, Washington, DC
A: Skidmore Owings and Merrill
ID: Charles Sister
The Remington on Post Oak Park (Rosewood), Houston, TX
A: Shepherd + Boyd USA
ID: Intradesign
P: Jaime Ardiles-Arce
Ritz-Carlton, Washington, DC
A: The Ehrenkrantz Group (addition); John Carl Warnecke and Associates (restoration)

THE RENOVATION

Doubletree, Tucson, AZ
ID: Barry Design
Grand Hyatt, New York, NY
A: The Gruzen Partnership, Der Scutt
ID: Dale Keller and Associates, GKR
P: Laura Rosen
Grove Park Inn, Ashville, NC
A: Daniels International
ID: Design Continuum
Inter-Continental New York, New York, NY
A: William B. Tabler
ID: Trisha Wilson & Associates
P: Bill Rothchild
The Mayflower (Stouffer), Washington, DC
A: Vlastimil Koubek
ID: Intradesign
Park Hyatt, Chicago, IL
ID: Hirsch/Bedner and Associates
Plaza Athenae (Trust House Forte), New York, NY
A: John Carl Warnecke and Associates
ID: Valarian Rebar, Corrigan Designs
Ramada Renaissance, Geneva, Switzerland
A and ID: SK Design International
P: Courtesy SK Design International
Sheraton O'Hare, Chicago, IL
A: Shayman & Salk
ID: Integrated Design Associates
P: Nakashima/Tschoegl
Sheraton Savannah, Savannah, GA
A: Rabun Hatch Portman McWhorter Hatch & Rauh
ID: Design Continuum
P: Gorchev and Gorchev

THE ADDITION

Holiday Inn Disney World, Orlando, FL
A: Lindy Associates
ID: Holiday Inns
Hyatt Regency O'Hare, Chicago, IL
A: John Portman and Associates
ID: Hirsch/Bedner and Associates (addition)
Inter-Continental Lusaka, Lusaka, Zambia
A: William B. Tabler
ID: Walter M. Ballard
Inter-Continental Nairobi, Nairobi, Kenya
A: William B. Tabler
ID: Walter M. Ballard
Sheraton on Harbor Island, San Diego, CA
A: Hendrick and Mock, Ballew and Associates
ID: Hirsch/Bedner and Associates, Integrated Design Associates

THE RESTORATION

The Adolphus, Dallas, TX
A: Beran & Shelmire
ID: Swimmer Cole Martinez Curtis
P: Courtesy The Adolphus
The Bellevue Stratford (Westin), Philadelphia, PA
A: Vitetta Group
ID: Graham Solano
Capital Hotel, Little Rock, AK
A: Cromwell, Truemper, Levy, Parker, & Woodsmall
ID: ABV & Associates
Four Season's Olympic, Seattle, WA
A: The NBBJ Group
ID: Frank Nicholson, John S. North
P: Richard Busher
Hermitage—A Park Suite, Nashville, TN
A: Gresham Smith and Partners
ID: Jerry Law
Inter-Continental Paris, Paris, France
ID: Neal A. Prince (IHC)
P: Courtesy Inter-Continental Hotels
Marriott's Hotel Galvez—Galveston, Galveston, TX
ID: Jeffrey Howard & Associates, Marriott Hotels
Mayfair Regent, Chicago, IL
A: Lawrence B. Berkley & Associates
ID: Ellen L. McCluskey Associates
P: Peter Paige
Mayfair Regent, New York, NY
ID: Ellen L. McCluskey Associates
P: Mark Ross
The Melrose, Dallas, TX
A: Shepherd + Boyd USA
ID: Trisha Wilson and Associates
P: Louis Reens
Netherland Plaza (Omni/Dunfey), Cincinnati, OH
A: Rabun Hatch Portman McWhorter Hatch & Rauh
ID: Ellen L. McCluskey Associates; Rita St. Clair (restoration consultant)
P: Courtesy Omni/Dunfey
Sheraton Jefferson, Richmond, VA
A: Vlastimil Koubek
ID: Hocheiser and Elias
Teller House, Central City, CO
A: Community Services Collaborative
ID: Bruce Bradbury, Janet Pile Designs
Willard Inter-Continental, Washington, DC
A: Vlastimil Koubek
ID: Tom Lee

ADAPTIVE REUSE

The Helmsley Palace, New York, NY
A: Emery Roth & Sons
ID: Tom Lee, Leona Helmsley (guestrooms)
P: Steven Zane
The Henley Park, Washington, DC
A: Smith Segreti Tepper
ID: Roger Sherman Associates, American Contract Designers
Hilton at Lackawanna Station, Scranton, PA
A: Buchanon and Ricciuti
ID: Buchanon and Ricciuti
P: Terry Connors
Hotel Roxborough, Ottawa, Quebec, Canada
ID: RTKL Associates
Hyatt Regency Buffalo, Buffalo, NY
A: The Gruzen Partnership
ID: Integrated Design Associates
P: Patricia Bazelon, Robert L. Smith
Marriott Omar Khayyam Hotel, Cairo, Egypt
A: Frizzell Hill Moorhouse Beaubois
ID: Ed Dann
P: Courtesy Frizzell Hill Moorhouse Beaubois
Meridien-Boston, Boston, MA
A: Jung/Brannen
ID: Jutras + Nobili Associates
P: Steve Rosenthal
Nova Park Elysees, Paris, France
A: Jean Jacques Fernier
ID: Rene Hatt
P: Courtesy Nova Park Elysees
Royal Crescent, Bath, England
A: William Bertram
ID: Julie Hodgess
Sheraton Greensboro, Greensboro, NC
A: Odell Associates
ID: Design Continuum
Stanford Court, San Francisco, CA
A: Curtis and Davis
ID: Andrew Delfino
P: Courtesy The Stanford Court

THE MEGA-HOTEL

Headquarters Hotel, Orlando, FL
A: The Nichols Partnership
ID: Intradesign
Hyatt Regency Grand Cypress, Orlando, FL
A: Killingsworth, Stricker, Lindgren, Wilson & Associates; Harward K. Smith
ID: Hirsch/Bedner and Associates
P: Peter Paige, Courtesy Killingsworth et al.
Orlando Marriott Resort, Orlando, FL
A: RTKL Associates
ID: Jutras + Nobili Associates, Marriott Hotels
P: Courtesy RTKL Associates

THE MULTIUSE COMPLEX

Bonaventure Place (Bonaventure Hilton International), Montreal, Quebec, Canada
A: ARCOP, William B. Tabler
ID: Design International
Carleton Centre (The Carleton), Johannesburg, South Africa
A: Skidmore Owings & Merrill
ID: Design International
P: Ezra Stoller © ESTO
Charles Square, Cambridge, MA
A: Cambridge Seven Associates
ID: Hirsch/Bedner and Associates
Copley Place (Boston Marriott Copley Place), Boston, MA
A: The Stubbins Associates
ID: Marriott Hotels
P: Bill Horseman
Copley Place (Westin Copley Place), Boston, MA
A: The Architects Collaborative
ID: Design International
P: Len Gittleman
Credit Lyonnais Tower (Francotel), Lyon, France

A and ID: Cossutta & Associates
P: Hamid Samiy
Drawings by Ursula Imhof
The Crescent, Dallas, TX
A: John Burgee with Philip Johnson, Shepherd + Boyd USA
Rendering by Patrick Lopez
Ecumed, Ft. Lauderdale, FL
A: RTKL Associates
ID: Hirsch/Bedner and Associates
P: Courtesy RTKL Associates
Embarcaderro Center (Hyatt Regency San Francisco), San Francisco, CA
A and ID: John Portman and Associates
The Galleria (Westin Galleria), Dallas, TX
A: Hellmuth, Obata & Kassabaum
ID: Design International
P: Courtesy Westin Hotels
Greenville Commons (Hyatt Regency Greenville), Greenville, SC
A: Thompson, Ventulett, Stainbeck & Associates
ID: Hirsch/Bedner and Associates
IDS Center (Marquette Inn), Minneapolis, MN
A and ID: Johnson-Burgee
Kensington Center (Sheraton Kensington), Tulsa, OK
A: WZMH Group
ID: Design Continuum
Koll Center (Irvine Marriott), Irvine, CA
A: Flatow, Moore, Brian & Associates
ID: Marriott Hotels
Lafayette Place, Boston, MA
A: Mitchell Giurgola
ID: Frank Nicholson
Rendering by Romaldo Giurgola
Marina Square (Marina Mandarin, Oriental, Pan Pacific Hotels), Singapore
A and ID: John Portman and Associates
ID: Dale Keller and Associates; Don Ashton Design-Asia
P: Courtesy John Portman and Associates
Millender Center (Omni/Dunfey Hotel), Detroit, MI
A: The Ehrenkrantz Group
ID: de Polo Dunbar
P: Courtesy Forrest-Dillon
One American Center, Austin, TX
A: Morris*Aubry
Pertama, Kuala Lumpur, Malaysia
A: John Portman and Associates
Raffles International Centre (Westin Stanford and Westin Plaza), Singapore
A: I. M. Pei & Partners
ID: Design International
Renaissance Center (The Westin Detroit), Detroit, MI
A and ID: John Portman and Associates
ID: Westin Service
P: Courtesy John Portman and Associates
Water Tower Place (Ritz Carlton-Four Seasons), Chicago, IL
A: Loebl-Schlossman-Hackl
ID: Armin Trattmann, Warren Platner

THE MEDICAL HOTEL

Children's Inn, Children's Hospital Med Center, Boston, MA
A: The Architects Collaborative
ID: Ahern and Schopfner
Houston Marriott Medical Center, Houston, TX
A: Sykes Jenning and Kelly
ID: Marriott Hotels
Wyndham at Travis Center, Houston, TX
A: Morris*Aubry
ID: Henry End/Jeffrey Howard & Associates

THE PLANNED COMMUNITY

Cityplace, Dallas, TX
A: Cossutta & Associates
P: Gorchev and Gorchev
Harbour Island, Tampa, FL
A: The Hillier Group
ID: Frank Nicholson
P: Courtesy The Hillier Group
Las Colinas (Mandalay Four Seasons), Irving, TX
A: WZMH Group
ID: Frank Nicholson

THE CASINO HOTEL

Golden Nuggett, Atlantic City, NJ
A: Joel D. Bergman
ID: Henry Conversano and Associates
P: Rod Hicks, Berry & Homer
Harrah's North Boardwalk Casino (Proposal), Atlantic City, NJ
A: Cambridge Seven Associates
P: Steve Rosenthal
Harrah's Marina, Atlantic City, NJ
A: BWB Associates
ID: The Stubbins Associates
P: Edward Jacoby
Harrah's at Trump Plaza, Atlantic City, NJ
A: Alan Lapidus Associates and David Jacobson Associates
ID: Belmuth Design Group
P: Paul Warchol; John A. Lynch
Hilton, Atlantic City, NJ
A: John Carl Warnecke and Associates, David Jacobsen Associates
ID: Kovacs-McElrath
Inter-Continental Kinshossa Casino, Kinshossa, Zaire
A: Auxelbeton
Loews La Naboule Hotel and Casino, Nice, France
A: Interplan, Orselli
ID: Atelier
Loews Monte Carlo, Monte Carlo, Monaco
A: Jean Ginsberg, Herbert Weisskamp, Jean Notari
ID: Ellen L. McCluskey Associates

OTHER CREDITS

Honeywell System 80
P: Courtesy Honeywell Commercial Division
Hotel Design Phases
Drawing by Daniel Rutes
International symbols
P: Courtesy Signs of Safety
Space hotel
P: Courtesy NASA
Union Hotel, Saratoga, NY
P: Courtesy Cornell University Library

INDEX

Italics indicate illustrations, tables, or diagrams.

Edited by Stephen A. Kliment and Susan Davis
Designed by Damien Alexander
Graphic production by Ellen Greene
Set in 9 point Century Old Style